Computers, Chess, and Cognition

T. Anthony Marsland
Jonathan Schaeffer

Editors

Computers, Chess, and Cognition

Foreword by Ken Thompson

With 97 illustrations

Springer-Verlag
New York Berlin Heidelberg London
Paris Tokyo Hong Kong Barcelona

T. Anthony Marsland
Computing Science Department
University of Alberta
Edmonton T6G 2H1
Canada

Jonathan Schaeffer
Computing Science Department
University of Alberta
Edmonton T6G 2H1
Canada

On the front cover: "Rook and Falling Bits" used courtesy of Alberta Government Telephones, Edmonton, Canada.
Photo credits: Plates 1, 3, 5, 11, 12, and 15: C. Vanzella; Plates 2 and 13: M. Newborn; Plates 4, 6 to 10, 14 and 16: J. Uiterwijk.

Library of Congress Cataloging-in-Publication Data
Computers, chess, and cognition / T. Anthony Marsland, Jonathan
  Schaeffer.
     p. cm.
  Includes bibliographical references and index.
  ISBN 0-387-97415-6 (alk. paper)
    1. Chess—Data processing. 2. Chess—Computer programs.
  I. Marsland, T. Anthony. II. Schaeffer, Jonathan.
  GV1449.3.C66 1990
  794.1'72536—dc20   90-44790

Printed on acid-free paper $\mathcal{TOC}$

© 1990 Springer-Verlag New York Inc.
All rights reserved. This work may not be translated or copied in whole or in part without the written permission of the publisher (Springer-Verlag New York, 175 Fifth Avenue, New York, NY 10010, USA), except for brief excerpts in connection with reviews or scholarly analysis. Use in connection with any form of information storage and retrieval, electronic adaptation, computer software, or by similar or dissimilar methodology now known or hereafter developed is forbidden.
The use of general descriptive names, trade names, trademarks, etc., in this publication, even if the former are not especially identified, is not to be taken as a sign that such names, as understood by the Trade Marks and Merchandise Marks Act, may accordingly be used freely by anyone.

Camera-ready copy prepared by the editors.
Printed and bound by R.R. Donnelley & Sons, Harrisonburg, VA.
Printed in the United States of America.

9 8 7 6 5 4 3 2 1

ISBN 0-387-97415-6 Springer-Verlag New York Berlin Heidelberg
ISBN 3-540-97415-6 Springer-Verlag Berlin Heidelberg New York

Foreword

Thirteen years have passed since the classic book on computer chess, *Chess Skill in Man and Machine†*, appeared and seven years since a later expanded edition. In this time, the field of computer chess has made remarkable strides forward. In the early 1980s only the best computers were playing at the master level. Now store-bought machines are competing with masters and the best computers are occasionally beating top Grandmasters. It is a mere 40 years since Claude Shannon published a paper laying the foundations for computer chess, and already the long sought goal of artificial intelligence, to defeat the World Chess Champion, is in sight.

The book has five parts and gives an excellent account of the most exciting recent advances in computer chess. It starts with a short history of computer chess activities, including some of the best man-machine and machine-machine games. This is followed by a section in which the secrets of three of the strongest chess programs around today are revealed. Actually, there are no real secrets here; all the programs are intensive applications of technology and known techniques. For research-oriented readers the major contribution is the section which describes some of the most promising new ideas that could lead to stronger programs of the future.

The penultimate part of the book examines the sometimes tenuous relationship between computer chess and artificial intelligence. Since the game of chess is steadily yielding to the onslaught of technology, the book closes with a description of the current attempts of computers to play the game of Go. There is the hope that Go will become the "*Drosophila* of artificial intelligence" where chess has perhaps not succeeded.

Ken Thompson
Bell Laboratories
Murray Hill

---

† Peter Frey (editor), 2nd edition, Springer-Verlag, New York, 1983.

AUGUSTANA UNIVERSITY COLLEGE
LIBRARY

Preface

During December 1989, in London, two opponents sat across from each other separated by a chessboard. After four tense games, International Master David Levy extended his hand in resignation; he had lost all four. Peter Jansen, a player of modest standards, accepted. Levy's opponent, however, was several thousand kilometers away in Pittsburgh, Pennsylvania, quietly sitting in a cold, dark room, oblivious to the historic event that had just unfolded. Jansen was the human representative for the chess playing machine *Deep Thought*. His job was to relay the machine's moves, as they were received through the phone lines. An era had ended; for twenty years Levy taunted the computer-chess community, daring them to defeat him. And now it was over, in a manner more decisive than most had imagined.

This marked the end of an era in many ways. Just a scant year before, the first human Grandmasters were defeated by their electronic counterparts. World Chess Champion Gary Kasparov, recognizing the strength of the budding computer prodigies, challenged *Deep Thought* to a match, which he won decisively. It is not yet time for machines to triumph over man completely, but it is clear that man's domination in this intellectual sport *par excellence* is rapidly drawing to a close. A new era of computer chess is about to dawn, one in which a combination of fast hardware and sophisticated software will conquer a domain thought to be uniquely human. It may still take a few years to defeat Kasparov, but inevitably the humans must concede.

In sight now is the long sought-after goal of artificial intelligence, a field of computer science devoted to creating the illusion of machine intelligence. The relationship of chess and artificial intelligence is long. Initially, the optimism of the field led to a prediction in 1958 that machines would defeat all humans within 10 years. Unfortunately, the complexity of the human thought processes and the difficulty of modeling this electronically were grossly under-estimated. The role of chess as a vehicle for exploring artificial intelligence has often been compared to the role of the fruit fly for genetics. Chess, the *Drosophila* (fruit fly) of artificial intelligence, has proven to be a fruitful application for investigating machine intelligence.

Just as computer chess enters its decisive era, a new successor *Drosophila* is emerging. The game of Go is arguably more difficult than chess. Not only does it have a larger space of possible board configurations (10^{100} versus 10^{43} for chess) but it does not appear to be easily amenable to the search-based methods successfully used for chess, needing more of a knowledge-based approach. Thus the end of one era for artificial intelligence is the dawning of a new, more challenging one.

We hope our book is timely. We have tried to present the state of the art in computer-chess research and outlined what still remains to be done before Gary Kasparov falls. As well, the emerging field of computer Go is highlighted. This area will receive a great deal of attention in the future.

This book was not possible without the help and support of a number of people. First and foremost, we would like to thank the authors of the chapters:

- Danny Kopec (University of Maine, Orono) for his review of advances in man-machine play.
- David Levy (London, England) for his suggestions on how chess programs will beat the best chess players.
- Thomas Anantharaman, Murray Campbell and Feng-hsiung Hsu (IBM, Yorktown Heights) and Andreas Nowatzyk (Sun Microsystems) for their description of the design of *Deep Thought*.
- Hans Berliner (Carnegie Mellon University, Pittsburgh) and Carl Ebeling (University of Washington, Seattle) for permission to adapt one of their earlier articles on *Hitech*.
- Bob Hyatt (University of Alabama, Birmingham), Bert Gower (University of Southern Mississippi, Hattiesburg) and Harry Nelson (Lawrence Livermore Laboratories) for a detailed description of *Cray Blitz*.
- John McCarthy (Stanford University, California) for permission to reprint his article on *Drosophilas*.
- Donald Michie (The Turing Institute, Glasgow) for revising his paper on *Brute Force in Chess and Science* to our needs.
- Misha Donskoy (Institute for Systems Studies, Moscow) for help in providing some perspectives on how computer chess fell from grace.
- Hermann Kaindl (Siemens AG and the Technical University of Vienna) for his original contribution to the understanding of tree-searching methods.
- Gordon Goetsch (Carnegie Mellon University, Pittsburgh) and Murray Campbell (IBM, Yorktown Heights) for permission to reprint their article on the null-move heuristic.
- Peter Jansen (Carnegie Mellon University, Pittsburgh) for his article on speculative play in chess.
- Bob Herschberg (Delft Technical University, The Netherlands), Jaap van den Herik and Patrick Schoo (Rijksuniversiteit Limburg, The Netherlands) for permission to reprint their article on the confirmation of Troitsky's results.
- Tony & Linda Scherzer and Dean Tjaden (SYS-10 Inc., Hoffman Estates, Illinois) for their description of *Bebe*'s rote learning mechanism.
- Ken Chen (University of North Carolina, Charlotte) and Anders Kierulf, Martin Müller and Jurg Nievergelt (ETH-Zentrum, Zurich) for their review of work on computer Go.
- Kiyoshi Shirayanagi (NTT Software Labs, Tokyo) for his proposal on knowledge-based search in Go.

To these contributions we have added our own brief history of computer chess and a report on the 6th World Computer Chess Championship, as well as a review of how contemporary programs compare on a standard test suite of problems.

Preparation of the manuscript was greatly aided by help from the following: Christine Vanzella, Monty Newborn and Jos Uiterwijk for making their photographs available, some of which are used here; Peter Fode and Tim Breitkreutz for assistance in typesetting the many diagrams for this book; Karen Gona for technical typing and editing; Patrick Schoo for supplying chess diagram software; Steve Sutphen for clarifying and simplifying the mechanism for inserting postscript figures; Carol Smith for considerable help in re-working troff macros to our needs; and Roy Hall of Cornell University for supplying a complete set of troff documentation macros for producing text to Springer-Verlag style specifications. The manuscript was prepared using facilities provided by the Department of Computing Science, University of Alberta.

We also gratefully acknowledge the constructive notes provided by Professor Monroe Newborn, Betty Shannon's finding of several important typographical errors in the final draft, and the detailed comments of Professor Jaap van den Herik in uncovering many mistakes and inconsistencies in an early draft of the manuscript. Despite their perfection we recognize our own inability to prevent new errors from arising.

This book grew out of the 6th World Computer Chess Championship held in Edmonton, May 28-31 1989, and the accompanying *New Directions in Game-Tree Search Workshop*. The Canadian Information Processing Society hosted the championship, with the Alberta Government Telephone Company as the principal sponsor. Financial support for the workshop was received from the Natural Sciences and Engineering Research Council of Canada and the University of Alberta. Without the backing of these organizations, the groundwork for this book would not have been possible.

Tony Marsland
Jonathan Schaeffer
Edmonton, Alberta, Canada

Further Information

In 1977, the computer-chess community formed the International Computer Chess Association (ICCA). For those wanting to keep abreast of this rapidly progressing field, we recommend subscribing to the quarterly *ICCA Journal* which follows the latest research advances and competitive results. Similarly, there is fledgling computer-Go association, whose publication is called the *Computer Go* Newsletter. For more information, contact:

ICCA c/o Dr. H.J. van den Herik Department of Computer Science University of Limburg, P.O. Box 616 6200 MD Maastricht The Netherlands	Computer Go c/o David Erbach 71 Brixford Crescent Winnipeg, Manitoba Canada R2N 1E1

Contents

Part I. Man and Machine

This opening section puts computer chess into perspective with its past, present and future.

Tony Marsland recounts the past with his brief history of computer chess. The article highlights the major milestones in machine-machine competition. Danny Kopec provides a complementary article, surveying the milestones in man-machine play. The article culminates in *Deep Thought*'s unsuccessful challenge of Kasparov and the final defeat of David Levy.

The present state of chess programs is discussed in Jonathan Schaeffer's article on the 6th World Computer Chess Championship. The event brought the strongest chess programs in the world together to determine who was best - with some surprising and not-so-surprising results.

Finally, David Levy forecasts the future with his idea of what is needed to finally defeat the human World Champion. Although his paper contains a simple, yet powerful idea, the realization of it is quite difficult. Nevertheless, the type of knowledge engineering advocated by David is an important, promising area for future research.

1 A Short History of Computer Chess

T.A. Marsland

1.1 Review

Of the early chess-playing machines the best known was exhibited by Baron von Kempelen of Vienna in 1769. As might be expected, they were all conjurer's tricks and grand hoaxes, as Bell (1978) and Levy and Newborn (1982) explain. In contrast, around 1890 a Spanish engineer, Torres y Quevedo, designed a true mechanical player for KRK (king and rook against king) endgames. A later version of that machine was displayed at the Paris Exhibition of 1914 and now resides in a museum at Madrid's Polytechnic University (Levy and Newborn 1982). Despite the success of this electro-mechanical device, further advances on chess automata did not come until the 1940s. During that decade there was a sudden spurt of activity as several leading engineers and mathematicians, intrigued by the power of computers, began to express their ideas about computer chess. Some, like Tihamer Nemes of Budapest (Nemes 1951) and Konrad Zuse of Germany (Zuse 1945), tried a hardware approach, but their computer-chess works did not find wide acceptance. Others, like noted scientist Alan Turing, found success with a more philosophical tone, stressing the importance of the stored program concept (Turing *et al.* 1953).[1] Today, best recognized are Adriaan de Groot's 1946 doctoral dissertation (de Groot 1965) and the much referenced paper on algorithms for playing chess by Claude Shannon (1950). Shannon's inspirational work was read and re-read by computer-chess enthusiasts, and provided a basis for most early chess programs. Despite the passage of time, that paper is still worthy of study, and is again readily available as a reprint (Levy 1988, pp. 2-13).

1.2 Landmarks in Chess Program Development

The first computer-chess model in the 1950s was a hand simulation (Turing *et al.* 1953). Programs for subsets of chess followed (Kister *et al.* 1957) and the

This chapter is a revised and updated extract from "Computer Chess Methods," *Encyclopedia of Artificial Intelligence,* S.C. Shapiro (ed.), Wiley 1987, pp. 159-171.
[1] The chess portion of that paper is normally attributed to Turing, the draughts (checkers) part to Strachey, and the balance to the other co-authors.

first full working program was reported in 1958 (Bernstein *et al.* 1958). By the mid 1960s there was an international computer-computer match, later reported by Mittman (1977), between a program backed by John McCarthy of Stanford (developed by Alan Kotok and a group of students from MIT) and one from the Institute for Theoretical and Experimental Physics (ITEP) in Moscow (Adelson-Velsky *et al.* 1970). The ITEP group's program won the match, and the scientists involved went on to develop *Kaissa*,[2] which became the first World Computer Chess Champion in 1974 (Hayes and Levy 1976). Meanwhile there emerged from MIT another program, *Mac Hack Six* (Greenblatt, Eastlake and Crocker 1967), which boosted interest in artificial intelligence. Firstly, *Mac Hack* was demonstrably superior not only to all previous chess programs, but also to most casual chess players. Secondly, it contained more sophisticated move-ordering and position-evaluation methods. Finally, the program incorporated a memory table to keep track of the values of chess positions that were seen more than once. In the late 1960s, spurred by the early promise of *Mac Hack*, several people began developing chess programs and writing proposals. Most substantial of the proposals was the twenty-nine point plan by Jack Good (1968). By and large experimenters did not make effective use of these works; at least nobody claimed a program based on those designs, partly because it was not clear how some of the ideas could be addressed and partly because some points were too naive. Even so, by 1970 there was enough progress that Monroe Newborn was able to convert a suggestion for a public demonstration of chess-playing computers into a competition that attracted eight participants (Newborn 1975). Due mainly to Newborn's careful planning and organization this event continues today under the title "The North American Computer Chess Championship," with the sponsorship of the ACM.

In a similar vein, under the auspices of the International Computer Chess Association, a worldwide computer-chess competition has evolved. Initial sponsors were the IFIP triennial conference at Stockholm in 1974 and Toronto in 1977, and later independent backers such as the Linz (Austria) Chamber of Commerce for 1980, ACM New York for 1983, the city of Cologne in West Germany for 1986 and AGT/CIPS for 1989 in Edmonton, Canada. In the first World Championship for computers *Kaissa* won all its games, including a defeat of *Chaos* program that had beaten the favorite, *Chess 4.0*. An exhibition match between the new champion, *Kaissa*, and the eventual second place finisher, *Chess 4.0* the 1973 North American Champion, was drawn (Mittman 1977). *Kaissa* was at its peak, backed by a team of outstanding experts on tree-searching methods (Adelson-Velsky, Arlazarov and Donskoy 1988). In the second Championship at Toronto in 1977, *Chess 4.6* finished first with *Duchess* and *Kaissa* tied for second place. Meanwhile both *Chess 4.6* and *Kaissa* had acquired faster computers, a Cyber 176 and an IBM 370/165 respectively. The

---

[2] Descriptions of *Kaissa*, and other chess programs not discussed here, can be found elsewhere, e.g., the books by Hayes and Levy (1976), and by Welsh and Baczynskyj (1985).

exhibition match between *Chess 4.6* and *Kaissa* was won by the former, indicating that in the interim it had undergone far more development and testing (Frey 1977). The 3rd World Championship at Linz in 1980 finished in a tie between *Belle* and *Chaos*. In the playoff *Belle* won convincingly, providing perhaps the best evidence yet that a deeper search more than compensates for an apparent lack of knowledge. In the past, this counter-intuitive idea had not found ready acceptance in the artificial intelligence community.

At the 4th World Championship (1983 in New York) yet another new winner emerged, *Cray Blitz* (Hyatt, Gower and Nelson 1985; Chapter 7 *Cray Blitz*). More than any other, that program drew on the power of a fast computer, here a Cray XMP. Originally Blitz was a selective search program, in the sense that it used a local evaluation function to discard some moves from every position, but often the time saved was not worth the attendant risks. The availability of a faster computer made it possible for *Cray Blitz* to switch to a purely algorithmic approach and yet retain much of the expensive chess knowledge. Although a mainframe program won the 1983 event, small machines made their mark and were seen to have a great future (Levy and Newborn 1982). For instance, *Bebe* with special-purpose hardware finished second (see also Chapter 12 *Learning in Bebe*), and even experimental versions of commercial products did well. The 5th World Championship (1986 in Cologne) was especially exciting. At that time *Hitech* seemed all powerful (see also Chapter 6 *Hitech*), but faltered in a better position against *Cray Blitz* allowing a four-way tie for first place. As a consequence, had an unknown microprocessor system, *Rebel*, capitalized on its advantages in the final round game, it would have been the first micro-system to win an open championship. Finally we come to the most recent event of this type, the 6th World Championship (1989 in Edmonton). Here the Carnegie Mellon favorite, *Deep Thought* won convincingly, even though the program exhibited several programming errors. Still luck favors the strong, as the full report of the largest and strongest computer chess event ever held shows in Chapter 3 *1989 World Computer Chess Championship*. Although *Deep Thought* dominated the world championship, at the 20th North American Tournament that followed a bare six months later it lost a game against *Mephisto*, and so only tied for first place with its deadly rival and stable-mate *Hitech*.

From the foregoing one might reasonably assume that most computer chess programs have been developed in the USA, and yet for the past two decades Canadian participation has also been active and successful in providing supplementary support. Two programs, *Ostrich* and *Wita*, were at the inauguration of computer-chess tournaments at New York in 1970, and their authors went on to produce and instigate fundamental research in practical aspects of game-tree search (for example, Marsland and Campbell 1982; Campbell and Marsland 1983; Newborn 1985,88a,89; Marsland and Popowich 1985; Marsland, Reinefeld and Schaeffer 1987). Before its retirement, *Ostrich* (McGill University) participated in more championships than any other program. Its contemporary, renamed *Awit* (University of Alberta), had a checkered career as a Shannon type-B (selective search) program, finally achieving its best result with a second place tie at New York in 1983. Other active programs have included *Ribbit* (University of Waterloo), which tied for second at Stockholm in 1974, *L'Excentrique* and *Brute Force*. Currently the strongest Canadian program is *Phoenix* (University of Alberta), a multiprocessor-based system using workstations (Schaeffer 1989a,b), which tied for first place with three others at Cologne in 1986.

While the biggest and highest performing computers were being used in North America, European developers concentrated on microcomputer systems. Especially noteworthy are now the Hegener & Glaser products with the *Mephisto* program developed by Richard Lang of England, and the *Rebel* program by Ed Schröder from the Netherlands.

1.3 Implications

All this leads to the common question: When will a computer be the unassailed expert on chess? This issue was discussed at length during a panel discussion at the ACM 1984 National Conference in San Francisco. At that time it was too early to give a definitive answer, since even the experts could not agree. Their responses covered the whole range of possible answers with different degrees of optimism. Monty Newborn enthusiastically supported "in five years," while Tony Scherzer and Bob Hyatt held to "about the end of the century." Ken Thompson was more cautious with his "eventually, it is inevitable," but more pessimistic was Tony Marsland who said "never, or not until the limits on human skill are known." Even so, there was a sense that production of an artificial Grandmaster was possible, and that a realistic challenge would occur during the first quarter of the 21st century. As added motivation, Edward Fredkin (MIT professor and well-known inventor) has created a special incentive prize for computer chess. The trustee for the Fredkin Prize is Carnegie Mellon University and the fund is administered by Hans Berliner. Much like the Kremer prize for man-powered flight, awards are offered in three categories. The smallest prize of $5000 was presented to Ken Thompson and Joe Condon, when their *Belle* program earned a US Master rating in 1983. The second prize of $10,000 for the first program to achieve a USCF 2500 rating (players who attain this rating may reasonably aspire to becoming Grandmasters) was awarded to *Deep Thought* in August 1989 (for more details see Chapter 5 *Deep Thought*), but the $100,000 for attaining world-champion status remains unclaimed. To sustain interest in this activity, Fredkin funds are available each year for a prize match between the currently best computer and a comparably rated human.

One might well ask whether such a problem is worth all this effort, but when one considers some of the emerging uses of computers in important decision-making processes, the answer must be positive. If computers cannot even solve a decision-making problem in an area of perfect knowledge (like chess), then how can we be sure that computers make better decisions than humans in other complex domains—especially in domains where the rules are ill-defined, or those exhibiting high levels of uncertainty? Unlike some problems, for chess there are well established standards against which to measure performance, not only through the Elo rating scale (Elo 1978) but also using standard tests (Kopec and Bratko 1982) and relative performance measures (Thompson 1982). (See also Chapter 13 *The Bratko-Kopec Test Revisited*.) The ACM-sponsored competitions have provided twenty years of continuing experimental data about the effective speed of computers and their operating system support. They have also afforded a public testing ground for new algorithms and data structures for speeding the traversal of search trees. These tests have provided growing proof of the increased understanding about how to program computers for chess, and how to encode the wealth of expert knowledge needed.

Another potentially valuable aspect of computer chess is its usefulness in demonstrating the power of man-machine cooperation. One would hope, for instance, that a computer could be a useful adjunct to the decision-making process, providing perhaps a steadying influence, and protecting against errors introduced by impulsive short-cuts of the kind people might try in a careless or angry moment. In this and other respects it is easy to understand Donald Michie's support for the view that computer chess is the "*Drosophila melanogaster* (fruit fly) of machine intelligence" (Michie 1980).

What then has been the effect of computer chess on artificial intelligence (AI)? First, each doubter who dared assert the superiority of human thought processes over mechanical algorithms for chess has been discredited. All that remains is to remove the mysticism of the world's greatest chess players. Exactly why seemingly mechanical means have worked, when almost every method proposed by reputable AI experts failed, remains a mystery for some. Clearly hard work, direct application of simple ideas and substantial public testing played a major role, as did improvements in hardware/software support systems. More than anything, this failure of traditional AI techniques for selection in decision-making, leads to the unnatural notion that many "intellectual and creative" activities can be reduced to fundamental computations. Ultimately this means that computers will make major contributions to Music and Writing; indeed some will argue that they have already done so. Thus one contribution of computer chess has been to force an initially reluctant acceptance of "brute-force" methods as an essential component in "intelligent systems," and to encourage growing use of search in problem-solving and planning applications.

2 Advances in Man-Machine Play

D. Kopec

2.1 Introduction

In 1968, *Mac Hack Six* (Greenblatt, Eastlake and Crocker 1967) became the first program to compete at the level of the average U.S. tournament player. At that time few people took the entry of programs into tournaments seriously. The programs were viewed primarily as a curiosity and, perhaps, a slight bother. Inevitably, the terminals on which the computer's moves were relayed to the tournament site were noisy, disturbing the other participants. Hence special arrangements had to be made for computer programs in tournaments such as separate rooms or tables. Fortunately, with the exception of a few vocal opponents, most people felt that the machines provided an interesting addition or sideshow to a tournament. Albeit relatively weak, computers scored a few points against humans in chess tournaments in the early 1970s. This started to cause some bad feelings from humans who lost points to the computers, feeling that they had been adversely affected by the participation of the programs.

The fascination with trying to develop a computer program to play strong chess has stemmed from the belief that if you can get a program to play chess well, then there may be no boundary separating man's creative abilities from those of machines (Leithauser 1987). Thus chess playing by computer was an early preoccupation of researchers in artificial intelligence. However two schools of thought have evolved within the artificial intelligence community, both driving research and progress in their own ways. One is performance (or technology) driven (see Chapter 16 *Perspectives on Falling from Grace*) and the other is problem (or competence) driven (Lehnert 1988; Rich 1983). Computer chess has for many years been successful in terms of performance with regard to the Elo rating system (Elo 1978). By and large Elo ratings have been a reliable way to measure the chess strength of both humans and programs. This has been both fortunate and unfortunate for computer chess. Since 1975, when *Chess 4.7* became the first program to break the expert (2000) level, improvements in playing strength appear to be linear with increases in the depth of tree searches, as Figure 2.1 shows. This increase in strength with search depth does slow down as ratings rise over 2200, since the rating system becomes logarithmic from that point on[1]. It is regrettable that there is little to say about how a top

---

[1] Throughout the chapter, United States Chess Federation (USCF) ratings are used. When International (FIDE) ratings are used, they are indicated appropriately. USCF ratings are roughly 100 points higher than the equivalent FIDE rating.

program decides on a move beyond the power of the alpha-beta minimax algorithm (Knuth and Moore 1975). Yes, the programs do know something about king safety, pawn structure, piece activity (mobility), center control and absolute values for pieces and pawns. Some programs know more about certain chess concepts than others, depending on the chess strength of the programmers and chess consultants. Various refined techniques are employed to make the search more efficient including parallel algorithms (Marsland and Campbell 1982) and singular extensions (Anantharaman, Campbell and Hsu 1988) but, due to the competitive priorities of most programs, little is revealed about how a program finally selects one move over another. This largely explains why computer chess has appeared to advance primarily as a competitive sport (performance driven) rather than as a science (problem driven).

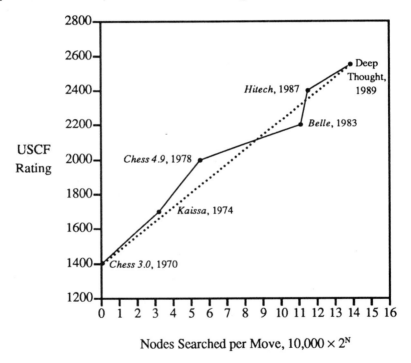

Figure 2.1: Increasing program performance (Newborn 1989).

This chapter reviews the major events in man-machine chess play. The emphasis will be on recent progress in the field. A detailed history of the early years of computer chess is provided by Frey (1977) and Newborn (1975).

2.2 Early Progress

The 1970s were highlighted by the reign of the *Chess 3.X* and *Chess 4.X* series of programs from Northwestern University, authored by David Slate, Larry Atkin and Keith Gorlen. Their programs won every ACM North American Computer Chess Championship in that decade except in 1974 (*Ribbit*) and 1978 (*Belle*). In 1978, *Chess 4.7* won the The Twin Cities Open in Minnesota with a perfect 5-0 score, raising its rating to an unprecedented 2040. The program was performing as well as a competent expert and was scoring regularly against human experts. The successes of *Chess 4.7*, its predecessors and successors, are well documented by Frey (1977).

The dominant human player in the United States in the 1970s was Grandmaster Walter Browne. In 1977, Browne had won the U.S. Invitational Championship three years in a row and was rated 2560. At this time he was full of energy and brimming with the success of a nationwide tour involving a series of 17 exhibitions, where he had only lost two games and drawn six. So it was only natural that *Chess 4.6* should be one of Browne's opponents in a 44-board simultaneous exhibition in Minneapolis. Michie (1983) contains a fully annotated description of that game. However, the game is so exemplary of the state of the art of computer chess play in 1978 that it is worth giving the score again here with light notes. *Chess 4.6* was running on the fast Cyber 176 computer, seeing over 2.5 million positions in three minutes of think time. Browne took his computer opponent seriously in this game, but it should not be overlooked that the handicap of playing 44 opponents did much to equalize the strength of the opponents. *Chess 4.6* does exhibit a few of the famed "computer moves," such as an inexplicable move (often with the king) in a perfectly normal position. These mistakes are probably due to the computer's inability to find another move which it believes could improve its position. Although at this time computers were reputed to be weak endgame players, *Chess 4.6* weathers the technical difficulties of the endgame through its tactical abilities, disguising its lack of special-purpose knowledge.

White: GM Walter Browne (2560 FIDE) – Black: *Chess 4.6*/Cyber 176 (2070)
Simultaneous Exhibition
1. d4 Nf6 2. c4 c5 3. Nf3 cxd4 4. Nxd4 e5 5. Nb5 Bc5 6. N1c3 *This variation was popular at the time. However, Chess 4.6 is now out of its book.* **O-O 7. e3 d6 8. Be2 a6 9. Na3 Nc6 10. Nc2 Bf5 11. O-O Qd7 12. b3 Kh8 13. Bd2 Rg8 14. Na4 Ba7 15. Bc3 h6** *Browne always tries to find active continuations and at the same time is trying to trade off the passive knight on c2. Browne, as a Grandmaster, always tries to find the "correct" move in a position. If he had a better understanding of the tendencies of computer play, he might have made a waiting move, expecting Chess 4.6 to weaken itself with g5.* **16. Rc1 Rad8 17. Nb4 Nxb4 18. Bxb4 Qc7 19. Qe1 Bc5 20. Bf3?! Bd3 21. Bxc5 dxc5 22. Be2 Bf5 23. f3 e4 24. f4 Bd7 25. Nc3 Qa5 26. Qh4 Bc6 27. Rc2 b5 28. g4 b4 29. Nd1 Rd6!** *Demonstrating the soundness of black's last three moves.* **30. Nf2 Rgd8 31. Rd1 Rxd1+ 32. Bxd1 Rd6!** *At this point Chess 4.6 had used 2 hours*

and 44 minutes of computation time to Browne's 22 minutes! **33. Qg3 Qd8** *Now
Chess 4.6 correctly predicts Browne's next 11 moves.* **34. Rc1 Rd2 35. g5 hxg5
36. fxg5 Nh7 37. g6 fxg6 38. Qxg6 Qh4!** *Now white is in great difficulty.
Browne spent a long time thinking, for the endgame after 39. Qg3 Qxg3 40.
hxg3 would be hopeless for white.* **39. Qf5 Bd7** *Leading to a won ending, but
even stronger was Ng5!* **40. Qf4 Qxf4 41. exf4 e3 42. Ne4 e2 43. Bxe2 Rxe2
44. Nxc5 Bc8** *Lacking special-purpose endgame knowledge, Chess 4.6 gets into
a little trouble. More aggressive is Bh3!? with ideas of mate.* **45. Rd1 Re8 46.
a3?! bxa3 47.Ra1 g5?!** *A dubious move because it offers to trade more pawns.*
48. fxg5 Re5 49. b4?! *49. Nxa6 Bxa6 50. Rxa3 would lead to the ending rook,
bishop and knight versus rook which is a theoretical win. However, the white
queen-side pawns might cause problems and it is questionable whether Chess
4.6 would have the technique required in any case.* **a5 !? 50. Nd3 Rxg5+ 51.
Kf2 axb4 52. Nxb4 Ra5 53. Ke3 Be6 54. Kd4 Ng5!** *This piece ends up playing
a vital role.* **55. Nc2** *Browne offered a draw which the Northwestern camp
turned down in the "interests of science."* **a2 56. Nb4 Ra4! 57. Kc5 Ne4+! 58.
Kb5 Bd7+! 59. Nc6 Nc3+! 60. Kc5 Bxc6 61. Kxc6 Rxc4+ 62. Kd6 Rd4+ 63.
Ke5 Rd1 0-1.**

2.3 The Power of Brute Force

If there is one lasting scientific impression left by chess programs, it is the power
of brute force. Brute-force tree searching methods have already accomplished a
lot more in terms of chess playing strength than many well-educated writers
would have opined (Hearst 1983; Michie 1983; Dreyfus and Dreyfus 1986).
When the Northwestern Chess series reached the expert level in the late 1970s
the skeptics were surprised. To many, it was as much of a revelation as a
disappointment to realize that the beauty in a forcing tactical sequence of moves
(a combination) could be reduced to efficient tree searching with the alpha-beta
algorithm. That is, the creative element in chess can be matched by a
computer's computations (Leithauser 1987). The accomplishments of brute-
force methods served to make us aware of how humans play strong chess, of the
importance of coming to grips with the hierarchical, heuristic, probabilistic
decision making which makes chess so appealing to us, and of the clear trade-
offs between knowledge and search. As the number of nodes searched by the
best programs increased, so did the number of surprises which resulted from
exhaustive brute-force searches of 5-ply and beyond.

A famous example occurred at the 2nd World Computer Chess
Championship in 1977 when, in Figure 2.2, *Kaissa* (black) against *Duchess*
(white) played 34 ... Re8 (!) instead of the "normal" 34 ... Kg7. This left an
audience of 500, including a former World Champion, quite perplexed for a few
minutes. What they had all overlooked was easily found by *Kaissa*'s brute-force
search: 34. ... Kg7 is met by 35. Qf8+!! Kxf8 36. Bh6+ Bg7 37. Rc8+ and mate!
Hence 34. ... Re8 was black's best chance for survival (Michie 1983).

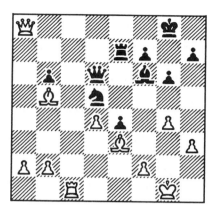

Figure 2.2: *Duchess – Kaissa* (black to move).

2.4 The Contributions of Endgame Databases

In 1977, at the 2nd World Computer Chess Championship, Ken Thompson came armed with a surprising weapon: his database for king and queen versus king and rook (KQKR). By having a search back up terminal positions with known values, Thompson was able to exhaustively enumerate all possible positions for any 4-men endgame. His database recorded all these positions and was able to determine whether any position for white or black was a win, draw or loss. If the position was won, the database provided the number of moves required to win given optimal play by both sides.

For the KQKR endgame, chess books allude to the technical difficulties involved in winning with the queen against a good defender of the rook's side. For example, Fine (1941) comments on a position that "This is a win, but from the general position the process is rather complicated." The stronger side tries to force a zugzwang position (one in which a side must move against its will relinquishing material or ground) whereby the rook must move away from the vicinity of its king. The only advice generally given to the defender is to "keep the king and rook together," avoiding any skewers or forks which might pick up the rook. Understandably, International Masters Hans Berliner and Lawrence Day were quite perturbed when, after about 20 minutes or so of trying with the queen's side, they were unable to win against Thompson's database. Furthermore, the database employed defensive techniques which were inexplicable. In particular, the program disregarded conventional wisdom and separated its king and rook, almost seeming to defy the human masters to find a forcing tactical sequence, which of course did not exist. This has been referred to by Donald Michie as "The Strange Case of Thompson's Table" (Michie 1983).

Ken Thompson was so convinced of the difficulties involved in winning KQ versus KR (the longest wins require 31 optimal moves) that he sought to test it against the strongest players. Grandmaster Robert Byrne declined, but Grandmaster Walter Browne thrust himself into the thick of things by agreeing to a bet for $100 to win with the queen's side against the database. Browne was given a time limit of 2.5 hours to play up to 50 moves, the maximum number of moves allowed by the laws of chess for this ending. However, challenged with a position that required 31 moves to win, Browne was unable to succeed against the database in the required number of moves, thereby losing the bet.

Browne's fighting spirit and ego were challenged by this experience. He carefully studied the computer's play and learned much about the KQKR endgame from his experience against it. A few weeks later he played a rematch from another 31 move position with the chance to regain his $100. This time he won, but exactly on move 50! (Actually Browne was allowed 5 extra moves in the rematch.) Play proceeds from Figure 2.3.

Figure 2.3: Walter Browne – KQKR database (white to move).

White: GM Walter Browne – Black: KQKR database
Exhibition
The number of moves to mate or win of the rook is indicated in parentheses. **1. Kb7 Rb4+ 2. Kc6 Rc4+ 3. Kb5 Rb4+ 4. Ka5 Re4 5. Qd6 Rd4 6.Qe5 Kd3 7. Kb5 Re4** (25) **8. Qf6 Ke3** (24) **9. Kc5 Rf4** (23) **10. Qg6 Ra4** (22) **11. Qg3+ Ke2** (21) **12. Qc3 Rf4** (20) **13. Kd5 Rh4** (19) **14. Qc2+ Ke3** (18) **15. Qd1 Kf2** (17) *Up to here Browne has played accurately and is making steady progress.* **16. Qd2+ Kf3** (17) **17. Qe1 Rg4** (19) **18. Qd1+ Kf4** (18) **19. Qe2 Rg5+** (20) **20. Kd4 Rf5** (19) **21. Qe3+ Kg4** (18) *Browne errs on moves 16, 17 and 19. Ken Thompson has found that lower rated players have trouble from a distance of 14 to 17 moves from the win. Usually the white king is trying to cross the "barrier" on the third or (as in this case) fourth rank. The books don't help here either.*

22. Ke4 Rf7 (17) **23. Qg1+ Kh5** (16) **24. Qg3 Rf8** (15) **25. Ke5 Rf7 26. Ke6 Rf8** (14) **27. Qa3 Rf4** (15) **28. Qh3+ Kg5** (16) **29. Qg3+ Rg4** (15) **30. Qe5+ Kh4 31. Qh2+ Kg5 32. Ke5 Kg6** (14) **33. Qh8 Rg5+** (14) **34. Ke6 Rg4** (14) *Browne has been stuck since move 26. He can only lose two moves now.* **35. Qg8+ Kh5 36. Qh7+ Kg5 37. Ke5 Rg3 38. Qg7+ Kh4 39. Qh6+ Kg4** (9) *Browne is now making steady progress but is still on a tightrope.* **40. Ke4 Rg2 41. Qg6+ Kh3 42. Qh5+ Kg3 43. Ke3 Rg1 44. Qg5+ Kh2 45. Qh4+ Kg2 46. Ke2 Ra1** (4) *Now 47. Qg5+ 48. Qh6+ 49. Qg7+ and 50. Qxa1 wins. Browne finds another way.* **47. Qe4+ Kh3 48. Qh7+ Kg3 49. Qg7+ Kh3 50. Qxa1 1-0.** *Browne just makes it within the normal rules and wins back his money.*

Despite the apparent tension, a little known fact is that the last 24 moves went exactly according to Browne's home analysis! Even though he thoroughly studied this ending for this re-match, he still made several mistakes, attesting to the difficulty of the endgame for human player.

As an addendum to this story, in 1895 the book *Analysis of the Chess Ending King and Queen Against King and Rook* authored by "Euclid" appeared. The author did the same kind of analysis as done by Thompson's program and arrived at the same conclusions: the longest win takes 31 moves (Sternberg, Conway and Larkins 1979). An insightful comment by the author was that:

> The view commonly held and expressed that there could be no practical difficulty in winning with queen against a rook was ... discarded as illusory. (Euclid 1895, pp. iv-v)

Clearly Euclid's book has been overlooked by both the chess and computer-chess worlds!

Another four piece endgame for which there already existed databases in the 1970s was king and rook versus king and knight (KRKN). Ströhlein (1970) developed such a database for his Ph.D. thesis. Between 1976 and 1979, considerable investigation was done into this endgame at the Machine Intelligence Research Unit, University of Edinburgh. Experiments with humans demonstrated that it requires a master strength player to hold a draw with the weak side (knight) and that it also requires a master level player to win with the strong side (rook) (Kopec and Niblett 1980). This research, combined with the KRKN database, helped uncover a number of errors in Fine's (1941) *Basic Chess Endings*. Many interesting KRKN positions required counter-intuitive separating moves between the weak side's king and knight to hold a draw. This was contrary to the standard advice from endgame texts to keep the weak side's king and knight as close together as possible.

More recently Thompson (1986) has extended this work to include all 5-men endings. This work has had great consequences for the game of chess as a number of special cases requiring more than 50 moves to win have been identified as a result of the database. These include: KBBKN, 66 moves; KQKNN, 63 moves; KQKBB, 71 moves; and KRBKR 59 moves. Thompson also made significant contributions to the knowledge about the endgame KQPKQ determining that in many cases more than 50 moves are required with best play. The few practical tests that have been done with the 5-men endings indicate that the order of magnitude increase in computational complexity in going from 4 to 5 men, comprises a jump in complexity which passes the threshold of human scrutability. In these cases, accounting for symmetries, rotations and reflections, the database size increases from roughly 3 million possible configurations (for 4-men endings) to over 100 million possible configurations (for 5-men endings). Clearly this is not an area which humans can learn easily and efforts to decrypt the databases into recognizable goal patterns promise no guarantee of success (Michie and Bratko 1987). Roycroft's difficulties in trying to make progress with the KBBKN database give further evidence for this. The problem is that these databases are the supreme example of the brute-force approach; there are no explanations of how a result is obtained. The databases only provide moves and the length of the solutions, but no insight into how a human might break the endgames into recognizable patterns to ease the difficulty of solving them.

One 5-piece ending which could use some decoding is KRBKR, since it occurs relatively often at the international level (Kopec, Libby and Cook 1988). A few basic winning and drawing positions have been known for several centuries, but little has been done to relate the database's moves to these known positions. The longest winning sequence is 59 moves, implying that some winning positions cannot be won because of the 50 move limit[2]. The world chess governing organization (FIDE) has reacted to these findings for optimal move sequences in peculiar ways. First the number of moves in which the defender could suffer in KRBKR was increased to 100, then decreased to 75, and now its not clear what FIDE intends to do. Surveying a handful of international games, Thompson was able to discover many examples of KRBKR where IM's and GM's had gone wrong. An interesting data point is the game *Deep Thought* versus Alex Fishbein from the 1988 Software Toolworks Open. *Deep Thought* did not have the KRBKR database yet scored the full point in this ending. However, at times being able to lookahead 10 or more moves, it may hardly have needed the database.

2.5 Expert Chess Programs

David Levy made a reputation for himself by betting on his chess skills against any machine. In this way he encouraged research and progress in computer chess. His famous 1968 bet for £1250 (then $2500) against four computer science professors was that no program could beat him in a six game match by August, 1978. In 1978, when Levy defeated his last challenger, *Chess 4.7*, he was simply too strong for the program. It is clear that he could beat it almost at will, although the final score of 3.5-1.5 somewhat belied this. In 1977 he easily

---

[2] The endgames KNNKP and KRP(a2)KBP(a3) also exceed the 50 move limit. More details on the KNNKP endgame can be found in Chapter 11 *Verifying and Codifying Strategies in a Chess Endgame.*

defeated the Russian program *Kaissa*. Then, just three weeks before leaving England for his match against *Chess 4.7*, Levy was challenged by Richard Greenblatt. His program, *Mac Hack Six*, had been supplemented with a hardware component called *CHEOPS*, which could analyze moves at the rate of 150,000 positions per second. A two game match was agreed on. Levy won the first game thereby rendering the second game unnecessary.

The first game of the match against *Chess 4.7* produced two surprises: the program's ability to find a piece sacrifice for two pawns and the outcome of the game, a draw. It was the first time that a program had drawn an international master under tournament conditions. However, Levy provoked his troubles with some passive opening play. This approach had proven successful in the past as computers never sacrificed against Levy and tended to weaken their position and beat themselves. *Chess 4.7* obtained a completely won game after the sacrifice but lost its way in the ensuing ending. Analysis of this famous game can be found in Levy and Newborn (1982).

The second game was more typical of the successful Levy formula for defeating chess programs: get them out of book early and into positions which depend more on understanding than tactics, and then exploit the weaknesses they have left behind.

White: *Chess 4.7* ($\approx$2100) – Black: IM David Levy (2300 FIDE)
1978 Match

1. Nc3 c5 2. e4 Nc6 3. f4 a6 *To take the program out of book.* **4. Nf3 g6 5. d4 cxd4 6. Nxd4 Bg7 7. Be3 d6 8. Nxc6?** *A typical error which programs have been making on the white side of the Sicilian Defense for many years. White relinquishes his well placed knight and strengthens black's center at the same time.* **bxc6 9. Be2 Rb8 10. Qc1 Qa5** *Black is already somewhat better.* **11. Bd2 Qb6 12. Na4 Qa7 13. Nc3 Bd4 14. Nd1 Nf6 15. c3 Bb6 16. Qc2 Ng4 17. Qa4 O-O 18. Bxg4 Bxg4 19. Qxc6** *Naturally the program goes after a pawn, but black has plenty of compensation in the resulting awkward position of the white king.* **Bxd1 20. Kxd1 Be3!** *See* Figure 2.4. **21. b3 Bxd2 22. Kxd2 Rbc8 23. Qa4 Qf2+ 24. Kd3 Qxg2** *Black now has a completely won game.* **25. Qd4 Qf3+ 26. Kc2 Qe2+ 27. Kc1 e5 28. fxe5 dxe5 29. Qxe5 Rfe8 30. Qg3 Rxe4 31. Qh3 Rd8 32. Qf1 Qd2+ 33. Kb1 Re2 0-1** *on move 54. It is worth adding that in the following years, computer-chess programmers have completely avoided playing the white side of open variations of the Sicilian Defense.*

Levy also won games 3 and 5, but experimented in game 4, allowing the program to emerge victorious.

In the late 1970s there were several instances of computer programs defeating strong players, including Grandmasters, at blitz chess. Not surprisingly, since this form of chess is primarily based on a quick and accurate tactical assessment, computers perform better than they do in slow tournament chess. Nevertheless, the differences in overall chess understanding, especially in the endgame, rendered top humans far superior to the top programs even at blitz chess.

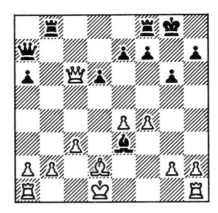

Figure 2.4: David Levy – *Chess 4.7* (white to move).

2.6 Master Level and Beyond: The Belle Era

The period 1979 through 1983 was marked by the dominance of the *Belle*
program, developed by Ken Thompson and Joe Condon (1982). The program
was characterized by speed facilitated by special-purpose hardware that allowed
it to analyze 30 million positions in 3 minutes of think time. *Belle* was a
powerful tactician able to exhaustively search to 8- and 9-ply in the middlegame.
In addition *Belle* had a vast opening library including a large portion of the five
volume Encyclopaedia of Chess Openings (Matanović 1989), totalling 375,000
positions, deftly typed in by Thompson himself. *Belle* seems to play well in
endings through its ability to see deeper as fewer pieces remain. *Belle* won the
3rd World Computer Chess Championship in 1980. Its rating peaked at just
over 2200 in 1983, officially becoming the first program to achieve the title of
master. Following are some representative examples of its play.

   Belle scored a major success at the 1983 U.S. Open, with a solid, master-
level, 8.5 points out of 12. In the following game, *Belle* crushes a strong player.

White: *Belle* (2075) – Black: Harry Radke (2321)
1983 U.S. Open

1. e4 d6 2. d4 Nf6 3. Nc3 g6 4. f4 Bg7 5. Nf3 c5 *A poor choice because it is
sharp, probably premature, and in Belle's book. Safer is O-O.* **6. e5 Ng4?** *Now
Nfd7 is necessary to maintain the tension.* **7. dxc5** *White gets an edge by
straightforward means.* **dxe5** *Black has only a choice of bad moves. If dxc5 8.
Qxd8+ Kxd8 9. h3 Nh6 10. Be3 and white has a big edge.* **8. Qxd8+ Kxd8 9.
h3 Nh6 10. fxe5 Nd7 11. Ne4!** *Keeping white's extra pawn with more
centralization.* **f5?** *A poor move, but it is already difficult for black to move.*
12. exf6 exf6 13. Nd6 *With the threat 14. Bxh6. White already has a won game.*
Ke7 *If Kc7 then 14. Bf4 and later O-O-O looks strong.* **14. Be3 b6 15. Bc4**

Belle has proceeded with strong developing moves. Again Bxh6 and Nf7 is threatened. **g5 16. O-O-O bxc5** *If Nxc5 then 17. Bxc5 bxc5 18. Rhe1+ Kd8 19. Nf5+ wins.* **17. Bb5** *Another simple and devastating move directed against the only defender of the black king.* **Ne5 18. Nxe5 fxe5 19. Rhf1** *Even stronger than 19. Bxg5+, as the bishop neatly aims at two loose pawns.* **1-0.** *All this was a direct consequence of black's poor opening play.*

In 1980, MIT Computer Science Professor Edward Fredkin established an incentive prize fund for the development and advancement of computer chess. The grand prize of $100,000 is to go to the first program to defeat the World Chess Champion. *Belle* was awarded the prize of $5,000 for becoming the first program to achieve a master rating. Hans Berliner has organized several Fredkin Incentive Prize tournaments, involving computers and humans competing together. The 1983 event involved only two programs, *Belle* and *Nuchess* (the successor to the Northwestern Chess series), competing with four humans in a three round event. An innovation used at this event was that the humans didn't know whether their opponent was a program or a human. *Belle* won all three of its games against expert opposition, although it was losing one of the games.

Soon afterwards, *Belle* tied for first in the 1983 New Jersey Open scoring an undefeated 5 out of 6. Here is its respectable draw against Steve Stoyko, the highest rated player in the tournament, allowing *Belle* to break the 2200 barrier.

White: Steve Stoyko (2345) – Black: *Belle* (≈2150)

1983 New Jersey Open

1. e4 e5 2. Nf3 Nf6 3. d3 *Stoyko, once a feared tactician, avoids any early tactical discussion with Belle.* **Nc6 4. g3 d5 5. Nbd2** *White is steering for a King's Indian Reversed, hoping that it might lead to strategic positions which Belle may not handle well.* **Bc5 6. Bg2 dxe4 7. dxe4 O-O 8. O-O Qe7 9. c3 a5 10. h3 Rd8** *Out of its book, Belle has developed soundly and nicely.* **11. Qc2 Be6?!** *Now a more provocative development is b6 followed by Ba6, eyeing the d3 square.* **12. Ng5 Bd7 13. Nc4 Nh5** *A neat idea, not for the threat of Nxg3 but because it forces white's next few moves.* **14. Kh2 b5 15. Na3 Bxa3** *This shattering of white's pawn structure is what Belle had foreseen.* **16. bxa3 Nf6 17. Nf3 Be6 18. Re1 Bc4** *Belle's bishop finds the a6-f1 diagonal anyway.* **19. Bf1 Bxf1 20. Rxf1 Qc5 21. Bg5 Rd6** *Belle surprisingly does not snatch the loose pawn on a3. Perhaps it feared (after Qxa3) 22. Bxf6 gxf6 23. Nh4 and 24. f4. Nonetheless, white's weak pawns will not go away and black again threatens to infiltrate via d3.* **22. Rab1 Rad8 23. Qe2** *Stoyko maintains an active policy which will assure some counterplay for the pawn.* **Qxc3 24. Rxb5 Qxa3 25. Rb7** *White has counterplay due to the pin on the N on f6 and pressure on the c-file.* **Rc8?** *Passive.* **26. Kg2 Qa4 27. Bxf6 Rxf6 28. Rc1 Qa3** *Black's pieces are not well coordinated in this middlegame.* **29. Rcb1 a4** *Black's back rank is too weak to play the desirable Nd4.* **30. Rd1 Qe7 31. Rd5 Re8 32. Qb5** *Threatening Nxe5 with a back rank combination, but also moving the P to a4.* **h6 33. Qxa4 Rd8 34. Rbb5 Rxd5 35. exd5?** *Better was Rxd5. Now Belle has a neat drawing combination (see* Figure 2.5). **Rxf3! 36. dxc6 e4 37. Qd4 Rf6 38. Re5 Re6 39. Rxe6 Qxe6 40. Qd8+ Kh7 41. Qxc7 e3 42. fxe3 Qxa2+ ½-½.**

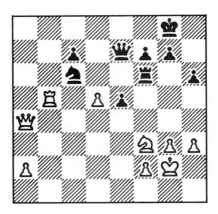

Figure 2.5: Steve Stoyko – *Belle* (black to move).

Although both sides made errors, this was a legitimate draw.
The source for the *Belle* game scores presented above is Welsh and Baczynskyj (1985) and some of the notes are based on Baczynskyj's comments.

To provide a balanced view of matters, a game from the 1981 Fredkin Challenge Match is presented below. *Belle*'s opponent, Carl Storey, won both games of a two game match for which he received $2500.

White: *Belle* (≈2100) – Black: Carl Storey (2206)
1981 Fredkin Challenge Match
1. e4 g6 2. d4 Bg7 3. Nf3 d6 4. Nc3 Nf6 5. Be2 O-O 6. O-O c6 7. a4 Qc7 8. h3 e5 9. Re1 Nbd7 10. Bf1 Re8 11. d5? *Not knowing any better, Belle plays this uncalled for move. It soon drifts into an endgame with few prospects.* **a6 12. Bg5 h6 13. Be3 cxd5 14. Nxd5 Nxd5 15. Qxd5 Nf6 16. Qc4 Qxc4 17. Bxc4 Nxe4 18. Bxh6 Bxh6 19. Rxe4 Bf5 20. Rh4 Bg7 21. Bd5 Re7 22. c3** *Belle does not realize that its rook is misplaced on h4. Rb4 was necessary and good.* **e4 23. Nd4 Bxd4 24. cxd4 Kg7 25. Rf4 Rae8 26. b4 Bc8 27. Ra3 f5** *The rook is trapped!* **28. Rg3 e3** *Better is Kf6.* **29. fxe3 Rxe3 30. Kh2 Rxg3 31. Kxg3 Re1 32. Bb3** *If 32. Rf3, then Rc1 33. Re3 Kf6 and black is still better.* **b6 33. Rf3 Re4 34. Rd3** *Rc3 is not played because of Rxd4!* **Bb7 35. Bd1 Re1 36. Kf2 Re7 37. Bf3?** *Not knowing much about rook endings, Belle drifts into a lost one. Better is Rc3.* **Bxf3 38. Kxf3 Rc7 39. Rb3 Rc4 40. a5 b5 41. Ke3 g5 42. Kd3 Kf6 43. Rc3 Rxc3+ 44. Kxc3 f4 45. Kd3 Kf5 46. d5 Ke5 47. Ke2 Kxd5 0-1.**

2.7 Cray Blitz versus David Levy

In 1983, *Cray Blitz* won the 4th World Computer Chess Championship, scoring 4.5 out of 5. The program ran on a Cray X-MP, world's fastest computer, and searched over 30 million positions in 3 minutes of think time. In 1984, the *Cray Blitz* team (Robert Hyatt, Albert Gower and Harry Nelson) challenged David Levy to a match during the 4th Advances in Computer Chess Conference.

This match was an indirect consequence of Levy's 1968 bet. The challenge was renewed with the support of OMNI Magazine, offering $5,000 (including $1,000 from Levy) to the first program to defeat David Levy at any time. For the match, opening and middlegame strategies were designed to befuddle the program which could search to 8 ply and beyond. Although he has never been rated more than 2375, David Levy's experience in playing against chess programs gave him a decided advantage.

As it turned out, *Cray Blitz* suffered from both communication and hardware problems causing it to fall into severe time trouble. Levy played surprisingly well after a 5 year layoff from chess, capitalizing on his "do nothing but do it well" strategy to score a 4-0 shutout. The complete details of the match and the games are well described by Levy (1986a) and by Welsh and Baczynskyj (1985). Levy and I, acting as his second, did extensive match preparation and planning. A position from the first game of the match is indicative of the success Levy had with this preparation. Levy chooses an opening which, although objectively unfavorable, proves difficult for *Cray Blitz*. White is drawn into a position with a blocked center where positional themes in the sub-center and wings become critical. *Cray Blitz* makes a number of serious strategical errors, and the position in Figure 2.6 arises:

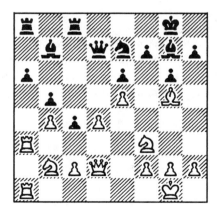

Figure 2.6: *Cray Blitz* – IM David Levy (white to move).

White: *Cray Blitz* ($\approx$2200) – Black: IM David Levy (2300 FIDE)
1984 Match

20. c3? *White's position has been steadily declining and the threat was simply*
20. ... c3. Best for white is probably Nd1. Instead, after the text the white knight
on b2 never gets back into play and white's position literally becomes split into
two halves. **Bxf3!** *Levy initiates an ideal pawn sacrifice. White's king-side*
pawn structure is permanently shattered, black obtains long-term positional
compensation and an initiative which the program finds difficult to evaluate
properly. **21. gxf3 Nf5!** *The P on a6 could not be defended anyway, and*
black's king-side initiative is about to begin. **22. Rxa6 Rxa6 23. Rxa6 Qb7 24.**
Ra5 Qxf3 25. Rxb5? *This is the culmination of the combination which began*
with 20. ... Bxf3!!. Levy knew that Cray Blitz would continue its greedy ways.
h6 26. Bf4 Qh3 27. Bg3 h5 28. Rc5 Ra8 29. Qc1? *Ra5 was the only defense.*
h4 30. Bf4? *This was white's last chance to put up resistance by Qf1, although*
it gives up a piece. **Qf3! 31. h3 Qxh3 32. Rxc4? Qf3 33. Bh2 h3 34. Qf1 Ra1!**
35. Nd1 Rxd1 36. Rc8+ Kh7 37. Rh8+ Kxh8 38. Qxd1 Qg2 mate 0-1.

2.8 The Reign of Hitech

In 1984 it was hard to foresee that *Cray Blitz* would soon be overtaken by
another program. At the 4th Advances in Computer Chess Conference in
London, Hans Berliner presented a paper on his "Five Year Plan for Computer
Chess at Carnegie Mellon University" (Berliner 1986). The approach presented
seemed a sensible hybrid of brute-force search and knowledge-based
approaches. He recognized the need for a powerful and deep exhaustive search,
but also advocated the development of a large incremental store of pattern-based
chess knowledge. Essentially, he had a clear plan for what had to be done, some
powerful methods for accomplishing his goals, a team of people which he could
rely on and work with (Carl Ebeling, Gordon Goetsch, Andy Palay, Murray
Campbell and Larry Slomer), and the support of an excellent university
(Carnegie Mellon) behind it. However, many remained skeptical since Berliner,
although having initiated his research into computer chess around 1970, had
never developed a strong program and even seemed to discontinue his work in
the area several times. His earlier software program, *Patsoc,* did not perform
particularly well at the 4th World Computer Chess Championship in New York,
1983.

Any remaining skepticism was completely dissolved when *Hitech* won the
1985 North American Computer Chess Championship with a perfect 4-0 score.
Its rating quickly rose well into the master class. Between 1985 and mid-1988,
Hitech was clearly the world's best program and in 1988 became the first
program to achieve a senior master (2400) rating. *Hitech* has won the
Pennsylvania State Championship three years in a row (1987, 1988 and 1989)
and is ranked amongst the top 150 players in the United States at 2413. More
details about *Hitech* and its performance can be found in Chapter 6 *Hitech*.

Since *Hitech* matured in 1987, with debugged software and more pattern recognition capabilities, it has achieved a large plus score against masters. It is generally regarded that *Hitech* plays the most human-like chess of the strong programs. The following game represents the highest rated player that *Hitech* has scored against and was quite an upset at the time. The play is wild with chances for both sides and illustrates what resourceful defenders the top programs can be.

White: IM Michael Rohde (2602) – Black: *Hitech* (≈2350)
1986 World Open

1. d4 Nf6 2. Nf3 g6 3. c4 Bg7 4. Nc3 d5 5. Qb3 dxc4 6. Qxc4 O-O 7. e4 Bg4 8. Be3 Nfd7 9. Qb3 Nb6 10. Rd1 Nc6 11. d5 Ne5 12. Be2 Nxf3+ 13. gxf3 Bh5 14. Rg1 *White has more space from his big center but black has no weaknesses.* **Qd7 15. Rg3 f5!** *An active move which creates weaknesses but also emphasizes some of the weaknesses in white's position.* **16. Bd4 Bxd4 17. Rxd4 Kh8 18. Rd1** *It's not so easy to suggest how white should continue because 18. e5!? f4 followed by 19. ... Rf5 may prove the white center pawns weak. Black starts to get some counterplay now.* **f4 19. Rg1 Qh3** *This looks offside, but black has just adequate resources for such a venture.* **20. Nb5 Qxh2 21. Rf1 c6 22. Qc3+ Rf6 23. Nc7 Raf8 24. Ne6 Ra8 25. d6!** *One senses that Rohde now feels he can win at will and he becomes just a little over-confident.* **Kg8 26. d7** *This should win, but perhaps 26. Qb3 first might be even stronger, virtually forcing exd6 27. Rxd6 etc.* **Nxd7 27. Rxd7 Rxe6 28. Bc4 Kf7 29. Ke2!?** *Again one gets the feeling that white thinks the game is over. Qe5 looks more effective, although after Qh3 30. Bxe6+ Qxe6 31. Qxe6+ Kxe6 32. Rxb7 Bxf3 black has plenty of play in the ending. Instead white could play 29. Rxb7.* **Qh3 30. Rxb7 Rd8** *Hitech has definite counterplay for the exchange, stemming from the bishop on h5.* **31. Rb3 Rd5!!** *An excellent defensive resource as the white king now becomes more of a target than its black counterpart.* **32. Ke1 Qg2 33. Bxd5 cxd5 34. Qh8 Rxe4+** *Forcing a draw which white could force in any case.* **35. fxe4 Qxe4+ 36. Kd2 Qe2+ 37. Kc3 Qc4+ 38. Kd2 ½-½.**

The play by *Hitech* in winning the next position is a wonderful technical and creative achievement and decided the 1988 Pennsylvania State Championship in *Hitech*'s favor.

White: IM Edward Formanek (2461) – Black: *Hitech* (≈2390)
1988 Pennsylvania State Championship

In Figure 2.7 *Black is up a solid pawn but it is not an easy position to win because the white knight is powerfully posted on d4 and the bishop is bad on b7.* **34. Rb1 Rc7 35. Rb6 Kf7 36. Re6 Qg5 37. Qg3 Rc2+!** *Forcing further simplification into a bishop versus knight ending which can only bring black closer to victory.* **38. Nxc2 Qxg3+ 39. Kxg3 Kxe6 40. Nd4+ Ke5 41. Kf3 h5 42. h4 g5 43. g3 Bc8 44. Nc6+ Kd6 45. Nd4 Bg4+ 46. Kf2 Ke5 47. Nb5 Bd7 48. Nd4 Ke4 49. Nc2 Bb5 50. Nd4 Ba6 51. Ne6 Bc8 52. Nd4 Bd7** *It appears the position is coming around full circle. Nevertheless, black is making steady progress in improving its position.* **53. Nc2 gxh4 54. gxh4 Bg4 55. Nd4 f5 56.**

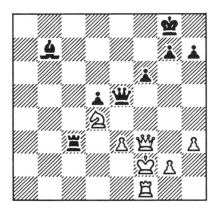

Figure 2.7: IM Edward Formanek – *Hitech* (white to move).

Ne6 f4!! *Such a wonderful move deserves a diagram,* Figure 2.8. *Hitech sees deeply into the position, as after 57. Nxf4 d4 58. Ng2 d3 59. Ke1 Kf3 wins.* **57. Nc5+ Kf5 58. Nd3 d4!!** *Transposing into the winning line described above.* **59. exd4 Ke4 60. Ne5 Kxd4** *A nice point is that if 61. Nxg4 hxg4, the black king can still stop the white pawn.* **61. Nf7 Be6 62. Ng5 Bd5 63. Nh3 Ke4 64. Ng1 Kf5 65. Ne2 Kg4 66. Kg1 f3 67. Nc3 Bc6 68. Kf2 Kxh4 69. Nd1 Kg4 70. Ne3+ Kf4 71. Nf1 h4 72. Nh2 h3 73. Nf1 Bb5 74. Ng3 h2 75. Nh5+ Kg4 76. Ng3 Bf1! 0-1.** *A beautifully played endgame.*

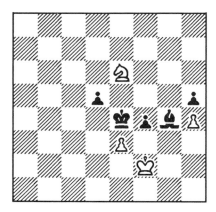

Figure 2.8: IM Edward Formanek – *Hitech* (white to move).

This section concludes with an example showing that humans are not to be out-done yet. Bear in mind that Kudrin is a Grandmaster and one of the twenty highest rated players in the United States. He also specializes in the Dragon Variation of the Sicilian Defense.

White: *Hitech* ($\approx$2390) – Black: GM Sergey Kudrin ($\approx$2620)
1988 National Open
1. e4 c5 2. Nf3 Nc6 3. d4 cxd4 4. Nxd4 g6 5. Nc3 Bg7 6. Be3 Nf6 7. Bc4 O-O 8. Bb3 d6 9. f3 Bd7 10. Qd2 Rc8 11. O-O-O Ne5 12. g4 b5 13. g5?! *In some sense, this variation is an ideal choice by black against a computer. There is plenty of deep theory and machines are likely to grab a pawn not realizing the long-term dangers to their king. In the meantime white's attack against the black king never gets off the ground.* **Nh5 14. Ncxb5 Nxf3 15. Nxf3 Bxb5 16. Bxa7 Bc4 17. Qe3 Bxb3 18. Qxb3 Nf4 19. e5 Qd7 20. Bb6?! Rb8 21. Qe3 Qa4** *Black has an excellent attacking position.* **22. Kb1 Rfc8 23. b3 Qc6 24. Ba7 Ra8 25. c4 Ng2 26. Qf2 Qe4+ 27. Kc1 Rxa7 28. Qxg2 Bxe5 29. Rhe1 Bf4+ 30. Kb2 Rxa2+ 31. Kxa2 Ra8+ 32. Kb2 Be5+ 33. Nxe5 Qxg2+ 0-1.**

2.9 The Master Micros

Through the 1980s, manufacturers of microcomputer chess programs had intensely pursued the goal of developing a master level program. The major companies involved in this effort have been Fidelity International, Hegener and Glaser (manufacturers of the *Mephisto* series) and *Novag* (manufacturer of the *Constellation* series). In retrospect, progress through the 1980s was superb. In 1980 the programs were still quite weak, playing no better than Class B (1600-1800) chess. By 1985 the *Fidelity Par Excellence* was officially rated 2100. The transition from the 6502 chip to the faster 68,000 chip, with its extended assembly language instruction set, special endgame knowledge and efficient software were primarily responsible for enabling *Fidelity* to surpass the coveted 2200 threshold in 1987. *Mephisto* followed suit in 1988. For this the programmers Dan and Kathe Spracklen (*Fidelity*) and Richard Lang (*Mephisto*) deserve tremendous credit. Their ability to compete with the best programs despite severe handicaps in memory size and CPU speed clearly attests to their superior software. *Fidelity* scored the first tournament win ever over an International Master at the 1986 U.S. Open[3].

White: *Fidelity* ($\approx$2180) – Black: IM David Strauss (2533)
1986 U.S. Open
1. e4 d5 2. exd5 Nf6 3. d4 Nxd5 4. c4 Nb6 5. Nf3 g6 6. Nc3 Bg7 7. h3 O-O 8. Be3 Nc6 9. Qd2 e5 10. d5 Ne7 11. g4 f5 12. O-O-O fxg4 13. Ng5 *This is all part of an extended book line prepared by Boris Baczynskyj which ends here.* **g3!? 14. c5 g2 15. Bxg2 Nc4 16. Qe2 Nxe3 17. Qxe3 Nf5 18. Qd2 Bh6 19. Nce4 Nh4 20. Rhg1 Bf5 21. Bh1** *A human might get tired of defending white's position, but of course a program is unaffected by such feelings.* **b6 22. d6 c6**

---
[3] *Chess 4.7*'s win over David Levy was under match conditions.

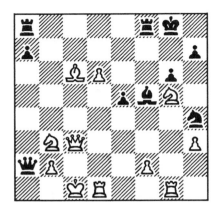

Figure 2.9: IM David Strauss – *Fidelity* (black to move).

23. Qe3 bxc5? 24. Nxc5 Qb6 25. Nb3 Qa6 *Strauss probably thought he was winning here.* **26. Qc3 Qxa2 27. Bxc6!** *See* Figure 2.9. *Computers know no dangers! A human would probably never dare to take this pawn.* **Rad8 28. Bd5+ Kh8 29. Nc5 Qb1+ 30. Kd2** *White now has a won game.* **Nf3+** *Black does not have enough for the piece.* **31. Bxf3 Rxd6+ 32. Ke2 Rxd1 33. Rxd1 Qc2+ 34. Qxc2 Bxc2 35. Rg1 Bf5 36. h4 Rb8 37. b3 Rc8 38. Nf7+ Kg7 39. Nd6! Rf8 40. Ra1 Kh8 41. Rxa7 Bf4 42. Nf7+ Kg8 43. Bd5 Kg7 44. Ng5+ 1–0.** *An efficiently played game by white.*

In 1989, a new man-machine event was christened, called The Harvard Cup. The 4 round event pitted four Grandmasters (Boris Gulko, Michael Rohde, Lev Alburt and Max Dlugy) against four computers (*Deep Thought, ChipTest, Hitech* and *Mephisto*). The games were played at the time control of 30 minutes sudden death. This seemed to handicap the computers more than the humans. The final score was 14.5 out of 16 in favor of the humans. In the following game, two-time U.S. Champion Alburt enters too many tactical complications and relinquishes half a point to *Mephisto*.

White: GM Lev Alburt (≈2696) – Black: *Mephisto* (≈2200)

1989 Harvard Cup

1. d4 e6 2. g3 Nf6 3. Bg2 Nc6 *Despite all their fine play, programs still often develop their knights in front of their queen's bishop pawns.* **4. Nf3 d5 5. O-O Be7 6. c4 O-O 7. Nc3 dxc4 8. e3 Na5 9. Qe2 c5 10. dxc5 Qc7 11. e4 Bxc5 12. Bg5 Ng4 13. e5 f6 14. exf6 gxf6 15. Bd2 Bd7 16. h3 Ne5 17. Nxe5 Qxe5 18. Qxe5 fxe5 19. Ne4 Bb6 20. Rad1 Ba4 21. Rc1 Bc6 22. Bc3 Rad8 23. Rc2 Rf5 24. Re2 h6 25. g4 Rf7 26. Bxe5 Rd3 27. Bc3 Kf8** *White now wins a pawn but lets black out of the bind.* **28. Bxa5 Bxa5 29. Nc5 Bxg2 30. Kxg2 Rd5 31. Nxe6+ Kg8 32. f4 b5** *With good technique white's king-side pawns should win, but Alburt makes the mistake of letting the game become an unclear and exciting*

race. **33. Re4 Bb6 34. Rfe1 Rd2+ 35. R1e2 Rfd7 36. Kf1?** *Inconsequential.*
**Rd1+ 37. Re1 Ba5 38. Rxd1 Rxd1+ 39. Kf2 Bb6++ 40. Kg3 Rd2 41. a4 a6 42.
Kh4 Rxb2** *Somewhere in the next few moves black should play Kf7, but the
machine can't anticipate white's mating idea.* **43. Kh5 c3 44. Kg6** *See* Figure
2.10. **Rb4!** *The ending now becomes tactical.* **45. Nd4 Kf8 46. Ne6+ Kg8** *Ke8
or Ke7 would be ideally complicated for Alburt's time pressure.* **47. Re5 c2 48.
Rd5?!** *Rf5 looks like a better winning try, e.g. Bc5 49. Nxc5!?, but after c1=Q
50. Rd5 Kf8 black may be winning.* **c1=Q 49. Rd7 Qc3 50. Re7** *Amazingly,
white still has a draw.* **Qc2+ 51. f5 Rxg4+ 52. hxg4 Qc6 53. Rg7+ Kh8 54.
Rh7+ Kg8 55. Rg7+ Kh8 56. Rh7+ Kg8 ½-½.**

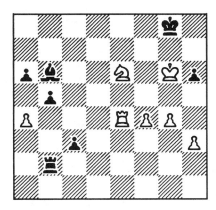

Figure 2.10: GM Lev Alburt – *Mephisto* (black to move).

2.10 Deep Thought Challenges Mankind's Best

In less than two years, *Deep Thought* has gone on a whirlwind tour through the
world of chess. Since the summer of 1988 its series of accomplishments,
including a number of Grandmaster victims and tournament victories, has been
remarkable. The program was developed by five researchers at Carnegie Mellon
University: Feng-hsiung Hsu, Thomas Anantharaman, Murray Campbell,
Andreas Nowatzyk and Peter Jansen. Hsu, Campbell and Anantharaman are
now working on a new *Deep Thought*, with the sponsorship of IBM. In the next
few years they hope that advances in parallel computing and VLSI technology
will enable *Deep Thought* to consider one billion moves per second, which
equates to an exhaustive search of about 14-ply. The version of *Deep Thought*
which played a match against David Levy in December, 1989, ran on four
processors in parallel and searched over 700,000 positions per second, or over
100 million positions (often over 10 ply) in 3 minutes. *Deep Thought's* speed
comes from its special-purpose VLSI chips, with the main program running off a

Sun 4 workstation. Its evaluation function is tuned using a database of 900
IM/GM games. The program consists of 100,000 lines of code and is written in
C. It evaluates king safety, mobility, development, etc. and employs an
important search concept called singular extensions (Anantharaman, Campbell
and Hsu 1988) to recognize moves which appear important enough to analyze
them more deeply. More details can be found in Chapter 5 *Deep Thought*.

Deep Thought won the 6th World Computer Chess Championship (Kopec
1989; Chapter 3 *1989 World Computer Chess Championship*) with a perfect 5-0
score. Its current rating is 2551 USCF and there are now only a few players in
the world strong enough to feel confident against the program. A few of *Deep
Thought*'s major games are presented below.

The program made history by tying for first at the 1988 Software Toolworks
Open with GM Anthony Miles, each scoring 6.5 out of 8. *En route*, the
program scored the first tournament win by a computer over a Grandmaster,
former World Championship candidate Bent Larsen. True, Larsen is no longer
in his prime, but neither can he be called a pushover with his 2580 FIDE rating.
The game score with annotations can be found in Chapter 15 *Brute Force in
Chess and Science*.

Deep Thought's strength lies in its deep searches. Figure 2.11 shows a
position that is bound to become historic in the annals of *Deep Thought*. It
illustrates, yet again, the stupefying power of brute-force search and how it can
lead to unexpected powerful, deep and devastating combinations.

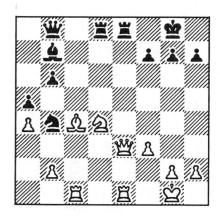

Figure 2.11: *Deep Thought* – Eric Cooke (white to move).

White: *Deep Thought* (2551) – Black: Eric Cooke (≈2250)
1989 Software Toolworks Open

White finds an unexpected and strong resource. **29. Qg5!!** *Prefaces the
carnage that follows. If Rxe1+ 30. Rxe1 Rxd4 31. Bxf7+! Kh8 (Kxf7 32. Re7+
and mates) 32. Re8+ wins. The threat of 30. Nf5 is now menacing and if 29. ...*

h6 then 30. Qg6 wins. **Rxd4 30. Bxf7+ Kxf7 31. Rc7+!** *A beautiful move, based on a simple mating theme which brute-force programs can find routinely and humans can overlook easily.* **Qxc7 32. Qf5+ 1-0.**

One area where *Deep Thought*'s play is weak is in the opening. Hence, it is probably wrong to alter one's style of play just to avoid *Deep Thought*'s book. That is what seems to happen in the following game. Former World Championship candidate Robert Byrne finds that out after he chooses the inferior Owen Defense to get *Deep Thought* out of book. Overall, Byrne's play is passive and he makes a number of inaccuracies (Byrne 1989).

White: *Deep Thought* (≈2550) – Black: GM Robert Byrne (≈2540)
USA Sports Center Match
1.e4 c5 2. c3 b6 3. d4 Bb7 4. Bd3 e6 5. Be3 Nf6 6. Nd2 Nc6 7. a3 d6 8. Qf3 g6 9. Ne2 Bg7 10. O-O O-O-O 11. b4 cxd4 12 cxd4 Qd7 13. Rac1 Rac8 14. h3 Ne7 15. Bg5 Rxc1 16. Rxc1 Ne8 17. Bb5 Qd8 18. Qg3 h6 19. Be3 d5 20. f3 Nd6 21. Bd3 b5 22. Rc5! *Seizing the initiative.* **a6 23. Bf4 Nc4 24. Bxc4 dxc4 25. Bd6 Re8 26. Rc7 Ba8 27. Rc5 Nc8 28. Be5 Bxe5 29. Qxe5 Nd6 30. a4 Qd7 31. Qf4 Kg7 32. h4 Bc6 33. d5 Ba8 34. dxe6 Rxe6 35. axb5 axb5 36. Nf1 Nxe4!?** *Desperation.* **37. fxe4 Rxe4 38. Qf2 c3 39. Nxc3 Rxb4 40. Ne3 Bc6 41. Ned5 Bxd5 42. Nxd5 Rb1+ 43. Kh2 Qd6+ 44. g3 Qe5 45. Nc3 Qe1 46. Qd4+ Kh7 47. Nxb1 Qe2+ 48. Kg1 1-0.**

These two adversaries have since played each other twice more, each with a win.

There are still times when a strong human player can make *Deep Thought* look confused. Walter Browne again finds himself the center of attention by "upsetting" *Deep Thought* at the 1988 Software Toolworks Open. *Deep Thought* makes some peculiar bishop moves and then Browne finds a deep, long-term tactical theme based on white's weakness on the h1-a8 diagonal.

White: *Deep Thought* (≈2450) – Black: GM Walter Browne (≈2650)
1988 Software Toolworks Open
1. e4 c5 2. c3 Nf6 3. e5 Nd5 4. d4 cxd4 5. Nf3 Nc6 6. Bc4 Nb6 7. Bb3 d5 8. exd6 Qxd6 9. O-O e6 10. cxd4 Be7 11. Nc3 O-O 12. Re1 Nd5! *Getting Deep Thought out of book since the normal moves in this position are Bd7 and Rd8, as Browne writes in* Inside Chess, March, 1989. **13. g3!?** *Unnecessarily weakening.* **Qd8! 14. a3?! Nxc3!** *White is now saddled with a long-term weakness on c3.* **15. bxc3 b6 16. Qd3 Bb7 17. Bc2 g6 18. Bf4?!** *For the next three moves, Deep Thought gropes to find the right square for its queen's bishop.* **Rc8 19. Bh6?!** *This would have been more natural last move.* **Re8 20. Bd2? Na5 21. Ba4** *See* Figure 2.12. **Qd5!** *Browne finds a winning idea which is simply beyond Deep Thought's depth of analysis. Such long-term positional themes still separate top human players from the best programs.* **22. Bxe8 Rxe8 23. Kg2 Nc4 24. Bc1 g5! 25. h3 h5 26. g4 e5!** *All of black's forces join the attack.* **27. Qd1 f5! 28. gxh5 g4 29. hxg4 fxg4 30. Kg1 Qxf3 31. Qxf3 Bxf3 32. Bh6 Kh7 33. Bd2?** *Another futile move with the bishop, but the threat was Rf8-f5-h5-h1 mate!* **Rf8 34. Rxe5 Nxe5 35. Re1 Nc6 0-1.**

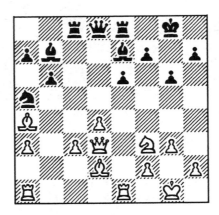

Figure 2.12: *Deep Thought* – GM Walter Browne (black to move).

In October, 1989, Gary Kasparov achieved the highest FIDE rating ever attained by reaching 2795 and eclipsing Bobby Fischer's mark of 2780. Shortly afterwards, Kasparov raised his rating over the 2800 mark. At the height of his confidence, he challenged *Deep Thought* to a two game match. Both sides played at the rate of two hours for all the moves. Kasparov took this challenge seriously (as he takes all chess-related matters) and prepared carefully for the match by studying *Deep Thought's* games. Kasparov convincingly won both games; it all looked so easy. However, this should not belittle the virtuoso performance by the human World Champion.

In the first game, Kasparov demonstrated his superior understanding of positional chess; *Deep Thought* was ground down in 52 moves. In the second game Kasparov won handily. A pawn sacrifice is too much for a gullible program to refuse and *Deep Thought* quickly finds the tactics overwhelmingly against it. That Kasparov should so handily defeat the best computer program shows there is still a long way to go to reach the level of the human World Champion.

White: Gary Kasparov (2800 FIDE) – Black: *Deep Thought* (2551)

Exhibition match

1. d4 d5 2. c4 dxc4 3. e4 Nc6 4. Nf3 Bg4 5. d5 Ne5 6. Nc3! c6 7. Bf4 Ng6 8. Be3 cxd5 9. exd5 Ne5 10. Qd4 Nxf3+ 11. gxf3 Bxf3 12. Bxc4! Qd6 13. Nb5 Qf6 14. Qc5 Qb6 15. Qa3! e6 16. Nc7+ Qc7 17. Bb5+ Qc6 18. Bxc6+ bxc6 19. Bc5 Bxc5 20. Qxf3 Bb4+ 21. Ke2 cxd5 22. Qg4 Be7 23. Rhc1 Kf8 24. Rc7 Bd6 25. Rb7 Nf6 26. Qa4 a5 27. Rc1 h6 28. Rc6 Ne8 29. b4 Bxh2 30. bxa5 Kg8 31. Qb4 Bd6 32. Rxd6 Nxd6 33. Rb8+ Rxb8 34. Qxb8+ Kh7 35. Qxd6 Rc8 36. a4 Rc4 37. Qd7 1-0.

2.11 End of an Era

In December, 1989, in a match billed as "The Ultimate Challenge," *Deep Thought* challenged David Levy for the $5,000 OMNI/Levy prize. A decade of chess inactivity was difficult for Levy to overcome and, perhaps surprisingly, he was overwhelmed 4-0 by *Deep Thought*. The second game pretty much summarizes the match as Levy had his best chance to score (a draw) and still came up empty-handed.

White: *Deep Thought* (2551) – Black: IM David Levy (2300 FIDE)
1989 Match
1. c4 d6 2. Nc3 g6 3. d4 Bg7 4. e4 a6 *This gets Deep Thought out of book, but the match plan was to play Nd7 with c5 or e5 to follow.* **5. Be3 Nf6 6. Be2 O-O** *I would prefer c5 either here or on the next move.* **7. f4!?** *Throughout the match, Deep Thought seemed to loved to create quartets with its pawns.* **c6** *Much too timid.* **8. e5 Ne8 9. Nf3 d5 10. O-O Nc7** *Ten moves into the game and black has no pieces beyond the second rank!* **11. Rc1 e6 12. Qe1 b5?** *Too weakening on a wing where white also has more space. I prefer dxc4 with Nd7-b6-d5 to follow.* **13. cxd5 cxd5 14. Nd1! Ra7 15. Nf2 Nd7 16. Qa5 Bd2 is very strong. Na8 17. Qa3?** *Trading queens followed by Bd2 was strong.* **Qb6 18. Bd2 a5 19. Qd6 b4 20. Rc6 Qd8 21. Rfc1 Bb7 22. R6c2 Ndb6 23. Qxd8 Rxd8 24. Be3 Rc8** *Black appears to nearly have equality.* **25. Rc5 Bf8 26. Bd3! Rd8 27. R5c2 Rc8 28. Rxc8 Bxc8 29. Ng4 Be7 30. Nf6+ Bxf6?** *Kg7 was essential.* **31. exf6 Rc7 32. Ne5 Rxc1+ 33. Bxc1 Bb7** *White's N/e5 and P/f6 are too strong.* **34. a3 Nc7 35. axb4 axb4 36. Bd2 Na4 37. Bxb4 Nxb2 38. Ng4!** *Announcing mate in 12!* **e5** *Desperation.* **39. Nh6+ Kh8 40. Nxf7+ Kg8 41. Nh6+ Kh8 42. f5 1-0.**

It was the end of an era in computer chess. The best programs are now playing at the strong master, weak Grandmaster level. Can it be long before advancing technology allows computers to successfully challenge Gary Kasparov?

Kasparov believes that he can "save mankind" for at least five years and probably ten. An unanswered question is how much of Kasparov's overwhelming success against *Deep Thought* was based on his preparation for the match and how much was based on his pure ability and technique? Kasparov believes that as computers become more of a threat to humans in the game of chess, so will humans learn new ways to exploit their weaknesses. This is undoubtably true, however the number of years where humans will be dominant must be very limited. In the meantime there will be some exciting chess battles ahead.

Acknowledgments. I would like to take this opportunity to thank those who have led me into the world of artificial intelligence and computer chess, particularly Larry Harris and Donald Michie, and those who have encouraged me to stay in it including Monty Newborn, Tony Marsland and David Levy, as well as George

Markowsky and Ed Northam. I would like to thank the late Harvey Brimmer for his careful corrections, and Ed Northam for his willingness to proofread the typescript carefully. Finally, I would like to thank Jonathan Schaeffer and Tony Marsland for asking me to be a contributor to this book and for their patience and concern as editors.

3 1989 World Computer Chess Championship

J. Schaeffer

3.1 The Opening

The story of an important event, such as the 6th World Computer Chess Championship, can be told from many points of view. From the scientific standpoint, the competitive results of the tournament and the papers presented at the accompanying Workshop best measure the scientific stature of the event. The participants measure the tournament in terms of their program's success and how much they enjoyed themselves. For the organizers, the costs, publicity and attendance of the event are their metrics. And, of course, from the audience's point of view, the event must be entertaining.

Rather than presenting yet another impersonal tournament report, this chapter provides a descriptive and anecdotal report of an important computer-chess event.

What is the recipe for organizing a World Computer Chess Championship? First, take one persuasive International Computer Chess Association (ICCA) president, David Levy. Second, take two naive people interested in computer chess, Tony Marsland and Jonathan Schaeffer. Mix the three together, with David saying all the right flattering things and applying subtle pressure. Finally, extract a commitment. It happened so fast, I'm still not sure how we were roped into this.

In fairness to David, the World Championship has traditionally alternated between Europe and North America and, within North America, between Canada and the United States. In 1986, David first broached the suggestion of holding the World Championship in Canada in 1989. The Championship has been held in the past in conjunction with a major computer conference. The obvious place to look was at the annual Canadian Information Processing Society's (CIPS) Congress. And where was it going to be held in 1989? Edmonton, May 28-31. How was it possible to avoid organizing the Championship if it was going to be held in your home town? I am sure David had a good chuckle over that.

It is difficult to appreciate how much work it takes to put on an international event like the World Championship. First and foremost was the problem of fund raising. CIPS guaranteed minimal support to put on the basic tournament; we needed more money to put on first class show. We were fortunate in that, early on, Alberta Government Telephones (AGT) was interested in the telecommunications aspects of the event. Six months after our initial contact, AGT agreed to be our principal sponsor. Their money, time and manpower ensured a successful tournament.

What do you have to do to organize such an event? The list seemed endless: finding volunteers, arranging facilities, finding computers, arranging commentators, contacting the participants, arranging the telecommunications, transportation, accommodation, tournament program, workshop, pre-tournament social event, post-tournament social event, invited guests, publicity, and a million little things. In short, everything. Neither Tony nor I properly appreciated the organizational task that lay ahead. Had we known ...

After the announcement of Edmonton as the site for the tournament, the most oft asked question was "Do I need to bring winter clothes?" The stereotype of Canada, winter and Eskimos, is just not true. In the summer, Edmonton has pleasant weather with little wind, no humidity, warm days and lots of sun. And that is what everyone was told. Unfortunately, we neglected to add the adjective 'unpredictable' to the list. As if in a self-fulfilling prophecy for those who believed Edmonton to be part of the Arctic, a week before the tournament began, a freak blizzard hit, covering the ground in a deep layer of wet snow. Jaap van den Herik (ICCA Journal editor) and his wife Lette arrived by plane that day into the midsts of a raging storm. It took considerable effort to dissuade them from turning around and going back to Amsterdam. Fortunately, the snow melted in a few days and the weather was perfect for the tournament.

The event officially started with a social on the eve of the opening round. A barbecue was held out in the country, a relaxing change of pace from the pressures of the city. In a comfortable atmosphere, with plenty of food, wine, music and friends, what do the participants talk about? After the perfunctory greetings, many of the programmers gather together and talk shop: What has changed in your program since the last event? Any new search ideas? What do you think of so-and-so's ideas? The wives and non-technical people quickly leave them alone and retire to an evening of ping-pong, amusements and pleasant conversation.

Some of the early tournament favorites included *Deep Thought*, whose recent results suggested it may be Grandmaster strength, *Hitech*, playing at the level of a U.S. senior master, *Cray Blitz*, the current computer champion and running on the world's fastest computer, *Bebe* and *Phoenix*, who tied for first in the 5th World Championship, and *Fidelity* and *Mephisto*, commercially available micros with some astounding results in the past year. Table 3.1 shows the tournament participants and Table 3.2 their specifications. Perhaps not surprisingly, the list of favorites correlates well with machine speed. Who would falter?

The first round produced a surprise, as *Mephisto* built up a promising position against *Waycool* and then deftly did an about face and lost.

In addition to the participants, the tournament brought together a number of prominent computer-chess researchers. John McCarthy and Donald Michie were the invited guests of the *New Directions in Game-Tree Search Workshop*

Program	Country	Authors
A.I. Chess	USA	Martin Hirsch
Bebe	USA	Tony and Linda Scherzer
BP	USA	Robert Cullum
Centaur	USSR	Victor Vikhrev
Cray Blitz	USA	Robert Hyatt, Albert Gower, Harry Nelson
Dappet	Netherlands	Dap Hartmann, Peter Kouwenhoven
Deep Thought	USA	Thomas Anantharaman, Mike Browne, Murray Campbell, Feng-hsiung Hsu, Peter Jansen, Andreas Nowatzyk
Fidelity X	USA	Dan and Kathe Spracklen, Ron Nelson
Hitech	USA	Hans Berliner, Murray Campbell, Carl Ebeling, Gordon Goetsch, Andy Gruss, Andy Palay, Larry Slomer
Kallisto	Netherlands	Bert Weststrate
Mephisto X	Germany	Richard Lang
Merlin	Austria	Helmut Horacek, Hermann Kaindl, Marcus Wagner
Moby	Britain	David Levy, Mark Taylor, Greg Wilson
Much	Netherlands	Jaap van den Herik, Roger Hünen, Harry Nefkens, Tom Pronk
Novag X	USA	David Kittinger
Pandix	Hungary	Gyula and Zsuzsa Horvath
Phoenix	Canada	Jonathan Schaeffer
Quest X	Netherlands	Frans Morsch
Rebel X	Germany	Ed Schröder
Rex	USA	Dan Dailey, Larry Kaufman
Shess	Netherlands	Ard van Bergen
Waycool	USA	Ed Felten, Rod Morison, Steve Otto
Y!89	Sweden	Lars Hjorth, Sandro Necchi, Ulf Rathsman
Zarkov	USA	John Stanback

Table 3.1: Participants.

held in conjunction with the tournament. McCarthy is well known in computer-chess circles for his early work on the alpha-beta algorithm. In the computing community, he is best known for the *Lisp* programming language. His fundamental research in artificial intelligence earned him the prestigious Turing Award, the "Nobel prize" of computing.

Donald Michie has done important work in computer chess for many decades. He has produced a prodigious number of research papers and books, with no sign of abatement to his hectic pace.

Program	Language	Code+Data K bytes	Book ×1000	Computer	Nodes/sec ×1000
A.I. Chess	C, Assembler	200+64	10	Dyna 8086	2.5
Bebe	Assembler	16+40	4	Sys-10	45
BP	C, Assembler	325	15	Unisys PW800	0.6
Centaur	Pascal	120+30	16	IBM PS2/80	1
Cray Blitz	Fortran, CAL	500+1M	5	Cray YMP	100
Dappet	Turbo Pascal	500	15	Toshiba	0.2-0.8
Deep Thought	C, Assembler	1M+23M	4.5	VLSI-Sys	1000
Fidelity X	Assembler	32+16	32-64	MC68030	10
Hitech	C	700+24M	5.8	VLSI-Sys	100
Kallisto	Assembler	20+8	6	Apple II	3-6
Mephisto X	Assembler	128	60	MC 68020	2
Merlin	Pascal	n/a	n/a	IBM 3090	0.5
Moby	Occam	n/a	8	Meikos Transp.	0.25
Much	C	170-2.5M	4.5	Sun 4	3
Novag X	Assembler	96+8	36	MOS 6502	2.8
Pandix	C, Assembler	50+10	7.4	Sanyo 386	0.30
Phoenix	C	200+2M	20	20×Sun 4	10
Quest X	Assembler	32+8	8	MOS 6502	8
Rebel X	Assembler	32+8	16	MOS 6502	2
Rex	Pascal	48	n/a	Unisys PW800	n/a
Shess	Fortran	60+2.5M	2	Vax 8600	0.4
Waycool	C	n/a	n/a	Intel 512-Cube	n/a
Y!89	Assembler	32+128	100	MOS 6502	5
Zarkov	C	100+200	16	HP 9000/835	2.5

Table 3.2: Technical specifications.

Claude Shannon, the father of computer chess, was on hand to present the newly created *Shannon Trophy* to be awarded to the World Computer Chess Champion. His visionary work in computer chess is now over 40 (!) years old, yet the ideas are still in practice today.

Another special guest was Ken Thompson, one of the principals (with Joe Condon) behind the *Belle* program. Ken is also well known for his extensive work in endgame databases. Outside computer chess, Ken is internationally recognized for his invention of the UNIX operating system, for which he (and Dennis Ritchie) received the Turing Award.

The chess commentator for the event was Canadian Grandmaster Kevin Spraggett. In 1989, he reached the quarter-finals for determining the challenger to the human World Champion. Although initially knowing little about computer chess, he learned quickly and left the event with a high regard for computer play.

The World Computer Chess Championship has been held every 3 years since 1974. The six events have produced five champions. One of the highlights of the Edmonton event was to be the uniting of all the World Computer Chess Champions. Of course, the winner of the 1989 event would be there, as would the *Cray Blitz* team, the 1983 and 1986 champions, who were participating in the tournament. David Slate was the representative for *Chess 4.6*, the 1977 champion, and Ken Thompson to support the 1980 champion, *Belle*. Unfortunately, the *Kaissa* team of Georgii Adelson-Velsky, Vladimir Arlazarov and Mikhail Donskoy, winners in 1974, had planned to attend but airline reservation problems forced a last minute cancellation. They eventually showed up, three months later!

In round 2, the first game between the top programs saw *Cray Blitz* defeat *Bebe*. Although *Bebe* played nicely for the first half of the game and built up a strong position, in the ensuing double rook and pawn endgame, it underestimated the paralyzing effect of doubled rooks on the seventh and was slowly ground down. *Phoenix* fell off the pace by dropping half a point to *A.I. Chess*. It has been said that all rook and pawn endgames are draws. *Phoenix* found this statement to be true, even when up two pawns!

3.2 The Middlegame

The stereotyped vision of a chess tournament is not unlike that of a library. Rows of tables occupied by people hunched over their chess sets in deep concentration. The sound of sliding chairs grating on the floor surface will echo through the room causing many to break their concentration briefly to give a withering glare at the offender. Typically, it is a gorgeous day outside and the sane observer wonders what these people are doing indoors.

Computer-chess tournaments have no need for the cardinal rule of human tournaments - silence. Since the competitors are electronic, they have little concern for the playing conditions. Noise, lighting, smoking and table mannerisms are all human factors that do not affect the electronic chess whizzes. All they need to keep them happy is a functioning plug and possibly a reliable telephone line.

The battles are fought on a chessboard using clocks, as in a human tournament. Alongside each board are the chess computers or the terminals used to connect the programmers to their machine in some far off place. Sometimes, each board requires at least 4 electrical outlets and two telephone lines.

Once the chess game starts, the operators become the program's baby sitter. There is nothing to do except relay the moves to and from the programs and occasionally answer its queries about the time used on its clock. Consequently, the programmers have no choice but to follow the emotional roller-coaster of the game, helpless to affect their "baby's" fate. I well remember the first time my program was entered in a tournament, feeling like an expectant father, unable to give help, but ready to hand out cigars when we won. Of course, losing is another matter. Except under unusual circumstances (such as machine crashes), whenever the program loses it's *your* fault and you must live with the burden. Did you chose the right opening? Why did it play *that* move? Why didn't it see this? Too many questions and, usually, too few answers.

The big game of round 3 was the *Cray Blitz - Hitech* encounter. *Hitech* was winning for most of the way but then finally let Cray off the hook; a draw. For some reason, *Hitech* has problems playing against *Cray Blitz*. A strong position for *Hitech* in the 5th World Computer Championship turned around and cost them the world title.

White: *Cray Blitz* – Black: *Hitech*
6th World Computer Championship (1989)
1. e4 e5 2. Nf3 Nc6 3. Bb5 a6 4. Bxc6 dxc6 5. O-O f6 6. d4 exd4 7. Nxd4 c5 8. Nb3 Qxd1 9. Rxd1 Bg4 10. f3 Be6 11. Be3 b6 12. a4 Bd6 13. a5 Be5 14. axb6 cxb6 15. Ra2 Nh6 16. Rc1 f5 17. Bxh6 gxh6 18. exf5 Bxb3 19. cxb3 Kf7 20. g4 Rhd8 21. Re1 Bh8 22. Nc3 Rd2 23. Re2 Rxe2 24. Nxe2 a5 25. Kf2 Rd8 26. Ke3 Rd1 27. Nc3 Bd4+ 28. Ke4 Re1+ 29. Kd5 Rf1 30. Nb5 Bg1 31. Kc6 Rxf3 32. Kxb6 Kf6 33. Ra1 Bxh2 34. Kxc5 Rxb3 35. Rxa5 Rxb2 36. Ra4 Kg5 37. Kc6 h5 38. gxh5 Kxf5 39. Ra7 h6 40. Rg7 Rd2 41. Rg6 Bf4 42. Nd6+ Bxd6 43. Rxd6 Rxd6+ 44. Kxd6 Kg5 45. Ke5 Kxh5 46. Kf5 Kh4 47. Kf4 ½ – ½.

Deep Thought made its mark with an interesting win against *Fidelity*. It was a hard game to understand - until *Fidelity*'s queen became trapped. As well, *Phoenix* fell from contention by drawing against *Novag* when up a pawn in a winning bishops of opposite color endgame. After 3 rounds, *Deep Thought* has a perfect 3-0 mark, a half point up on the field.

It is interesting to watch chess programmers during their games. They can be divided into three distinct classes based on their knowledge of what is happening in the game. Many of the programmers fall into the "ignorance is bliss" category. They know little about chess and cannot appreciate the "quality" of their program's play. As their program walks a fine line between victory and defeat, they calmly sit at the board oblivious to the drama unfolding in from of them. The *Bebe* team, Tony and Linda Scherzer, are good examples of this school. Their (quite sensible) attitude is to have a few glasses of wine during the game, some pleasant conversation and enjoy themselves. Afterwards, as an after-thought, they ask who won.

A small group of programmers belongs to the "knowledge is power" category. These members are strong chess players and can appreciate the subtleties in the game from move to move. They smugly grin when they see some good analysis appear on their terminal screen, and are riveted in horror as the program changes at the last minute to something awful. There is nothing quite like the feeling of seeing your program make a terrible move, being forced to play it on the board, and listening to the howls of laughter or murmurs of astonishment from the audience. Hans Berliner (*Hitech*) falls into this group. When *Hitech* makes a beautiful move, Hans radiates pride. When a bad move is made, he has a distinctive scowl that hides his deep concentration as he tries to diagnose the problem.

The last group represents a compromise between the two extremes. These members know something about chess; not enough to be considered a strong player, yet enough not to be considered ignorant. An example is Feng-hsiung Hsu of the *Deep Thought* team. Although he knows little about chess, he is competitive and wants to win. Unable to trust his own assessment of a chess position, he religiously follows *Deep Thought*'s evaluations, riding a roller-coaster as the scores fluctuate.

Ken Thompson has suggested that members of the local chess club should operate the programs while all the participants retire to the lounge. When the games are over, we would be permitted back into the tournament hall and told the game results. I suspect this would prevent more than a few of the gray hairs that seem to be appearing on the heads of some of the hardened tournament veterans (too late to help David Slate, however).

Round 4 saw *Deep Thought* overwhelm *Cray Blitz*. After some opening inaccuracies, *Deep Thought* aggresively pursued the initiative, giving the opponent no respite.

White: *Deep Thought* – Black: *Cray Blitz*
6th World Computer Championship (1989)
1. d4 Nf6 2. Nc3 d5 3. Bg5 Bf5 4. e3 Ne4 5. Nxe4 Bxe4 6. f3 Bf5 7. c4 c6 8. Qb3 Qa5+ 9. Kd1 Bc8 10. Bf4 Nd7 11. cxd5 Qxd5 12. Bc4 Qf5 13. g4 Qf6 14. g5 Qf5 15. Ne2 e6 16. e4 Qg6 17. h4 h6 18. gxh6 gxh6 19. Kc2 b5 20. h5 Qf6 21. Bd3 e5 22. dxe5 Nxe5 23. Qc3 Bd6 24. a3 Bd7 25. Bg3 Bb8 26. f4 Ng4 27. e5 Qe6 28. Nd4 Qd5 29. Rae1 Rg8 30. Bh7 Rg7 31. Be4 Qc4 32. Qxc4 bxc4 33. e6 fxe6 34. Nxe6 Rg8 35. Bg6+ Rxg6 36. hxg6 Bxe6 37. Rxe6+ Kd7 38. g7 Bxf4 39. Rg6 Ne3+ 40. Kc1 Bxg3 41. Rxg3 Rg8 42. Rxe3 Rxg7 43. Rxh6 Kc7 44. Ree6 1-0.

With a hard fought victory over *Fidelity*, *Hitech* moved into sole possession of second place (3.5/4), a half point behind *Deep Thought* (4/4).

3.3 The Endgame

Three years ago in Cologne, the last round saw the two favorites battle it out for the title. Back then, it was *Hitech* with a full point lead over *Cray Blitz*. History records that lady luck was not kind to *Hitech*. In 1989, the two favorites battled it out for the title in the final, fifth round. This time it was *Deep Thought* with a half point lead on *Hitech*. Once again, fate did not favor *Hitech*:

White: *Hitech* – Black: *Deep Thought*
6th World Computer Championship (1989)
1. d4 d5 2. Nf3 Nf6 3. Bf4 e6 4. e3 Nc6 5. Nbd2 Be7 6. h3 O-O 7. Be2 Nh5 8.
Bh2 g6 9. O-O f5 10. Be5 Nxe5 11. Nxe5 Nf6 12. c4 c5 13. Ndf3 Bd6 14. a3
Qc7 15. Rc1 a5 16. Qb3 b6 17. Qa4 Bb7 18. Rc2 Kh8 19. cxd5 Bxd5 20. Rd1
Rad8 21. Bb5 Ne4 22. Nd7 Rg8 23. Nfe5 Rg7 24. Rd3 Be7 25. Rd1 h5 26.
Rdc1 Bg5 27. Re1 Bh4 28. Rf1 Be7 29. Rfc1 g5 30. f3 Nf6 31. Kf1 g4 32.
hxg4 hxg4 33. f4 Be4 34. Rd2 Nd5 35. Re2 Rh7 36. Ree1 Nxe3+ 37. Kg1 Nd5
38. Ng6+ Kg7 39. Nxe7 Qxf4 40. Nxf5+ exf5 41. Rxe4 Qxc1+ 42. Bf1 fxe4 43.
Qb3 Rh1+ 44. Kxh1 Qxf1+ 45. Kh2 Rh8+ 46. Qh3 g3+ 47. Kxg3 Qf4++ 0-1.

A month after the event was over, Jaap van den Herik was hosting former
World Champion Anatoly Karpov and Grandmaster John van der Weil for an
evening of bridge. After the game, the conversation turned to chess and the
World Computer Championship. Jaap was willing to show Karpov the *Hitech-
Deep Thought* game, but Karpov had to guess the moves made by each side.
Unfortunately, Anatoly did not do so well on this test! This may have been his
first in-depth exposure to chess played by computers and he was not impressed.
In particular, he was not kind to *Hitech*'s 10. Be5.

The Edmonton event was a fitting climax to the meteoric rise of the *Deep
Thought* program. It was only 18 months earlier that *ChipTest* (*Deep Thought*'s
software and hardware predecessor) established itself as a force in computer
chess by winning the North American Championship. In the past year, *Deep
Thought* rocked the security of the human chess world by being able to
challenge Grandmasters as an equal. With new hardware in the works and the
financial support of IBM, *Deep Thought* can only get better.

In a quiet, unassuming manner, *Bebe* assured itself of a prominent place in
computer-chess history. *Bebe* debuted in the 1980 World Computer
Championship, going undefeated. In the 1983 event, they shared second place.
In 1986, it was a share of first place. And in 1989, undivided second place. Add
to that a string of second place finishes in the North American Championships.
Truly a remarkable record. And don't count them out for 1992!

One can feel sympathy for the *Hitech* team. They were the undisputed best
chess program over the period 1985-1987. In dramatic fashion, they took
computer play against humans to new, dizzying heights, approaching (and
eventually breaking) the 2400 USCF barrier. But in computer events, all they
have to show were victories in the 1985 and 1989 North American Computer
Chess Championships. *Hitech*'s chess knowledge makes it a formidable
opponent against human players but against other computers, it seems to make
little difference. Maybe this suggests that there is little to be gained by "human-
like" play; "computer-like" play is just as good and, in some cases, better.

The *Cray Blitz* program is, in some ways another enigma. With the world's
most powerful computer at their disposal, one would have expected them to
dominate computer chess. However, their record shows only one North
American Championship (1984), the 1983 World Championship and a last round

comeback to tie for first place in the 1986 World Championship. Although ranked among the leaders in the tournament, they never really seemed to contend for top prize.

The commercial manufacturers continued to impress. Both *Mephisto* and *Fidelity* were considered strong contenders. *Fidelity* put up creditable fights against both *Deep Thought* and *Hitech* before succumbing. *Mephisto* was upset in the first round but came back to go undefeated the rest of the way. When one considers the capabilities of their hardware in comparison to that of *Deep Thought*, *Hitech* and *Cray Blitz*, one can only be impressed at the quality of their software.

Table 3.3 shows the final results of the 6th World Computer Chess Championship.

3.4 The Post-Mortem

A tournament such as this is not without its share of stories and anecdotes:

The juggler

Claude Shannon is a man of many talents. Unknown to most of the participants, Claude is a juggling enthusiast and has even built a machine capable of juggling 3 balls! After the event, a windup social was held at Tony Marsland's house. We were all tired of computer chess and, of necessity, the conversation turned to other things. When someone mentioned Claude's juggling skills, popular demand required a demonstration. Of course, no one had any juggling balls. What to use? We needed something round, hard and light. Well, there were some week old baked potatoes left over from the opening social ...

Dr. Claude Shannon, world famous scientist and father of information theory and computer chess, became the pioneer of a new form of juggling. With amazing skill and grace, he became the first man to successfully juggle 3 baked potatoes. Battling his disintegrating juggling "balls," he managed to keep parts of the potatoes in mid-air for 30 seconds. It was a triumph of skill that left the audience clamoring for more! This virtuoso display had the unfortunate side effect of leaving a mess all over the carpet.

Quote of the tournament

The winner is Dr. Timofeev of the Soviet team. After round four (with *Centaur* reeling from four consecutive lop-sided losses), he was asked whether he was enjoying his visit to Edmonton. He paused for a moment of reflection and then slowly replied in his distinctive Russian accent: "Yes. We very much enjoy our visit to Edmonton. But, we not enjoy our visit back to Moscow."

Place	Participant	Round 1		Round 2		Round 3		Round 4		Round 5		Total
1	*Deep Thought*	b23	1	w16	1	b6	1	w3	1	b4	1	**5**
2	*Bebe*	b20	1	w3	0	b18	1	w16	1	w7	1	**4**
3	*Cray Blitz*	w15	1	b2	1	w4	½	b1	0	w11	1	**3½**
4	*Hitech*	b11	1	w13	1	b3	½	w6	1	w1	0	**3½**
5	*Mephisto X*	b18	0	w17	1	w8	1	b10	½	w12	1	**3½**
6	*Fidelity X*	w21	1	b7	1	w1	0	b4	0	w10	1	**3**
7	*Merlin*	b24	1	w6	0	b19	1	w9	1	b2	0	**3**
8	*A.I. Chess*	w22	1	w9	½	b5	0	b12	½	w16	1	**3**
9	*Phoenix*	w12	1	b8	½	w10	½	b7	0	w14	½	**2½**
10	*Novag X*	b17	½	w18	1	b9	½	w5	½	b6	0	**2½**
11	*Much*	w4	0	b14	½	w15	1	b21	1	b3	0	**2½**
12	*Zarkov*	b9	0	w22	1	b13	1	w8	½	b5	0	**2½**
13	*Quest X*	w14	1	b4	0	w12	0	b22	1	w20	½	**2½**
14	*Y!89*	b13	0	w11	½	b17	½	w18	0	b9	½	**2½**
15	*BP*	b3	0	w20	1	b11	0	w19	½	b23	1	**2½**
16	*Rebel X*	w19	1	b1	0	w21	1	b2	0	b8	0	**2**
17	*Kallisto*	w10	½	b5	0	w14	½	b20	½	b19	½	**2**
18	*Waycool*	w5	1	b10	0	w2	0	b14	0	w24	1	**2**
19	*Rex*	b16	0	w23	1	w7	0	b15	½	w17	½	**2**
20	*Pandix*	w2	0	b15	0	b23	1	w17	½	b13	½	**2**
21	*Dappet*	b6	0	w24	1	b16	0	w11	0	w22	1	**2**
22	*Shess*	b8	0	b12	0	w24	1	w13	0	b21	0	**1**
23	*Moby*	w1	0	b19	0	w20	0	b24	1	w15	0	**1**
24	*Centaur*	w7	0	b21	0	b22	0	w23	0	b18	0	**0**

The letter indicates the player's color, white or black. The number identifies the opponent that faced. The next number shows whether the player won (1), lost (0), or tied (½).

Table 3.3: Final results.

Taking from the rich

At the opening social, participants were served barbecued steak. My dogs, Casanova and Caissa[1], spent the evening pretending to be starving to attract any and all available table scraps. The only loser was Jan Louwman of the *Rebel* team. He made the mistake of leaving his steak unattended, whereupon Casanova took advantage of the opportunity to clean Jan's plate. Quipped one amused spectator: "It's not the dog's fault. Jan left the steak *en pris*."

---

[1] Mikhail Donskoy, of the *Kaissa* team, quips that if I can name my dog after his chess program, then he can name his dog *Phoenix*, if he ever buys one.

Diminishing returns

A little competitive spirit never hurts. So, in the last round Tom Pronk and Jos Uiterwijk of the *Much* team and myself, *Phoenix*, made a bet as to who would finish with more points in the tournament. *Much* had 2.5 points to *Phoenix*'s 2, but had to play *Cray Blitz* while *Phoenix* was paired against *Y!89*. At stake was dinner and a lot of pride.

The games started out well for both gamblers. *Much* played a strong game and was holding off the deeper searching *Cray Blitz*. *Phoenix* quickly got the better of the opening and began to dominate. It played a combination that won material, and then ...

During the last round, special awards were presented to Monty Newborn and Tony Marsland for their two decades of service to the computer-chess community. I had the privilege of presenting the awards. In the middle of the presentation I had to be called away: my program had crashed. When one runs on 30 computers, as *Phoenix* does, many are envious of the computational resources at hand. A cynic, such as myself, realizes that there are 30 times the chances for something to go wrong. At this critical point, a sub-network of the machines was now unavailable, so the program was restarted with 20 machines. When *Phoenix* crashed, it was about to play a crushing zugzwang move, winning a rook, two bishops and a dominating position for a queen. When the program restarted, it did not have enough time to search as deeply as it had before the crash, moved quickly and did not find the winning move. Instead it went into a semi-blocked position with 2 bishops for a rook. Meanwhile, *Much* had simplified into an endgame where it stood at least equal.

Both games are still going strong 5.5 hours after starting. At 1 am, *Phoenix* crashes again. Several more of the machines are unavailable as the system starts doing back-ups. Re-starting with 8 machines ...

At 2 am, more machines become unavailable, until ... there was only one. This important last round game was finished on one processor. *Phoenix* had a winning position throughout but lacked the search depth to see the winning combination. Finally at 3 am, the game was stopped for adjudication.

Things took a turn for the worse for *Much* after 2am. They overlooked a tactical shot (easy to do against *Cray Blitz*) and lost a pawn. By 3 am it was over.

Meanwhile, analysis of the *Phoenix-Y!89* game continued all night. At 9 in the morning, Mike Valvo, the tournament director, rendered his decision: a draw. In the final position, *Y!89* has an incredible drawing resource (which neither computer could find). So *Phoenix* and *Much* finished with 2.5/5 and the bet was a stand-off.

David and Goliath

Before round 5 was to begin, an exhibition match between *Deep Thought* and Grandmaster Kevin Spraggett was arranged. This match was largely for the media's sake; pitting the human David versus the electronic Goliath would be of greater interest to audiences than any machine versus machine competition.

Consequently, this exhibition match seemed to attract more publicity than the World Championship itself.

Playing one game with 30 minutes per player per game and a second with 10 minutes per player per game, the match ended with a draw and a win for Spraggett. Asked afterwards why he didn't win both games, Kevin replied that it was more important not to lose than it was to win. Does this mean Grandmasters are finally learning to respect their electronic counterparts?

World famous in their own minds

David Slate, who was part of the team that produced *Chess 4.6*, the 1977 World Champion, took a side trip to the spectacular West Edmonton Mall. After an uneventful shopping trip, David was returning to the hotel on the bus. Deeply absorbed in reading the pamphlets he had picked up, he was startled to hear someone calling his name. To his surprise, the passenger beside him recognized him and knew all about his computer chess successes!

Three months after the event, I was taking a short holiday in the Canadian Rocky Mountains, about 500 kilometers from Edmonton. Out in the middle of nowhere, hiking along a trail to a scenic lake, I came across a couple and their child, no more than 5 or 6 years old. Suddenly the child became quite excited and started pointing at me. He whispered something to his father. As I continued along the trail, I was startled to hear: "Excuse me. Are you Jonathan Schaeffer?" It seems the child had been reading about the World Computer Chess Championships and had seen my picture in the paper. Three months later, he still remembered what I looked like. And the child had a question. He wanted to know the result of *Phoenix*'s last round game, since it finished too late to be included in the following morning's newspaper!

3.5 And Finally

Although it is difficult to be objective, the consensus appears to be that the tournament was a big success. The event attracted over 100 spectators each round and received prominent local, national and international publicity. The participants left with stories to tell and adventures to share. As always, the events are a lot of fun, whether you win, lose, or draw. It is only a scant three years until the next World Championship, never enough time to get ready.

Through computer chess, I have made many friends. The whole experience from conception of a chess program to competition for a world title has been a rewarding experience. And I think I can say that for all the competitors.

Acknowledgments. A World Computer Chess Championship is not possible without the help of numerous people and organizations. Tony Marsland and I were the co-organizers. CIPS Edmonton provided us with enormous help in planning, organizing and carrying out the work. As well, we were fortunate in having many dedicated volunteers, to whom we sincerely extend our thanks.

The Canadian Information Processing Society hosted the event. Alberta Government Telephones were our principal financial sponsors. The event could not have been as successful as it was without their people, advice, advertising and financial support. Finally, the Natural Sciences and Engineering Research Council of Canada and the University of Alberta provided funds to allow the *New Directions in Game-Tree Search Workshop* to be help along side the tournament.

Highlights from the 1989 World Computer Chess Championship

Plate 1: Tournament Hall, Edmonton Convention Centre.

Plate 2: K. Thompson, C.E. Shannon, and D. Slate.

Plate 3: H.J. Berliner and M.S. Campbell.

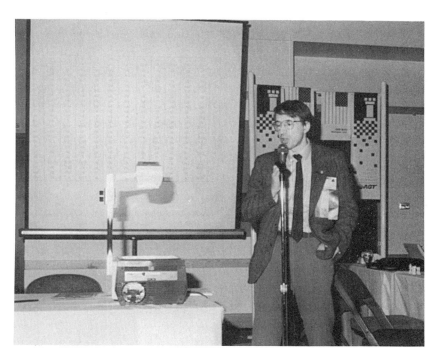

Plate 4: T.A. Marsland.

Plate 5: K. Spraggett.

Plate 6: M.M. Newborn, M. McCarthy, K. Thompson, and J. Nievergelt.

Plate 7: C.E. Shannon.

Plate 8: J. van den Herik
and R. Herschberg.

Plate 9: D. Kopec.

Plate 10: M.M. Newborn.

Plate 11: J. Schaeffer.

Plate 12: T. Scherzer.

Plate 13: H. Nelson and R. Hyatt.

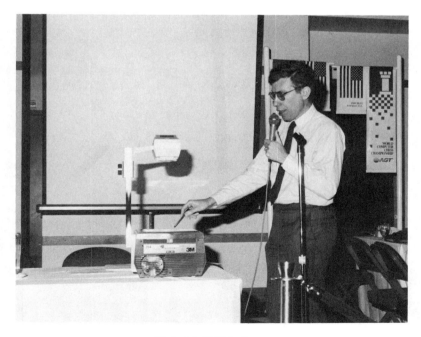

Plate 14: D.N.L. Levy.

Plate 15: D. Michie and J. McCarthy.

Plate 16: M.S. Campbell, F-h. Hsu, P. Jansen, and Bob Sutcliffe.

4 How Will Chess Programs Beat Kasparov?

D.N.L. Levy

During the closing weeks of the 1980s two significant events occurred in the world of computer chess. In a two game match played in New York, the reigning World Chess Champion, Gary Kasparov, soundly thrashed the reigning World Computer Chess Champion, *Deep Thought*. A few weeks later *Deep Thought* crushed the author of this chapter, a retired International Master who had hitherto never lost a match against a computer program.

Kasparov indicated his respect for his opponent by studying its games in advance of his match, as though he were preparing for a contest with a human Grandmaster. He now believes that his mission in life is to stave off defeat by computers, remaining as the last human World Champion who could defeat the very best that computer technology can muster. Two important questions are raised by this prospect: When will it happen and how will it happen? In answer to the first question the author speculates that 20 to 25 years will be needed. The purpose of this chapter is to attempt to throw some light on the second of these questions.

In my opinion the major breakthrough to super-Grandmaster class will be due more to new ideas in chess software than to increases in hardware power. The singular extensions algorithm (Anantharaman, Campbell and Hsu 1988), a major leap forward for chess software, can readily be compared with the analysis process of strong human players who extend their search along lines which, to them, are obviously important. I believe that quantum leaps can be obtained in all three phases of chess, by additional modeling of the thought processes of human Grandmasters.

4.1 The Ideas Behind the Chess Openings

This is the title of a book by the American Grandmaster and former World Championship contender Reuben Fine, and his words point to one of the notable weaknesses of computer play. Many chess programs have enormous openings books to call upon, ensuring that at some stage during the opening they will arrive at a position which is theoretically acceptable, or even good, for them. What most of these programs lack is any understanding of what to do next. We can sympathize with Capablanca who wrote:

> Chess books should be used as we use glasses - to assist the sight; although some players make use of them as if they thought they conferred sight.

In a more cynical vein, we can even applaud Tarrasch's biting comment on a move made in a World Championship match:

> Up to this point White has been following well-known analysis, but
> now he makes a fatal error - he begins to use his own head.

The problem on which we focus in this part of our discussion is: How can a chess program be endowed with an *understanding* of the *ideas* behind the opening that it has played in a game?

Each chess opening has its own themes and ideas. A player who possesses a sound understanding of these ideas will often hold sway over one who merely learns the book moves by rote. We would like our programs to do both - play the book moves and then understand what to do next.

The approach being proposed here was first suggested by the author in 1980, and used in the *Chess Champion Mk V* program which won the Commercial section of the 1981 World Microcomputer Chess Championship. The foundation of the idea is to provide the program with a list, called GOODLIST, of "mini-plans" that it should try to put into operation. Here is a simple example.

After the moves 1. e4 c5, the program's GOODLIST might consist of the following:

$$P1: c5xd4; P2: d6/Nf6/a6/e6/Be7/O-O/Qc7;$$

The first entry means that if the program reaches a position in which the move c5xd4 is legal, it gives this move a bonus which encourages the program to play it. P1 is an identifier for this particular mini-plan in this particular position. A semi-colon separates the various mini-plans on GOODLIST. The second entry, for which the mini-plan identifier is P2, means that if the program reaches a position in which the move d6 is legal, this move gets a bonus and, once the move d6 has been played, the move Nf6 gets a bonus and, once Nf6 has been played, then a6 gets a bonus, ... and so on. In other words, the syntax:

$$move1 / move2 / move3 / ... ;$$

encourages the program to play all these moves but in a particular order.

Mini-plans can be added to or deleted from GOODLIST dynamically, according to what happens during the game. Later in the program's openings book one can add new mini-plans and, if desired in some situations, delete the remnants of old ones. For example, after the moves: 1. e4 c5 2. f4, it might be thought desirable for black to adopt a different setup from that advocated in mini-plan P2, so we could write:

$$-P2; P3: g6/Bg7/Nc6/e6/Nge7/O-O,d5;$$

which would mean: remove mini-plan P2 from GOODLIST, replacing it with the new mini-plan beginning with g6. (Note that the moves O-O and d5, which are separated by a comma, are each given the "GOODLIST bonus" once the move Nge7 has been played).

What should be the magnitude of the GOODLIST bonus? When a mini-plan was added to GOODLIST, the bonus was between 0.25 and 0.33 of a pawn, perhaps rather large. The GOODLIST bonus for each mini-plan was decremented for each move played, if and only if the move was *not* part of the mini-plan. This decaying factor, which was in the range 0.01 to 0.02 pawns per move made by the program, prevented the program from being encouraged to play ideas which were no longer called for - moves which had been thematic in one type of position but possibly wrong in the given situation. Since each mini-plan could have different sized bonuses at the same point in the game, the program would prefer moves that were part of recently introduced mini-plans to moves that were part of a mini-plan added to GOODLIST many moves ago.

It would be easy to extend the syntax to include, for example, rule formats such as: "Do not play the following mini-plan if your opponent has already played move *x*," or "Play the following mini-plan if your opponent has played move *y*." It would also be possible to create a BADLIST of moves, to be avoided. Even with the simple syntax described so far, programs would have a much better understanding of the ideas behind the chess openings than they do at the present time. It is easy to see that a human chess Master or Grandmaster could use and even enrich this syntax to explain to a program the ideas behind the chess openings in a simple, straightforward manner.

This approach provides the program's openings book with a rule based expert system, into which human experts can add new rules quickly and effectively after seeing examples of misplayed positions from the opening or early middlegame. To illustrate the potential of this system we present the following game. If the reader is a strong chess player (good club strength or above) it will be obvious to him that the player of the black pieces had an excellent understanding of the ideas behind the Modern Benoni Defense.

White: *Savant* – Black: *Chess Champion Mk V*
2nd World Micro Championship (1981)
1. d4 Nf6 2. c4 c5 3. d5 e6 4. Nc3 exd5 5. cxd5 d6 6. Nf3 g6 7. e4 Bg4 8. Bb5+ Nbd7 9. h3 Bxf3 10. Qxf3 a6 11. Bxd7+ Nxd7 12. 0-0 Bg7 13. a4 0-0 14. Bf4 Qb6 15. Qe2 Rab8 16. a5 Qc7 17. Rfe1 Bd4 18. Be3 Rfe8 19. Bxd4 cxd4 20. Nb1 b6 21. axb6 Nxb6 22. Rxa6 Nxd5 23. Rd1 Nf4 24. Qf3 Qc2 25. Nd2 d3 26. Kf1 Ne2 27. Ke1 Rxb2 28. Rxd6 Nc3 29. Rxd3 Nxd1 30. Rd7 f5 31. Qxd1 Qxd1+ 32. Kxd1 fxe4 33. Rd4 e3 34. fxe3 Rxe3 35. Rd8+ Kf7 36. Nc4 Ke7 37. Rd4 Rb1+ 38. Kd2 Rg3 0-1 on time.

4.2 The Correct Strategy in the Middlegame

The GOODLIST syntax could be extended to middlegame play to encourage a program to plan in accordance with the demands of the position. Up to the end of the 1980s, programs relied almost entirely on a linear evaluation function for their middlegame play. Many chess programmers have discussed the possibility of non-linear evaluation, so that the weightings assigned to the various terms of the evaluation function depend on the type of position on the board, but so far as the author is aware no-one has implemented this idea. To a strong human player the concept is obvious. A strategy (and hence an evaluation function) which works well in one type of position will often fail in a different type of position.

One form of non-linear evaluation is to bias the program's evaluation function according to the type of position currently on the board. This could be achieved using the GOODLIST approach. A chess program could store many hundreds or even thousands of *fragments* (or *chunks*) of positions. Each fragment would contain those elements which are essential for distinguishing between positions of differing character. Typically, a fragment would be a common part of a very large number of positions of a particular type. For example, the fragment in Figure 4.1 would probably fit tens of thousands of master chess games (it is taken from the King's Indian Defense - one of the more popular defenses to 1. d4).

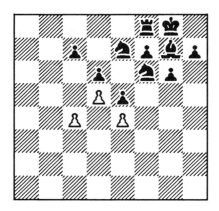

Figure 4.1: Fragment of a King's Indian position.

For each fragment the program stores one or more mini-plans, which are put onto GOODLIST when the fragment is first recognized in the tree. At deeper nodes in the tree the GOODLIST bonus is in effect. This allows a program to take advantage of its understanding of a particular type of position even before that type of position has actually appeared during the game. In the middlegame the GOODLIST bonus should be smaller than that for the openings - it is necessary to experiment to determine a suitable range of values.

Human experts would provide the information to be encoded in the various mini-plans, in much the same way that they give chess lessons: "In this type of position you should do this, that and the other. But if your opponent plays Re8 then do not play h4." The power of this idea is limited only by the richness (or lack of it) of the syntax and the number of fragments at the program's disposal.

This idea was seen in a much more primitive form in the Zobrist and Carlsson (1973) program. Their idea of snapshots (corresponding to our fragments) was too rigid to have any real hope of success. The GOODLIST method provides much more flexibility and power.

4.3 How to Win in the Endgame

As everyone knows, computers cannot play endgames well. At least, that used to be the conventional wisdom. Nowadays we recognize that in some endgame situations computer programs can play perfectly while human experts, even Grandmasters, can falter. While database programs can instantaneously play the optimal move in endings such as rook and bishop versus rook, human masters and Grandmasters often manage to lose from drawn positions or draw games which they should have won. But 5 or 6 piece endings, those that are susceptible to database analysis, do not form the major part of the problem of playing a good endgame and, in comparison with Grandmasters, *Deep Thought* and its colleagues are patzers when it comes to playing most endgames. How can this situation be rectified?

In chess it is the endgame, more than any other aspect of the struggle, which best distinguishes the strong players from the weak. The reason why top Grandmasters are so much better at the endgame than their weaker colleagues is that they are better at generalizing from a wealth of knowledge and experience. To endow the chess programs of the future with similar abilities, we must make available to them the vast amount of knowledge about the endgame which has been built up over a century or more of master play.

An endgame annotated by a Grandmaster can provide a wealth of information. It will usually be possible to deduce from the Grandmaster's comments the status of the game at every moment - whether it is a win for one side or the other or whether it is a draw. The moves of the game, combined with the annotator's exclamation marks, question marks and comments, indicate what should or should not be played in a particular position. Any comments by the Grandmaster as to the plan which either side should be adopting provides data for GOODLIST. The problem with all this, of course, is that the chances of the program ever reaching a position which arose in this game, or in the annotations to it, are extremely remote. In more than a decade of international experience I can not recall ever having an endgame which could be found in one of the standard works on the subject. I often had positions which were similar, and for which the examples presented and the general advice offered by the books were useful, but how could this type of information be used by a computer program?

Ultimately I believe the answer to lie in fuzzy matching. A program reaches a leaf node in its endgame analysis and needs to evaluate the position. It looks in its database for any positions which are, in some sense, close to the position in question, and computes its evaluation from a combination of the proximities and known values of these positions. This evaluation could be augmented by information which is part of conventional evaluation techniques, such as penalizing a defending king which is "outside the square" of a passed pawn.

When not faced with the problem of leaf node evaluation, a program's endgame module would use fuzzy matching to find mini-plans to go on GOODLIST. The bonus for a particular mini-plan would depend on the proximity of the two positions, so there could be many different mini-plans, each with a different bonus. The endgame mini-plans themselves would need to be expressed differently from those used in the opening and middlegame. Rather than state that a certain move should go on GOODLIST, the syntax would allow the human knowledge engineer the flexibility to state that a certain piece should perform a certain function. For example, "the white rook should be placed on the f-file between f1 and f5; the black king should attack the square in front of the c-pawn and, if possible, the square two in front of the c-pawn as well; the black bishop should control the a1-h8 diagonal."

4.4 Conclusion

Up to now chess programmers have only scratched the surface of knowledge engineering within their chosen environment. With a large number of Grandmasters willing and able to provide expert advice, it is surprising that this rich source of information and ideas has remained largely untapped. The GOODLIST concept is a simple, flexible and powerful idea for endowing chess programs with understanding. The author speculates that when most of the chess knowledge currently enshrined in books has been made available to programs in this format, Kasparov's remaining period of supremacy will genuinely be measured in years, rather than decades.

Part II. Chess Programs

There are many parameters in the equation for producing a strong chess program. Unfortunately, it is not clear what all the parameters are and how to weigh them. In this part, detailed descriptions of three chess programs are presented. In comparing the descriptions, one can see the large variety of ideas used. With one exception, there appears to be little consensus between the programs on what the parameters for success are. The exception is speed; the three programs represent the deepest searching chess machines currently available. Is this the only parameter required for success?

The chapter on *Deep Thought*, by Feng-hsiung Hsu, Murray Campbell, Thomas Anantharaman and Andreas Nowatzyk, describes the hardware and software of the current World Computer Champion. At the heart of the system is a *Belle*-like move generator (Condon and Thompson 1982); new, improved and integrated into a single chip. The speed of the hardware allows the program to search to extraordinary depths. But this is not the sole reason for *Deep Thought*'s success. Careful note should be taken of the tool used to tune the evaluation function. Instead of the traditional *ad hoc* methods, the *Deep Thought* team can tune their program's evaluation function to maximize the number of times the program's move choice agrees with that of a Grandmaster, for a given test set. Although not perfect, as the *Deep Thought* team admits, the results represent a significant advance in the technology used for construction of chess programs. However, this introduces an important philosophical dilemma. Computers have different strengths and weaknesses than humans. Is it appropriate to tailor the play of a machine to approximate that of a human?

Hitech is also built around special-purpose VLSI chips. However, as Hans Berliner and Carl Ebeling write, the design is radically different from *Deep Thought*'s. Perhaps the most novel part of the architecture is the *pattern recognizers*, allowing complex patterns to be recognized and evaluated. The paper provides an interesting data point; two years of improvements to the search algorithm and chess knowledge resulted in a gain of 200 rating points, without any increase in program speed.

Finally, Robert Hyatt, Harry Nelson and Bert Gower describe their work on the *Cray Blitz* program. As in the previous papers, the emphasis on performance is clear. In *Cray Blitz*'s case, this is achieved by using multiple processors on the Cray YMP, the world's fastest computer. However, this paper gives us something the previous two did not: a detailed description of the chess knowledge used. It is interesting to compare *Cray Blitz*'s knowledge with that of *Chess 4.7* (Slate and Atkin 1977), a program written over a dozen years ago. It would appear, from a macroscopic perspective, that little has changed in chess programs. However, a decade's worth of experience has carefully refined the set of knowledge considered beneficial for the effort expended in calculating it. As well, we now have a better idea on how much to weight each component of an evaluation function.

Although these chapters describe three of the major chess programs existing today, they do not necessarily cover the spectrum of what is possible in a chess program. Certainly there is much disagreement on what the best combination of search methods are and, indeed, whether alpha-beta is all that we would like it to be. On the knowledge side, there still remains the large gap between the advocates of increased knowledge in chess programs versus those that forsake the knowledge for deeper search. Ultimately, both philosophies must be correct. The only question is which one will succeed first in building a program capable of defeating the human World Champion. The verdict is not yet in.

5 Deep Thought

F-h. Hsu, T.S. Anantharaman, M.S. Campbell and A. Nowatzyk

5.1 Introduction

Deep Thought is the first chess machine to achieve Grandmaster performances against human opposition. In November 1988, the machine tied for first in the Software Toolworks Championship with Grandmaster Anthony Miles, defeating four-time World Championship candidate Grandmaster Bent Larsen along the way. Since then, the machine has been successful against other Grandmasters.

This level of performance is due in large part to a sizable jump in hardware speed, but incremental improvements in the position evaluation and some new thinking on selective search algorithms also play important roles. This paper gives a brief history of the development of the program, and discusses some of the aspects of the project that differentiate it from previous chess machines.

5.2 History

Deep Thought was developed by a group of computer science graduate students at Carnegie Mellon University. It was not part of an official project, and no faculty were directly involved. These factors permitted the team members a great deal of autonomy which, combined with their diverse backgrounds, led to some of the non-traditional approaches used in the project.

The development of the program began in June 1985, when Feng-hsiung Hsu concluded that a single-chip chess move generator could be built even using the somewhat obsolete 3-micron VLSI (Very Large Scale Integration) technology available to the university community, and that rapidly advancing technology would make a World Champion level chess machine a possibility in the near future, The new chip design was based on the *Belle* move generator (Condon and Thompson 1982), but the circuit size was significantly reduced over a direct VLSI implementation of the *Belle* design.

After six months of design, simulation and layout work, the chip was sent for fabrication. Four months later the first working chips were received.

This paper contains revised portions taken from "A Two-Million Moves/s CMOS Single-Chip Chess Move Generator" by F-h. Hsu (1987), *IEEE Journal of Solid-State Circuits,* vol. 22, no. 5, pp. 841-846.

Measurements showed that the chip was about ten times faster than the 64 chip module used in the *Hitech* chess machine (Ebeling 1986), and allowed a maximum throughput of 2 million moves per second (Hsu 1987).

To test the chip's functionality, Hsu built a simple chip interface for Sun workstations. Thomas Anantharaman, a fellow graduate student, had written a toy chess program as a pastime. Hsu and Anantharaman quickly got together and the chip interface was put into a Sun 3/160 workstation. After the software move generator was replaced by the hardware, the program was able to search roughly 50,000 positions per second, and the chip was verified to work correctly within a real chess program.

With only seven weeks to the 1986 North American Computer Chess Championship, the team became ambitious and decided that it might be interesting to enter an enhanced version of the chip tester. There were two major improvements that were considered important. First, a more sophisticated evaluation function was desirable and Campbell, who had at one time been a competitive chess player, agreed to work on it. The second and more difficult task (especially given the time constraints) was to augment the hardware so that it could act as a simple searching engine. This engine would run at much faster speeds than the workstation, and could use the potential speed of the move generator chip better. To have the machine completed in time, it was decided to ignore castling and repetition detection in the searching engine. To compensate for the omission, a hybrid search emerged as the most appropriate architecture, with the early levels of the search taking place on the host computer and the last few levels occurring on the search engine. Since the vast majority of the work of a brute-force program takes place near the leaves of the game tree, this method exploited the speed of the searching engine effectively.

Work was begun immediately on the new chip tester, which would become known as *ChipTest*. Since the project had no budget, the new tester was built by scrounging up spare parts from other projects. Unfortunately, the microcode was not running and the host software was not fully debugged in time for the Championship. Consequently, the slow and buggy *ChipTest* only managed an even score in the tournament. For a chip tester that was not intended to be a real chess machine, it was nonetheless a respectable debut.

The experience of the 1986 Championship led to an important change in *ChipTest* and influenced the later design of *Deep Thought*. During the Championship, two other programs played into a forced line without realizing the outcome. A series of informal discussions about the problem between Campbell and Hsu resulted in Hsu proposing what he called the singular extensions algorithm (Anantharaman, Campbell and Hsu 1988). This algorithm, in simplest terms, extends the search (searches deeper) along the line where the opponent has only one single good reply. The increased search depth along forcing (tactical) lines led to a significant improvement in the program's tactical abilities.

Meanwhile, a working microcode program was also completed. Searching at 400,000 to 500,000 positions per second, *ChipTest* won the 1987 North

American Computer Chess Championship in a clean sweep, defeating, among others, the then World Computer Chess Champion *Cray Blitz*.

It was clear from the *ChipTest* experience that the hardware could be sped up and made "smarter." A small amount of funding was acquired for building a new machine, which became known as *Deep Thought*.

The raw speed of a *Deep Thought* processor is about the same, on a per processor basis, as the *ChipTest* processor, but it searches about 30% faster because of refinements in the microcode search algorithm. The main difference between the processors is the enhanced hardware evaluation function. This evaluation function consists of four components: piece placement (the only component that was in *ChipTest*), pawn structure, passed pawns and file structure.

The *Deep Thought* machine first played in May 1988, when the Fredkin Foundation held the Fredkin Masters Open chess tournament. This was a special event designed to match some of the top machines against human master players. *ChipTest* and *Deep Thought* received provisional USCF ratings of 2521 and 2599, respectively, at that tournament, breaking by far previous computer rating records. *Deep Thought*'s performance was especially surprising, even to the authors, as the machine was still being wired just the day before the event.

Two months later, at the 1988 US Open held in Boston, the first among several "unthinkables" happened. In the 9th round, the program routed the Canadian co-champion and perennial US Chess Grand Prix winner, IM Igor Ivanov. Rated at USCF 2641, Ivanov became the first player generally considered Grandmaster class to lose to a computer under tournament conditions. The 1987 US Open Champion, Grandmaster Lev Alburt (2652), then had a close call in the 10th round against *Deep Thought*. Because of a bug in the program, a trivial repetition draw was missed and the program ended up losing the game. Despite the respectable showing, this was still a bug ridden event for the machine. In another game, in a winning position the program allowed a one move mate by a player rated under 2100[1]. The new dual processor version of the machine was found to reverse the sign of the checkmate value under certain conditions. Instead of being checkmated, the machine thought it was checkmating the opponent! It was also discovered after the event that the bulk of *en passant* pawn captures were not being generated.

Over the 1988 Thanksgiving weekend, the Software Toolworks Championship was held in Long Beach, California. With a total prize fund of $130,000, it was one of the top 3 US chess tournaments in 1988. Beside several strong American Grandmasters and International Masters, former World Champion Mikhail Tal (then number 16 in the world) and Danish Grandmaster Bent Larsen (number 42 in the world) were also playing. After winning its first two games, *Deep Thought* was then paired against Larsen. We were bracing for a loss and hoping for a draw. Larsen was out-calculated in a tactically

---

[1] After the game, the opponent said "Thank you! Thank you!" and ran off, delighted at the turn of events!

complicated position and lost (the game score can be found in Chapter 15 *Brute Force in Chess and Science*). It turned out this was only the first of the two big surprises in the tournament. With the exception of the fourth round loss against Grandmaster Walter Browne and the fifth round draw against International Master Vincent McCambridge, the program won all the other games in the 8 round tournament and tied for first with the British Grandmaster Anthony Miles. Since computers are not eligible for tournament prize money, Miles took home the $10,000 first prize[2].

The program played 42 rated games in 1988 and the performance over all the games, including early games where it suffered from bugs, was 2598 USCF. Because of the heavier weight placed on the first 20 games in the USCF rating formula, it received an established rating of 2551, roughly equivalent to the bottom rung of active Grandmasters. Its best 25 game performance over the period was 2655. For this result, *Deep Thought* was awarded the $10,000 Fredkin Intermediate Prize for the first program to achieve a performance rating over 2500 for 25 consecutive games (see Chapter 1 *A Short History of Computer Chess*). It is interesting to note that the program's average performance steadily improved over this period as its searching speed was increased from 450,000 to 700,000 positions per second.

In February 1989, *Deep Thought* was invited to assist Canadian Grandmaster Kevin Spraggett in his preparation for the World Championship Candidate Quarter Final match. The program's last minute participation did not affect the match, but did establish a precedent of human-computer cooperation at the highest level of chess (Jansen and Schaeffer 1990).

Three months later, *Deep Thought* became the new World Computer Chess Champion by winning all of its games in the Championship held in Edmonton, Canada. The wins included another victory over the previous title holder, *Cray Blitz*.

In October 1989, a two game exhibition match was played in New York City against World Chess Champion Gary Kasparov of the Soviet Union. This match, which attracted a great deal of world-wide media attention, marked the first appearance of a 6-processor version, capable of searching over 2 million positions per second. In spite of the hardware boost, Kasparov defeated the program rather easily in each of the two games. Though the result was not unexpected given Kasparov's much higher rating, the computer's play was somewhat disappointing. Serious bugs, one of them related to castling, were introduced in the new six-processor code, and only uncovered 2 months later. A game from this match can be found in Chapter 2 *Advances in Man-Machine Play*.

Another historic match took place in December 1989, in London, England. *Deep Thought* played four games against International Master David Levy. Levy is well known in computer-chess circles for his 1968 bet in which he stated that no computer would beat him at chess in the following decade. Levy, who

---

[2] A year later, *Deep Thought* won an exhibition "playoff match" against Miles.

has since retired from competitive chess, has considerable knowledge of the inner workings of chess programs. He won his bet handily in 1978 and the challenge was extended such that the first machine to defeat him would collect a prize offered jointly by him and OMNI magazine. The last challenge that Levy faced was in 1984 from *Cray Blitz*, running on the Cray XMP supercomputer. Levy easily won all four games of the match, drawing upon his knowledge of computer play to "frustrate" the machine. But in 1989, *Deep Thought* turned the tables and beat Levy 4-0, seemingly without effort (see Chapter 2 *Advances in Man-Machine Play* for the Levy saga).

Anatoly Karpov, 1975-1985 World Chess Champion, visited Harvard University in February 1990 and played an exhibition game against *Deep Thought*. Because of unresolved bugs in the four- and six-processor versions of the machine, a decision was made to revert to the two-processor configuration. The program played one of its best games for the first 50 moves, and then blundered away a clearly drawn position. Ironically, the six-processor version would have had enough speed to avoid the blunder.

In addition to these major events, a number of exhibition games against Grandmasters have been played, including wins against Robert Byrne (twice) and Anthony Miles. *Deep Thought*'s current record against International Masters (under regular tournament conditions) stands at eleven wins, two draws and one loss, and against Grandmasters, four wins, two draws and four losses.

5.3 VLSI

The ascent of the brute-force chess machines back in the late 1970s made one thing crystal clear: there is a strong causal relationship between the search speed of a chess machine and its playing strength. In fact, it appeared from machine self-test games that every time a machine searches one extra ply, its rating increases by about 200-250 rating points (Gillogly 1978; Thompson 1982). Since each extra ply increases the searched tree size by five to six times, every two-fold increase in speed roughly corresponds to a 80-100 rating point gain. Ratings obtained by machines against human players indicate that this relationship holds perhaps all the way up to the Grandmaster level where *Deep Thought* currently resides. The presence of this causal relationship was the reason the project was started in the first place.

The record breaking search speed (over 900,000 positions/second for the basic two-processor version after the latest microcode revision), is primarily due to custom hardware (Hsu 1987,90). Central to this custom hardware is a VLSI single chip chess move generator.

5.3.1 Move Generators

Deep Thought is a natural extension of the trend towards faster computing for chess machines. The past decade has seen chess programs move from

AUGUSTANA UNIVERSITY COLLEGE
LIBRARY.

mainframes to multi-processor machines and special-purpose hardware. Machines built specially to play chess progressed from LSI, to bit-slice and VLSI technologies. There have been successful (Condon and Thompson 1982; Ebeling 1986) and less successful (Moussouris, Holloway and Greenblatt 1979; Babaoglu 1977; Schaeffer, Powell and Jonkman 1983) attempts at building hardware move generators. Both *Belle* and *Hitech*, built around their hardware move generators, are tremendously successful chess machines, and were the top rated chess computers in the periods of 1980-1984 and 1985-1987 respectively.

The *Deep Thought* move generator is similar to *Belle*'s (Condon and Thompson 1982). However, two important improvements have been made on that design. First, *Belle* required a *disable stack* for each square, to disable moves that have already been generated. This has been eliminated by calculating this information from the previous move made. Second, *Belle* used a *priority network* to arbitrate between moves, essentially providing ordering information. This was replaced with a distributed arbitration mechanism. As a result of these two improvements, the chip area is reduced by more than a factor of four over the direct implementation of a *Belle*-like design.

5.3.2 Chip Overview

The chip is composed of an 8×8 array of similar combinatorial circuits and a two-level arbitration network. Each combinatorial circuit consists of a transmitter that sends out attack signals to its neighbors according to its own piece type and a receiver that accepts signals from its neighbors. The combinatorial circuits are customized according to their corresponding square address, and have up to around 550 transistors per cell. The first level of the arbitration network is embedded into the array. Two operations are provided, *FIND-VICTIM* and *FIND-AGGRESSOR*. In the *FIND-VICTIM* cycle, the chip locates the highest valued unexamined piece under attack. In the *FIND-AGGRESSOR* cycle, the chip finds the lowest valued unexamined piece attacking a given square, which is normally the last located victim square. Making a move or unmaking a move is achieved by writing appropriate piece types into the piece registers resident on each combinatorial circuit cell.

Typical move processing sequences, as shown in Figure 5.1, consist of a *FIND-VICTIM* cycle, a *FIND-AGGRESSOR* cycle, a move making cycle, and sometime later, after the resultant position has been processed, a move unmaking cycle. The figure has been simplified and contains only the more frequent sequences. When a new position is reached, a *FIND-VICTIM* cycle is executed with a *FIRST-MOVE* mask that enables all the victims. If the *DEFENDER-IN-CHECK* status is asserted by the chip, then the last move made is illegal and should be unmade. If no victim is found, then there are no legal moves left for the current position and the unmaking of the previous move is in order. After a victim is found, a *FIND-AGGRESSOR* cycle is executed with a *FIRST-MOVE* mask to find the first aggressor. For both *FIND-VICTIM* and *FIND-AGGRESSOR* cycles, the chip generates a *HAS-MOVE* status signal in

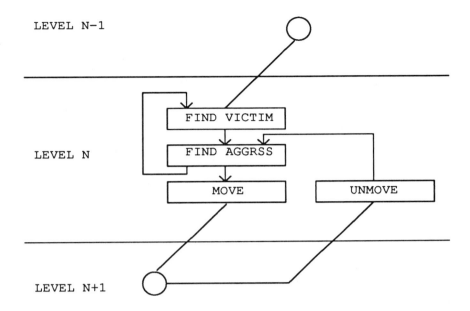

Figure 5.1: Typical move processing sequences.

roughly half a cycle to give the external controller sufficient time to decide on the operation to be performed in the next cycle. The *DEFENDER-IN-CHECK* signal is also generated within half a cycle for the same reason. After the newly found move is made and the resultant position processed, an unmove cycle is executed. Subsequent to each unmove cycle, a *FIND-AGGRESSOR* cycle is first executed to find additional aggressors for the same victim in the move just unmade. The aggressor part of the move is used to mask off previously searched aggressors on the same victim. If no new aggressor is found, then a *FIND-VICTIM* cycle is executed using the last victim as the mask, and so on.

The above sequences describe the processing of normal moves. The basic cells have been enhanced to facilitate the processing of special moves. Third rank and fifth rank squares have special logic to handle two-square pawn moves. First rank and eighth rank squares are modified to utilize the edge effects and to handle pawn promotions. Castling moves and *en passant* captures are processed by loading shadow pieces and then testing the move generation status. Pawn promotions are processed right after each move made by executing a *FIND-VICTIM* cycle with the *PROMOTION-ONLY* flag asserted. This special cycle usually fails to locate any promotion square and is essentially an overhead. It is possible to eliminate most of this overhead by keeping track of the seventh rank pawns and only executing the special cycle when there is at least one seventh rank pawn on board. The *PROMOTION-ONLY* flag when turned off will exclude the promotion moves from the normal move generation process. The

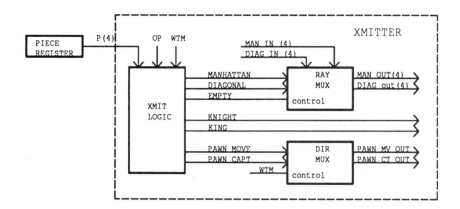

Figure 5.2: Transmitter circuit.

DEFENDER-IN-CHECK status signal is correctly generated whether the
PROMOTION-ONLY signal is asserted or not.

5.3.2.1 The Transmitter

The block diagram of the transmitter is shown in Figure 5.2. The transmit logic
generates the primary attack signals based on the resident piece type, whether
white is to move (WTM) or not, and the current operation type. If the operation
is *FIND-VICTIM*, then only the attack signals of the resident piece are asserted.
If the operation is *FIND-AGGRESSOR* and the square has been selected as the
victim square, then the attack signals are asserted as if a super-piece that is the
union of all pieces is on the square, with the exception that pawn move signal is
generated only if the square is empty and pawn capture signal is generated only
if the square is not vacant.

The manhattan and diagonal signals, generated by the ray pieces (bishops,
rooks and queens), are propagated through each square via the ray multiplexors.
Each square has eight ray multiplexors, one for each direction. A direction
multiplexor is used to select the direction of pawn move signals and pawn
capture signals. The WTM signal decides whether the signals should go up or
down the chessboard.

5.3.2.2 The Receiver

The receiver receives the incoming attack signals and generates appropriate
priority signals to the arbitration logic. As shown in Figure 5.3, all the attack
signals are first grouped and *OR* ed together according to their types. The
concentrated attack signals are then sent to the main receiving logic.

The main receiving logic first latches the concentrated attack signals and
then computes the output priority signals based on the latched signals, the
resident piece type, WTM and the operation code. If the operation is *FIND-*

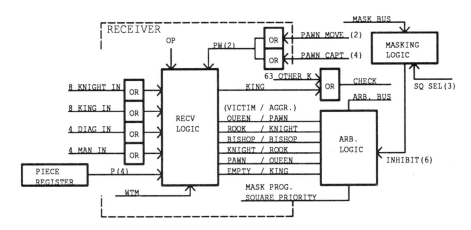

Figure 5.3: Receiver circuit.

VICTIM, the output priority signals will be asserted according to the piece type whenever there is at least one input attack signal asserted. Six different types of victim priority signals can be generated: queen, rook, bishop, knight, pawn and empty square. A king attacked signal may also be generated during the *FIND-VICTIM* cycle. If the operation is *FIND-AGGRESSOR,* then the output priority signals will be asserted if and only if there is an input attacking signal matching the piece type. Also in *FIND-AGGRESSOR* cycles, the ordering of the priority lines are inverted as shown in Figure 5.3. That is, the queen priority signal becomes the pawn priority signal, the rook priority becomes the knight priority and so on.

During *FIND-VICTIM* cycles, the king attacked signals are *OR* ed over the entire board to generate the status signal *DEFENDER-IN-CHECK*. The other priority signals are wired to the on-square arbitration logic which is part of the first level arbitration network. The other status signal *HAS-MOVE* is generated as the first output bit of the arbitration process.

5.3.2.3 The Move Masking Scheme

To avoid generating previously examined moves, some way to mask off moves must be provided. This is achieved by providing the chip with the last generated move during the move generation cycles. The chip then generates appropriate masking signals and inhibits examined cells from the arbitration process.

To facilitate the masking process, the priorities of the chess squares are assumed to be row-major; that is, among squares with the same piece priority, squares belonging to the same row will always have either higher priority or lower priority compared to squares of a particular different row. Now given the last victim or the last aggressor tried from the current position, the squares with higher piece priority and the squares with the same piece priority but higher or equal square priority will have to be disabled.

The mask generation logic generates, based on the input piece type in the last move tried, piece priority masking signals that are broadcast over the mask buses running through the squares. Squares with higher piece priority than the masking signals are then inhibited from the arbitration process.

The square address of the last victim, or the last aggressor, simultaneously gets decoded into 8 column select signals, 8 row select signals and 8 row enable signals. Each square receives one column select signal, one row select signal and one row enable signal. The three control signals are used to modify the inhibit signals going into the arbitration logic. The global address decoding logic and on-square mask logic are designed such that the combined effect causes squares with the same piece priority as the input piece but with higher or equal square priority to be eliminated from further considerations.

The move masking computation is overlapped with the operations of the transmitter and the receiver.

5.3.2.4 The Arbitration Logic

The priority signals from the squares are arbitrated via a two-level arbitration network. As shown in Figure 5.4, the first level arbitration network consists of 8 arbitration buses running through the squares, one bus per row. The two-level design reduces the bus loading and also allows partial overlapping of the time spent on row arbitration and the time spent on column arbitration.

The arbitration on each arbitration bus is done with the wired-or distributed arbiter scheme. Each square has a multi-bit arbitration element, one bit for each bus line. In the chip, the first level arbitration buses are 7 bits wide and the second level arbitration bus is 10 bits wide. After all the arbitration bus lines settled down, the priority of the highest priority element competing will appear on the bus.

The highest priority bus line of the arbitration network is used to provide the *HAS-MOVE* status signal. The piece priority outputs from the arbitration network are properly re-encoded at the chip output stage to give the correct piece type encoding for both the *FIND-VICTIM* and the *FIND-AGGRESSOR* cycles. Since this re-encoding is overlapped with the arbitration of the square priority signals, the chip throughput is not affected.

5.3.2.5 Piece Registers

For every position searched by the chess machine, a move and an unmove operation must be executed. A normal chess move affects two squares and, if the piece registers are single ported, it is necessary to execute four register write operations for every position. To improve speed, the piece registers are all dual ported. The masking buses and the arbitration buses double as the piece loading buses during the register loading cycles.

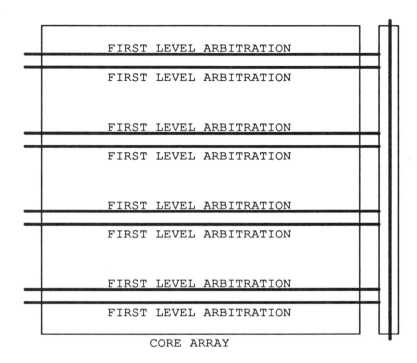

Figure 5.4: Two-level arbitration network.

5.3.3 Circuit Implementation and Evaluation

At the time the design was started, the only CMOS process easily accessible by the University community was a 3-micron, two-metal, p-well process, and the design was therefore implemented in this technology. However, the layout was done in such a way that it is relatively easy to migrate to a denser technology later. With the 3-micron process, the die size is 6812×6912 microns. The exact transistor count is 35,925. The chip is packaged in a 40 pin DIP. Ten of the pins are used for power and ground to reduce switching noise. Power consumption is less than 0.5 W. The measured minimum cycle time is around 120-150 nanoseconds (ns) for *FIND-VICTIM* and *FIND-AGGRESSOR* cycles. The cycle time is somewhat shorter for move making and move unmaking cycles. The maximum throughput is roughly 2,000,000 moves per second.

5.4 The Chess Machine

The chess hardware is one single large wire-wrapped board measuring 40 centimeters by 36.7 centimeters. It is a triple height, full depth VME card that

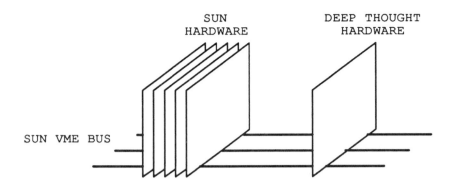

SUN   DEEP THOUGHT
HARDWARE   HARDWARE

SUN VME BUS

Figure 5.5: System configuration.

can be plugged directly into a Sun workstation. Figure 5.5 shows the system configuration. Two chess specific processors are on the wire-wrapped board. A printed circuit board version of the machine, with some further enhancements, has been designed and successfully built. The following descriptions refer to the wire-wrapped version.

The Sun host software views the chess hardware as memory mapped peripherals. Besides various debugging and table down-loading operations, the host software can issue the following commands to either one of the chess processors.

(1) Obtain a new move from the current position.
(2) Make a move.
(3) Unmake a move.
(4) Check the legality of a move for the current position. (This is used for trying out transposition-table moves and killer-table moves.)
(5) Start searching the current position to a depth of N plies. N is usually set to 3 or 4.
(6) Return the value from the just completed search.
(7) Return the best move from the just completed search.

The commands only affect the accessed processor. The decision to disallow simultaneous access from the host to the processors is estimated to cost a 1-3% reduction in overall speed, but it simplified the design.

The first four commands are used for host software tree traversal, and the last three commands are the interface to the hardware search coroutine. A software readable status register tells the host software whether the processors have completed their searches. The host software searches the first few plies with a hardware assist, and calls the hardware search coroutines when the software tree is N plies from leaf nodes. The transposition table and the killer table are also maintained by the host in software. The bottom N plies searched directly by the hardware processors are searched without using the transposition table or the killer table. When N is 3, the main effect of this omission of

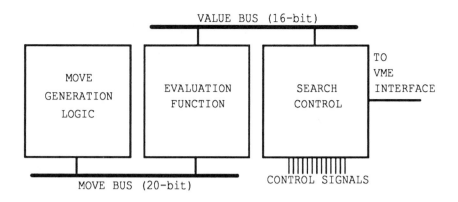

Figure 5.6: Interconnections between the processor main blocks.

hardware transposition/killer tables is an increase of up to 10% in the tree size. A side effect, which is somewhat harder to evaluate, is that repetitions are no longer detected in the bottom N plies. The current software/hardware combination does about 700,000 evaluations per second for the original wire-wrapped version.

Each hardware chess processor itself can be broken into three main parts: the move generation logic, the evaluation function and the search control. The main interconnections between the three parts are shown in Figure 5.6. The move generation logic and the evaluation function and connected by a 20-bit, bi-directional move bus, and the evaluation function and the search control are connected by a 16-bit value bus. The communications from and to the host go through the search control.

5.4.1 Move Generation Logic

The move generation logic centers around the single chip chess move generator described earlier. Figure 5.7 shows the main components. A 20-bit move bus is used to transfer information between the main components. Connected directly to the move bus are a 256-word deep move stack, a special-move constants generator that produces the move constants for *en passant* and castling moves, and an interface to the move generator. The special-move constants generator acts as a small ROM storing the special-move constants. The move stack, besides storing the moves themselves, is also used to store move generation status information such as the castling rights status and whether the current position has any legal moves. The move generator interface is just a collection of latches and multiplexors controlled by a move generation sequencer. The sequencer is a finite state machine that takes as inputs the status bits from the move generator itself and commands from the search control.

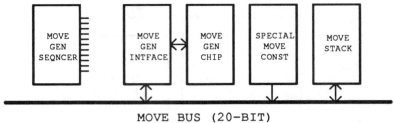

MOVE BUS (20-BIT)

Figure 5.7: Move generation logic.

5.4.2 Evaluation Function

The philosophy behind the design of the evaluation function hardware is somewhat unusual. The overriding concerns are the circuit size and the feasibility of future integration, possibly in a somewhat different form. Sacrifices in the knowledge content of the evaluation function were deemed justifiable if they simplified the circuit design significantly. Nonetheless, most of the terms existing in typical chess evaluation functions are either implemented or substituted with something easier to implement in hardware. The resulting evaluation function was determined, to some degree, by the whims of the hardware designer[3]. It is unclear whether the right balance had been struck in the trade-off between the simplicity of the hardware design and the knowledge content of the evaluation function. *Deep Thought*'s performance indicates that its evaluation function is more or less comparable to other research machines.

One common chess evaluation term that is noticeably missing is a direct measurement of space and mobility, usually considered the most important positional evaluation heuristic for a chess program. The term alone has been observed to correspond to almost an extra ply of search (Schaeffer and Marsland 1985; Schaeffer 1986). There is no evidence to say that *Deep Thought* would not improve significantly with the term introduced. The term was, however, considered too expensive to implement without building a custom chip. Recent software simulation seems to indicate that the missing term may have a major impact on the program's performance. A version of the program with a simulated mobility term defeated by a win/loss margin of about 2 to 1 the normal version that did not have the term.

5.4.3 Hardware Evaluation Capabilities

Deep Thought's evaluation function, like that of *Belle*, can be logically divided into an incremental evaluation function and a slow evaluation function. Unlike *Belle*'s evaluation function, which uses ROMs for its evaluation tables and

---

[3] Who has never been known to have great aptitude for playing chess.

therefore cannot be easily reprogrammed, the *Deep Thought* evaluation function uses RAMs for all its evaluation tables and is normally modified for each new root position. The software uses this hardware feature by pre-computing the evaluation tables and effectively removing some of the evaluation computation out of the hardware inner loop.

The incremental evaluation function is nothing more than lookups of the piece placement table. The piece placement table holds a value for each chess piece on any of the 64 board squares. For a typical move, up to two subtractions and one addition may be needed to update the incremental score. The moving piece value at the *FROM* square and the victim piece value at the *TO* square may have to be subtracted, and the moving piece value at the *TO* square has to be added. To improve the speed, the incremental evaluation function is pipelined in two stages. With a clock of 60 ns, the result of the incremental evaluation is available within one 180 ns move generation cycle after the move is executed. The incremental evaluation is a catch-all for heuristics not handled by the slow evaluation. The main heuristics used in the incremental evaluation at the moment include: material value, piece centralization, pawn advancement, rooks to the seventh rank, king tropism (moving pieces near opponent's king), and so on.

Computation of the slow evaluation is triggered whenever a move is executed. The microcode can elect to ignore the slow evaluation when the incremental evaluation score is nowhere near the search window. Conceptually, the slow evaluation is an 8-cycle, one cycle per file, operation. In reality, the computation is a 14-cycle one, including a 6-cycle latency resulting from the actual pipeline stages. The cycle time is 60 ns, and the total slow evaluation time is therefore 840 ns.

Figure 5.8 shows the main logic blocks of the slow evaluation. The *PAWN BITMAP* block is implemented with two Xilinx Logic Cell Arrays (LCA). Each LCA maintains the pawn bitmap for one color, implemented as six circular 8-bit shift registers, which fit nicely with the LCA internal structure. Each cycle, the *PAWN BITMAP* LCAs generate 3 groups of different output signals: the bitmap of the current file, the *OR* ed bitmap of the two adjacent files and the *OR* ed bitmap of the three files. The bitmap of the current file also gets sent to the *FILE COND* block which detects whether the current file is open or semi-open and whether there are pawns blocked on dark or white squares. The *ROOK_CNT* block is two additional LCAs that maintain the number of rooks on each file for either side. The current file number is also generated at the *ROOK_CNT* block. The bitmap, the file status, the rook counts and the file number are grouped together to index five slow evaluation tables. The outputs of the slow evaluation tables are then summed and accumulated in the pipelined adder tree block, which is implemented with another LCA. It is interesting to note that the throughput of the pipelined adder tree is of the order of 100 million additions per second. The whole slow evaluation function takes less than 20 off-the-shelf chips, roughly 20% of the total chip count for each processor. It also reduces the effective search speed by about 30%.

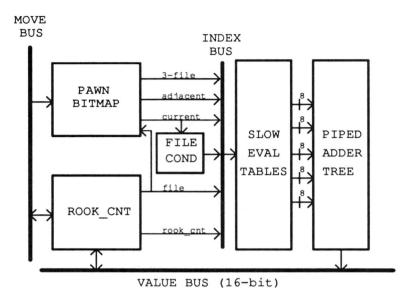

Figure 5.8: Slow evaluation function.

The five slow evaluation tables can be divided into three groups: pawn structure tables, passed pawn tables and the file table. The main inputs of the pawn structure tables are the bitmaps of the current file and the *OR*ed bitmaps of the two adjacent files. Isolated pawns, backward pawns and doubled pawns are recognized by the pawn structure tables. The passed pawn tables take as inputs the bitmaps of the current file and the *OR*ed opponent 3-file bitmaps. The file table assigns a value to each file based on the status of the file and the numbers of rooks occupying the file.

5.4.4 Search Control

The search control consists of a simple microcontroller and a typical datapath. The microcontroller used is very primitive. There is no microcontrol stack and no subroutines are allowed in microcode. The branching is done by multiplexing the condition signals directly into the lowest two control store address bits. The design has one advantage: it can be clocked almost at the memory speed. The microcycle used is 60 ns, which is beyond the easy reach of available microcontroller chips. The writable microcontrol store has 8K of 64-bit words.

The search control datapath is used to handle the alpha-beta ($\alpha\beta$) computation. The value stack, shown in Figure 5.9, has 1K of 16-bit words, but is organized as a 256 deep stack with 4 word frames. The $\alpha\beta$ values and the incremental evaluation score are stored on the value stack. The one remaining

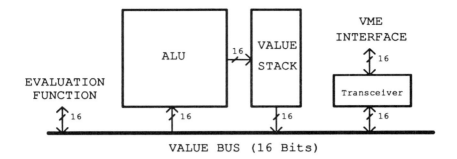

Figure 5.9: Search control datapath.

word in each value stack frame is used for microcode debugging. The ALU is an IDT49C402 16-bit ALU containing sixty-four 16-bit registers. The large number of registers allows various constants to be stored directly in the ALU. The datapath is clocked with the same 60 ns clock as the microcontroller.

Each chess processor in *Deep Thought* can search about 500,000 positions per second on their own. Both the move generation logic and the evaluation function can sustain throughput more than twice that. The slowdown mainly results from the search control mechanism. The generic ALU used is not really the optimum datapath for doing the $\alpha\beta$ search. There are also some mismatches among the three main blocks that aggravate the problem.

5.4.5 In Perspective

The move generator itself is between a factor of 100 to 1,000 times smaller than *Hitech*'s (Ebeling 1986) and *Belle*'s (Condon and Thompson 1982) in terms of chip count, and yet is faster by a factor of 10 and 2 respectively. With two processors of about 100 chips each, the chess machine as a whole is about a factor of 10 smaller than the other two chess machines. At 700,000 nodes per second, *Deep Thought* is about 5 times faster than the other machines in raw speed, and also 200 rating points stronger. With current VLSI technology, it should be possible to produce single chip machines with yet another 5- to 10-fold speedup.

5.5 Software

Many of the software ideas in the program are similar to those used by others. In this section, some of the major differences and innovations of *Deep Thought* are described.

5.5.1 Evaluation Pre-Computation Software

The so-called software evaluation function of *Deep Thought* is not a traditional evaluation function at all. It performs the pre-computation of the hardware evaluation tables, instead of the actual computation itself. As well as taking into account the usual evaluation issues, it also functions as a sort of planning facility. This type of pre-computation is not exactly original; the *Chess 4.X* group apparently had done it, as did Schaeffer (1983b) with his planning component *Planner*. What really distinguishes *Deep Thought*'s evaluation software is its design from the outset for automatic tuning.

The evaluation software computes the hardware evaluation table entries as linear functions of the evaluation parameters multiplied by arbitrarily complicated functions of positional features. Because of uncharacterized interactions of the positional features, the evaluation parameters are not independent variables from the tuning program's point of view. It would be desirable to reduce the interdependency of the evaluation parameters in order to improve the stability of the tuning process.

Given the limited time actually spent on coding the evaluation software, it is surprising how well the evaluation software does. The evaluation software has not really explored all the possibilities inherent in the hardware evaluation function, and yet the program's positional evaluation seemed to be no worse than the better research programs. Among the research programs, *Phoenix* appeared to be the only program that caused *Deep Thought* problems with positional play. It is suspected that the lack of a real mobility term might be a factor in this case, since *Phoenix* is reported to have an effective mobility term (Schaeffer 1986). One possible explanation for *Deep Thought*'s apparent equity in evaluation against most of the other research programs is the diminishing returns effect when adding knowledge to a chess program (Schaeffer and Marsland 1985; Schaeffer 1986). Once a sufficient amount of knowledge is added to a chess program, the addition of further chess knowledge produces very little gain. *Deep Thought*'s evaluation apparently has reached the typical saturation point. Finally, it should be pointed out that the best commercial chess programs appear to have measurably better evaluation than the research ones at this point in time.

5.5.2 Evaluation Parameter Tuning Software

It is difficult to improve any sufficiently complex evaluation function by manually adjusting the weights of its components. For *Deep Thought* in particular it was even harder, since none of its authors had a working chess knowledge comparable to the program's strength. Moreover, the interactions between the 100+ weights in the evaluation function would have made adjustments by hand hopeless anyway. Thus it was decided early in the project to automatically tune the evaluation parameters.

The first part of any tuning problem is deciding what to tune for. One basic assumption behind the current automatic tuning procedure is that if the program's moves at a shallow search depth match good players' moves more frequently, the program will in general play better even for the normal search depths. Tuning under this assumption is not equivalent to optimizing tournament level play. A simple example where this assumption can go wrong is as follows. Assume that in a Grandmaster (GM) game, the GM pushes a pawn to open up a file for attack. The opening of the file might require up to three pawn moves and one pawn exchange to achieve. The tuning procedure, not realizing the true objective of the pawn advancement, might decide that the pawn gains high values as it advances. Eventually, it will be able to match the 3 pawn moves at the cost of missing the pawn capture, because the pawn would gain so much value that the program refuses to give it up. Despite the flaw in the assumption, it is the simplest one to make and is the basis of various proposals for automatic evaluation function tuning procedure (Nitsche 1982; Marsland 1985; Meulen 1989).

The development of *Deep Thought*'s parametric evaluation function tuning was based on two separate approaches. In the first approach, a standard hill climbing algorithm was encoded that uses the chess hardware to execute 5- or 6-ply searches on each position of a Grandmaster game database[4]. The number of "correct" move selections is recorded as the figure of merit. According to a predetermined schedule, one weight of the evaluation function is changed. If a better figure of merit is obtained, the modified weight is kept, otherwise it is changed back, and the process repeats. To avoid getting stuck at local optima, a probabilistic method known as *simulated annealing* could be applied. Unfortunately, even with plain hill climbing, the run time for this optimization process on a database of about 900 games (roughly 65,000 positions) is measured in years. By the time one hill climbing run was completed, *Deep Thought* would be an obsolete machine. Nevertheless, the figure of merit used by the hill climbing algorithm proved to be extremely useful in verifying the second tuning method described below.

The second tuning procedure evolved from the simple notion of finding the least square fit of the machine's evaluation with respect to the *true* values of the positions (Nitsche 1982; Marsland 1985). The *true* values of the positions might be approximated by using the values returned from deep searches; however, the approximation falls short when evaluation concepts new to the machine are to be added. The other obvious alternative is to assign values to positions based on the moves chosen by good players. Nitsche (1982) used the crude approximation of simply assigning a '1' to the position after the database move, and a '0' to all alternatives, and reported satisfactory results for tuning simple

---

[4] The game database used consists of 900 GM and master level games collected by Kees Roos and distributed by Hartmann (1987a,b) to other computer-chess researchers. The games used are perhaps not quite as high in overall quality as, say, Chess Informant games, but the observed move matching rate correlates well with the matching rate against a recently acquired Informant database. This leads us to believe that the game database used is of sufficiently high quality to draw valid conclusions about the tuning procedure.

endgame play. This approximation, however, has at least two major flaws. First, it is too simple minded for full chess game applications. Second, it is not really necessary to assign *absolute* values to the positions. The partial move ordering provided by the training database games gives a strong hint about the *relative* values of positions: a position reached after a GM move is likely to be better than the ones reached after alternative moves. This leads to either an over-constrained system of inequalities or an over-constrained system of equalities with undetermined right-hand-side relative positional values. The system of inequalities formulation is closely related to the linear discriminant problem found in the field of pattern recognition. Two early proposed tuning approaches (Marsland 1985; Meulen 1989) considered solving the linear discriminant problem or its variants. The tuning approach actually used in *Deep Thought* was based on the system of equalities formulation. As will be seen later, this allows finer control of the tuning process. One additional major departure from the early proposals (Nitsche 1982; Marsland 1985; Meulen 1989) is that the positions being compared are not the positions one ply from the root position, but rather the *dominant* positions, possibly several plies from the root position. The *dominant* position after a top level move is defined to be the position which gives the minimax value for the subtree.

As a preliminary step, the evaluation function was modified to provide conditional compilation. In normal play mode, calling the evaluation function down-loads a complete set of values into the hardware evaluation tables. In tuning mode, the evaluation function returns the symbolic evaluation in the form of a vector with one component for each sub-function without applying any weighting. Since a normal evaluation function call is quite costly (because the evaluation tables are large), in tuning mode the evaluation function switches to a lazy evaluation method that computes only those table entries that are required for a given position. This results in a considerable reduction in CPU time required. It was essential to have only one version of the source code to avoid discrepancies between the actual evaluation function and the one being tuned.

The tuning process starts by using *Deep Thought* to create a tuning database that contains a shallow game tree for each of the 65,000 training positions. The game trees were pre-pruned to contain only moves that lead to quiet, roughly balanced positions. This requires including trees generated by the quiescence search. Past approaches that did not include the quiescence search (Marsland 1985; Meulen 1989) must ignore moves which lead to unbalanced positions, for example, capture moves or moves which allow captures. As will be seen below, without the quiescence search it is difficult to establish relationships between some types of parameters.

The tuning program uses an initial set of parameters that evaluate each leaf tree position. This value is used as the first approximation to an oracle. In this procedure, the oracle is a difference in the value between 2 positions, and not an absolute value. This approach avoids the need for absolute values that are more susceptible to systematic errors at the expense of more complex computations. Given the value difference and the vector of sub-function value differences, a least square procedure computes a new set of parameters.

Without further modifications, this new set would be identical to the initial set of parameters. However, this is a rather expensive way of computing the identity and is similar to fitting a straight line through a set of points that were generated by the equation for a straight line. Besides aiding in debugging, this procedure prepares the stage for the actual tuning process.

Tuning is accomplished by comparing the preliminary oracle value differences for pairs of positions. One position is always the leaf node that corresponds to the GM move while the other leaf node is reached by an alternate move. The GM leaf node value is expected to dominate the values of the other positions. If the alternate move scored lower (i.e. the difference is negative), the oracle was correct and no adjustment is necessary. If the GM move scored lower, the preliminary oracle value will be adjusted before it is used in the fit for the new parameter set. The amount of adjustment determines how much the new parameter set will differ from the previous iteration. Experiments showed that too much correction leads to radical changes.

This tuning procedure changes all parameters simultaneously. It could be understood as determining the direction of the optimum in the 100 dimensional parameter space and then moving a certain distance in that direction.

The next iteration does not necessarily compare the same positions, because the new parameter set may result in a different path through the game trees. This can lead to some instabilities of the iteration process. This is caused by the need to search deeper than one ply, which is the only way to establish a relation between some of the weights. For example, comparing the values of a knight to that of a bishop requires comparing positions that differ in the number of knights and bishops and therefore are separated by several moves.

This basic procedure was refined by several heuristics that deal with the selection of the proper adjustment. For example, it turned out to be beneficial to correct small errors more forcefully than large errors. At first glance, it may seem counter-intuitive to choose the correction term to be inversely related to the evaluation error. Large evaluation errors are more likely caused by a structural deficiency of the evaluation function that can't be fixed by changing weights. There are certain positional concepts that simply are not yet part of *Deep Thought*'s evaluation function. A small mis-evaluation, on the other hand, may very well be correctable by modest parameter changes.

It was observed that correcting only erroneous evaluations led to a reduction in the range of values returned by the evaluation. This does not affect the number of correct inequalities (the primary objective function). However the reduction in variance reduces the precision of the evaluation function and was observed to negatively impact the search behavior at deeper search depths. This problem was addressed by applying a uniform force to all correct evaluation differences that is a function of the total amount of correction applied to incorrect evaluation differences. This factor permits the variance of an evaluation function to be kept in the right range.

The typical tuning process starts with an initial parameter set that is created by the author of the evaluation function. The tuning process is applied for about 10 to 20 iterations, each requiring about 2 hours CPU time on a Sun 3/260 (lately this time has increased considerably because the evaluation function has become more complex). The best results are selected on the basis of move matching rates using 5- or 6-ply searches. The final results are then tried in self-play games with earlier versions. Initial experimental results are quite encouraging, but further experimentation is required. For example, the optimal parameter set depends on the actual search depth. Parameter sets that score best in shallow searches don't necessarily do likewise in deeper searches. High move matching rates on human GM games don't necessarily correlate with better scores in self-play. And self-play may lack significance because of the structural similarity of the opponent.

5.5.3 Search Software

The search software consists of about 15,000 lines of code written in C for the host and 3,000 lines of microassembly code for the chess hardware. The host code is unusually large, makes extensive use of goto's and macros, and has been known to choke most C compilers. The microcode, being microcode, is, of course, a mess. Part of the problem in the host code can be traced to constraints imposed by the microcode. The search software as a whole is complex enough to make it likely that bugs remain in the code. Nonetheless, the program works well enough to allow Grandmaster-level play.

The search is split between the host and the hardware, with the last three plies of search being executed on the hardware and the remaining part of the search executed on the host. This allows the search to run at close to the raw speed of the hardware. In theory, this arrangement should also make it easy to do experiments on new search algorithms on the host because of the availability of high level languages.

To understand the search behavior and, in particular, the machine's apparent success with selective search extensions, it is necessary to know what has been done in the microcode search. *Deep Thought* uses a simpler than normal quiescence search. It only searches capture moves in the quiescence tree. Check evasion is extended for internal nodes, but checks are not even detected in the quiescence tree. A checkmating move right before the quiescence search will not be detected as a mate. Intrinsically, this means that the search is less stable than most other programs. The microcode also implements two kinds of pruning mechanisms: futility cutoffs (Schaeffer 1986) and a variant of the null-move pruning mechanism (Beal 1989; Chapter 9 *Experiments with the Null-Move Heuristic*). The effects of the pruning mechanisms are such that for off-balance positions, the size of the search tree drops dramatically and search extensions for off-balance positions are cheap.

The relative instability of *Deep Thought*'s brute-force search makes it imperative that some sort of selective search extensions be implemented.

Without selective extensions, at least a handful of other much slower machines will occasionally be able to find checkmates earlier than *Deep Thought*. The extensions could be applied at both the microcode level and the host level. The microcode level offers better observation of the search instabilities near the search horizon, and the host level search extensions are easier to implement and less time critical. Other than check evasion, the existing microcode does not implement any other search extensions, and most of the extensions go on at the host level.

Central to the derivations of the selective search extensions is a change of mindset from the search efficiency oriented, brute-force search paradigm. The elevated search capability of the hardware leads to the observation that search is relatively cheap compared to static analysis and could also be used for information gathering. Once the mindset has been changed, ideas such as singular extensions (Anantharaman, Campbell and Hsu 1988) come naturally. In its simplest form, the singular extensions algorithm deliberately offsets the search window for the sibling moves of the principal variation move in the hope of finding whether the Principal Variation (PV) move is significantly better than all its sibling moves. When the PV move is verified to be "singular," its search depth is increased by one, and hence the name "singular extensions." Beside singular extensions, several other related search extensions have also been proposed by various members of the team and incorporated into the host search code.

Measuring the effectiveness of the selective search extensions implemented on *Deep Thought* had turned out to be a difficult problem. Conflicting results were obtained. Private communications with outside groups indicate that the beneficial effects are minimal to non-existent for other programs. This could be a combination of the higher instability of *Deep Thought*'s quiescence search and the existing search extensions already in other programs. Measurements with the program itself returned conflicting, though positive, evidence. Self-test matches between various versions of the program indicated that up to about 30 rating points can be gained over the vanilla brute-force version. Anantharaman (1990) developed an indirect rating measurement scheme, and found a collection of search extension heuristics that appeared to improve *Deep Thought*'s performance by about 86 USCF ratings points over the vanilla brute-force version. There is some debate within the group whether this measurement can be taken at the face value. It is a promising result nonetheless, although it certainly needs to be verified independently by direct measurements.

As a final note, the last two plies of the software search (i.e. plies 4 and 5 from the leaf) are programmed separately to take advantage of the two hardware processors available. Since the code used to juggle around the two processors is fairly complicated by itself, most of the selective search extensions are restricted to the remaining upper part of the tree, plies 6 and upward from the leaf nodes. The parallel algorithm used is not remarkable, but gives reasonable speedup because of the small number of processors involved.

5.6 Conclusions

Combining advances in hardware design with some innovative software algorithms has allowed *Deep Thought* to be the first chess machine to achieve Grandmaster-level play. In particular, the VLSI move generator chip and the selective searching algorithms are unqualified successes, and the evaluation function tuning is promising. In spite of the successes, there are strong indications from the play of the top commercial chess machines that further improvements are possible, even with the existing hardware. The top commercial machines are now at least 200 rating points higher than top research machines of comparable speed. Projecting this gain into *Deep Thought*'s rating range is dangerous, but it is conceivable that a further 100-200 rating point increase can be achieved.

Where can such gains come from? There are multiple possible sources. First, *Deep Thought* is well known for the poor quality of its opening book. Second, the evaluation function is not up to par with the best commercial machines. There is, however, a limit to the improvement that can be achieved in the evaluation function, as the hardware imposes certain constraints on what can be implemented. A refined automatic tuning mechanism might allow this limit to be reached more easily. Third, the search mechanism is suboptimal: the quiescence search is known to be too simple-minded, and the existing search extensions do not seem to be as good as were originally thought. It is, unfortunately, difficult to make significant changes to the quiescence search on the existing hardware without impacting the search speed. And finally, it is certain that bugs still exist in *Deep Thought*, with unknown impact on its performance.

Credits and Acknowledgments. Hsu designed the *ChipTest* and *Deep Thought* hardware, and wrote the microcode for both machines. Anantharaman wrote the majority of the chess software for both machines, and developed an early version of the *ChipTest* microcode. Campbell wrote the *Deep Thought* evaluation function and created the initial opening book for both programs. Nowatzyk wrote the microassembler used in both machines, and wrote the evaluation tuning code.

The authors would like to acknowledge the contributions of Peter Jansen (endgame databases, opening and evaluation assistance), Mike Browne (opening book processing programs) and Larry Kaufman (opening book). Additional support was provided by John Zsarnay and Lawrence Butcher. We would also like to thank H.T. Kung for financial assistance that enabled the *Deep Thought* hardware to be built in the first place. Raj Reddy and Randy Bryant provided additional financial assistance in the later phases of the project. And finally, we would like to thank Jonathan Schaeffer and Tony Marsland for their help in putting the material for this chapter together.

6 Hitech

H.J. Berliner and C. Ebeling

6.1 Introduction

Hitech was Carnegie Mellon University's first truly potent computer-chess competitor. It burst onto the scene in May 1985, when it achieved a score of 3.5-1.5 in its first competition in a human tournament, losing points only to Masters. By September it was good enough to share first place in a tournament which included four Masters, and thereby raised its USCF rating to 2233, thus eclipsing *Belle*'s high-water rating mark of 2206. It went into the North American Computer Chess Championship of 1985 as the highest rated program of all time, and duly won the tournament, though not without some assists from lady luck. Since that time *Hitech* has played in dozens of events, and won 70% of all its games, almost all of which were against Expert and Master competitors.

The program has won several tournaments including the Pennsylvania State Chess Championship three consecutive years running (1987-89). It has also tied for first in both the 1986 World Computer Championship and the 1989 ACM North American Computer Championship. It has drawn with some of the top 30 ranked US players.

Hitech has performed excellently in match play. It has never lost a match of two games or more and only drawn three of these while winning five. Most notably it defeated former US Champion Arnold Denker 3.5-0.5 in 1988, and defeated World Under-14 Champion Joel Lautier 2-0 in 1987. Today, the program has a rating of 2413 USCF.

The chess machine *Belle* pioneered the use of special-purpose hardware (LSI chips) to enhance the speed at which chess positions could be processed. The *Hitech* design took this one step further: building special-purpose VLSI chips. The resulting machine can analyze 175,000 positions per second. Search alone is not enough to play Grandmaster chess; knowledge is essential. The hardware includes the novel use of pattern recognizers to detect interesting features on the board and include that information in the evaluation of a position.

This chapter is an updated, abbreviated version of "Pattern Knowledge and Search: The SUPREM Architecture" which originally appeared in *Artificial Intelligence,* vol. 38 (1989), pp. 161-198.

The research was sponsored by the Defense Advanced Research Projects Agency (DOD), ARPA Order No. 4976, monitored by the Air Force Avionics Laboratory under contract F33615-84-K-1520, and by an IBM graduate student Fellowship.

Here the hardware, software and pattern recognizers that make up the *Hitech* chess machine are described. Additional contributions of the design team have been documented by Berliner (1989).

6.2 Architecture

The system architecture has four major parts, as Figure 6.1 shows:
- The Oracle is the primary repository of knowledge that the system needs to operate. The Oracle has production-like rules which define interim goals for both sides and the patterns that are needed to recognize achievement of these goals during the search.
- The Searcher is given a task by the Oracle. It then invokes the Move Generator and the Evaluator to do the search and evaluate the leaf nodes.
- From a given position, the Move Generator generates subsequent positions extremely rapidly by considering, in parallel, all feasible moves.
- The Evaluator assigns numerical values to each reached position by comparing selected patterns of position components to pre-tabulated patterns in its memory.

These four parts are organized into two separate subsystems. The Oracle is a general-purpose computer while the other three components include a special-purpose processor.

6.2.1 Operation

The Oracle has rules that define position classes, and the knowledge required to evaluate properly the positions likely to be reached by a search, starting from the current position. Knowledge takes the form of patterns plus conditions under which the pattern knowledge can be applied.

The Oracle is smart but slow, and somewhat resembles a rule-based system, looking for those patterns that are most likely to be useful in the evaluation process. To do this well, the Oracle must be reasonably knowledgeable about chess. At the start of a search, the Oracle analyzes the position that is actually on the game board, and selects the appropriate knowledge. It compiles the patterns into a form that can be evaluated by a simple table lookup, and then down-loads the compiled patterns into units within the Evaluator that perform pattern recognition and evaluation. This strategy avoids the recomputation of pattern values during the evaluation process, and so significantly speeds the evaluation.

After down-loading the patterns, the Oracle selects the depth of search and delegates control to the Searcher. Search then proceeds as follows:
(1) At each new node, the Move Generator proposes the best move to try next.
(2) The Searcher broadcasts the candidate move on the bus so that *Pattern Recognizing and Evaluation units: recognizers*, and any other position-maintaining units, can update their individual position descriptions.

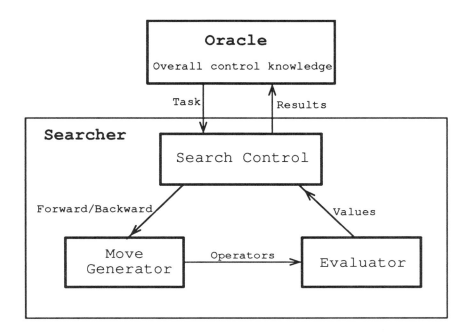

Figure 6.1: The architecture.

(3) The Evaluator scores relevant position features via independent recognizers that consult their internal pattern tables for values. One key advantage over other searching systems derives from the use of numerous recognizers operating in parallel. The Evaluator combines recognizer outputs in an adder tree and returns the new position's value.

(4) The Searcher decides whether to continue along the current branch or backtrack to some earlier point. Control recycles to step (1).

When the Searcher completes the specified search, control returns to the Oracle. The Oracle then decides whether to probe further or to accept the solution returned by the Searcher.

6.2.2 System Description

A Sun 4 workstation is the host computer for *Hitech* and contains the host software, which is written in C and consists of about 55,000 lines of code. About 50% of the software is the Oracle program which contains pattern selection information and the pattern library. The pattern library encompasses about 40 down-loadable patterns. The remainder of the host software controls the chess program, and maintains the top-level activity representation, an opening book and user interface.

The custom hardware in the Searcher can process about 175,000 chess positions per second. This includes generating a move, incrementally maintaining all representations and the values that these produce, and retracting all these when the time comes to back-track in the search.

The hardware includes 14 general recognizers. These are units that are capable of detecting patterns that encompass up to 36 bits. Recognizers are used to detect the presence of partial-board patterns. Each recognizer has a set of patterns for which it is responsible. Included in the armory of a recognizer are tables for detecting the presence of the patterns, and tables for interpreting the meaning of detected patterns. The interpretation of a pattern may involve assigning a value to it, or mapping it into a class of patterns, so it can be combined with other patterns that have been detected to make larger patterns. There are three levels of interpretation in the recognizers, although there is nothing fixed about this. It would seem that the larger the recognizers and the more levels of mapping, the better. Our design was influenced primarily by cost.

There are also 8 Global State recognizers, which monitor certain variables that may be crucial to deciding whether a certain pattern is significant, or determining the degree of significance. These recognizers feed their values into the final interpretation of any general recognizer, and are intended to provide global context. Details of this can be found in Section 6.5.3 *Application Coefficients and the Role of Context.*

The Oracle analyzes the root position to be processed and determines the type of knowledge that is most appropriate. Since recognizers are a finite resource, only a fraction of the available patterns can be down-loaded, and it is the task of the Oracle to do this effectively. The Oracle determines the stage of the game and other salient features of the root position in order to make its decisions. Once the best set of patterns have been identified, they are down-loaded into the appropriate recognizers and the search can begin.

6.2.3 Searching

Hitech, like most successful chess machine/programs, executes an $\alpha\beta$ *iterative-deepening* search (Slate and Atkin 1977). This *full-width* search involves examining all alternatives at a node except those that can be mathematically eliminated as having nothing to do with the solution. The search must know what the complete set of alternative moves is at any stage in the search, and keep track of those already tried as well as those remaining to be tried.

Iterative-deepening involves doing a complete search to depth N, followed by a complete search to depth N+1, followed by another to depth N+2 and so on as time allows (Scott 1969). It has been shown that this method does not waste time, as may at first appear. Its efficiency results from the information that is computed during each iteration and then saved to be available during succeeding iterations. One item of information saved is the best move in each position, as remembered from the last time the position was visited. Since the effectiveness of $\alpha\beta$ is dependent on the order in which moves are tried, it is an important advantage to consider the likely-best moves first. Another item of information is the value of the subtree below each node and the depth to which it was searched. If the identical position should be found again in the tree, it may be possible to avoid searching it altogether.

6.3 The Searcher

6.3.1 The Move Generator

The speed of the operator that provides the means to move from one point in the search space to the next places an upper bound on the size of the search space that can be examined. In chess this is often the factor that limits the search size since the rules that govern how pieces may move are rather complicated.

The move generator also plays a crucial role in the speedup obtained by the $\alpha\beta$ algorithm. It can be shown that optimal efficiency is achieved if the best move is examined first at each node in the search tree (Knuth and Moore 1975). Moreover, at many nodes of the tree, only one move needs to be generated if it provides a refutation. Thus the order in which moves are generated has a great effect on the speed of the search. Unfortunately, typical software move generators are forced to generate all moves since it is difficult to determine *a priori* which move to generate first.

6.3.2 A Fast Parallel Circuit for Move Generation

All previous software and hardware move generators have been concerned with only the moves of the pieces that are actually on the board in a given position. Software move generators generally compute the entire set of moves in the most convenient order and then sort them according to some set of heuristics. In contrast, *Hitech*'s move generator examines in parallel every move that could *ever* be possible, and computes the subset of those moves that are actually legal in the current position. It then selects what it projects to be the best move from this set of legal moves one at a time, as required.

We call the set of all moves that exist the *ever-possible* moves, and they can be described as the set of triples {piece, origin, destination} in the cross product (*Piece* × *Square* × *Square*) that are allowed by the rules of chess. This set can be enumerated by examining all the moves that could ever be made by each piece in turn. For example, one can place the queen on each of the 64 squares in turn, listing those destination squares to which the queen could move on an empty board. Another way to enumerate this set is to examine each square in turn and list all the moves that can be made to that square by the different pieces. We have chosen the latter method. Figure 6.2 shows all the ever-possible moves to the square e4.

An ever-possible move is legal in a position if the following three independent conditions are satisfied:

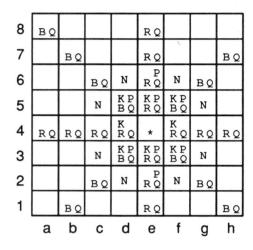

Figure 6.2: The set of ever-possible moves to the single square e4.

- The *origin* condition: The appropriate piece must be on the origin square.
- The *destination* condition: The destination square must either be empty or be occupied by an opponent's piece.
- The *sliding* condition: For sliding moves (queen, rook, bishop and two square pawn moves), the squares between the origin and destination square must be empty.

As an example, consider the move of a black queen from b4 to e4. For this move to be legal, the piece must first be on the square b4, the square e4 must be empty or contain a white piece, and the squares c4 and d4 must be empty.

There is a fourth condition that the move generator ignores: The player's king must not be in check after the move is made. This condition is computed after making the move by checking whether the king is attacked. The moves generated by the first three conditions are often called *pseudo-legal* moves; we will continue to call them legal with the understanding that the fourth condition is checked elsewhere.

The computation required to decide whether each of the ever-possible moves is legal is straightforward, requiring only a handful of gates operating on information about the state of the squares affecting the move. A move generator made from one of these simple circuits for each ever-possible move can compute the entire set of legal moves quickly in parallel. A key observation made years ago by Allen Newell is that there are only about 4,000 ever-possible moves for each side. Although this still represents a large circuit, VLSI technology can make this kind of parallel solution attractive.

6.3.3 Computing the Ever-Possible Moves

Each ever-possible move can be thought of as a pattern to be recognized. This pattern involves some small subset of the board state and recognizing the pattern instance that corresponds to a legal move is straightforward. Thus the move generator really consists of many pattern recognizers, one for each ever-possible move. Moreover, these pattern recognizers can all fire in parallel to determine the set of legal moves.

Each move recognizing circuit operates on a subset of the state variables that represent the board position, producing as output a boolean value indicating the legality of a single move. The straightforward implementation of the state variables is an 8×8 array representing the board, where each array location is a 4-bit value encoding the piece occupying that square of the board. The state variables are easily maintained incrementally as the game state changes. With the exception of the relatively rare cases of castling and *en passant,* moves affect only two squares and thus two writes into the array are sufficient to update the state variables when a move is made or backed up[1]. Each of these writes is called a *half move* and either places or removes a piece on a square.

The problem with this implementation is the communication of the state variables to the move recognition circuits. Since each of the 4,000 move recognition units requires about 5 inputs, on the order of 20,000 wires are required for communicating the state variables to the recognition circuits. One of the characteristics of VLSI circuits is the high cost of communication. This comes about because the size of the active devices has been reduced to the point that the wires between adjacent devices require as much, or more, area than the devices themselves. If signals are required to go any distance at all, the space they consume can overwhelm that used by active circuitry. Moreover, the delay attributed to long wires can dominate the gate delay for VLSI circuits. This disparity is even more pronounced if signals must cross chip boundaries.

The key idea of the move generator architecture that permits a reasonable VLSI implementation is that of duplicating the state variables throughout the move computation circuits so that the inputs to those circuits are available where they are used instead of being communicated through many different wires. Of course the state variables themselves must be maintained as moves are made, but this requires far less communication. Only 10 wires are required to communicate the address and data when writing the state variable array. Although these 10 wires must be routed throughout the circuit to all state variables, this can be done with a regular layout to minimize wiring space. This transformation in the circuit is represented in Figure 6.3. The tangled wiring network that carries the state variables to the function circuits in the first circuit is replaced by a single event bus that communicates the change in the state

---

[1] Moves made when extending a branch of the tree are reversed when the search back-tracks. An alternative solution would be to maintain the state variables in a stack.

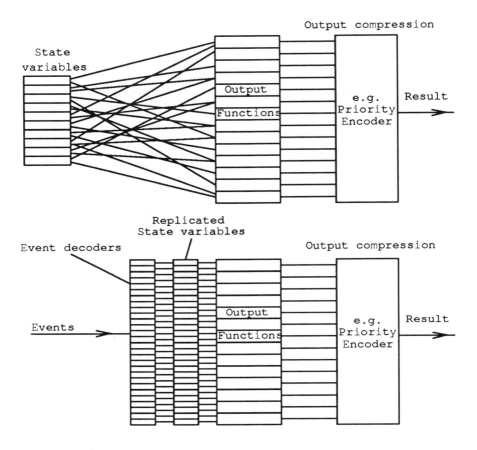

Figure 6.3: Communication of state variables.

. variables. Copies of the state variables used by each function are kept within the function circuit itself.

There are some important points to be made about this circuit transformation. First, it makes a single chip implementation more feasible by drastically reducing the communication between circuit elements on the chip. Second, if the entire circuit is too large to fit on one chip, the circuit can be partitioned almost arbitrarily onto several chips. This is in contrast to many parallel circuits that are constrained by the communication pattern to an all-or-nothing approach where the circuit is not feasible if it does not fit on a single chip. This also allows the implementation to track advances in technology. While the initial implementation was done using 64 chips, it could be done with just 4 chips using current technology.

One can view the move generator as a write-only memory where the memory output is a set of functions of the memory state. The memory is not the usual one, however. A single write instruction modifies many different memory locations and, since a single memory value is used by many different functions, each location is replicated in each function circuit to minimize the amount of wiring required. One can also view move generation as a large pattern recognition problem for which there are 8,000 possible features (4,000 moves for each side) to be recognized in a board position. Each of the 8,000 circuits acts as a feature recognizer that looks for one particular pattern corresponding to one ever-possible move. As the board changes, the information about the change is broadcast to all the recognizers, each of which determines whether a feature is present or absent.

6.3.4 Move Selection

The move generator as described thus far consists of a large parallel circuit that computes the legality of the approximately 4,000 ever-possible moves for each side. There remains the task of isolating the few moves that are actually legal. This process of move selection is important since the order in which moves are tried makes a large difference to the efficiency of the $\alpha\beta$ search.

One solution would be to use a suitably modified priority encoder to identify the legal moves in a serial manner. The drawback of this method is that it imposes a static ordering on the set of ever-possible moves. This static ordering cannot take into account dynamic factors such as square safety that can drastically change the value of a particular move.

Static ordering can be done, however, on a square by square basis. That is, the dynamic factors that affect the value of moves affect all moves to one square in the same way. For example, if the opponent is guarding the square, the value of all moves to the square is reduced because of the likelihood that the moved piece will be captured. Thus the move generator is partitioned into 64 parts, one for each square, with a priority encoder used to select the moves to each square without sacrificing search efficiency. In the process of generating moves to a square, the value of each move is estimated by noting the value of the moving piece, the captured piece, if any, and the safety of the destination square. This safety calculation is possible because the parallel move computation circuit computes the entire set of legal moves. The moves are then dynamically ordered among squares based on the value associated with each move.

6.3.5 Maintaining the Context of Active Positions

The $\alpha\beta$ search traverses the search tree in depth-first order so that at any position the first move is made and its subtree examined before the subtrees of the remaining moves are examined. At about half the nodes in the search tree only one move is examined and thus the move generator produces moves one at a time when required. Thus the context of the move generator must be saved from the time one move is generated until the next move is requested, during which time the move generator is processing positions in the subtree. The move generator context includes the state variables that represent the board position, which are restored automatically by performing inverse moves when the search backs up the tree, and information about which moves have already been generated in each position. This latter information is kept by each chip in a stack that remembers the most recent move tried from a position. The priority encoder then uses this to generate the next untried move.

6.3.6 Special Operations

The move generator supports several operations that serve to speed up the search algorithm. The first is used during the part of the search that attempts to play out the active components of a position. This *quiescence* search is done after the pre-determined search depth is reached and examines only capture moves and responses to check. A control signal from the chess machine is asserted during the quiescence search which informs the move generator chips to generate only capture moves. This signal is not asserted if the side to move is in check so that all escaping moves are allowed. However, the move generator also is able to avoid most of the illegal moves that arise when escaping check.

Another special operation allows the chess machine to query the move generator about the legality of a particular move. This is used to verify whether a move suggested by another module such as the hash table or killer table is actually legal. This operation can be done quickly since the move generator has a list of all legal moves.

6.3.7 The Move Generator Chip

The current implementation of the move generator consists of 64 chips, one for each board square. Figure 6.4 shows the block diagram for this chip. Besides the move computations, each chip contains a maskable priority encoder, a stack of move indices for representing the current search context, a PLA for performing the dynamic move priority calculation and a distributed voting circuit that is used in conjunction with the other chips for selecting the move with the highest value. The voting is done by having each chip place the priority of its move on a bus that all chips can examine. When the chip with the highest valued move recognizes that no other chips have a better move, it presents its move. More details of the move generator chip can be found in Ebeling's (1986) thesis. The chip was designed so that it can generate the moves to any of the 64 different squares. Each of the 64 chips is assigned to a different square of the board during initialization. Designing just one chip and using 64 copies takes advantage of the inexpensive replication costs of VLSI chips. In so doing, there are some inefficiencies, especially at the edge of the board where there are fewer legal moves than at the center. While this particular implementation was convenient for prototyping the design, the move generator architecture allows a range of implementations using fewer chips or even wafer-scale integration to decrease board area, power consumption and delay. This architecture is thus suitable for a variety of technologies with different circuit densities.

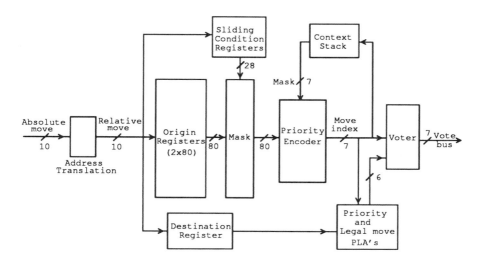

Figure 6.4: Move generator chip block diagram.

6.4 Position Evaluation

The third component of the classic chess program that goes along with the search control and move generation is position evaluation. In theory, the search terminates only at nodes whose values are win, loss or draw, but such a termination condition cannot be used in practice since complete game trees for most interesting positions consist of at least 10^{100} nodes. The evaluation function is used to approximate the result of a complete search by computing values by which different positions can be compared. Each leaf node, as determined by some *a priori* depth limitation, is assigned a value by the evaluation function to produce an ordering on the set of all leaf nodes with respect to the probable outcome of a complete search from that node. While material is the most important consideration, many more subtle factors arise when comparing positions, since a winning position can be created without any win of material. An evaluation function that does not recognize these *positional* factors is sure to lose, even to an average player, given the present search depth limits.

If one examines a typical winning line of play in a game between good players, there is a gradual progression in the value of the evaluation function from an even position to the final win. At first the advantage is subtle, with one player having a positional advantage because their pieces are deployed more effectively than the opponent's. As the game progresses, this positional advantage is increased until at some point a player actually establishes a material advantage. Eventually the winning player is able to use superior forces to engineer a mate. Positions in which the material balance is at stake are called *tactical* while those in which the players are jockeying for control of space are called *positional*.

Computers tend to be very good at tactical play since the material computation is simple, and to maintain complete accuracy in deep calculation may strain even a human World Champion. It is in computing the subtle positional factors that computers have difficulty. Computers often use their superior tactical ability to save weak positions that were reached because of an inadequate understanding of the positional defects of earlier decisions. The problem is that these positional defects manifest themselves only after many moves so that no reasonable search can hope to discover their eventual effect. As more than one programmer has discovered, the only advantage that a deep search has in these cases is that the positional problem becomes apparent somewhat sooner, with a slightly better chance of survival.

Evaluation, then, comprises many different factors, all of which must be taken into consideration when comparing two positions. While it is possible to carry the result of this evaluation as a vector of values, each representing some component of the evaluation, the values are typically combined into a simple scalar that represents the weighted sum of the components. These weights are assigned according to the relative importance of each component (Samuel 1967). Choosing the correct weights is difficult because components may be more or less important depending on the exact position. In these cases, a correct evaluation requires that the weights be themselves the result of some "higher-level" evaluation. These dynamically computed weights are called *application coefficients* (Berliner 1979a). The problem of combining the evaluation components into one scalar is difficult even for human players, involving decisions such as what constitutes sufficient positional compensation for some loss of material. How the application coefficients are computed is a matter of judgment and experience.

There is a complex relationship between the evaluation function and the depth of search. Because the search is able to see deeper, the evaluation function needs to know less about tactical factors other than simple material. For example, a capture is discovered by a 1-ply search which knows only about material, the concept of a double attack is discovered by a 3-ply search and the threat of a double attack by a 5-ply search. Thus the evaluation function used by an 8-ply search has less need to know explicitly about a double attack than a 6-ply search. Other positional factors, such as board control and piece mobility, appear to be less important when searching deeply. The key to building an effective evaluation function is deciding which factors are indeed important relative to the power of the search.

There are three related considerations involved with designing an evaluation function. The first is the identification of the knowledge required to understand positions sufficiently well. The level of play of the program ultimately depends on how well the evaluation function can distinguish good and bad positions.

Identifying the components that the evaluation must understand is the job of an expert who knows the problem intimately and can identify and correct deficiencies discovered through experience with the program. The second consideration is whether these components can be computed efficiently, and this depends on the complexity of the evaluation and the power of the computational method. Finally, a decision must be made about which evaluation components to include in the final evaluation function. This decision must consider the trade-off between search speed and the extent to which the evaluation should understand each position. This again is the product of the experience and judgment of an expert but also depends on how efficiently the evaluation can be implemented.

The trade-off between search speed and knowledge is a classic one: including more knowledge in the search necessarily slows down the search. In computer chess, the emphasis has shifted over the past decade in favor of speed. Since 1980, the fast searchers, *Belle* and *Cray Blitz*, have dominated computer chess, as against the more knowledgeable programs such as *Nuchess*. This reflects the difficulty of encoding the relevant chess knowledge and bringing it to bear efficiently. In many cases, the time required to analyze some complex facet of a position slows the search to the point where the overall play of the program is diminished instead of enhanced. The problem is how to increase the knowledge without decreasing the speed. It is just this ability of *Hitech* to perform complicated analysis extremely quickly that allows it play at such a high standard.

6.4.1 Evaluation Complexity

The different components of the evaluation function have widely varying computational requirements. We classify an evaluation function as first-order, second-order or higher-order based on its computational complexity. An evaluation function, $f(S)$, is defined as first-order if, and only if,

$$f(S) = \sum_i g(i, s_i) \tag{6.1}$$

where i ranges over all the squares of the board in position S, and g represents the value of piece s_i on square i. In other words, a first-order evaluation can be computed by examining the state of each square of the board independent of the other pieces and squares. Moreover, the overall value is computed as the linear sum of the values of the separate squares. This means that the function f can be computed incrementally during the search. That is, if the difference between two positions S^i and S^f involves only one square, δ, then

$$f(S^f) = f(S^i) - g(\delta, s_\delta^i) + g(\delta, s_\delta^f) \tag{6.2}$$

since

$$f(S^f) = \sum_{j \neq \delta} g(j, s_j^f) + g(\delta, s_\delta^f)$$

and

$$f(S^i) = \sum_{j \neq \delta} g(j, s_j^i) + g(\delta, s_\delta^i)$$

Once the initial value of the evaluation function is established, computing its value at new positions is accomplished by computing the function g on the s_δ's that describe the difference between neighboring positions in the search. There is a close relationship between the s_δ's used here and the half move operators that we have used previously to describe the incremental change from one position in the search to another. A *remove piece* half move corresponds to the negative term in Eq.(6.2) and a *place piece* half move to the positive term. Since most moves affect two squares, a total of four half moves are required to move the search from one position to another. If $g(i, NULL) = 0$, where NULL represents the state in which no piece occupies the square, then only two half moves are needed for non-capturing moves, and three for captures.

The prime example of incremental evaluation is that of material evaluation which totals each player's material. In this case the function g is defined simply by

$$g(\delta, s_\delta) = Value(s_\delta)$$

where values are assigned to each piece based on their relative strengths. By contrast, determining whether a pawn is isolated cannot be done incrementally, since it requires information about the presence of pawns on three adjacent files.

A second-order evaluation function is one that depends on the relationship between two or more squares and thus cannot be computed incrementally. It cannot be described by Eq.(6.2) and must take the more general form

$$f(S) = g(s_1, s_2, \cdots, s_k), \quad k > 1. \tag{6.3}$$

In the worst case, g may be a function over the entire board, but generally second-order evaluations depend on a subset of the squares. For example, each legal move computation performed by the move generator is a second-order evaluation. The legality of a move depends on the state of the origin, destination and possibly intervening squares. This second-order evaluation operates over a small subset of the board state, which led to the simple parallel architecture based on distributed state described in Section 6.3.1 *The Move Generator*. We will now show that this architecture can be generalized to perform position evaluation.

6.4.2 The Role of the Oracle

The Oracle is located in the host computer and cooperates with the Searcher. It is invoked at the start of a search to perform a detailed analysis of the root position to determine:

(1) the present position-class of the root, and
(2) the position-classes that are likely to be encountered during the search, and which would therefore require evaluation.

The Oracle allows the evaluation to be tuned to the region that the search is likely to cover. This was not required in the case of the move generator since the set of ever-possible moves does not change. The ability to determine the patterns relevant to the search locale greatly increases the efficiency of the pattern recognition architecture.

The Oracle must be both knowledgeable about chess and be an excellent resource allocator. Typically, there is more knowledge that could be put into recognizer units than there are units. However, certain simplifying assumptions help here. For instance, once the amount of material for one side drops below a certain threshold, it is unlikely that considerations of the opponent's king safety will come into play. This allows the focus to be gradually shifted to the endgame, and recognizers would be assigned such tasks as they are freed from performing other tasks. This type of tracking of what is important allows the same recognizer units to change gradually the patterns they are monitoring, providing increased flexibility with few units.

This flexibility is achieved by generality in the hardware which can receive down-loaded tables at the start of the search to deal with a large variety of situations. There is some risk in using the Oracle to decide what knowledge is to be used. For instance, in one branch of the search many pieces could be swapped off, reaching a simplified position, far away from the root, for which the designated knowledge would not be suitable. Also, it is possible for material on the board to *increase* due to pawn promotion, and thus king safety could again become a consideration, after having been dismissed as inconsequential in the Oracle analysis. However, such occurrences are rare.

This effect can be lessened by making the evaluation less dependent on assumptions made at the root. This trades increased evaluation hardware for more precise evaluation. Given a fixed evaluation time, the Oracle is always faced with the decision about which components to include for any one search. This decision is much easier if the hardware is not too cramped.

6.5 Implementing the Evaluation Function

First-order evaluation is interesting since it is extremely easy to compute, requiring only the specification of the function g in Eq.(6.1) The domain of g is the cross product of the set of pieces and the set of squares. Since there are 12 different pieces and 64 squares, g can be completely specified by a table with 768 entries. Moreover, many different first-order evaluations can be combined into one since

$$f_1(S^f) + f_2(S^f) =$$

$$f_1(S^i) - g_1(\delta, s_\delta^i) + g_1(\delta, s_\delta^f) + f_2(S^i) - g_2(\delta, s_\delta^i) + g_2(\delta, s_\delta^f)$$

and thus

$$g(i, s) = g_1(i, s) + g_2(i, s), \quad \text{for all} \ \ i, s.$$

Since it is inexpensive to compute a first-order evaluation, it is advantageous to cast as much of the evaluation function as possible in this form. Although at first glance there appears to be little besides simple material computation that is first-order, second-order evaluations can often be approximated by a first-order evaluation. Although the result is less precise, in cases where the second-order evaluation is difficult to compute or not important enough to warrant the extra computation, the first-order evaluation can provide a performance gain if it adds any additional understanding at all, since it does not slow down the search.

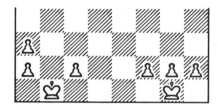

Figure 6.5: The king is safe behind the pawns.

Figure 6.6: Function g for a king's pawn shelter.

As an example, consider the problem of king safety. In Figure 6.5 the king on the right side of the figure is safely hidden from attack behind the three pawns. Removing one of these pawns would put the king in some jeopardy, removing two would expose the king to serious threats, but removing all three would be a disaster. Advancing the pawns one square would weaken the shelter somewhat. This simple king shelter evaluation can be approximated by defining the function g in terms of the six squares in front of the king, as shown in Figure

6.6 (where a pawn is worth about 100 points). This definition of g gives the pawn shelter at the right side of Figure 6.5 a bonus of 75 points. Advancing one pawn loses 9 points, losing one pawn costs 25 points, and losing all three costs 75 points. Since the loss of the second and third pawn is more serious than the loss of the first, a more precise pawn shelter evaluation would adjust the amount each pawn is worth *based on how many of the others are still present*. Moreover, capturing from b2 to a3 (as shown on the left side) is much worse than advancing from h2 to h3, but this cannot be reflected by this first-order evaluation. However, the first-order approximation does give some idea about the value of these pawns, and although it is not as good as second-order evaluation, it is better than no evaluation at all.

Using an Oracle and first-order evaluation to approximate second-order evaluation yields surprisingly good play when used in combination with deep search. In fact, *Hitech* initially used only incremental evaluation in conjunction with an Oracle, attaining an estimated rating of about 2100. But it would sometimes make serious mistakes because it did not understand some things about chess that involve second-order evaluation that cannot be reasonably approximated by a first-order evaluation controlled by an Oracle. The primary deficiency involved some basic ideas about pawn structure such as doubled and isolated pawns. These concepts, which are crucial to playing high-caliber chess, simply cannot be computed without second-order evaluation.

6.5.1 Computing Second-Order Evaluations

As defined by Eq.(6.3), a second-order evaluation must be expressed as an arbitrary function over the state of more than one square. Such an evaluation can be computed serially, as is usually done, but only at a cost to the search speed. The move generator has the same problem since the legal move computation is a second-order evaluation. This section describes an architecture for the evaluation function that is similar to that used for move generation. In the case of the move generator, each legal move computation operates on the set of state variables consisting of the origin square, the destination square, plus intervening squares for sliding moves, resulting in a boolean value indicating whether the move is legal. The state information for each move is maintained by a set of registers that are updated incrementally by half moves broadcast over the move bus.

In the case of an evaluation function, the computation operates over the state relevant to the particular evaluation component, and the result is a number representing the value of a particular state assignment. If the state over which the function operates is relatively small, then the function can be computed by table lookup. For the king safety example of Figure 6.5, the state can be represented as six bits, one for each pawn shelter location, and thus a 64-entry table is sufficient to compute the second-order pawn shelter evaluation precisely. The overall evaluation function is divided into several different evaluation components such as pawn structure and king safety, each of which is analyzed

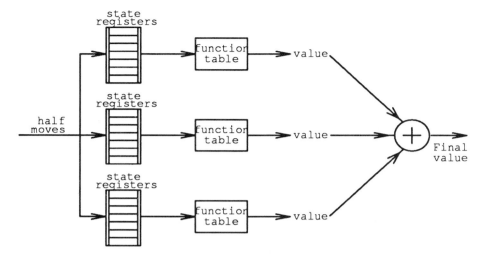

Figure 6.7: Parallel evaluation and combination of components.

separately and the results added together to reach a final value. This overall evaluation architecture is summarized in the simple block diagram in Figure 6.7.

For most second-order evaluation components encountered in chess, the amount of relevant state is too large for simple table lookup to be used as the evaluation method. In these cases, the evaluation is divided into subcomponents that can be analyzed separately and then combined. For example, the evaluation of king safety can be divided into the evaluation of the pawn shelter, the location of the king with respect to the castling privilege and the attacking opportunities of the opponent. The subcomponents are defined such that the state under analysis is small enough to allow a table lookup evaluation. Moreover, each subcomponent evaluation reduces the total state under consideration by discarding redundant and irrelevant facts. For example, we reduce the pawn shelter state from about 8,000 possible categories to only 16 final categories of shelter. A similar reduction takes place with respect to king location and opponent's attacking chances. Finally, all these factors are combined to produce 256 categories of king safety. This allows table lookup to be used to combine the results of the individual subcomponents into a final value. This mapping-down process is illustrated in Figure 6.8, where complex evaluations are performed in a series of steps that map the overall state down to a final value.

The above method amounts to a recursive factoring of the evaluation function into sub-functions that have limited input. Our implementation uses an 8K byte memory for each mapping unit which limits the sub-functions to 13 bits of state input. The current hardware uses three levels of mapping to reduce a total of 36 bits of state and context information to an 8-bit value. These tables can be specified before each search which allows the Oracle to decide which evaluation components are most important within the scope of the search.

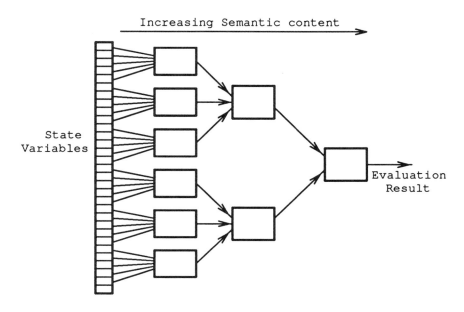

Figure 6.8: Position evaluation.

6.5.2 The State Variables

Each evaluation component operates over a subset of the entire set of state variables. The representation to be used for this subset must be specified as part of the function specification. As in the move generator, the values of these variables are modified incrementally as the search makes and unmakes moves while traversing the search tree. The state variables are kept in a set of state *accumulators* whose contents are defined and updated using a table of values called the state description table. This table contains an entry for each possible half move, specifying the amount to be added to the accumulator when a piece is placed and the amount to be subtracted when the piece is removed.

The entries in the table determine the meaning of each bit in the accumulator. In practice, the accumulator is divided into a number of fields, each representing some relevant set of facts about a position. A field may represent a pattern or a sum. For example, one field may count the number of pawns, another may keep track of the location of the king and another may indicate whether a bishop is on a particular square. The carry chain of the accumulator can be broken at predetermined points in order to keep signed data from overflowing from one field to another. The data that is stored in the state accumulator is not raw, but already encoded via the state description table. By knowing that certain states cannot exist or are not of interest, the number of field entries can be reduced. If we are interested in a pattern of 3 elements, but only whether or not they are all present, it would be wasteful to assign a bit to each element. Instead, one uses the arithmetic power of the accumulators to assign a value of "1" to each element. Then when all are present, the accumulator will indicate "3", and no other value will be of interest. In this way only two bits are used to compute this function instead of three, as would be required by the naive method.

6.5.3 Application Coefficients and the Role of Context

We have assumed up to this point that each evaluation component can be analyzed independently and the results summed into an overall value. Often, the results cannot be combined linearly. That is, there are non-linear relationships between the components that affect how the results are combined. For example, the relative importance of the king safety component depends on the amount of material remaining. Or if the king is under severe attack, it may not matter much that the pawn structure is strong. This contextual information can be applied via *application coefficients* (Berliner 1979a), which specify how much weight a component carries in light of other factors.

We have built into our evaluation hardware the ability to include the results of other evaluation components as part of an evaluation. Up to three results from other evaluation units can be selected with which to perform a final mapping on the component evaluation value. This obviously has the opportunity for feedback paths, but we do not allow this since the time for the circuit to settle would become unbounded. One might note the resemblance of these context connections to the lateral inhibition connections in neural networks.

Figure 6.9 gives the overall design of one of our second-generation evaluation units. Two levels of mapping are used to compute an intermediate value from the current state, and a final mapping applies selected context information to produce a final value. *Hitech*'s evaluator contains 14 of these general recognizer units and 6 additional recognizers that are dedicated to pawn structure. Another 8 smaller recognizers are used for computing the global state such as total material, material balance and the number of remaining pawns. This global state provides context whereby the interpretation of the other recognizers can be modified.

This second-generation hardware differs from our first-generation hardware in size, but not basic design. The amount of state has been extended from 20 to 24 bits, the ability to use context information has been added, the number of units has been increased from 8 to 14, and 8 global state recognizers have been added. We should point out that the global state recognizers can be used either to provide context information to the evaluation or to extend the amount of board state used by a recognizer. This gives the new evaluation hardware a great deal more flexibility than the original design.

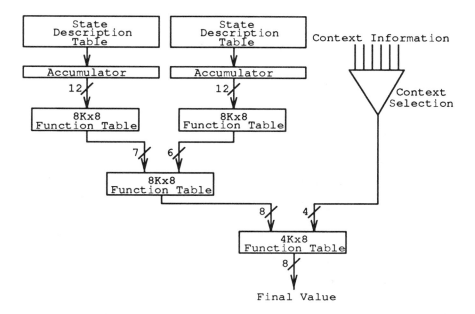

Figure 6.9: The design of a single evaluation unit.

6.6 The Chess Machine

The previous sections have described *Hitech*'s parallel architecture for move generation and position evaluation, and presented the details of their implementation. These functions must be augmented by other functions such as αβ search control and repetition detection for the program to be fully operational. This section describes the chess hardware and software that makes up the balance of the *Hitech* chess machine.

The structure of the chess machine, shown in Figure 6.10 is similar to that used by other special-purpose machines such as *Belle* (Condon and Thompson 1982). The chess machine consists of modules that operate under microprogrammed control and communicate over two shared busses. A controller runs the αβ algorithm using specialized hardware units to perform the computationally complex tasks of move generation and evaluation. The first data bus is the move bus, which communicates the half move operators used to move from one position in the search tree to the next. The second is the value bus, used to communicate values between the evaluation function and those modules that use values to perform the αβ decisions. Each module may generate status signals indicating the presence of specific conditions that are used by the controller to modify the flow of control.

The structure of the controller is shown in Figure 6.11. Microprogram control flow is specified by a next address field in the microinstruction.

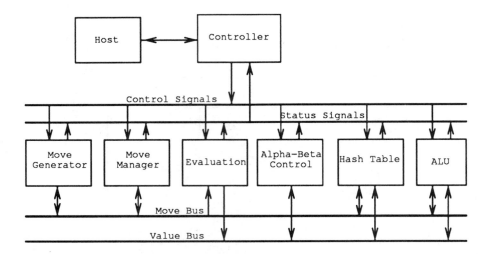

Figure 6.10: Structure of the chess machine.

Branches are performed by *OR* ing selected status signals into four bits of the next address field. By assigning branch targets appropriately, 2-way, 4-way, 8-way and 16-way branches can be performed based on any subset of the four status signals. Microsubroutines are supported by a return address stack.

The controller interfaces to a host, currently a Sun 4 workstation, via an interface to the host bus. This interface contains several registers that are written and read by the host program to communicate data to and from the chess machine and to initiate execution of microprograms. Data is passed between the host and chess machine via registers connected to the move and value busses. Commands executed by the chess machine are regarded as subroutine calls by the host, where the arguments are written into the move and value bus registers before writing the command register and the results are read back when the operation is complete.

6.6.1 Move Generator

The move generator used by *Hitech* is built from 64 of the VLSI chips described in Section 6.3.1 *The Move Generator*, with additional special hardware to generate castling and *en passant* moves, which are not handled by the chips. These special moves are only rarely legal and thus are handled as exceptional conditions by the controller. If one of the special moves is legal, a status flag is asserted which causes control to be diverted to a special routine that generates the corresponding half moves. In the case of castling, for example, the hardware asserts a status flag if the player still has the castling privilege and there are no pieces between the king and rook. The controller then queries the move

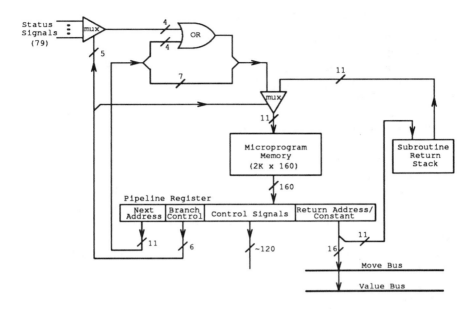

Figure 6.11: The chess machine controller.

generator to determine whether the opponent controls any of the squares that the king must cross.

Another special case is that of pawn promotion. Although the move generator produces pawn advances to the last rank, it does not perform the actual promotion. This is done by special hardware that recognizes any pawn move to the last rank and raises a status signal to force the controller to intervene and promote the pawn to each of the four possible major pieces in turn.

6.6.2 Evaluation

Position evaluation is divided into two parts: incremental, first-order evaluation using a simple table defined by the oracle, and general second-order evaluation performed by the hardware described in Section 6.5.1 *Computing Second-Order Evaluations*. The actual programming of the second-order evaluation hardware is specified using a compiler that allows one to define the functionality of each unit in a straightforward manner. The Oracle determines before each search which evaluation components to include. This decision is based on the number of available units, the phase of the game and the board position itself. Compiling and down-loading the evaluation tables can take 15-20 seconds, but the host software recognizes cases where tables have already been set up and the startup time averages less than 5 seconds per search.

6.6.3 The Transposition/Refutation Hash Table

The hash table is an optimization that allows results that have already been computed earlier in the search to be used to reduce the search time (Zobrist 1970a). One function of the hash table is to detect transpositions, i.e. positions that are reached via two different paths in the search tree. By saving the result of each sub-search in the tree, the effort to search a position when it is reached a second time can be saved. The use of the hash table is complicated by $\alpha\beta$ cutoffs that result in values that are bounds and not exact values. We maintain only one value for each position along with flags indicating whether the value is an exact value, a lower bound or an upper bound. In some cases it is necessary to re-search a subtree if the $\alpha\beta$ values have changed since the previous search.

The second use of the hash table is to extend the usefulness of iterative-deepening by using the information gained during previous search iterations to improve the move ordering. The hash table saves not only the result of previous searches, but also the move that achieved the result or forced an $\alpha\beta$ cutoff. Searching this move first when searching the position to a greater depth yields near-optimal move ordering. Moves produced by the hash table are checked for legality by the move generator, since ignoring the possibility of collisions in the hash table could be fatal.

Hitech employs a depth-based replacement algorithm for positions in the hash table. Nodes that root a deep search subtree have precedence over nodes that root shallower ones, since one wants to keep the information that is likely to be the most expensive to replace. Our measurements showed that depth-based replacement outperforms simple replacement by a factor of two. Also, our experiments show that good move ordering by the move generator combined with the ordering information provided by transposition table yields an $\alpha\beta$ search efficiency that is only about 40% worse than the optimal ordering. That is, on average, the program searches only about 1.4 times the number of nodes that an $\alpha\beta$ search with perfect move ordering would search.

6.6.4 The ALU

A general-purpose 16-bit ALU (AMD 29116) allows microprogramming of arbitrary computations on moves and values within the machine. The ALU is connected to both the move and value data busses, and condition codes generated by ALU operations can be tested by the controller. The ALU is typically used to experiment with modifications to the search algorithm. When the experiments verify the utility of some refinement, then explicit hardware support can be provided. Currently the ALU is used to discover recapture sequences and to implement a hybrid hash table replacement algorithm.

6.6.5 Microprogramming Support

Microprograms are written as C programs using predefined macros that are then compiled, linked with a microassembler and executed to produce the object microprogram. This allows the programmer to use C constructs in the microprogram as well as the C preprocessor for macros and conditional assembly. The microassembler module assigns addresses to microinstructions based on branch conditions so that the minimum amount of memory is used. It also uses information about the timing requirements of the various modules to generate automatically the correct clock timing based on the operations performed by each microinstruction.

6.6.6 Executing the Search

Figure 6.12 shows the operation of the hardware during the inner loop of the $\alpha\beta$ search. This is an elaboration of the standard depth-first search, showing those tasks that are performed in parallel.

The move generation phase consists of computing the dynamic priority of the next move and voting to determine the chip with the best move. This move is made by executing three half moves, which are saved on a stack and used to unmake the move when the search backtracks. This making and unmaking of moves forms the backbone of the search. All modules that depend on the state of the search change that state when half moves are executed. After a move has been made, each of the modules computes new results based on the new position. The move generator calculates whether the new position is legal and whether the side to move is in check, and if the escape check mechanism should be invoked. The evaluation hardware computes a new value based on the new state, and the hash and repetition tables read the entries corresponding to the new position.

At this point, the search control decides whether a leaf position has been reached or whether the branch should be extended another ply. This decision is based primarily on depth and quiescence considerations, although the hash and repetition tables may provide an immediate value for the position. If indeed a leaf has been reached, the most recent move is reversed using the half moves saved on the stack and an entry is written into the hash table depending on the replacement algorithm. Otherwise the move generator or possibly the hash table produces the move with which to extend the tree.

6.6.7 Software

The software comprises a combination of a microprogram that performs the inner loop of the standard $\alpha\beta$ search; a host program that performs the Oracle analysis, time control and user interface; and interface routines that pass information between the host and the chess machine. The microprogram includes a standard quiescence search that examines all captures and responses to check. Moves that escape from check are not counted as a ply since they are considered to be forced moves. Recapture moves are also detected and not counted as a ply under the assumption that the recapture was forced. Our definition of a recapture is one that re-establishes the material to the level that is

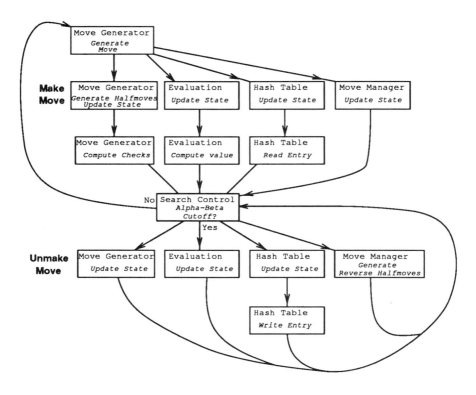

Figure 6.12: Execution of the αβ search.

considered to be the value of the root position. This definition means that
recaptures in lines of play that maintain the material status of the root position
are not counted. For instance, if the tree search starts out with a capture of a
knight, and a re-capture of a knight comes either immediately or after some
intermediate non-captures, it will not be counted, as it re-establishes the
equilibrium that existed at the root.

The Oracle in the host program performs an analysis before every search
and down-loads information to the evaluation hardware. The host program then
builds the first level of the search tree and orders the root moves using shallow
searches to establish exact values for each position at the first ply. From there,
the program does iterative-deepening using the chess hardware until the time
allocation algorithm decides that there is not enough time for another iteration.
This algorithm decides how much time to spend on any one move based on the
amount of time and number of moves left in the game and an estimate of the
difficulty of the position. After a move is made, the program assumes that the
opponent will make the expected response and begins a new search. If the
opponent makes a different move, this search is discarded. The user interface
allows the operator to set the game parameters, and entertains the operator with a

variety of interesting information about the progress of the search including the current prime variation.

6.7 Performance

Our experience with the *Hitech* chess machine shows that the architecture successfully combines high expertise levels with extremely fast search. It can examine about 175,000 positions per second, 10^6 times more positions than a human player. This ability has resulted in excellent moves that even Masters at the scene could not predict. The program has risen rapidly into the top 0.5 of 1% of ranked US chess players, and it is still climbing, as shown in Figure 6.13.

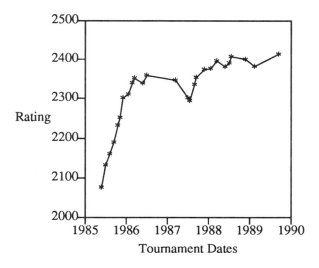

Figure 6.13: Performance history.

As of October, 1989, *Hitech* had played 175 serious tournament games, principally against human competitors and achieved a record of 122.5-52.5 (70%). It has won the Pennsylvania State Championship tournament three years running from 1987-1989, each time with strong contingents of human Masters participating. It has also won several other human tournaments. By 1987 *Hitech* had the unique experience of obtaining draws in tournament play against three players ranked among the top 30 US players, one of whom was among the top ten US players. In 1988 the program defeated former US Champion and Grandmaster Arnold S. Denker by a score of 3.5 - 0.5 in the AGS Challenge Match. While we have not felt that computer versus computer competitions are very revealing about how strong a particular machine really is, *Hitech* has participated in some computer events. It won the 1985 North American

Computer Championships with a perfect score of 4-0, and tied for first in both the 1986 Computer World Championships and the 1989 North American Computer Championship. During most of this time the program's published rating was a good 150 points higher than that of its nearest computer competitor.

Hitech's current US Chess Federation rating is 2413, making it a Senior Master, the highest title that a national Federation can award. By mid-1986, it had surpassed all previous chess program's ratings by about 170 points. If one averages *Hitech*'s rating increase from the initial 2076 it earned in its first tournament in May, 1985, to its present rating, over the set of games it has played, it averages out to a gain of about 2 rating points per game. However, progress has not always been steady. We consider *Hitech*'s career to be divided into 4 epochs:

(1) May - September, 1985 without any pattern recognizing capability.
(2) October, 1985 - July, 1986 with the first-generation pattern recognizers.
(3) February, 1987 - July 1987 with the second-generation pattern recognizers, marred by many software problems.
(4) Since August, 1987 when the software problems associated with changing hardware seem to have been overcome.

Table 6.1 shows that during epoch 1, the program won 30% of its games against Masters. In epoch 2, when we added pattern-based evaluation, the success rate against Masters rose to 79%. However, its success rate against super-masters (those rated above 2400 in the USCF rating scale) was not noteworthy. In epoch 3, results were uneven because of problems associated with insufficiently tested software for the new pattern recognizers. We feel results from this epoch are best ignored, and this view is substantiated by comparing the results against Experts, Masters and Super-Masters across epochs 2, 3 and 4. In epoch 4, the program's potential can again be seen, as the second-generation pattern recognizers discussed in this chapter begin to take effect. Here it improves its performance against every class of player, including beating some super-masters. *Hitech*'s percentage of wins does not increase from epoch to epoch, because the quality of competition keeps getting better, as can be seen in the individual columns.

Epoch	All games	Experts	Masters	Super-Masters	Performance
1	13-4	1-0	1.5-3.5	0-0	2158
2	34.5-11.5	12-2	13.5-3.5	1-6	2383
3	13-8	7-3	2-4	0-1	2216
4	62-29	21.5-1.5	29-13	8.5-14.5	2467

Table 6.1: *Hitech* rated-tournament record.

Of most significance in Table 6.1 is the Performance Rating column. This is the statistical estimate of the most likely strength of player that would have achieved the same result. *Hitech* plays chess well enough to be among the top half of 1% of all registered chess players in the World. It generally has an Expert (the rank below Master) level understanding of chess concepts and strategy. However, its tactical ability, the ability to calculate the direct consequences of a move, is close to that of a Grandmaster (the highest level of human play). This potential comes from its powerful search, which is more thorough, though not always as deep, as that of the best humans. *Hitech*'s search causes sparkling things to happen from time to time:

- It has made at least 10 moves, in tournament settings with several good players watching, that were both excellent and *not anticipated* by *any* of the expert spectators.
- It has found dozens of refutations of textbook examples that have been in the literature for many decades.

6.8 The Usefulness of the Recognizers

For *Hitech* to operate effectively it is necessary to evaluate leaf nodes in the search very quickly. This is accomplished in about 1 microsecond. Further, the structure as described in Section 6.5 *Implementing the Evaluation Function* does evaluations in essentially constant time, regardless of the number of recognizers and the patterns they are seeking to detect.

We believe the structure of the recognizers to be general. This structure evolved from direct experience with *Hitech* and is still evolving. The important issues are:

- They are able to compute second-order knowledge which is essential.
- They are fast.
- They are implementable at reasonable cost and space.
- Evaluations can be factored into pieces small enough to fit into a recognizer and then recombined at will. This allows dealing with complex situations.
- Application coefficients, which are needed to provide context information can be readily computed.

However, there are some disadvantages to our scheme, that should be noted, although presently none of them appear to be important.

- The recognizers are loaded once for each root search. This means that if the situation during the search were to change drastically, so that the down-loaded knowledge were no longer applicable, the evaluation of such leaf nodes would be inaccurate since new knowledge could not be down-loaded. This problem rarely appears, and there is no immediate remedy, nor do we see an urgent need for one.
- Each recognizer has a limited size; i.e. 13 bits in each branch. This allows a great deal of information to be dealt with. For instance, to compute the safety of a king, one recognizer deals with the pawn shelter, location of king, open lines available to the opponent and whether one's own rook is locked in by the king. The Global-State recognizer then provides

information on the amount of material on the board, which modulates the final value. However, it is clear that expertise comes through better understanding, and there will always be more features that could be incorporated. Thus, there is pressure for ever-larger recognizers.

• The interconnection scheme among recognizing units is not completely general. This would be too expensive. The Oracle software knows exactly which recognizers can be connected to which others, and while, in principle, it would be desirable for results to be shared among the recognizers, this lack has not yet become an important hindrance for progress.

Our theory of "recognizing" as evinced by the recognizers is as follows:

(1) Top level bits are extracted from the current state according to the needs of the pattern that is to be detected. As stated above, the number of bits is governed by cost considerations. The adequacy of any particular width must be dependent upon the domain. However, we have found that the present 12 bits plus one external signal in each main branch of the recognizer is capable of a great deal. Tables that are down-loaded into a recognizer are capable of detecting three or four distinct but related patterns.

(2) Mapping-down from 36 bits of information to at most 8 is necessary to get an eventual interpretation of the top level bits. It should be noted that as classes or interpretations are found, it is possible to aggregate values, classes, or interpretations. Thus a class at the second level could represent a compound of inputs from several patterns in the same branch of the recognizer. In effect, each mapping-down step abstracts some meaning from the level above it, until a final meaning in the form of an evaluation is produced. The three-fold mapping with approximately a two-to-one reduction of bits in each mapping step appears to be adequate in most cases.

(3) The restrictiveness introduced by going to fewer bits in each map-down step is quite similar to what one would expect in a learning paradigm. The need to represent what is known in fewer bits forces generalization and thus learning. In our application there is no machine learning, and the representations we use are probably much too terse to be discovered by today's learning algorithms. However, in principle, a structure of this type could be taught, either by experience or by a tutor.

(4) The ability to extract meaning gradually from a set of bits provides great flexibility in knowledge encoding. For instance, in the typical pattern loaded into a recognizer, there are 2^{24} states times 2^{12} global states which are mapped down to one of 2^8 interpretations. To extract meaning from so much data, the input of which has already been filtered in 1 microsecond, puts competitive systems at a tremendous disadvantage.

Although it is not always possible to encode every facet of every potential pattern, we have found that in general we are able to encode any item of knowledge that we have striven hard to encode. Since the inception of pattern recognizers, we have continued to add successful patterns to the knowledge base at the rate of one or two a month. We believe that *Hitech*'s knowledge can be increased to produce further growth in performance.

6.9 Summary and Conclusions

The architecture of *Hitech* differs in important ways from previous efforts. It combines large searches with the power of pattern recognition. The former allows visiting any node that could contain a solution within a limited, but large, search horizon. The latter allows detecting complex conditions that help assess the value of a node. Pattern recognition provides the ability to ascertain relations among elements in a domain state, and is thus considerably more powerful than the application of heuristics that merely indicate that the presence of some element of a domain state is good to a prespecified degree. Without pattern recognition, large amounts of additional search would be required to find the properties of a domain state that patterns can encode.

Now it can be readily seen that *Hitech* was the dominant force in computer chess from mid-1985 to mid-1988. During this time, no hardware speedups were made, and the program advanced in rating purely because of the ever-increasing knowledge in the system. This knowledge related to a greater understanding of chess, greater understanding of using time, and improvements in the efficiency and effectiveness of the search. These efforts blended to produce a rating gain of over 200 points on the USCF scale, from the time the fleshed out program first showed it was capable of beating Experts with amazing consistency.

Acknowledgments. A machine of this complexity could not have been built by two people; it is the result of a team effort. The hardware has been designed and built by Carl Ebeling; the Oracle is based largely on the chess program *Patsoc*, by Hans Berliner. The above concepts and implementation are the result of much interaction between the two principals. Other students and department employees have contributed significantly in the design of the searching software, the programming of the control system, testing of the whole structure and other facets. Persons who deserve mention are Gordon Goetsch, Andy Gruss, Murray Campbell, Larry Slomer and Andy Palay. Since this research involves the two areas of artificial intelligence and VLSI, not every Computer Science Department could have supported this project, and we are grateful for the opportunity provided by Carnegie Mellon University and its Research Sponsors.

7 Cray Blitz

R.M. Hyatt, A.E. Gower and H.L. Nelson

7.1 Introduction

Cray Blitz began playing in computer-chess events when it entered ACM's 1976
North American Computer Chess Championship. It has participated in nearly
all major computer-chess events since then using the name *Blitz* and later *Cray
Blitz*.

The program became a serious competitor in 1980 when it was moved to a
Cray-1 supercomputer, becoming the first chess program to use such a powerful
machine. Three years later (1983, New York City) it became the World
Computer Chess Champion. By successfully defending this title in 1986
(Cologne, Germany) *Cray Blitz* became the only program so far to win back-to-
back World Championships.

Like many other chess programs, *Cray Blitz* grew out of the ideas developed
by Slate and Atkin (1977) and their successful *Chess 4.X* program that
dominated the early years of computer-chess competition. In spite of these
common roots, diverse research has resulted in many improvements that cause
current chess programs to bear little resemblance to their ancestors. The weakest
machines of the present generation would be serious competition for the
strongest programs of the middle to late 1970s.

Increased hardware performance is partially responsible for this improved
playing ability, but programming improvements have also significantly raised
the level of playing skill. For example, there are now microcomputer/program
combinations that are significantly faster and stronger than *Chess 4.X* running on
a CDC Cyber 176 supercomputer, even though current microcomputers do not
approach the speed of such machines. Improvements in search strategies, in
selectivity (mainly in quiescence searching) and in evaluation routines resulted
in programs that are formidable opponents to anyone.

This chapter describes the current version of *Cray Blitz* and gives details
about the evaluation routines and the search strategy used. Additional details
about the program can be found in an earlier paper (Hyatt, Gower and Nelson
1985).

7.2 Tree Search

Cray Blitz divides the tree search into three distinct regions: the basic full-width
search region, the tactical quiescence-search region and finally a simple

quiescence-search region. Evaluation occurs at all end points in the tree not classified as checkmates, stalemates or draws.

Cray Blitz searches these three regions consecutively so that after completing region one, the algorithm then switches to the search heuristics for region two, and finally uses special heuristics for region three to complete final quiescence before applying the evaluation procedures.

7.2.1 The Basic Full-Width Search (Region One)

The first stage is a full-width search where Cray Blitz considers all moves as long as the variable ply is not greater than the current nominal search depth, the variable rdepth. After the search begins, rdepth is iteratively increased by first doing a 2-ply search, then a 3-ply search, and so forth until time is exhausted.

During an iteration, rdepth also changes when the search notices that the side to move is in check. Since there are normally only a few moves that get out of check, these positions are easier to search (in terms of nodes required). The reason for searching such variations a little deeper lies in the effect a check has on search accuracy. Occasionally a check simply delays the inevitable (horizon effect), but sometimes, by following the variation to its conclusion, it leads to a tactical win of material or checkmate. For these reasons, Cray Blitz always extends the branches of checking variations deeper into the tree. This search strategy sometimes causes significant search-depth extensions. For example, a nominal 9-ply search could extend to a 17-ply search if every move by one side is a check.

7.2.2 Move Ordering in Search Region One

Since the $\alpha\beta$ algorithm is sensitive to move ordering (in terms of pruning efficiency), Cray Blitz expends considerable effort ordering moves to maximize cutoff possibilities, as the following sections explain.

7.2.2.1 Null Move

A null move is a "pass" where the side making a null move simply does nothing. It seems to have been introduced successfully by Ken Thompson in his Belle program, but many people including Kozdrowicki, Donskoy and ourselves experimented with essentially the same idea during the 1970s. The basic approach is to give up the move to see what threats, if any, the opponent has. Gradually these ideas were refined and formalized by Beal (1989) and by Goetsch and Campbell (1988) (see also Chapter 9 Experiments with the Null-Move Heuristic). The null move allows one side to make two consecutive moves without any response by the opponent. In Cray Blitz, making a null move decreases the variable rdepth by one and also disallows the null move at any other node in the current variation. The idea is that if one side makes two moves in a row and still cannot obtain an advantage, then the first move of the two move sequence should be rejected because it seems unlikely to be strong/good. The advantage is that decreasing *rdepth* by one makes the resulting tree significantly smaller, speeding up the search. On the other hand, the null move assumes that not moving is bad, an assumption that fails when the side to move is in zugzwang.

This heuristic typically reduces the size of the trees searched by as much as 75%, although the average is between 25% and 50%. This makes the program about twice as fast as it is without the null-move heuristic.

The null move is only allowed in region one of the tree search (never in the quiescence) and it is only tried when there is enough material for both sides that zugzwang is unlikely.

7.2.2.2 Transposition-Table Move

A transposition-table entry, retrieved at most positions, holds a move and information about the score or search bound in effect when the search placed that entry in the transposition table. This move is either the best move backed up to the current position, or else it is the move that caused a cutoff (a refutation move) in the current or a previous iteration.

The search first checks the move for legality (to avoid making an illegal move obtained from a transposition-table collision) and then makes the move on the game board to continue the analysis. No move generation is done until after this move fails to cause an $\alpha\beta$ cutoff. Statistics gathered in *Cray Blitz* indicate that trying these moves first eliminates move generations at over 33% of the nodes in the tree search, increasing the program's performance significantly.

The search avoids re-examining the transposition-table move (after generating the complete set of moves) by simply deleting it from the move list.

7.2.2.3 Capture Moves

Next the move generator produces the complete set of *pseudo-legal* moves for the current side (these are chess moves that ignore the requirement of not leaving your own king in check). From this set of moves, the search extracts those that capture pieces and pawns and examines them with a static exchange evaluator to determine how effective each capture is.

The search uses a fast static exchange evaluator, *ripoff*, to determine the effective material score for all possible captures. *Ripoff* does not understand tactical subtleties, such as pins, and only considers the possible series of captures on the destination square of the current capturing move. *Ripoff* produces a material score by adding/subtracting the values of the pieces exchanged on a square using the minimax procedure. The resulting score measures the relative win/loss of material. Next the search sorts the list of non-losing capturing moves (*ripoff* scores not less than zero) into descending order based on the material balance score. The capture search examines them in that order.

Losing captures are searched along with non-capturing moves later in the search. Pawn promotions are also treated as captures, even though they might not capture anything, since promotions change the material balance. Another exception is that moves of passed pawns to the sixth or seventh rank are treated as captures that gain a small amount of material (one-half pawn to be exact). Then, if the pawn push is unsafe, the material score shows a loss (score less than zero) so that these moves will not be tried until later.

7.2.2.4 Killer Moves

Killer moves (Slate and Atkin 1977) are moves that were good in similar positions, therefore the search tries them here to determine if they refute the previous branch. Whenever backing up a move as best, or any time a move causes a cutoff (a refutation move), the search enters it in one of two slots for the current ply. If the move is already in one of the two slots, the search increments its use count by one. Whenever adding a new move, the new move replaces the old move with the lowest use count. Whenever the search increments the variable *ply*, it zeros the use count for the killer moves at the new *ply*. This is done to prevent one killer move from developing an extremely large use count, making replacing it impossible. If it remains useful, its use count is incremented regularly.

If the tree search tries both of the killer moves for the current ply without obtaining a cutoff, it then tries all the other killer moves (for the correct side on move) starting at the killer moves for ply 1 or ply 2 as appropriate. For example, if searching at ply 9 and the current two killers do not cause a cutoff, the search tries the killers for ply 1, then the killers for ply 3 and so on up to *rdepth*.

7.2.2.5 Other Moves

If none of the preceding moves cause a cutoff, the remaining moves are searched in the order they are produced. This is not random because the moves toward the center of the board are generated first, then moves toward the opponent's king and developing moves appear before other less active moves are generated.

7.2.3 Capture Search in Region Two

For the capture search, region two extends exactly four plies beyond the end of the region one search. During these four plies, the program tries captures that win material and captures that appear to be equal exchanges. In this phase, the search ignores captures that lose material according to *ripoff* unless they fall into the group of moves that check the opponent, as described below.

Search region two provides a transition from the full-width basic search to a selective quiescence search. The primary function of region two is to extend those variations where a king seems to be in some difficulty so that the search does not miss a checkmate or win of material. The search tightly constrains region two except when examining certain types of chess positions using a problem-analysis mode. To reach region two, the search follows the current variation to the point where *ply* is greater than *rdepth*, indicating that the full-width part of the search is over.

The control routine for region two counts the number of checks made in region one of the search. The search uses the smaller of this number and two (currently) to control how many plies for the current side it includes in region two. For example, if the program delivers checks at plies 1 and 5 in region one, so that region one terminates at ply 11 (assuming a 9-ply nominal search depth plus two in-check extensions), then the search includes all checking moves at plies 13 and 15. This further extends checking lines to be sure that the king is safe before applying the static position evaluator to a position. It should be mentioned that since regions two and three are not full-width, certain considerations apply when analyzing checking moves like these. Specifically, if the search deliberately checks the opponent at ply 13, then it flags ply 14 as full-width to make sure that the king escapes without getting mated or losing material (if possible). That is, the attacker can be selective but the defender is exhaustive to verify the attacker's material gain. It might turn out that the checking move is not the best winning move, but at least it establishes a good lower search bound to help the search compare different branches.

Along with the series of capturing and/or checking moves, *Cray Blitz* also includes some moves that advance passed pawns. Passed pawn moves to a safe square are included in the capture search for region two. This is particularly helpful in endgames where passed pawns are serious threats, but it also uncovers various tactical opportunities in the middlegame as well. With region two, the simple 9-ply search (previous example) which became a 17-ply search with the check extension algorithm, is now equivalent to a 21-ply search with these two additional checking plies included. This lets a 9-ply search find some mates in 11 full moves. Search region three extends the analysis even further.

7.2.4 Move Ordering in Search Region Three

Search region three is the normal capture-only type of quiescence search. In fact, search regions two and three overlap, so that at any ply, after trying the region two checking moves, the search continues with the moves that are normally part of region three.

7.2.4.1 Capture Moves

Capture moves in region three are similar to those in regions one and two, but specifically include only those captures that appear to win material.

7.2.4.2 Plies Where One Side Is in Check

The search uses the flag *inchk* to indicate that the current side is in check and possibly mated. This forces the current side to try all legal moves regardless of the current search region. Since some inane captures are also checks, this flag results in many additional full-width nodes, unless care is taken to restrict its use to those positions where it is relevant.

The rule for using the *inchk* flag is as follows. If, after completing the region one search, the current side is in check at every ply from that point to the current ply, then the search continues to set *inchk*, if appropriate. Since this forces the current side to try all legal moves at every ply beyond the full-width region, it denies the current side the ability to stand pat as in the normal quiescence search.

If the variation contains non-checking quiescence moves, then the search does not set *inchk* for plies beyond the first such move. There is no reason to look for mates and material gain if the side under attack can simply stand pat at a ply where it was not in check, and thereby avoid the sequence of checks and the resulting mate or whatever. A player who is in check at every ply cannot stand pat, and so it is beneficial to continue pursuing the king.

As in search region two, safe passed-pawn advances are included in region three also. This is a "last attempt" to promote the pawn or force the opposing side to give up material to stop it.

7.3 Parallel Processing

In the early 1980s, *Cray Blitz* used a single processor Cray computer, but with the introduction of the dual processor XMP line new possibilities arose. These led to new issues of how best to use shared memory for communication and for transposition tables, and how best to divide the tree-search work. At this stage Harry Nelson joined our team to help develop and debug parallel processing support software for the XMP and YMP (8 processor) computers.

The design of *Cray Blitz* takes maximum advantage of shared memory multiprocessing computer systems. The messages and requests (described later) passed from processor to processor are simply flags stored in a shared memory word that all processors test at the beginning of a node expansion. The overhead to send such a message is therefore zero, and the maximum delay before a processor responds to a request is the amount of time that it takes one processor to expand a single node (roughly 40 microseconds on a Cray YMP, which includes move generation, evaluation and updating the various data structures used to support the tree search itself). Additional details can be found in Hyatt's (1988) thesis .

The current algorithm, called Dynamic Tree Splitting (DTS), extends the Principal Variation Split (PVSplit) algorithm described by Marsland and Campbell (1982), Marsland and Popowich (1985), and Newborn (1985). Like DPVS introduced by Schaeffer (1989b), DTS addresses two major problems exhibited by the PVSplit algorithm:

(1) PVSplit requires that all processors split work up at the nodes on the Principal Variation (PV), and

(2) all processors synchronize at the end of these parallel searches before any can proceed to other work.

7.3.1 Who Owns a Node?

A simple example illustrates the first design problem encountered during the development of DTS. Suppose processors A and B are searching through subtrees and processor B runs out of work to do. B must then ask A if it can help search the remainder of A's tree. A and B split the remainder of this tree at some node and they both then proceed to finish the work below that node. If A finishes first, it should be able to help B with whatever it has left and vice-versa. This makes the issue of who "owns" the node (or who can back up into the portion of the tree above the node) significant. With DTS, the last active searcher at a node "owns" the node.

The data structures to support this are intricate, but the complexity is more than offset by eliminating the synchronization that normally occurs at the end of these parallel searches. DTS requires absolutely no synchronization at these points.

7.3.2 DTS in a Nutshell

Whenever a processor exhausts the work (subtree) that it is doing, it broadcasts a help request to all busy processors. These processors make a quick copy of the *type* of each node they are searching in the current subtree and the number of unsearched branches at each node, and give the information to the idle processor. The busy processors then resume searching where they were interrupted. The idle processor (or processors if more than one is idle) examines the data and picks the most likely split point based on the amount of work left, and the depth of the node. The following description uses the terminology of Marsland and Popowich (1985), to describe these actions. Subtrees are made up of PV, CUT and ALL type nodes (these correspond exactly to the minimal game-tree notion of type = 1, 2 and 3 nodes used by Knuth and Moore (1975)). Thus the idle processor selects a PV or ALL node, but never a CUT node, and then forces the selected processor to split at the chosen node. The busy processor arranges to share the data at the selected split point and then both processors continue searching from that point in parallel.

Each processor compares its newest result with those from previous parallel searches. If the new value is better, the current search path and score are written over the previously best. Other conditions are also possible. If a processor discovers a refutation to the branch that leads to a split point node, other processors working at that split point are doing unnecessary work. The processor informs the others and they immediately stop and try to find more useful work to proceed with, by broadcasting a help request. As a processor finds a new best score for a split point, it shares the value with other parallel searchers at that split point to improve their $\alpha\beta$ cutoff performance. These issues are dealt with more deeply in Hyatt's (1988) thesis.

7.3.3 Parallel Performance

Performance can be measured in many ways (Hyatt, Suter and Nelson 1989). One common measure is how much idle time accumulates as the search progresses. In particular, how much time a processor spends idly waiting for other processors to send data so that it can find a satisfactory split point. In *Cray Blitz*, running on a Cray YMP with eight processors, it is uncommon for the total idle time for a three minute search to total more than a second; more typically the time is down in the 0.01 second range.

A more useful performance measure is how much does the size of the tree increase when comparing the sequential search with the parallel search. This is a more revealing comparison that points out the deficiency that other parallel algorithms exhibit. In theory, the search analyzes PV and ALL nodes completely; however, it normally searches only one descendant from a CUT node. In practice such analysis breaks down because the perfect move ordering assumption only applies to minimal game trees, although recent analysis (Reinefeld and Marsland 1987) of average game-tree search now makes it possible to address this issue directly.

The DTS algorithm always tries to split ALL nodes, a reasonable goal since they are normally completely searched. What happens, however, is that when the branch chosen from a CUT node is not best, allowing one of the branches from the successor ALL node to refute it, then the ALL node behaves like a CUT node, since almost any branch searched reveals the bad move ordering at the previous supposedly CUT node. If the search chooses such an ALL node for a split point, processors will do unnecessary work since any one branch might refute the previous branch. This increases the search overhead significantly.

Some tests with *Cray Blitz* produce trees that increase in size very little, and for typical positions each processor seems to add less than 10% extra nodes to the total searched. However, other positions produce trees that are sometimes two to three times the size of the sequential search. This keeps the processors busy, but they stay busy searching unnecessary parts of the tree. In summary, the only significant points are that most positions run much faster using a parallel search, and also no positions require more time for the parallel search than the sequential search.

To better measure search overhead, two other performance tests were run. First, the evaluator was modified to generate incrementally increasing numbers, so that the search traversed the tree in absolutely worst order (changing the $\alpha\beta$ search to a simple minimax search). With this change, DTS provides nearly optimal speedup for up to eight processors, where eight processors divides the search time by almost exactly eight. These results can be compared with those of Feldmann *et al.* (1989). The second test was to modify the evaluator to generate constantly decreasing evaluations, making the tree search move ordering perfect. Once again DTS again produced nearly optimal speedups, showing only 1-2% loss because of communication delays and memory conflicts. This associates the search overhead problem with choosing poor split nodes for parallel searching. Unfortunately, a search is the only method discovered so far that identifies bad split nodes. Several possible solutions are currently under test, but clearly this is a problem that must be solved if parallel searching is to provide uniformly good results.

Testing shows that a four-processor machine provides an average speedup of about 3.2 over the entire game (there is not yet enough YMP data to determine average performance for eight processors, although an educated guess would place the average speedup between 5 and 6). Some moves are near a factor of 4.0 and others drop down below 2.5 and even lower. Occasionally a move actually speeds up by more than a factor of 4.0 producing the so-called "super-linear speedup" anomaly.

Cray Blitz will soon use both distributed and tightly-coupled multiprocessor systems. In the future a cluster of Cray computers connected over a local area network may provide even more performance.

7.4 Evaluation Procedure

The evaluation procedures in *Cray Blitz* have evolved over the years and are a direct result of analyzing the many games played by the program. Some of the ideas are well-known and came from the early days of computer chess programs (for example, Shannon (1950) and Slate and Atkin (1977)). Other ideas address specific weaknesses that the program exhibited at some point during tournament play. For an alternative assessment of evaluation function performance, see Ebeling's (1986) thesis.

The following sections explain the scoring ideas for each piece. However, the descriptions do not include the actual point scores because they are too specific to *Cray Blitz* and the machine it runs on. In fact, the numbers might actually lead the beginning computer-chess programmer completely astray because there is a specific interaction between search strategies, search speed and evaluation.

The basic scoring unit in *Cray Blitz* is a pawn worth 1,000 points. Following elementary chess theory, knights and bishops are worth 3,000 points, a rook is worth 5,000 points, a queen is worth 9,000 points and the king is worth infinitely many points. Since current chess knowledge indicates that bishops are worth more than knights, the program does contain such knowledge. However, the knowledge is dynamic rather than static so that in certain cases a knight can be better.

In the following sections, if the program is playing white, bonuses for white pieces are positive numbers and bonuses for black pieces are negative; the opposite holds true for penalties.

7.4.1 King Scoring

King scoring recognizes two distinct phases in the game. If the opposing side has no more than 13,000 points of material (not counting pawns), then the king uses endgame scoring (described later in this section). If the opposing side has more than 13,000 points of material (a queen and rook, for example) then the king uses middlegame scoring. The middlegame scoring quantifies the safety (or lack thereof) of the area around the kings. The location of friendly pawns governs the king safety.

The absolute location of the king is the first scoring component for king safety. The king prefers either knight file with the rook or bishop file a second choice; the kings dislike the two central files even though in some positions they might actually be better. In addition to the preferred files, the kings prefer the back rank as first choice; successive ranks are worse in a linear manner. The optimum square for the king is therefore on the first rank on either of the knight files; alternatives are worse in proportion to the distance from the "optimum" square. This number represents a starting point for the king safety score, other values can easily outweigh the initial approximation and make the king stay in the center or move somewhere else, as needed. (See also Chapter 6 *Hitech* for another discussion of king safety.)

Holes in the pawn structure or open lines leading to the king are positional weaknesses that lead to attacking chances. The program penalizes holes in the pawn structure surrounding the king. For example, pawns at e3, f2, g3 and h2 leave weak squares or holes at f3 and h3. The program carefully examines the status of files around the king, specifically the files from the edge of the board to the file one past the king. For a king on the knight file, the safety zone includes the bishop through the rook files. For a king on the rook file, the safety zone still includes the same three files. For a king on the kings bishop file, the zone would include the king, bishop, knight and rook files. There are three levels of penalties associated with king safety. For completely open files, the penalty is substantial since enemy pieces have direct access to the king. If the king does not have a friendly pawn in front of it, but an opposing pawn is blocking the file, the penalty is less, but still substantial since opening the file is under the opponent's control. If the opponent has a half-open file bearing on the king (no opponent pawn but the king does have one), then the penalty is less because it is somewhat harder to force the file open.

Another safety consideration is *luft*, or breathing space. A king trapped on the back rank with the three squares on the second rank in front of it blocked by friendly pieces/pawns or else controlled by the opponent earns a penalty. This avoids those positions where *Cray Blitz* overlooks back-rank mates at nodes near the maximum depth of the tree.

The final safety term penalizes moving the king and/or rooks before castling. Moving the king earns the largest penalty, moving the king-rook is next and moving the queen-rook earns the smallest penalty. Upon reaching the endgame phase (13,000 points) *Cray Blitz* disables the above penalties. From this point forward, the only scoring concerns centralizing the king. As described later, passed-pawn scoring depends on king location, but since pawn positions drive this heuristic, the pawn module computes the score.

7.4.2 Queen Scoring

The queen-scoring routine recognizes three basic positional features:
  (1) centralization,
  (2) king tropism (closeness to opponent's king) and
  (3) the opponent's king safety.

Of the three considerations, the last needs clarification. The value of a queen is directly related to the safety of the opponent's king. If the opponent has an exposed king position, then the program's queen becomes more valuable and vice-versa. This gives the program some sense of when a queen trade is advantageous and when it is not.

7.4.3 Rook Scoring

The rook-scoring routine recognizes five basic positional features:
  (1) king tropism,
  (2) open and half-open files,
  (3) rooks on the 7th rank,
  (4) rooks behind a passed pawn and
  (5) rook mobility.

Rook mobility is a recent addition that attempts to eliminate tactics based on a rook that is trapped, or a rook that cannot move without losing material. The mobility term penalizes a rook that cannot move horizontally because of friendly pieces, pawns and/or the edge of the board. An example would be playing Ra2 to defend a pawn at b2. The rook at a2 incurs a penalty for no horizontal mobility. Although this heuristic evaluates some cases incorrectly, it does eliminate some awkward rook moves that later cause the program great difficulty. (An example of this problem can be found in *Cray Blitz - Hitech* from the 6th World Computer Chess Championship in Edmonton, Alberta. *Cray Blitz* won a pawn, but then defended a pawn on b2 with Ra2 and later lost the b2 pawn as a result.)

Half-open files and king tropism are really long-range heuristics that try to anticipate attacks and file openings long before the search actually reaches the position. This attracts rooks to places where they will probably be useful later, although at times the rooks end up on squares where they have to move again.

7.4.4 Bishop Scoring

The bishop-scoring routine recognizes three basic positional features:
  (1) the presence of two bishops,
  (2) "good" and "bad" bishops and
  (3) open diagonals.

The concept of "good" and "bad" bishops is a measure of how many friendly pawns are on the same colored squares as a bishop. The more friendly pawns there are on the same colored squares, the more restricted the bishop becomes. With enough of these pawns, a bishop can become worth less than a knight since the knight does not "slide" and cannot be blocked by pawns.

Open diagonals are similar to open files for rooks except that it is easier to close a diagonal than it is to close a file. This makes diagonals more difficult to evaluate, but it helps to recognize when a bishop attacks the king zone along with other pieces.

7.4.5 Knight Scoring

The knight-scoring routine recognizes three basic positional features:
- (1) central control,
- (2) king tropism and
- (3) outpost knight.

The concept of an outpost knight is a knight on the opponent's side of the board that is occupying a square that cannot be attacked by a pawn. The only exception is that a knight on the edge of the board cannot be an outpost.

7.4.6 Pawn Scoring

Nimzovitch said that "pawns are the soul of chess," and to that ideal a significant part of the programs's total positional evaluation time is devoted to pawn positions. The pawn-scoring routine recognizes eleven basic positional features.
- (1) center pawn movement,
- (2) advancement,
- (3) pawn rams,
- (4) presence of eight pawns,
- (5) doubled/tripled pawns,
- (6) isolated pawns,
- (7) backward pawns,
- (8) passed pawns,
- (9) outside passed pawns,
- (10) square of the king and
- (11) king against king and pawn(s).

The center pawn movement term produces a large penalty if both the king-pawn and queen-pawn stand on their original square. Only one center pawn standing on its original square produces a smaller penalty. This encourages advancing the central pawns to create the open type of positions that the program plays best.

Pawn-advancement scoring is a dynamic system that varies depending on the type of opening, always with the idea of favoring open positions where the program's tactical ability is most useful. An example is that for openings when *Cray Blitz* plays d4 for white, the program strives to follow with c4 when possible to open the position (the same is true for d5 as black). This idea of altering the scoring based on the opening is described in more detail later.

The match between *Cray Blitz* and David Levy in 1984 led to the development of the pawn-ram term. In that match, Levy won each game easily by blocking things up so well that the program could find no tactics since no open lines were available. Ivan Bratko suggested this term which adds a penalty for each pawn ram (where two pawns of opposing sides are "face to face" on the same file).

The presence of eight pawns incurs a penalty to encourage at least one pawn exchange (this is an asymmetric scoring term that only evaluates rams from the program's point of view). This term attempts to avoid locked positions in a manner similar to the pawn-ram term. (Note that Ken Thompson developed this idea for *Belle* '80).

The isolated-pawn term evaluates pawns with no friendly pawns on adjacent files. An isolated pawn with no opposing pawns in front of it receives the largest penalty since it is easy to attack from the front with rooks and queen. An isolated pawn with enemy pawns in front of it is not as bad, because it is harder to attack and win it. This scoring routine also evaluates the special case of artificially isolated pawns which occurs when a pawn advances so far that other pawns are unable to support it.

Backward pawns are simply special cases of isolated pawns. A backward pawn has adjacent pawns advanced far enough that they cannot defend it. If the backward pawn is on an open file, the penalty is the same as that for an isolated pawn on an open file, otherwise it is the same as that for an isolated pawn on a closed file.

Passed pawns are surprisingly difficult to evaluate in middlegame positions. For example, is an isolated passed pawn weak or strong? For this reason, isolated passed pawns earn no special bonus as long as the opponent has more than 13,000 points of material (pieces only) since enough pieces can be used to attack the pawn continually, and perhaps eventually win it. On the other hand, when forced to accept such a weak pawn, the program understands that trading pieces makes the pawn more valuable.

The outside passed pawn is a well-known positional advantage which in simple king and pawn endings is almost always a win for the side with such a pawn. This evaluation is complex and also handles the case where both sides have an outside passed pawn. The program correctly assesses these positions under all circumstances and generates the appropriate bonus for the correct side.

When one side has passed pawns and the other side has no pieces (or when both sides have passed pawns and neither side has pieces), the evaluator quickly determines whether the resulting position is won or lost by counting squares and noting where the pawn(s) queen. The simplest idea is the square of the pawn, where the pawn can race to promotion without being caught by the opposing king. Variations on this theme include both sides having passed pawns (where one or both are unstoppable). Here, the program correctly understands concepts such as "queening at least two moves before the other side wins" (unless the opposing king is supporting the opposing pawn to promotion which results in a draw), understanding queening with check or queening and simultaneously attacking the opponent's queening square (unless the opposing king is also defending the queening square, resulting in a draw for KPK endings). The program can solve any type of pawn race position without searching a tree of any type.

The one principle adhered to rigidly in the evaluation is correctness. If there is any doubt in the outcome, then the passed-pawn score produces nothing. If the scoring term produces a bonus, then one side is definitely winning (as opposed to "probably" winning). The bonus is more than a rook, but less than a queen so that obtaining a queen is better than simply being able to queen. The insistence on correctness here is important, in that if the position cannot be classified as won or lost, then a deeper tree search (before applying this routine) may clear things up and allow proper evaluation.

In simple king against king and pawn(s) endgames, current programs can solve the resulting positions easily and quickly. The difficulty comes when trading pieces and/or pawns and reaching such a position deep enough in the tree that a search to the conclusion is impossible. This evaluation routine allows *Cray Blitz* to play these endings correctly with no tree search whatever, or conversely to reach such a position anywhere in the tree search and still correctly assess the resulting position as won or lost.

7.4.7 Miscellaneous Scoring

Several special-purpose scoring routines are used to handle opening development, to assess cases where both sides have a bishop and pawns and finally to evaluate endings with opposite color bishops and a rook-pawn. During opening development, *Cray Blitz* penalizes moving any piece twice before moving all pieces once. This is done by examining the current search variation and penalizing moves that do not move pieces/pawns from their original squares. The penalty is dropped either after move fifteen, or after developing all pieces and castling the king. Although such a concept seems almost too primitive to include in a former World Champion, the program's ability to find tactical forays before completing development (without this heuristic) still amazes its authors. The program has won (and lost) games where one piece never moved from its original square. An example was the queen bishop in the game against *Belle* in the 1981 ACM North American Computer Chess Championship and the game against *Deep Thought* in the 6th World Computer Chess Championship in Edmonton, Canada. This simple idea eliminates these premature skirmishes and results in more logical play during the opening. The routine also implements the common opening knowledge for the particular opening it is playing. For example, it penalizes blocking the c-pawn with a knight in queen-pawn openings. This guides the program along usual book opening theory, even when its opening book does not include an early reply by the opponent. It also prevents the program from trying to exploit some tactical weakness of the opponent without having all its pieces developed, so that it later falls into tactical difficulty itself. Note that this is one of the few asymmetrical scoring terms in the program, applying only to the program's pieces and not the opponent's.

The next special-purpose scoring routine evaluates certain types of drawn endgames such as bishops of opposite color and endgames with a rook-pawn. When in a bishop of opposite colors endgame, the positional score is reduced, since drawing is probable, unless one side is significantly ahead (two pawns or more). The program correctly evaluates king against king and rook-pawn, and also king and rook-pawn against king and bishop (with other pawns present or not). The essence here is that it is possible to be material ahead, but in reality be in a drawn ending. This routine alters the score to reflect a draw, even though one side is ahead in material. An example here would be to avoid a position with king, rook-pawn and bishop of the wrong color against a lone king where one side is 4,000 points ahead in a drawn position. Using this routine, the program avoids numerous swindles by strong humans who found other programs susceptible to these traps. It appears that the idea can be generalized to other known draws.

7.4.8 Draw Scoring

A heuristic added several years ago was to not assign draw scores a value of zero, but rather assign them a value *equal* to the ply where the search reports a draw. This makes the program accept a draw when it is behind, but it forces it to follow the longest possible drawing sequence it can while still maintaining the forced draw. Against humans, delaying the draw for as long as possible gives them ample opportunity to blunder the draw away and lose. For the program, since a two-fold and three-fold repetition are identical, this heuristic also allows the program to find a way around the first two-fold repetition and perhaps avoid the draw altogether if it is possible (and if it is desirable to do so).

To implement this heuristic, the program reserves a scoring window between 0 and 100 and uses these values exclusively for draws. If a real score is greater than zero, 100 is added to it. This leaves a hole in the scoring range that contains no positional component. Thus, a positional score of 1 is reported as 101, leaving a 100 point range and preventing the draw scores from interacting with or duplicating positional scores.

The only negative aspect comes from the transposition-table scoring where the score might indicate that there is a draw in n-ply from the stored position. In fact, the looked-up draw score can be false because a shorter draw occurs somewhere in the variation. This difficulty caused Slate and Atkin to avoid storing *any* draw scores in the transposition table. While this design is inherently inaccurate, program performance improved dramatically in positions where draws occur frequently (Nelson and Hyatt 1988). Even though both draw scoring methods have inaccuracies, both will always find the draw and accept or decline as the score dictates.

7.4.9 Hash Scoring

Since the king safety and pawn scoring is so complex and time-consuming, the program reduces the computational overhead that these routines consume by storing the values in a hash table and re-using them as needed (Slate and Atkin 1977).

For pawn scoring, the locations of all pawns on the board are used to compute a hash key for each resulting pawn formation encountered during the tree search (as opposed to Slate and Atkin which used three adjacent files to form a key to retrieve a score for the three files only). The hashing routine uses the complete pawn structure to form the hash key so that more interactions between pawns can be included than were in the early Slate and Atkin's program. The search updates the hash key dynamically when moving, capturing, or promoting pawns. The program keeps all pawn scoring terms in the hashed scoring table, except for those that depend on the locations of pieces (since piece locations are not used for forming the hash key). During a typical 10-ply middlegame search, 99% of all pawn positions are retrieved from the table, reducing the pawn scoring overhead to 1% of its original total. The evaluation routines compute the remaining pawn scoring terms at each of the remaining nodes and then add the result to the value retrieved from the hash table. This allows us to implement almost any type of pawn-evaluation strategy without considering the computational time required. In a typical chess competition, $2^{17} = 131,072$ entries for pawn positions are used, where each entry is one 64-bit word.

For king safety, the location of all pawns on the board and the king position are used to create a hash key. This key is dynamically updated as the board changes. The search then uses the key to save the computed king safety for later reuse. In typical 10-ply middlegame searches, over 95% of the positions reached require no king safety evaluation since the value comes from the hash table. In a typical chess competition, $2^{18} = 262,144$ entries are used for king safety positions, where each entry is one 64-bit word.

7.5 Miscellaneous Features

7.5.1 Scoring Parameter Blocks

The scoring parameters were recently moved to a common block in lieu of the hard coding used in the past. This provided two immediate benefits. The first is that it makes tuning the program's scoring values simpler and eliminates the constant re-compiling that hard-coded values required. It is now possible to alter a value, test the new code against the old and tune the value as necessary, all without re-compiling the source code.

A second benefit is the ability to tune the evaluation parameters to more closely fit the game. For example, most programs, if not all, play Nc3 after d4 when not using an opening book. Now, the program uses one parameter block for e4 openings, another parameter block for d4 openings and so forth. In this way, the opening book dictates which basic plan the program follows by loading the appropriate parameter block depending on the book line played. Previous to this change, *Cray Blitz* played e4 openings better because they result in more open (and tactical) positions. Now it is possible to train the program to play any opening system by adjusting the various positional parameters to make the program follow the known plans for such openings.

7.5.2 Tree Search Hashing

Cray Blitz uses the transposition/refutation table hashing briefly described by Slate and Atkin (1977), and in more detail by Marsland (1987). The search stores real search scores as well as search bounds since the real score is frequently unknown when using the alpha-beta algorithm. The differences in the implementation by *Cray Blitz* from *Chess 4.X* will be described here.

First, a complete hash-table entry occupies 96 bits, of which 40 bits are used to hold the hashed board value. The low order bits of a 64-bit hash key are used for the hash address and the high order 40 bits are stored in the table to resolve collisions. For typical transposition table sizes (2^{26} entries on a Cray YMP), the entire 64 bits are used. In 1974, *Cray Blitz* pioneered the concept of storing a hashed board representation rather than a true representation of the board to save memory; after years of testing most other programs now subscribe to this method as well. The only danger inherent in this technique is that two different positions can produce the same 64-bit hash key. Since the program stores a "best" move in the transposition-table entry, the move is validated to further "prove" that the two positions are identical. Hours of simulation produced almost no collisions with the current hashing algorithm that follows the ideas presented by Zobrist (1970a). The only concern is that as machine speeds continue to improve, a 64-bit hash key might soon be insufficient. In 1974 simulations using 32 bits produced no collisions due to the slow processor speeds available then. However, Warnock and Wendroff (1988) proved that 32 bits are completely inadequate for the size of tree searched by today's faster processors.

The next part of the entry is either the true score or the appropriate upper or lower search bound if the true score is not known. The search only needs one bound if the real score is not known, and it does not need either bound if the real score is known.

The third piece of information, called the *draft* by Warnock and Wendroff (1988) (authors of *Lachex*), is the search depth below the current position that the search penetrated to. For example, when doing an 8-ply search and storing a position at ply three, the draft is five.

The last useful piece of information kept in the table is the best move from the current position. This move is always tried first in the search to improve the move ordering and is saved, even in the quiescence analysis. The only requirement is that the type of move must match the search region. For example, a simple piece move (not a capture) is not allowed in region three.

Deciding what to keep and what to discard in the table is a difficult issue. The first decision made was that a single probe (as made by Slate and Atkin) into the transposition table is not sufficient. The program retrieves several hash-table entries with a negligible time penalty by utilizing vector operations on the Cray computer system. The hashing routine uses the low order N bits of the hash key as the base transposition table address and the middle ten bits as the random offset for the re-hash of the second through the eighth entries (it currently uses eight possible table entries to store and/or look up positions). From the list of eight possible transposition table locations, the following criteria select the best table entry for replacement (stopping with the first criterion met, if any):

(1) store over a position from a previous search (NOT the same thing as the current iteration),

(2) store over a position that has a smaller draft (i.e. retain the one that saves the most work later) and

(3) do not replace real scores by search bounds.

These rules let *Cray Blitz* find about 30% of typical middlegame positions in the transposition table, and well beyond 90% in certain endgame positions.

One important implementation detail (that most chess programs avoid) is that the transposition table is never cleared. The table carries information from move to move in a continuous manner. The program recognizes that a position comes from a previous search so that it may be overwritten first, but the table is never cleared since it contains potentially useful information.

7.5.3 Time Utilization

Another area where *Cray Blitz* has been innovative is in the utilization of time during tournament play (Hyatt 1984). Using this timing algorithm, the program goes into a "deep think" when it finds itself in trouble. The search remembers the value returned from an iteration. It is possible that the next iteration finds that the best move really loses material when searching deeper. If the next iteration fails low but the search reaches the target time for the move before completing the iteration, the program continues to think beyond the time limit to find a move that does not lose anything. The amount of extra time used is proportional to the material lost. This algorithm was developed to avoid the circumstance where the program sees a loss of material and the programmers are on the edge of their seats hoping that the program finds the saving move before exhausting the search time. This overflow algorithm minimizes these occurrences and generally helps save material at least once in each game played. Avoiding one weak move is ample justification, even though the program sometimes "deep thinks" when forced to give back a pawn it "won" earlier, after finding that the pawn really cannot be held.

To assist with the time overflow algorithm, the program attempts to accumulate extra time during the search. First, the program attempts to save a fixed amount of time (set by the operator and normally 20 minutes for tournament games). The large opening book and thinking on the opponent's time usually saves enough time to meet this requirement. Until saving the required amount of time, the program computes the target time by taking the total time allowed, subtracting the operator overhead (normally 10 minutes) and dividing by the total moves in the time control. As it gets ahead on time, it continues to use this target until it saves the amount of time required (20 minutes here). Once this has been saved, it then computes the target time as the time left on the clock less the 20 minute deep think buffer, and divides this by the number of moves remaining. Thereafter, as it saves time by correctly predicting the opponent's move, the average time per move increases steadily.

Another timing issue is the decision of whether to start the $n+1$th ply iteration when it is hopeless to finish the iteration. The next iteration is always started for an important reason. Since the program uses the aspiration search and computes the lower and upper search bounds for iteration n from the iteration $n-1$ score (plus and minus a quarter of a pawn), a fail-low condition happens quickly (if it is going to). The program therefore starts the next iteration and gives it a chance to fail low. This invokes the deep think time overflow algorithm to let the program search for a solution to the problem that it would not have seen had it stopped after the last iteration. This allows the program to more or less verify that the move and score from iteration n are reasonable, even though it really cannot search iteration $n+1$ within normal time constraints. This also happens at least once per game, although sometimes it is impossible to avoid the material loss an iteration discovers.

Also, starting the next iteration and then aborting it on a time-out interrupt does not waste the time, even if the search does not fail low. After announcing the move, the search is re-started and the transposition table prevents searching the parts of the tree already examined, effectively skipping the search back to the point at which the interruption occurred.

7.6 Future Work

Future work on *Cray Blitz* encompasses four distinct areas. First, maintaining the opening book is a never-ending task because playing the same exact opening twice is tantamount to committing suicide. As the program improves, more and more opponents prepare for it by studying old games and openings played, looking for some tactical shot or positional advantage they might find by playing some unexpected move. Also, opening books are rife with errors and cannot be trusted, even though Grandmasters edit and use them. The program does not agree with many of the current opening book analysis and cannot play some of the opening styles with success. Constantly altering the book to keep it innovative and surprising is difficult and time-consuming.

Second, the program will never have enough chess knowledge. This continuing task of improving the program's playing skill through enhancing its knowledge is extremely difficult. General knowledge is fairly easy to develop, but as the knowledge base grows, additional knowledge becomes more specific and difficult to embody in programming algorithms. The endgame logic has already passed the point where it is comprehensible and changes now require hours of study to make sure that they do not adversely interact with other code.

Third, the selective part of the tree search needs refining and enhancements. It seems clear that a 5-ply exhaustive search is better than a 3-ply exhaustive with three additional selective plies added on. However, as the depth increases, a 8-ply exhaustive search with five selective plies added on would almost certainly be better than a 10-ply exhaustive search with no selective search (assuming it tries reasonable selective moves). A significant exhaustive search is necessary, but how deep it must go before tapering off into a selective search is open for conjecture. To find some of the deep moves that World Champion class humans find, the program must use some type of selective heuristics because it will never search 20 plies deep in common middlegame positions if all 20 plies are exhaustive. This strategy will determine just how strong the program becomes.

Finally, newer and better machines will become available that offer greater parallelism. The next machine from Cray Research will have sixteen processors, and sixty-four will not be too far behind. Current algorithms are simply not up to using this many processors efficiently. Although search speed is the least important of the four areas discussed in this section, it is always important because sometimes one more node would be enough to determine that a move wins or loses. It is a continuing struggle to make more and more processors work together more effectively.

Part III. Computer Chess Methods

This section describes some of the commonly used techniques and interesting new ideas for constructing chess programs. There are two principal components of chess programs: search and knowledge. In the following discussion, it is interesting to consider how each chapter contributes to these areas of artificial intelligence (AI).

Hermann Kaindl provides a thorough overview of tree searching. The paper describes all the conventional search methods commonly used by chess programs, as well as many of the important alternatives. By providing a balanced view of the many techniques available, Kaindl provides food for thought. It is easy for a new chess programmer to follow the well-trodden path of his predecessors without realizing the rich diversity of ideas that the search of chess trees has evoked. For those readers who are interested in more detail and are fluent in German, Kaindl's (1989) book is an excellent followup.

Gordon Goetsch and Murray Campbell provide a detailed analysis of the performance of the null-move heuristic. Although not a new idea, it has recently gained prominence as a means of achieving large reductions in search tree size. The cost is the introduction of a small amount of error into the search. Given the large errors already present in search trees (for example, the values returned by an evaluation function), the disadvantage appears insignificant compared to the gains. The null move has the potential for applicability in more ways than described in this paper, and will be an active research topic in the coming years.

Emmanual Lasker is often described in the chess literature as a "psychological" player. He would occasionally play objectively inferior moves, counting on the surprise value to upset his opponent's equanimity. Computer programs, on the other hand, only play the move deemed best by a minimax search; any psychological surprise is accidental. Peter Jansen explores the fascinating area of speculative play. He argues that there are classes of positions where programs should not play the best minimax move. For example, knowing that programs often out-search their human counter-parts, Jansen suggests programs might play second-best moves that contain traps the opponent is unlikely to see. In a sense, it is a gamble; the opponent might see through the trap. On the other hand, didn't Emmanuel Lasker win a lot of points using the same technique?

The last decade has seen enormous progress in the computation of chess endgame databases. Bob Herschberg, Jaap van den Herik and Patrick Schoo describe some of the magic involved in solving one of the most difficult chess endgames. The king and two knights versus king and rook pawn endgame has generated extensive human analysis and speculation on which positions are won and in how many moves. To computers, this endgame is no longer a mystery;

they can play it perfectly now. To mere mortals, it will always remain a difficult endgame to play. As we discover, the Russian problemist A.A. Troitzky was not a mere mortal!

Superficially, it appears that Chapter 12 *Learning in Bebe* addresses the mainstream AI concerns about computer-chess research. Unfortunately, no. Tony and Linda Scherzer and Dean Tjaden describe a learning technique implemented in their chess machine *Bebe*. Their results are impressive, showing how a chess program can use results from previous games played to create the effect of learning. Although a useful technique for computer-chess practitioners, this form of rote learning seems to be largely ignored by the AI community. The obvious question to ask is "Why?" Perhaps it illustrates the usual gulf between theory and practice, so often seen in computer-chess research and elsewhere.

Finally, Tony Marsland compares program performance on the most oft-used and abused benchmark in computer chess - the Bratko-Kopec set of positions. Although we all recognize the importance of benchmark testing, it remains a difficult problem to come up with a fair test. Comparing the test results of the major chess programs from two time periods nearly a decade apart, Tony is able to make some general conclusions on the progress of computer chess.

And what of the issues of knowledge? Conspicuously absent from this section on computer chess methods is anything to do with the acquisition, representation and weighting of the chess knowledge used by the programs. This remains one of the most challenging areas of computer chess and artificial intelligence research. Perhaps its absence is a consequence of the *ad hoc* techniques used by most chess programmers. They work well in practice but cause the AI purists to shudder.

Perhaps the objectives of AI need to be modified. Instead of searching for the elusive true machine intelligence, AI research should be satisfied with creating the *illusion* of intelligence. Under this scenario, computer chess gets top marks!

8 Tree Searching Algorithms

H. Kaindl

8.1 Introduction

Much of the work on search in artificial intelligence deals with trees. These are usually defined implicitly by a so-called problem representation, and the process of searching for a solution of the given problem can be represented by a search tree (more generally an acyclic graph, because of transpositions). For instance, in games like chess, the board positions correspond to nodes (or vertices) and the moves to directed arcs. This chapter reviews and critiques search algorithms for two-player game trees. The emphasis is on those algorithms which are currently most useful in computer-chess practice.

8.2 Background

While the game of chess could be solved in principle, this is not possible within any practical time and space limits. Hence we have to make decisions for a "good" next move without knowing the game theoretic values of the positions resulting from the legal moves available from the current position. These decisions usually have to be based on heuristic estimates, which are normally represented simply by point values ranging over an interval of integer numbers (or, for theoretical purposes, real numbers). Given that the game theoretic values are win, loss and draw, what is the exact meaning of these heuristic approximations?

Most of the interpretations of heuristic values in the AI literature are rather vague. Such a value estimates the situation for one player according to its *quality* (Winston 1977), *worth* (Nilsson 1980), *merit, strength* or *probability to win* (Pearl 1984). While the last of these interpretations is the most concrete one, it is also rather problematic (Horacek, Kaindl and Wagner 1987). Palay (1983) presents an interpretation as an approximation of a *delphic value*. This would be supplied by an oracle using the same scale as the evaluation function that is used to estimate the values heuristically.

Regardless of the interpretation of these point values, their assignment to the game situations induces a partial ordering. Of course, it is conceptually questionable to represent everything about the value of a position by a single number, especially since there is no information about the reliability of the estimates involved. Here we will also sketch approaches using intervals and probability distributions as values. However, since point values are most frequently used, we will primarily emphasize methods based on them.

Given an evaluation function, we could make our move decision at the root quite simply. All the children nodes (immediate successors) are generated and evaluated, and one of them leading to the maximal value is chosen. Unfortunately, experience shows that move decisions based on this method are usually bad. Hence, the usual paradigm is to select the next move on the basis of *bounded lookahead search* which normally cannot proceed all the way to goal nodes (known wins, losses, or draws). It is interesting to note that for single agent problem solving, nearly all work is centered around finding complete solutions. Although the idea of bounded lookahead search has been occasionally used for guiding the search for a complete solution (Rosenberg and Kestner 1972), only recently (Korf 1990) pointed out that for single agent problem solving in a real-time setting, actions must be committed before their ultimate consequences are known.

However, when the search probes deeper and the leaf nodes are assigned heuristic values, the question arises what to do with these. How can they be used appropriately for the decision at the root? Let us assume that one of the moves to a child position with maximal value is chosen. The question remains, how are these *dynamic* values computed from the *static* values of the corresponding leaf nodes? Usually this is done according to so-called *back-up rules*.

8.2.1 Minimaxing

In practice, the most successful approach for backing up point values is *minimaxing*. It can be considered a generalization of the game theoretic relationship between accurate values, possibly even for an infinite set of values. Although these values are normally heuristic, they are used as if they were accurate.

The key assumption is that in a game between two players, MAX and MIN, MAX on move always selects the *maximum* of the values of his children nodes, whereas MIN takes the *minimum*. Applying this rule recursively over the entire game tree, a *minimax value* can be computed.

Instead of looking at all the values in the tree from one side's point of view, it is usual to assume that the *static evaluation function* $f(n)$ represents its value from the viewpoint of the side on move in the evaluated position. Hence, the following definition of the back-up rule uses this *negamax* formulation to compute the value MM of a tree:

(1) $MM(n) := f(n)$ for leaf node n, and

(2) $MM(n) := max_i (-MM(n_i))$ for all children n_i of n.

Figure 8.1 shows a simple example of how these values are propagated in a tree. The path connecting the root with the leaf node whose static value becomes the minimax value is called the *principal variation*.

Usually, the primary interest is not the minimax value of the tree itself, but rather the move to be selected at the root. In accordance with this back-up rule,

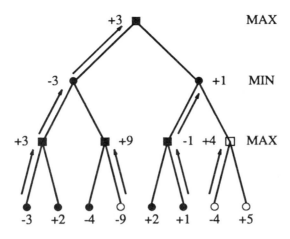

Figure 8.1: A minimax tree.

the choice is one of what may be several moves leading to the maximum
(backed-up) value of the children (multiplied by −1).

8.2.2 Modifications and Alternatives to Minimaxing

The *M and N backing-up procedure* was introduced by Slagle and Dixon
(1969). It is motivated by the inherent uncertainty associated with heuristic
values and therefore assumes that using only one back-up value (the maximum
or the minimum) is somewhat risky. The idea is to keep one's options open by
backing up a function of the M (N) greatest (smallest) values. Unfortunately, in
this way the possibilities of backward pruning (see below) become more
complicated and less efficient.

The back-up rule presented by Slagle and Bursky (1968) interprets the point
values as independent probabilities to win. This idea was again proposed later
by Pearl who called it *product propagation*. Of course, this method presupposes
that the values are in the range [0,1]. For chess, Pearl (1984) proposes a
mapping of the material count into the [0,1] range by use of a function based on
the arctan. Unfortunately, it is not clear whether the resulting values represent
probabilities to win in some realistic sense (Horacek, Kaindl and Wagner 1987).
Moreover, these values are in practice rarely independent.

Another alternative to pure minimaxing is *average propagation* which
combines the values of minimaxing and product propagation by taking the mean
value of them (Nau, Purdom and Tzeng 1986). This is one of the many possible
hybrid algorithms between the extremes of minimaxing and product
propagation. The comparison showed that the advantages and disadvantages of
these different methods depend heavily on the properties of the evaluations, in
particular their degree of uncertainty.

However, all these investigations compared the alternatives to minimaxing without its refinements, which we will discuss below. Moreover, all methods were used to the same fixed search depth. Unfortunately for product and average propagation, tree pruning schemes, such as those available for minimaxing (as discussed below), are not possible. After all, since the backing-up of all the children's values are required, shouldn't the comparisons between algorithms be made on a fair basis of equal time allotment? This could be approximated by allowing the same number of nodes searched.

8.3 Depth-First Search

Besides the rules used for backing up values, the order of tree traversal is important. The computation of a minimax value $MM(n)$ for a node n is usually done by a *depth-first search* (realized by *backtracking*). For example, the numbers assigned to the nodes in Figure 8.2 show the order of node generation in a tree of fixed search depth 2. The main advantages of this search strategy are the *linear* storage requirement, since it only needs a stack of the nodes on the current path, and the simple control strategy.

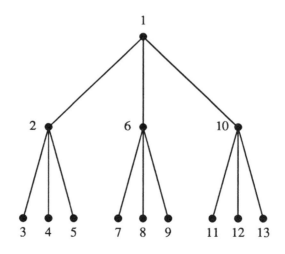

Figure 8.2: Order of node generation in a depth-first search.

8.3.1 The αβ Algorithm

The oldest and best known method for efficiently computing a minimax value is the alpha-beta algorithm (called αβ here). The following example illustrates the basic idea of how effort can be saved in comparison to actually looking at all the nodes in the tree.

Consider the part of the tree from Figure 8.1, as shown in Figure 8.3. The left subtree has resulted in a value of +3 for the root. Since we strictly maximize, only values $> +3$ are of any interest. Values $\leq +3$ cannot change anything at the root. This information can now be used when searching the right subtree. After the right subtree's left subtree has been searched, a value of +1 can be claimed there. This implies that only values $> +1$ are of further interest at this node. What does this now mean relative to the situation at the root? Using negamaxing, we already have $-1 \leq +3$ and so those values yield no change. The left child of the root still has the best value available (+3). However, since the value of the right child can only get worse from the viewpoint of the root (it could become < -1), further investigations of the right subtree cannot change the value of the root. Why then should the search continue there?

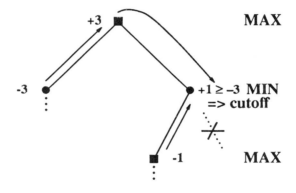

Figure 8.3: An $\alpha\beta$ cutoff.

We can also look at this search reduction idea in the following way. If a player has already found one *refutation* to a move of the opponent, there is no point in searching for a better one. Such a termination of the search is called a *cutoff*. This whole process of riskless pruning the search tree is called *backward pruning*.

The pseudo-code for the $\alpha\beta$ procedure, called *FAB* (Fishburn 1981), is shown in Figure 8.4. SelectNextMove returns legal moves, one after another. It returns the special value *null* when there are no more moves left, and also when some artificial termination criterion is fulfilled (e.g., the maximum search depth). ∞ denotes a value that is $\geq \mid$ StaticEvaluation(Position) $\mid$ for all leaf *Positions* of the game. The recursive call takes as a parameter the position which results from playing the move M in *Position*, written as M (*Position*). Of

```
function FAB( Position, Alpha, Beta ) : integer;
      M := SelectNextMove( Position );
      if M = null then
            return( StaticEvaluation( Position ) );
      end if;
      Best := −∞;
      while M ≠ null do
            Value := −FAB( M( Position ), −Beta, −max( Alpha, Best ) );
            if Value > Best then
                  Best := Value;
                  if Best ≥ Beta then
                        return( Best );
                  end if;
            end if;
            M := SelectNextMove( Position );
      end while;
      return( Best );
end function FAB;
```

Figure 8.4: FAB (Fail-soft $\alpha\beta$).

course, the move leading to the best value is a result at least as important as the value itself. For reasons of brevity we omit that additional code here.

The parameters α and β represent the bounds for the cutoffs. Using the negamax formulation, β is the current bound and α serves as a kind of intermediate storage saving the other bound for the next level of the tree. In fact, β is not only the best value achieved by the opponent at the parent node, but at all nodes on the current path with the opponent moving (multiplied by -1). α is the best value from all the nodes on the current path with the same player to move as at the currently investigated node. Figure 8.5 shows the relationship between these bounds and *Best,* the current best value at this node. α and β delimit the range of those values which are still of interest at the current node. *Best* can only become greater and eventually reach or exceed β, which would cause a cutoff.

The $\alpha\beta$ algorithm seems to have been discovered independently by several people even before 1960, but only in a weaker form without taking advantage of all possible cutoffs (see, for example, the works of Brudno (1963) and Newell, Shaw and Simon (1958)). The term $\alpha\beta$ was coined by John McCarthy (but related to a heuristic extension). Knuth and Moore (1975) presented the sketch of a proof that this method in fact returns the same value as exhaustive minimaxing, when called with initial values of $-\infty$ and $+\infty$ for the bounds. Their version included the so-called *deep cutoffs,* allowing bounds information obtained at depth i in the tree to cause cutoffs at depths greater than i.

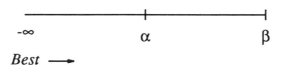

Figure 8.5: The bounds of FAB.

FAB in Figure 8.4 corresponds to a small modification proposed by Fishburn and Finkel (1980) which they called *falphabeta* (Fail-soft Alpha-Beta). In contrast to the original version of $\alpha\beta$, where *Best* would be initialized to α, FAB sets *Best* to $-\infty$. This change allows FAB to return a VALUE $< \alpha$ or $> \beta$. Of course, FAB never searches more nodes than the original $\alpha\beta$ procedure. However, when using an aspiration window (see the next section) it can occasionally provide better bounds for an eventual re-search.

8.3.2 Using a Window

The effort for an $\alpha\beta$ search decreases the smaller the interval between α and β. Moreover, for many applications, it is possible to obtain a reliable estimate, before the search begins, of a range that will contain the minimax value. This narrower window *aspires* to contain the correct value and is called an *aspiration window* (later we discuss some methods for estimating it). Hence, $\alpha\beta$ is often used in its *AAB* (Aspiration Alpha-Beta) variant, where the FAB window at the root is initialized to artificial bounds:

> Value := FAB(Position, Alpha, Beta);

Of course, there is some risk that the estimate turns out to be wrong and the minimax value lies outside the aspiration window. In this case, the search has to be repeated with a different interval, usually in the following way:

> **if** Value $\leq$ Alpha **then**
>   Value := FAB(Position, $-\infty$, Value);
> **else if** Value $\geq$ Beta **then**
>   Value := FAB(Position, Value, $+\infty$);
> **end if;**

When searching to variable depth, more information than that provided by FAB can be gained from such search trees. Barth (1988) proposed an algorithm that, under certain conditions, is not only able to tell how far a value is away from a given window (like FAB), but also bounds its maximum distance from the window. Hence, in such cases an interval results. Although it does not help for computing a minimax value, our main purpose is to find the best move. Barth (1988) uses such intervals for the move decision, based on the idea of the top level procedure of B*. (B* is discussed later in Section 8.5.2 *B* and PB*.*)

In principle, the use of aspiration windows offers a simple possibility for parallelism. For example, three processors can simultaneously search the tree using the windows $(-\infty, \alpha)$, (α, β) and $(\beta, +\infty)$. One processor is guaranteed to find the solution and, because it used a narrower window, will do so faster than in the sequential case. Although this approach can be easily extended for use by n processors, Baudet (1978a) showed that even with an infinite number of processors, the speedup would be bounded by a constant factor (about 5). Every processor must search at least a minimal-sized game tree and, consequently, this limits the effective parallelism.

8.3.3 PAB, SCOUT and PVS

A slightly different approach for the efficient computation of exact minimax values is represented by *Palphabeta* (Fishburn and Finkel 1980) and *SCOUT* (Pearl 1980,84). These algorithms initially search along a path towards a leaf node to which they assign a static value. Assuming then that this path already contains "good" moves for both players, they only test whether one of the alternatives has a better value. Such tests can be done cheaper than the computation of a minimax value for all these subtrees. However, when alternatives yield better values, *re-searches* of these subtrees are necessary to determine their correct value.

Figure 8.6 shows pseudo-code for the *PAB* algorithm (Principal variation Alpha-Beta). The first move is investigated by a recursive call. The loop over the remaining alternatives contains calls to FAB. The first (unconditional) one gets a *minimal window.* Assuming integer values v, the interval $(v, v+1)$ contains no value at all. The call to FAB with this minimal window only serves the purpose of testing whether one of the alternatives has a better value. Whenever this is the case, FAB is called again with a wider window to compute the value.

The following example shows how PAB can save effort compared to FAB. However, when re-searches are necessary, PAB may be less efficient, depending on the characteristics of the trees. The tree in Figure 8.7 results from that in Figure 8.1 by changing the order of moves of the right successor node of the root (as indicated by an arrow). PAB searches the same nodes as FAB in the left subtree of the root. Consider the node marked by an asterisk. FAB cannot prune this node after the investigation of the first child, since there is no appropriate bound (other then $+\infty$) available. In contrast, PAB calls FAB with a minimal window and, consequently, with an artificial bound (+4). This is sufficient for a cutoff because $+4 \geq +4$ is given. In fact, evaluating the expression $max(-max(+4, -y)), +1)$ results in the correct value for the right child of the root (+1), independent of the value y.

```
function PAB( Position ) : integer;
        M := SelectNextMove( Position );
        if M = null then
                return( StaticEvaluation( Position ) );
        end if;
        Best := −PAB( M( Position ) );
        M := SelectNextMove( Position );
        while M ≠ null do
                Value := −FAB( M( Position ), −Best−1, −Best );
                if Value > Best then
                        Best := −FAB( M( Position ), −∞, −Value );
                end if;
                M := SelectNextMove( Position );
        end while;
        return( Best );
end function PAB;
```

Figure 8.6: PAB (Principal variation αβ).

It is interesting to consider how well FAB with artificial bounds searches this tree. A call to FAB with *Beta* = 4 results in the same cutoff as the application of PAB. However, *Beta* > 4 causes the same behavior as if *Beta* = +∞.

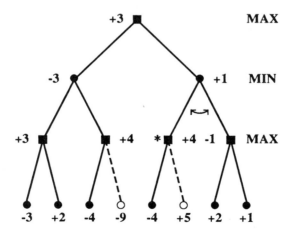

Figure 8.7: A PAB search tree.

```
function SCOUT( Position ) : integer;
        M := SelectNextMove( Position );
        if M = null then
                return( StaticEvaluation( Position ) );
        end if;
        Best := -SCOUT( M( Position ) );
        M := SelectNextMove( Position );
        while M ≠ null do
                Search := not TEST( M( Position ), -Best-1 );
                if Search then
                        Best := -SCOUT( M( Position ) );
                end if;
                M := SelectNextMove( Position );
        end while;
        return( Best );
end function SCOUT;

function TEST( Position, Value ) : boolean;
        M := SelectNextMove( Position );
        if M = null then
                return( StaticEvaluation( Position ) > Value );
        end if;
        while M ≠ null do
                Search := not TEST( M( Position ), -Value-1 );
                if Search then
                        return( Search );
                end if;
                M := SelectNextMove( Position );
        end while;
        return( Search );
end function TEST;
```

Figure 8.8: SCOUT and TEST algorithm.

The idea of testing the alternatives in SCOUT is based on different considerations. The algorithm is adapted from one used to solve games and distinguishes between values which are greater than a given one and the others, rather than between win and loss. The resulting procedure has been named *TEST* by Pearl (1980), where it is described in a minimax formulation. The SCOUT algorithm is given in Figure 8.8. Contrary to FAB, TEST (without enhancements) cannot return information about the actual value for re-searches.

Although SCOUT and PAB are similar, there is a notable difference between them in the way re-searches are done. PAB uses FAB, while SCOUT calls itself recursively. Campbell and Marsland (1983) were the first to re-work SCOUT into an αβ framework. Later, this was refined into the Principal Variation Search (PVS) algorithm (Marsland 1983) which, with its search depth control, became a popular choice for many chess programs (see Figure 8.9). Independently, Reinefeld (1983) published his *Negascout* algorithm, a formulation which introduced an additional deep cutoff when the evaluation function used always returns a value and not a bound on a position.

```
function PVS( Position, Alpha, Beta, Depth ) : integer;
        if Depth = 0 then
                return( StaticEvaluation( Position ) );
        end if;
        M := SelectNextMove( Position );
        if M = null then
                return( StaticEvaluation( Position ) );
        end if;

        Best := -PVS( M( Position ), -Beta, -Alpha, Depth-1 );
        M := SelectNextMove( Position );
        while M ≠ null do
                if Best ≥ Beta then
                        return( Best );
                Alpha := MAX( Best, Alpha );
                Value := -PVS( M( Position ), -Alpha-1, -Alpha, Depth-1 );
                if Value > Alpha and Value < Beta then
                        Best := -PVS( M( Position ), -Beta, -Value, Depth-1 );
                else if Value > Best then
                        Best := Value;
                end if;
                M := SelectNextMove( Position );
        end while;
        return( Best );
end function PVS;
```

Figure 8.9: PVS (Principal Variation Search).

Based on the underlying idea of PAB and SCOUT, some approaches for parallel search have been developed (Marsland and Campbell 1982) and tested (Marsland and Popowich 1985). Assuming a good move ordering, these algorithms try to split the tree appropriately. Although this way of using parallel hardware is already much more successful than that using several windows, its performance for many processors is not completely satisfactory (Schaeffer 1989b).

8.4 Depth-First Iterative-Deepening

It is usual in practice to perform depth-first minimax searches successively deeper and deeper *(iterative-deepening)*. The first mention in the literature seems to be by Scott (1969). Mainly it was used to cope with the real-time situation of playing time controlled games. Even if an $\alpha\beta$ search is controlled by a fixed depth limit, its duration is often difficult to predict. It depends on properties of the given position which are difficult to assess, and it is related to the frequency of cutoffs. However, if the duration of a search to depth i is known, it is easier to predict how long the subsequent search to depth $i+1$ will last.

Although this was the only aspect of iterative search discussed by Scott (1969), there are also some other benefits for computer chess. The additional effort of repeating the shallower searches is relatively small, and the asymptotic complexity is the same as that of a pure depth-first search, given an exponential search space. Further, this method can even help save effort when used within bounded lookahead search in two-player games. This observation is due to Slate and Atkin (1977), who describe the following procedure: Starting with a first iteration to depth two (plus quiescence search), each subsequent iteration is one ply (one move by one player) deeper than the preceding one. This series of iterations are terminated when a preset time threshold is exceeded. (Some programs increase the search depth by two plies.) Each search (to depth i) saves the principal variation, which is tried first in the subsequent iteration (to depth $i+1$). Since it is likely that this principal variation is also a good move sequence for both players for the next iteration, this often results in an improvement of the move ordering as compared to directly searching to depth $i+1$. This move ordering has, in general, a strong influence on the efficiency of $\alpha\beta$-type algorithms, because it influences the frequency of cutoffs. (In Section 8.6 *The Efficiency of the Minimax Algorithms*, some theoretical results on this issue are presented.) Similar and even stronger effects can be achieved by use of specific tables which store useful information for use in later iterations (see Section 8.7.1 *Achieving a Good Move Ordering*).

Depth-first iterative-deepening can also help when using an aspiration window (AAB for instance). The minimax value of iteration i can serve for determining an appropriate window for iteration $i+1$. Since this value is normally stable from one iteration to the next, there is only a small risk that the search will have to be repeated with another window.

8.5 Best-First Search

Most of the programs for two-player, perfect information games use depth-first search integrated into iterative-deepening. The main advantage of this method is the low storage requirement. However, from a theoretical point of view there are some interesting approaches using best-first search. They can be categorized into two groups, based on whether they minimax the values or search using a different backup rule.

8.5.1 SSS* and DUAL*

Stockman (1979) developed a best-first search algorithm, called *SSS** (State Space Search), for computing minimax values. This name is derived from the search space defined by states which are represented by specific triples. It is closely related to a search algorithm for AND/OR-Graphs called *AO** by Nilsson (1980).

SSS*'s best-first search strategy *dominates* $\alpha\beta$ in the following sense. When some node n is searched by SSS*, $\alpha\beta$ also has to search it, but not vice versa. $\alpha\beta$ is restricted by its depth-first search strategy and consequently cannot use the same amount of information for its cutoff decision. A formal proof of this dominance can be found in Stockman (1979) but requires the modification found by Campbell (1981) to ensure nodes are expanded in the appropriate order. Below we will sketch how much more efficient SSS* would be under practical conditions. However, because of its exponential storage requirements, SSS* is normally not used in chess programs.

Based on considerations and investigations of parallel search by Kumar and Kanal (1984), Marsland, Reinefeld and Schaeffer (1987) propose an algorithm called *DUAL**. This algorithm has a directional (left-to-right) search of the root node moves (like $\alpha\beta$ does), while searching the subtrees using a "dual" of SSS* (exchanging the respective actions of MAX- and MIN-nodes). Of course, these cannot alter the enormous storage requirements. An interesting approach for reducing the storage requirements was described by Marsland and Srimani (1986) in the form of an algorithm called *PS** (Phased Search). It partitions the children of MAX nodes into k groups, which are searched in phases one after another. The amount of storage required depends on k. PS*(k) can be viewed as a balance between the respective advantages and disadvantages of SSS* and $\alpha\beta$. In the extreme, it becomes SSS* when using only a single phase, and it resembles $\alpha\beta$ when assigning a phase to each child.

8.5.2 B* and PB*

All the algorithms mentioned above use point values and, although those based on minimaxing achieve good results, the projection of all the information about the quality of a position into a single number is generally considered conceptually doubtful. In particular, it is impossible to represent information about the uncertainty of the evaluations, despite their heuristic nature.

The *B** algorithm of Berliner (1979b) represents an evaluation with an *optimistic* and a *pessimistic* value. These are upper and lower bounds on the "delphic value" of the position. Ibaraki (1986) calls a model based on such intervals "informed" and presents corresponding generalizations of $\alpha\beta$ and SSS*.

Usually, we are more interested in finding the best move in the root position, rather than its minimax value. B* uses its bounds to prove that one move is the best (relative to the heuristic evaluations). The termination condition of this algorithm is fulfilled when the pessimistic value of one child of the root (the "best" one) is not worse than the optimistic value of all the other children of the root. This can happen even if the interval at the root has not been reduced to a single value, and hence some effort may be saved.

The search control of B* tries to achieve the termination condition as fast as possible. Conducting a best-first search, it tries to expand the node with the best evaluation. This way the pessimistic value of the "best" child of the root may be raised to become equal or better than the optimistic values of all its alternatives, which would prove it to be best. Hence, this search strategy is called PROVEBEST. B* also uses the DISPROVEREST strategy by trying to lower the optimistic values of all the alternatives to fulfill the termination condition. Because the search investigates parts of the tree which are not assumed to contain the "best" positions, strictly speaking, B* exceeds the scheme of a classical best-first search.

Detailed descriptions of B* have been given by Berliner (1979b) and Palay (1982,83). The main difficulty of B* comes from the problem of reliably estimating optimistic and pessimistic bounds on a position. Although it is easier to estimate bounds than point values, this algorithm is more dependent on accurate estimates than those based on minimaxing.

Whereas such intervals can represent uncertainty, they do not indicate by themselves where the delphic value is in the interval. Hence, Palay (1982) assumed certain distributions for guiding the search appropriately. As a next major step, Palay (1983) used probability distributions to represent evaluations in an algorithm based on B*, which he called *PB** (Probability-based B*). The back-up rules for distributions are, of course, more complicated. Although the one developed by Palay is somehow related to minimaxing in the negamax formulation, it multiplies probabilities much like the product propagation rule mentioned earlier, also making use of the independence assumption. However, the meaning of probabilities in these approaches is quite different. While here uncertainties are expressed, the point values are assumed to represent probabilities to win. Unfortunately, estimating such probability distributions is difficult, and PB* seems to be rather sensitive to their accuracy.

8.6 The Efficiency of the Minimax Algorithms

As well as using concrete implementations of algorithms for specific domains like chess, the efficiency of the various algorithms for computing minimax values can also be compared on a more abstract level. In fact, much work has been devoted to their mathematical analysis using simplified models. Since these results often cannot be satisfactorily related to the observations in practice, we will emphasize those studies which help us understand the empirical data.

The usual models assume game trees with a constant number of children at each node; that is, a branching degree b. The algorithms compared compute the (exact) minimax value of trees with constant depth d. In general, algorithms like $\alpha\beta$ will not generate every node in such a tree. We would like to know how many of them each algorithm actually generates, as a means of comparing algorithm performance. Usually, the leaf nodes at depth d are counted and this number is taken as a measurement of the efficiency. This measure is often called NBP (Number of Bottom Positions) in the literature. Related to this is the average number of children generated at each node, which is called the branching factor (a formal notion of its asymptotic growth rate was given by Knuth and Moore (1975)). Since the efficiency of these algorithms depends heavily on the ordering of the nodes and their evaluations, we also have to make certain assumptions here as well.

8.6.1 The Worst and Best Case

Actually, there exist trees where $\alpha\beta$ cannot cutoff at all. In such a worst case it has to search all b^d leaf nodes. However, such cases are contrived and are irrelevant from a practical point of view.

In the best case, $2b^{d/2} - 1$ leaf nodes have to be visited if d is even, while $b^{(d+1)/2} + b^{(d-1)/2} - 1$ leaf nodes are examined when d is odd (Slagle and Dixon 1969; Knuth and Moore 1975). Figure 8.1 shows a simple example. With perfect ordering, $\alpha\beta$ only has to visit 5 $(= 2^2 + 2^1 - 1)$ leaf nodes there. The tree of minimal size that has to be searched in any case is called the *minimal tree,* which is outlined by the bold squares and circles in Figure 8.1. Algorithms such as PAB, SCOUT, SSS* and DUAL* can do no better than this best case. Although the savings are great, we must be aware that the tree still grows exponentially, albeit with a reduced exponent. This perfect ordering would allow a search to nearly double the search depth compared to the worst case.

There is an approach for parallel search based on the knowledge that the minimal tree always has to be searched (Akl, Barnard and Doran 1982). First, the nodes which cannot be pruned anyway are searched, thus getting useful bounds for the subsequent search.

8.6.2 The Average Case

Since neither the best nor the worst case are achieved in practice, it is interesting to get an idea of the behavior in the "average" case. However, an important question is how to define average properly. It should not only model the behavior in practice, but also allow for theoretical investigation. Usually, mathematical analysis as well as computer simulations are applied here. (Benchmark tests with existing programs in domains like chess can also be used, but the potential for generalizing these results is questionable.)

Essentially, there are two main directions to be distinguished, according to the modeling of node ordering. One assumes that it is completely random.

Hence, each of the possible orderings is equally likely, and the average is taken over all possible node orderings. The other assumes that, based on empirical observations, there is a good ordering achieved using appropriate heuristics. Of course, this case is even more difficult to model and analyze.

Although the mathematical model of random ordering is simpler to analyze than the others, the results for $\alpha\beta$ have only been achieved in steps (Fuller, Gaschnig and Gillogly 1973; Knuth and Moore 1975; Baudet 1978b; Pearl 1982). The main results can be summarized as follows. Under given conditions, $\alpha\beta$, SSS* and SCOUT achieve the same (asymptotic) branching factor. While SSS* dominates $\alpha\beta$ in the sense described above, both algorithms are *asymptotically* equivalent. A result of Tarsi (1983) even renders them *asymptotically optimal*. Compared to the worst case, the search depth can be increased approximately by a factor of 4/3 under these conditions.

However, observations from computer-chess practice show that much more can be saved as a result of good ordering heuristics. Also, these theoretical investigations assume node evaluations to be independent, which they are not. Approaches to model the dependencies in practice (but not heuristic ordering) are described by Knuth and Moore (1975) and Fuller, Gaschnig and Gillogly (1973), and some analysis of $\alpha\beta$ using these models have been done by Newborn (1977) and Darwish (1983). Reinefeld and Marsland (1987) have compared $\alpha\beta$ and Negascout analytically, using a simple model which integrates the ordering aspect. Their results also support the slight preference of Negascout over $\alpha\beta$, as observed in practice.

The model of a *strongly ordered tree* proposed by Marsland and Campbell (1982) can be related best to the trees searched in practice. In such a tree, the first move from each position is best 70% of the time, and 90% of the time the best move is within the first quarter of all the moves from this position. The first of these conditions can be easily and cheaply checked during a search, if the definition is slightly modified so that a cutoff is also counted as best. Using this first parameter of the strongly ordered tree definition for generating search trees, simulations for several algorithms have been run. For the cases of 50% and 80% see the paper by Campbell and Marsland (1983), and for 60%, the work of Marsland, Reinefeld and Schaeffer (1987).

What are realistic values of this parameter? Since no statistics about it are widely available, the chess program *Merlin* was used to gather some data (Kaindl 1988a). While *Merlin* incorporates many ordering heuristics, the result was nevertheless unexpectedly high. Out of 438 move decisions (most of them under tournament conditions) a mean value of 90.3% (with a standard deviation of 8.2%) resulted for the relative frequency of the first move from each node being best or achieving a cutoff. To give some comparison with other programs, an attempt was made to estimate this parameter for the chess program *Tech* from the data given by Gillogly (1978). One can conjecture that, despite the simple structure of this program, a value between 70% and 80% was achieved there.

For this reason, Kaindl, Wagner and Horacek (1989) investigated strongly ordered trees with a chance > 70% that the move searched first at a node

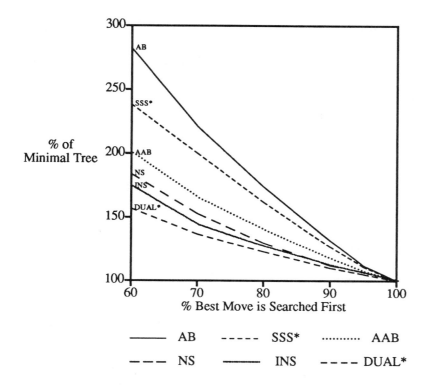

Figure 8.10: Search of strongly ordered trees ($d = 5$ and $b = 20$).

achieves the best value or a cutoff. Consider the consequences of varying this parameter. Figure 8.10 shows the behavior of a variety of algorithms on a uniform tree of search depth 5 and branching factor 20. The horizontal axis is the frequency with which the first move from a node is best or causes a cutoff. The vertical axis shows the average percent node count relative to a minimal tree. *AB* represents the original version of $\alpha\beta$, which gives equivalent results here as FAB, while *NS* indicates the performance of Negascout. *INS* (Informed NS) is a Negascout variant that stores extra information to reduce the cost of a re-search, in a similar way to using a transposition table as discussed below (Marsland, Reinefeld and Schaeffer 1987). For odd search depths, there is a clear separation in algorithm performance. When the search depth is even, the algorithms have nearly equal performance (with the exception of $\alpha\beta$ which is still significantly worse). The differences between odd and even search depths is partially a consequence of the odd-even nature of the formula for the minimal search tree size.

Studies of even and odd search depths (for example, Figure 8.10) show that the savings with increasing ordering can be quite high when approaching the optimum. The diagram also shows that the linear storage algorithms (the ones used in practice) are not the best in terms of NBP considered. However, as we will discuss below, their performance can be improved most by achieving a good move ordering through the use of tables, resulting in increased storage requirements. One can conjecture that at even and odd search depths different algorithms are most efficient.

Let us compare AB and AAB, with the window size and frequency of re-searches estimated from practical experience with *Merlin*. Although AB in its pure form is always the least efficient method, AAB does much better. The question of how much the other algorithms can profit from such a window is an issue currently under investigation. Kaindl, Wagner and Horacek (1989) show that AAB gets more efficient with increasing search depth, relative to the other algorithms. However AAB benefits less with improved ordering than do the others.

8.7 Additional Aspects and Heuristics

Besides the pure functionality of the various search algorithms and their efficiency, there are many additional aspects of interest here. For instance, it is important to achieve a good ordering but at an acceptable cost.

8.7.1 Achieving a Good Move Ordering

The usual heuristic for move ordering is to search those moves whose values are best from the viewpoint of the player moving first at the node. In general, this method increases the frequency of cutoffs. Unfortunately, during the search, the programs cannot distinguish those nodes where this ordering helps from those where it has no effect at all. Nevertheless, experience shows that the application of this heuristic is useful.

Historically, Slagle and Dixon (1969) investigated a method which they called *fixed ordering*, using $\alpha\beta$ for trees of the game of *kalah*. All children of a node are generated, assigned a static evaluation, and ordered according to these values. Occasionally, when searching the subtree of a "good" child it may turn out not to be good because of newly discovered information. Another method investigated by Slagle and Dixon (1969), which they called *dynamic ordering*, reacts in such a situation by terminating the search of this subtree and continuing in a different one. Note that by doing this globally in the tree after each node generation and evaluation, the depth-first search is done in the same order as a best-first search. In effect, $\alpha\beta$ searches the tree in the same order as SSS*.

Compared to random ordering, large improvements in search efficiency have been observed using fixed or dynamic ordering. However, there are two reasons why these methods are not the best for computer-chess practice. First, in the case of a cutoff, the superfluous generations and evaluations are costly. Second, the usual static evaluation functions for positions are often less appropriate for the purpose of ordering than cheaper methods evaluating the moves leading to these positions. Such methods can either use domain specific heuristics (e.g., related to capture moves), or, more generally, information gathered dynamically by the search itself (using tables to store this information).

Important information, such as whether a move resulted in a cutoff, is used by the *killer heuristic* (Slate and Atkin 1977). When move y refutes move x, it is quite likely in domains like chess that y is also able to refute other moves in "similar" positions. Consequently, it is empirically useful to store the move y in a *killer table*. At nodes of the same depth in the tree, the killer move, if legal, can be tried as one of the first.

As we have already discussed above, such tables are also useful for depth-first iterative-deepening. Tables can be used to store the best move in a particular position, amongst other information. In most cases, this move is also good in the next iteration and should therefore be searched first. However, such tables are also important for another reason. They enable a tree-searching algorithm to treat more general graphs appropriately, in that they allow for the recognition of transpositions to the same successor positions. Greenblatt, Eastlake and Crocker (1967) called these transposition tables. Of course, the advantage of this kind of table is that identical positions need be searched only once. Unfortunately, because of changing $\alpha\beta$ bounds it may not always be possible to use the stored value as it is and so avoid the re-search. Moreover, one must be aware of the storage requirements of such a table which can far exceed those of pure backtracking. However, in contrast to an implementation of, for instance, SSS*, the usual realization of a transposition table as a hash table is much more efficient and flexible, since it allows for handling overflows by simply overwriting less valuable entries.

A recent idea is to store information about the usefulness of the moves in the previous parts of the search in a *history table* of all possible moves (indexed by their from- and to-squares). This *history heuristic*, introduced by Schaeffer (1983a,89a), uses this information to sort the moves at all interior nodes. This approach is general, since it stores and uses information abstracted from positions throughout the tree, while the killer heuristic is usually restricted to the same level. At the other extreme is the use of the principal variation, which stores and uses an exact move sequence for one specified position. The transposition table is designed to keep exact information for all the positions it can store.

Slate and Atkin (1977) give a detailed description of the move ordering mechanisms in a chess program. In general, each of the mentioned heuristics results in large savings compared to random ordering. However, when they are combined, one must be aware of some overlapping in the effects, which is supported by computer-chess practice as well as the experiments reported by Schaeffer (1989a).

8.7.2 Static Evaluation Functions

Although the exact meaning of the heuristic values estimated by the static evaluation functions for chess is not really clear, we will sketch how these functions are or should be constructed. Actually, this is an issue of knowledge representation rather than search, but we will include it here for a better understanding of the search aspects.

In general, one tries to model features of positions in an attempt to quantify some estimate of the advantages for one or the other of the players. By combining the estimated values, an overall value is computed. Historically, this is done in the form of a linear combination:

$$V = \sum_{f \in F} c_f \times f$$

with F the set of all the used features, whose respective value f is weighted by the corresponding constant factor c_f. Usual examples of such features in chess and checkers are, for instance, the "material balance" or "mobility."

A basic problem arises when certain features are not equally important in every phase of the game (e.g., the king's distance from the center in the middlegame in contrast to the endgame). Of course, it is possible to build several functions, one for each phase. However, the transitions between them are problematic, because it is difficult to get them smooth. In general, large changes of the values artificially built into the evaluation function resulting from small changes of a feature, can lead to the *blemish effect* (Berliner 1979a; Ackley and Berliner 1983).

Linear functions can only represent average relations between features, and are insufficient for describing special situations. For this reason Samuel (1967) used *signature tables* in his famous checkers program, rather than the original linear polynomials (see also Samuel 1959). These tables represent the values of the function for each feature vector. Despite an efficient implementation, it was necessary to restrict the value ranges of the feature values, and for this reason Berliner (1979a) conjectures problems from the blemish effect even in this approach.

Non-linear functions have their own problems, however. The increased sensitivity can result in stability problems. For example, the multiplication of two variables in the range 0..50 can cause the result to fall in the much larger range 0..2500. The following example illustrates another problem. Let I express the *intensity of pain* and D its *duration*. Minimizing the product of I and D, setting $D = 0$, may be the solution: *suicide*. Berliner (1979a) calls a construction which allows for unwanted manipulations of variables a *suicide construction*.

As a consequence of these problems, Berliner developed the method *SNAC* (Smoothness, Non-linearity, Application Coefficients), while working on his famous backgammon program *BKG* (Berliner 1979a,c). An *application coefficient A* is a variable whose value changes slowly in relation to a single move. A typical example is a variable expressing the phase of the game. These variables A_f (corresponding to the feature f) substitute or supplement the constants c_f in the polynomial. This way global non-linear relations result, as well as smooth transitions and local linearity. For more details the reader is referred to Berliner (1979a) and Ackley and Berliner (1983).

Horacek (1984) discusses more problems with static evaluation functions, in particular the ignorance of the *uncertainty* of the values. Unfortunately, with the current state of the art it is nearly impossible to construct a purely static evaluation function for an interesting domain like chess which would satisfy the requirements of B* or PB*. For this reason, mechanisms have been designed to integrate some handling of uncertainty for special features into the framework of minimaxing (Horacek, Kaindl and Wagner 1986; Horacek 1989).

In practice, there is a major constraint for constructing large and complex evaluation functions given by the enormous number of calls to it within a deep search. Making the evaluator too slow, the speed of the search is reduced significantly, which has consequences for the quality of tactical moves in chess. Making the evaluator too fast may mean that inadequate knowledge is present, influencing the quality of positional moves. Fortunately, an implementation using parallel hardware can improve this situation (see Condon and Thompson 1982). Another possibility is to evaluate only the root position extensively, and use stored information from this analysis efficiently for the evaluations within the tree. Ebeling (1986) gives a comprehensive treatment of this approach and its support by special-purpose hardware.

It is important to realize that today's evaluation functions for chess include almost exclusively static features. The features on the current board are relevant, while the dynamic aspects of how things will develop from there are usually ignored (sometimes with the exception of a static analysis of exchanges). More complicated attempts have failed because of the expense of the computations as well as the large error rate compared to deeper search. Detailed descriptions of evaluation functions used in successful programs are given by Slate and Atkin (1977) and Ebeling (1986).

8.7.3 Quiescence and the Horizon Effect

In theory, minimaxing is mostly investigated within full-width searches (except cutoffs) up to a fixed depth, where the resulting positions are evaluated statically. Strictly doing so in computer-chess practice, however, leads to the well-known *horizon effect* (Berliner 1974). Unrecognized problems are pushed over the search horizon by means of objectively bad actions within the search tree. It is often thought to be caused primarily by the fixed boundary, but fundamentally it is related as well to the evaluation function and its interplay with the search.

When looking at the values returned by the usual static evaluators for chess (and also checkers or kalah), an important property of them can be easily observed. In most cases, the values can be changed dramatically by moves or move sequences. For instance in chess, consider a move which captures a queen. Whether or not this queen is actually lost by the opponent, the static value of the resulting position differs significantly from that of the position before the capture move. Hence, positions with more stable values are of special interest (e.g., those where the side to move cannot profitably capture). For such positions the term *quiescent* was coined by Shannon (1950). Independently, Turing *et al.* (1953) derived the same concept from their considerations about chess programming; they called such positions "dead."

However, abstracting from the issues of specific games, what is the domain-independent concept of *quiescence* all about? Essentially, it can be viewed as a property of the static evaluation function related to its stability with regard to further search. For use in theoretical investigations of the benefits of minimaxing, formal definitions modeling this concept are given by Kaindl (1988b) and Scheucher and Kaindl (1989).

Whenever a leaf node at a fixed horizon is not quiescent, the horizon effect can lead to a bad decision. Since state-of-the-art static evaluators cannot estimate dynamic situations well, currently the best method of avoiding the horizon effect is to search to variable depth.

8.7.4 Searching to Variable Depth

The goal of searching to variable depth is not only the avoidance of the horizon effect, but more generally greater efficiency. After all, backward pruning can at best reduce the exponent but never avoid the exponential growth of the trees. Moreover, most of the legal moves are "bad" anyway. Chess players find it absurd to consider every move to a constant depth.

Even Shannon (1950) and Turing *et al.* (1953) proposed to search *forced* variations beyond the horizon of the full-width search in chess (notably captures and checks). The goal of such *selective* searches is to find positions which can be evaluated more accurately by the static evaluation function, since they are (more) quiescent (as they relate to the dominant material term). In this sense, the notion of *quiescence search* was coined.

It is interesting to note that most of today's competition programs for chess do not include significantly more move selection criteria in their quiescence search than those already proposed some decades earlier. Their full-width search, however, has become much deeper as a result of better search techniques and faster hardware. As a consequence, overt occurrences of the horizon effect have become rare. Berliner (1981) showed why this effect does not directly influence the move decision at the root of a deep search tree often.

Nevertheless, a more advanced quiescence search can be useful. Kaindl (1982a,b) presents a model and its realization in the chess program *Merlin*. The results with this approach are quite good for the considered criteria, but it is rather expensive to provide a complete set of such criteria. In particular, the control of such a search is hard and has been achieved only through elaborate mechanisms.

Another approach has been called *forward pruning*, which involves only the search of "plausible" moves, with the remaining ones simply discarded.

(Note, this has to be distinguished from backward pruning which demonstrably does not alter the results.) Of course, the principal problem of this approach is that a move may initially look "implausible," but is in fact good (e.g., a sacrifice). Hence, there is always the possibility of making a wrong decision because of the omission of an important move. For this reason forward pruning is no longer used throughout a search tree, but has proven successful by building a full-width tree to a fixed depth and then continuing the search in a selective fashion. Consequently, the distinction from a quiescence search is somewhat fading.

One can distinguish between different forms of forward pruning. *Tapered forward pruning* selects a predetermined number of moves depending on the level in the tree; the deeper the tree, the less the moves considered (Greenblatt, Eastlake and Crocker 1967). *Aspiration forward pruning* estimates values for the moves and compares them with the current values of α and β. If an estimate is outside this interval then the corresponding move can be omitted because it would not influence the result, given that the estimate is correct (Berliner 1974). Although this method is conceptually more interesting, tapered forward pruning is easier to implement. Another approach is called the *method of analogies,* which tries to avoid searching moves again in "analogous" situations (Adelson-Velsky, Arlazarov and Donskoy 1975). Unfortunately, this ambitious approach, although more closely paralleling the human example, seems difficult to implement successfully.

The most promising approach for searching to variable depth appears to be making the horizon of the full-width search variable. A simple but effective implementation of this idea in many of today's competition programs is not to count replies to check as a ply of depth. In effect, whenever such half moves are contained in a path, it will be searched the corresponding number of plies deeper. This way the horizon is made variable in certain forced variations but, unfortunately, also in cases where the value cannot influence the result of the search. (Because of the usually small number of legal moves in check situations this is not important here. But with other criteria, for instance in relation to captures, this is critical.) For this reason, the method has been refined in *Merlin* in such a way that an optimistic estimate of the value has to be greater than the best value up to this point (*Best* in Figure 8.4). This made the additional inclusion of forced checks and of certain captures possible. For more details and a general model for extending the horizon, see Kaindl (1983).

The basic problem with such estimates is that they require considerable domain knowledge and are, nevertheless, rather uncertain. Therefore, the dynamic discovery of such information is a useful idea, for instance to find out whether a variation is forced. Using *minimal windows* (like PAB in Figure 8.6), this approach gives excellent results, especially with fast hardware. In particular, the *singular extensions* algorithm has potential (Anantharaman, Campbell and Hsu 1988), although considerable work remains to be done (Anantharaman 1990). Moreover, a combination of knowledge and such searches may be useful.

The approaches to implement searching to variable depth sketched above are all based on minimaxing. Recall the scheme of B*, which does not require artificial bounds for the search depth at all. Unfortunately, the difficulty of coming up with appropriate evaluations is even greater there. Nevertheless, there exist two successful implementations on this basis, albeit for a restricted domain of tactical chess (winning material or checkmating).

The first was in the program *PARADISE* (Wilkins 1982), whose search method corresponds more closely to *SB** (Palay 1983), a variant of B*. There are additional mechanisms for search control involved, partly based on the work of Berliner (1974) and partly related to planning. Basically, considerable domain dependent knowledge in the form of patterns was used. The results are rather good, when deep search is necessary. However, this application of knowledge is slow, and errors may occur because of a missing piece of knowledge. Unfortunately, it is not clear how this approach could be extended to a tournament chess program.

The implementation of PB* by Palay (1983) is based on a completely different idea. The evaluation process itself uses shallow searches. For obtaining optimistic and pessimistic bounds of a position, the *null move* is used (a "move" which only alters the side to move). Though, of course, not being legal in chess, in the general situation it leads to a worse result than the better legal moves. In this way the null move helps the program recognize threats for both sides. The results (using the variation PSB*) are better than those of *PARADISE,* but this is partially a consequence of using distribution functions instead of intervals for representing the evaluations. The approach of combining searches at two levels, instead of the explicit manipulation of domain knowledge, is appealing. However the dynamic computation of evaluations via search is expensive.

It should be noted, that the null move idea has already been used widely. Although Adelson-Velsky, Arlazarov and Donskoy (1975) and Beal (1989) describe uses for forward pruning, Wilkins (1982) and Kaindl (1983) show the possibility of handling threat situations within quiescence searches based on it. Further details can be found in Chapter 9 *Experiments with the Null-Move Heuristic*.

Finally, let us mention approaches that guide the search to variable depth in a domain independent way. McAllester (1988) proposes a method of keeping track of the number of leaf nodes whose values have to change for the value at the root to change by a certain amount. Schaeffer (1989c) presents an algorithmic formulation and the first results in the domain of chess using these *conspiracy numbers*. While this method is based on minimaxing, Rivest (1988) proposes approximating the max and min operators by generalized mean-valued operators. These allow for determining the leaf node for selection, on whose value the (approximate) value at the root most highly depends. Both these methods will have to be investigated more thoroughly to allow for an accurate assessment.

8.8 The Decision Quality

By far, minimaxing is the most widely used method for implementing games like chess on a computer, and it is the most successful method in practice. For a long time, there was also universal agreement on its usefulness. However, the discovery of *minimax pathology* by Nau (1980) (and the subsequent work of several authors) demonstrated that in certain game trees minimax search can also have detrimental effects. It has been proven that under certain conditions the move decisions based on minimaxing can become systematically *worse* with increasing search depth.

In principle, the discovery and investigation of this phenomenon is quite important. Many practitioners use minimaxing without questioning its utility or thinking about alternatives. Unfortunately, most of the theoretical investigations trying to show the reason(s) for the observed effectiveness of minimax search in practice are not really convincing. Occasionally, the theoretical work is even interpreted in such a way as to imply this method would be bad in principle. Although a comprehensive treatment of this topic is impossible here, a critical overview exists (Kaindl 1988b). Nevertheless, let us briefly sketch the basic problem.

Pearl (1984) emphasizes the following conceptual defect of the minimax back-up rule: computing a function of the estimates, as if they were the true values, instead of an estimate of the function. Pearl also constructed a "real" game reflecting exactly the structure and properties of a theoretical game tree in which the true values of the nodes are completely independent of each other. The initial configuration of such a game is constructed by randomly assigning each square of its board one of two possible values, independently of the values of the other squares. The rules of this game are such that these values correspond exactly to the (true) leaf values of a tree with constant branching degree and constant depth. In this game, pathological behavior of minimaxing has shown up. Investigations by Nau (1983a,b) show that by introducing certain dependencies between the values, the pathology disappears (essentially the same thing is shown by Beal (1980,82) and Bratko and Gams (1982)). Although originally independent distributions were assumed for the true and heuristic values, introducing dependencies between the true values in some form of "clustering" changed the results.

Even these theoretical investigations cannot convincingly explain the enormous utility of minimaxing observed in practice. For instance, the tables in Nau (1983a) show only modest improvements in decision quality using minimaxing with increasing search depth. Unfortunately, the models of "improved visibility" and "traps" investigated by Pearl (1984) was much simplified, so that their relationship to practice is questionable (Kaindl 1988b).

None of these models takes the properties of the usual evaluation functions in dynamic domains into consideration; they almost exclusively include static aspects. The search has to cope with the dynamic aspects. For this reason, the tree model of Kaindl (1988b) is based on the concept of quiescence. The additional new assumptions reflect observations from computer chess practice. The errors of statically evaluating quiescent situations are usually smaller than those of evaluating non-quiescent ones. (Why else are resources spent for quiescence search?) Moreover, in such dynamic domains most of the situations are non-quiescent (relative to the existing evaluation functions). More recently, Scheucher and Kaindl (1989) have defined another formal model of quiescence and investigated the class of tree models based on this and the previous one. The behavior of these models generally corresponds quite well to observations in practice, particularly the model based on the more restrictive definition of quiescence. This approach may help to bridge the gap between theory and practice for the decision quality of minimax lookahead, which has proven essential for the success of today's chess machines.

9 Experiments with the Null-Move Heuristic

G. Goetsch and M.S. Campbell

9.1 Introduction

The strength of the current generation of chess programs is strongly correlated with their search speed. Thus, any improvement in the efficiency of the tree search usually results in a stronger program. Here we describe a technique, called the *null-move heuristic,* that can be effectively used to improve search speed with only a small chance of error. Although the technique has been previously used in specialized programs for chess tactics, this chapter describes an implementation suitable for general chess programs.

9.2 The Null Move

The null move changes only the side to move in the game state. It is not a legal move in the game of chess, but is legal in other games such as Go. Even if legal, it would rarely be the best move in a chess position. The class of positions where the null move would be best are named *zugzwang* positions. For the vast majority of chess positions, the right to make the next move is advantageous because at least one of the legal moves available to the player would strengthen the position.

The null move is effective in practice in identifying positions in which one side is lacking in tactical threats. For example in a position with white to move, if white can give black an extra move without significantly impairing the position it is usually the case that black has no tactical threats against white. If black's extra move seriously impairs white's position then tactical threats for black may or may not exist. White can often use the move to solidify the position, thereby eliminating black's threats, though it may also be the case that black has threats even after white makes a move.

An earlier version of this chapter appeared in the 1988 AAAI Spring Symposium Proceedings, pp. 14-18.

The research was sponsored by the Defense Advanced Research Projects Agency (DOD), ARPA Order No. 4976 under contract F33615-84-K-1520 and monitored by the Air Force Avionics Laboratory.

Since the null move is almost always worse than the best move, the value it returns can serve as a lower bound on the value of the current position. Frequently this value serves as a reasonably tight lower bound. If the value returned causes a cutoff (or narrows the window), and is computationally cheaper to evaluate than the best legal move, we can speedup the search. It is possible to conduct a full search (to the normal depth) beneath the null move, but this is unlikely to be computationally cheaper than evaluating a legal move. To make the null move evaluation cheaper, we do a limited search of the null move to a shallower depth than the legal moves in the position.

The null move can form the basis for a family of forward-pruning algorithms. The principal theme is that the null move can be evaluated with a *reduced depth search* and used to *estimate* a *lower bound* on the heuristic value of the position. The null-move search has the effect of causing a cheap cutoff of the search, if one side is behind (below the window) and has no "threats," with the definition of threat determined by the results of the search.

It must be emphasized that using null-move search as a forward-pruning mechanism can reduce the accuracy of the minimax computation. It is assumed that the null-move value is not greater than that of the best legal move. If this assumption is violated, it may be pruned away incorrectly. By selective use of the null-move search, the frequency of errors can be reduced to a such a level that their effects are dominated by errors in the heuristic evaluation function.

9.2.1 Advantages

The advantage is reduced search effort. If we perform a reduced depth search of the null move to a depth one less than a normal search of a legal move and the branching factor is five, for example, then the null move evaluation costs roughly one fifth that of evaluating a legal move (to the normal depth). If the value returned by the null-move search is sufficient to cause a cutoff then it would be faster to examine it in preference to any of the legal moves.

9.2.2 Disadvantages

(1) Wasted effort when the null move fails to produce a cutoff (or raise the bottom of the search window).
(2) The value returned by the null-move search may not be a lower bound on the value of the position. This failure could be due to one of the following:
   • Zugzwang. A zugzwang position is one in which a player would be lost (or badly weakened) if forced to move next, yet might be winning if the opponent were to move next. In these positions, a player desires to forfeit the move. These are positions where having the next move is a disadvantage. There are subclasses of the zugzwang positions:
   Mutual zugzwang.
      Both players are in zugzwang and whoever must move next will lose. Allowing the null move will change the outcome.

Single zugzwang with waiting move.

The player in zugzwang will lose, since the opponent can safely make a waiting move that will then compel the player in zugzwang to move.

Single zugzwang without waiting move.

The player in zugzwang will lose only if on move, otherwise the opponent must make a move that will release the zugzwang.

- Horizon Effect (Berliner 1974). This is a consequence of reducing the number of moves available to the opponent in the null-move search. If black has an unstoppable 2-move threat, a 4-ply search will recognize it. If the reduced depth search for the null move is too shallow, the program will not recognize the threat. Consequently it will think that the null move allows it to avoid the threat. This gives the program the option of limiting the search horizon to avoid an unstoppable threat. Consider the position in Figure 9.1 with white to move. A program that evaluates each of the legal moves with a 3-ply search will recognize that white is lost, e.g. 1. Qb3, Qh3 2. Qxb7, Qg2 mate. A program with reduced depth null-move searching would evaluate the null move with a search of 2 ply or less (for example, 1. null, Qh3 2. Qb3, and evaluate white as being ahead a rook). Thus the program would incorrectly estimate that white stands better by at least a rook in the diagrammed position. The search reduction associated with the null move allows the program to fool itself by not allowing black to complete the mating attack.

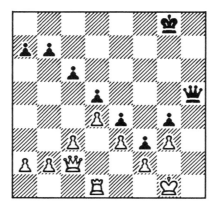

Figure 9.1: The horizon effect.

The frequency of failure of the null-move heuristic varies with the characteristics of the position. Positions encountered during a chess game can generally be categorized as one of the following:

- Opening game positions: characterized by the undeveloped state of the board, with many pieces still on their original squares. Tempi are extremely valuable in these positions and no errors resulting from the null move have been observed.
- Open middlegame positions: characterized by open pawn structures and the presence of many pieces. Errors caused by the horizon effect occur very rarely, allowing use of the null move.
- Closed middlegame positions: characterized by locked pawn structures. Horizon effects occur occasionally, e.g. as one player slowly builds an unstoppable attack against a weak pawn. Errors can occur, but are sufficiently rare to allow the use of the null move.
- Endgame positions: characterized by having few pieces of the board. Zugzwang positions are common, and the lack of highly mobile pieces leads to horizon effect difficulties as pawns and kings plod across the board. The null move frequently fails miserably in these positions preventing its safe use.

9.3 Implementation

To evaluate the utility of the null-move search, a series of experiments were performed with a modified version of the *Hitech* chess machine (see Chapter 6 *Hitech*). The *Hitech* machine consists of special-purpose chess specific hardware communicating with a microcode engine that operates under the control of a software program running on a host Sun 3[1]. To avoid undue complications in testing alternative versions of the program, no modifications were made to the hardware or microcode. All subtrees encountered during the search with search depths of 5-ply or less were evaluated by the *Hitech* hardware with a standard $\alpha\beta$ minimax search. Control of the program in manipulating the shallower portions of the search tree were retained by the software with which alternative implementations of the null move were explored. The program was tested over sets of positions from *Hitech*'s recent tournament games.

9.3.1 Basic Hitech Implementation

Suppose the search arrives at a node with a window (α, β) and a remaining search depth of d-ply. Before searching the legal moves to depth $d-1$, the null move is searched to some reduced depth $d-1-r$ and returns a value v. The returned value, v, is treated as if it were returned for a normal search on a legal move, either causing a cutoff, raising the bottom of the window, or having no effect. The null move is disallowed if any of the following are true:
- The moving side is in check. Playing the null move when in check does not result in a legal chess position.

---

[1] *Hitech* has since been upgraded to a Sun 4.

- The search is at the root of the search tree. At the root of a tree, a move is being selected rather than a value being computed. Thus including the null move makes no sense, since a null-move cutoff does not help select a move.
- A previous move on the current variation was a null move. This simplifies the implementation.

9.3.2 The Transposition Table Refinement

A program using a transposition table to cache results of partial searches (Slate and Atkin 1977) can use the following refinement to improve the effectiveness of the null-move search. The critical assumption made with the null move is that the right to move is advantageous. The value of a tempo (move), t, is assumed to be ≥ 0. We can apply this assumption to eliminate some of the null-move searches. Consider a position n with white on move. The transposition table may contain information on this position based on searches made in previous iterations. Assume that the transposition table contains a value, v_h, that is an exact value or an upper bound, and that the position has been previously searched to depth d_h. A search will be made to evaluate the position, n', resulting from making the null move in position n. Since the two positions are identical except for the loss of the right to move for white, we know that the value of position n' should not exceed $v_h - t$ provided that the null move is searched to at least depth d_h. Therefore, if $(v_h - t) < \beta$, the null move should fail to cause a cutoff, and if $(v_h - t) \leq \alpha$, it should fail low. Under these circumstances, we do not make the null move.

9.3.3 Other Uses of the Null-Move Search

The *Kaissa* program (Adelson-Velsky, Arlazarov and Donskoy 1975) used a null-move search to the normal depth in positions where one side was significantly ahead. The idea was that the null move might produce smaller subtrees that would be evaluated faster than legal moves and would still produce a cutoff, although there is no evidence that it had a significant effect.

Palay's (1983) work on adding probabilities to the B* algorithm (Berliner 1979b) used null-move searching to a fixed depth to calculate the lower and upper bounds for a position (as B* requires).

Beal (1989) proposes using the null move to enhance the quiescence search of a chess program. He created a second-order quiescence search to evaluate leaf nodes. Lower bounds for nodes within the quiescence search tree were estimated by making the null move and employing a conventional first-order quiescence search to the resulting position. The second-order quiescence search was not limited by depth, but stopped when sufficient convergence of the bounds was achieved.

Schaeffer (1987,89b) uses the null-move search in *Minix*, a tactical searcher that runs in parallel with the chess program *Phoenix*. The *Minix* implementation differs from the *Hitech* implementation in two ways:

- *Minix* uses a material-only evaluation function.
- *Minix* has a maximum depth for the null-move search (Schaeffer 1988).

9.4 Analysis

Assuming application of the null-move heuristic at a single position, we can estimate the reduction in search effort as follows. A standard d-ply search with an effective fixed branching factor of b should require the evaluation of b^d leaf nodes. A null-move search conducted with a null-move depth reduction r would require the evaluation of b^{d-r} leaf nodes. If the search results in a cutoff with probability p, the evaluation of pb^d leaf nodes will not be required because of the null-move cutoffs. The remaining $(1-p)b^d$ leaf nodes must be evaluated when the search fails to produce a cutoff. Therefore the total number of leaf nodes to be evaluated will be $b^{d-r} + (1-p)b^d$. Thus if $p = 0$, then the null-move searches are pure overhead ($b^d + b^{d-r}$). If $p = 1$, then the cost is reduced to that of the null-move search (b^{d-r}). From the above, we can determine that if $p > b^{-r}$ the total search effort will be reduced. For a realistic set of values, for example $p = 0.5$, $r = 1$, and $b = 4$, the overall search cost will be reduced. The effort expended on the null-move portion of the search would be nearly 25% of a conventional search, but will reduce the conventional search effort by roughly 50% for a net reduction in total search effort by approximately 25%.

A more complex analysis can be made allowing for the recursive application of the null-move search within each subtree. A standard assumption for such analysis is that the probability of the null move causing a cutoff is independent of its location in the search tree. Our experience suggests that this assumption is inaccurate. We refrain from further detail, in the belief that it would be misleading.

9.5 Experimental Results

The null move was initially evaluated by shallow fixed depth searches. Early experiments showed that shallow depth search evaluations of the null move were flawed because of horizon effects. Many threats could not be recognized by shallow depth searches. For example, a mate in 2 threat could not be detected by a 2-ply search.

The use of a fixed depth search to evaluate the null move is a form of forward pruning. Forward pruning in this context has the same disadvantages as when used in selective searches, i.e. the program will inadvertently prune away critical lines of play. In the case of the null move, it will evaluate a position as satisfactory since the null-move search reveals no threats for the opponents when, in fact, a few extra ply would show that the position is inferior. The bound from the null move is in error because of the horizon effect, and if the null move is always evaluated to the same depth, later iterations searching this position to a deeper depth will make the same mistake. For example, in Figure 9.1, a fixed-depth 2-ply null-move search will *always* overlook the forced mate for black.

We have used reduced depth searches ($r = 1$) to evaluate the null move, minimizing the horizon effect difficulties with fixed depth searches. These deeper depths allow the search to discover many non-obvious threats and defenses that would elude a shallower search.

If the null move is determined to be better than any of the legal moves in the position it indicates a failure of the heuristic. This could occur because of zugzwang or horizon effects as previously mentioned. If the null-move search returns a value within the search window, $\alpha < v < \beta$, and is determined to be the best move, we know that the heuristic has failed and the node should be re-searched without the null move. If the search returns $v \geq \beta$, we cannot determine if the true value lies below β without a full search that nullifies the advantage of performing the null-move search. Consequently we must accept null-move cutoffs as genuine.

Our current best implementation of the null-move search employs a minimal window search centered about β. This foregoes the opportunity to narrow the $\alpha\beta$ search window since a fail-low of the null-move search provides no information with which to narrow the bounds. The advantage is that the null-move search requires the least time with the narrowest possible window. The cumulative benefits of a small speedup of the frequent null-move searches dominate the less frequent benefits of narrowing the search window.

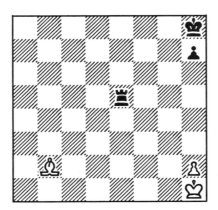

Figure 9.2: White to move, null-move search works.

Experience suggests that the null move should be tried even when the current evaluation is significantly below α. Far too often the losing side has a forced win of material (say it has pinned a piece) that cannot be avoided. For example, in Figure 9.2 suppose the expectation is that the position is about even.

White is currently behind in material, but allowing the null move will cause a cutoff: 1. null, any 2. Bxe5.

Although the null-move search seems well suited to detecting threats against material, it also functions well in detecting positional threats. In Figure 9.3 white stands to gain the advantage with 1. Rd7, moving the rook to the seventh rank and confining the black king to the back rank. If black attempts a null move after 1. Rd7, the null-move value will fail low. The value after 1. Kc2 and many other moves, will also fail low. If white plays 1. Rh1, then black may attempt a null-move search and the value will fail high. White has an advantage because of the opportunity for placing a rook on the seventh rank. While 1. Kc2 does not achieve that advantage immediately, it does maintain the threat of 2. Rd7 which Black cannot ignore, as indicated by the fail low of the null-move value. Alternatives, such as 1. Rh1, squander white's advantage by eliminating the threat of 2. Rd7. The fail high of the null-move search value recognizes this. In our experience a significant fraction (roughly half) of all null-move cutoffs are caused by values that are only slightly greater than β (less than a quarter pawn).

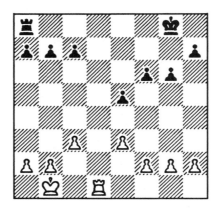

Figure 9.3: White to move, positional case.

The improvement discussed in Section 9.3.2 *The Transposition Table Refinement* has also been tested on *Hitech*. With this enhancement, the null move tends not to be attempted along the principal variation where it is least likely to be of benefit. Experience shows that occasional speedups of 5-10% will result in some positions, and that a slow down will almost never result. Over the span of test positions a small speedup of 1-2% was achieved.

The real benefit comes from minimizing the number of errors caused by null-move searching. Roughly half of all errors caused by null-move searching take place in positions that this technique identifies. Inadvertent cutoffs occur frequently in competitive positions which tend to occur on or near the principal variation. Positions that are not competitive because one side is dramatically ahead generate far fewer inadvertent cutoffs. By not attempting the null-move search in these positions, we drastically reduce the frequency of errors. Errors are infrequent, perhaps 1 position in 1,000 in endgames, but have a nasty habit of propagating changes in the values of subtrees up to the root. This may cause the program to choose an inferior move with unacceptable frequency.

We have found the performance of the null-move search to be variable from one position to the next. The magnitude of the total search reduction typically varies from 0% to 50%. Because of this great variability, we have characterized the performance of the heuristic in general terms only.

Our current best implementation of the null-move search results in an approximate 25% reduction of search effort in opening and middlegame positions for the *Hitech* program. We do not use null-move searches in endgame positions since the frequency of incorrect cutoffs has been excessive. We believe that reductions of up to 50% in the total search effort are obtainable with the null-move search heuristic.

9.6 Future Research

There are many promising ideas to improve the effectiveness of the null-move algorithm described in this paper:
- Shallower searches, e.g. $r = 2$, can be tried, reducing the overhead of the null-move search. Hopefully, the frequency of additional erroneous null-move cutoffs resulting from horizon effects will be acceptable. Initial experiments confirm additional speedups, but the effect on accuracy has not yet been fully explored.
- It can be assumed that the minimal value of a tempo, t, is greater than or equal to some small positive integer rather than ≥ 0. This permits a cutoff if the value returned by the null-move search exceeds $\beta - t$. This allows a greater proportion of the null-move searches to cause cutoffs, reducing the overall search time. The minimal value of a tempo, t, must be a lower bound on the value of a tempo to avoid inadvertent cutoffs. An appropriate value for t must be determined empirically. It would be dependent on the evaluation function and could vary during the course of a game.
- Generally if a null move fails to cause a cutoff in an early iteration, there is a high probability that it will fail in later iterations as well. For example, if the opponent is attacking a queen, the null move will generally fail miserably to the queen capture. By recording this information in the transposition table entry for a position, null-move searches can be avoided in positions where there is little hope for success.
- Allowing the null move to cause a cutoff can be dangerous, particularly in positions where *zugzwang* is possible. It might be reasonable, instead, to continue the search with a reduction in the search depth if the null move fails high. For example, if a null-move search with depth reduction $r = 2$ fails high, search the legal moves with depth reduction $r = 1$ instead of the

normal depth. Only if this reduced depth search fails to find a cutoff is the node searched to its normal depth. This idea may allow the use of the null-move heuristic in endgames.

9.7 Conclusions

Tournament chess programs face real-time constraints in making their specified time control. They desire to maximize the value of their computations per unit time. The null-move heuristic allows a program to examine a search tree in less time with an acceptable reduction in accuracy for most phases of a chess game.

Previously the null-move heuristic had been used in specialized tactical chess programs. This article has shown that this heuristic can be usefully employed in general chess programs, with potential savings of up to 50%.

10 Problematic Positions and Speculative Play

P. Jansen

10.1 Introduction

When commentators annotate chess games, they make use of various symbols to show their evaluation of moves or positions. For example, one might find something like 23. Re1? −+, indicating that white's 23rd move was bad ('?') and the position is now lost ('−+'). Whereas '?'s can have game-theoretic significance, '!'s ("very good moves") and '!!'s ("excellent moves") do not (since it is not possible to turn a game-theoretically lost position into a draw or win). The meaning of a '!' (and other evaluative symbols) must therefore be found, not in a game-theoretic analysis of the game, but rather in its "psychological" aspects.

In a little-known paper, Simon (1974) discusses the difference between what is perceived as a bad move ('?') by human chess players, and the game-theoretic concept of a losing move. A main parameter in Simon's exposition is the proportion of moves that are *problematic* as distinguished from *obvious*. In his model, Simon assumes that a player makes mistakes only in problematic positions, but then with a probability of at least 50%. He does not attempt to further characterize this concept or investigate under what circumstances other evaluative comments besides question marks would be used.

It seems that such problematic positions deserve more attention. Indeed, it is precisely in these positions that the best move would be called "very good" or "excellent." Even though chess annotators seem to have widely different conventions for deciding when to use an exclamation mark, most people agree that the best moves in problematic positions should be both (1) better than the alternatives and (2) hard to find. Sometimes (especially in studies or problems) it is required that the move be the only move to preserve the game-theoretic result.

This chapter is a revised version of a paper in the *New Directions in Game-Tree Search Workshop* proceedings, T.A. Marsland (ed.), Edmonton, May 1989, pp. 122-134.

This research was sponsored by the Defense Advanced Research Project Agency (DOD), ARPA Order No. 4976, Amendment 20, under contract number F33615-87-C-1499, monitored by the: Avionics Laboratory, Air Force Wright Aeronautical Laboratories, Aeronautical Systems Division (AFSC), United States Air Force, Wright Patterson AFB, Ohio 45433-6543.

In spite of the efforts of several researchers to incorporate fallibility of the opponent into their search models (McAllester 1988; Michie 1986a; Russell and Wefald 1988; Teague 1988), minimax search has not conclusively been shown to be inferior for real games (Teague 1988). Minimax also remains the only method for which significant speedups can be obtained (with the $\alpha\beta$ algorithm).

How can we then, in the context of a minimax search, take game-tree dynamics into account to come up with an explanation of why some moves are considered good? This chapter is an attempt to describe the meaning of a *good move* and *problematicity* in psychological terms. As a first approximation, we look at the relation with search effort, and show how this information could be gathered and applied in programs used for tournament play or annotations.

Here we try to characterize what would lead a chess commentator to use an exclamation mark in his analysis, and how we could use this information for practical play.

Although no chess game can be won without mistakes of the opponent,[1] people prefer to ascribe a win to their own merits rather than to such mistakes. How this credit is assigned is not an obvious matter, however. The chess encyclopedia and informants (Matanović 1989) limit exclamation marks to "very good" and "excellent" moves, subject to the interpretation of the annotator.

Note that, somewhat counter-intuitively, whether a move deserves an exclamation mark is not so much a characteristic of the move (and the resulting position) itself, but rather from the initial position from which the move was made. It seems logical therefore to define *problematicity* as a characteristic of a *position* rather than of a move. This leads to a strongly related concept, the *difficulty* of a position.

In this chapter, problematicity is, as a first approximation, linked to the evolution of values during the search. Two intuitive classes of problematic positions are described. A few example positions are analyzed, and the possibilities and appropriateness of speculative play discussed.

10.2 Extracting Information from Search Statistics

First we review some basics of iterative-deepening $\alpha\beta$ search. More detailed descriptions can be found in Chapter 8 *Tree Searching Algorithms*.

Using *iterative-deepening* in game-tree search (especially in combination with $\alpha\beta$ search and the use of a transposition table) has proven to be beneficial in several respects. In the worst case it uses only slightly more time than a direct search up to a given depth, allowing a progressive reordering of moves (speeding up $\alpha\beta$ by allowing more cutoffs), as well as search termination at arbitrary times (with obvious advantages in tournament play).

Even more time can be saved when *aspiration search* is used. In aspiration search, the assumption is made that the principal value v_d for a search to depth d

---

[1] Assuming that the initial position is a draw, of course!

(or d-ply) is probably not very different from the value v_{d-1} of a $(d-1)$-ply search. Thus time can be saved by using a small $\alpha\beta$ window around the v_{d-1} to obtain the initial $\alpha(d)$ and $\beta(d)$ parameters for the next level d. When the actual v_d lies outside this window, however, only a bound will be obtained. This is called *fail high* when $v_d \geq \beta(d)$ and *fail low* when $v_d \leq \alpha(d)$. In the latter case the tree has to be re-searched with a new window.

In an abstract sense, the meaning of fail-high and fail-low at the top level is that expectations, based on previous search information, are violated. In other words, nodes in one or more branches in the search tree turn out to have been evaluated incorrectly (at least in comparison with what we know at this point in the search), and it was necessary to search down to the current depth to detect this fact.

If we assume that the most important terms in the evaluation function used in a computer program (material balance, for instance) correspond more or less to the terms used by humans most of the time, the search effort spent by the program to discover the change in evaluation can be assumed to be roughly proportional to the search effort needed by a human player. In fact, since humans are not all that good at searching, the human will need *much more* time to reach the same conclusion.[2]

At least one component of the (human) opponent's behavior can therefore be modeled by considering the *evolution* of values of moves in terms of search depth (and therefore search effort required). Taking simple search statistics into account (like fail-highs and fail-lows) provides a much more reliable basis for estimating probabilities that the fallible opponent will select certain moves, than just taking a function of the final values only. Furthermore, since searching seems to be a major weakness in human players, it seems logical to concentrate on this information for a first approximation.

10.2.1 Computing Problematicity from Search Data

What is a good move in terms of search characteristics? Important elements that characterize a move as being good, are
(1) the difference in final evaluation with alternative moves and
(2) the (negative) difference in evaluation with alternatives up to some certain large depth D.
To incorporate at least some element of the human forward pruning, we add:
(3) the (negative) initial difference in evaluation with the alternatives.[3]
Note that this definition is dependent on the evaluation function, search method and search depth of the program, as well as on certain apparently arbitrary

---

[2] Note that we ignore the human's strong points here: the right piece of knowledge may be equivalent to a deep search, and some Grandmasters can work out extremely long lines (but selectively). The given assumptions are therefore bound to fail from time to time, which is why a program should not aim for speculative play in general (see Section 10.4 *Speculative Play*).
[3] In practice this could be the result of a shallow search.

parameters (such as D). Experimentation is necessary to show their appropriateness.

10.2.2 Two Types of Problematic Positions

At this point we can make a rough distinction between several classes of problematic positions, roughly corresponding with an intuitive classification. For example, one class is "the best move is not obvious" and a second, "the obvious move is not best."[4] Looking at it from the point of view of the opponent, whose move led to the position under consideration, we can call these *swindle positions* and *trap positions* respectively, even though they need not follow necessarily from inferior moves.

To simplify the exposition, assume A and B are are two alternatives being considered, of which A is the "good" move. Figure 10.1 and Figure 10.2 give the values of the moves (V) as a function of search depth (positive values are good for the player now on move). The shaded area is an indication of the deceptiveness of move A. Move S, the values of which are also shown in the figures, is the best move in the (hypothetical) alternative position that would have arisen when the opponent had played the best move.

In a *swindle position* (Figure 10.1) the (eventually) best move A seems to be worse than alternative B when searching less than some critical search depth D ("the best move is not obvious"). A reason for bringing opponents to this position, rather than some quiet and objectively better alternative position (with best move S), may be that under some circumstances we do not expect them to find A, leading to a potential net gain of $V_S - V_B$. In other words, we are *swindling* our opponents; we hope they won't find the best continuation. Note that in the example, by playing B the opponent thinks our move was best (since the $\min(A, B)$ looked inferior to S, because the search depth was inadequate).

In a *trap position* (Figure 10.2), B appears to be an excellent move as long we search less than D-ply deep ("the obvious move is not best"). Such a situation may arise when we set a trap for our opponent and hope that he goes for the obvious move. If the alternative was S, the opponent thinks we blundered (since A looks much better than S). Again we can hope for a gain of $V_S - V_B$.

Psychologically speaking, this pure version of a trap may not be effective (since it is "too obvious," which might make an opponent suspicious). However, for now it seems best to leave it at this simple classification, and defer a more complex analysis until more experimental data is available.

Ideally, statistics should be gathered both about which depth D is appropriate (as a function of playing strength) and about how significant evaluation differences are with respect to the outcome.

As a first step, we propose to include the following parameters into a measure of goodness:

---

[4] Thanks to Bert Enderton for this concise description.

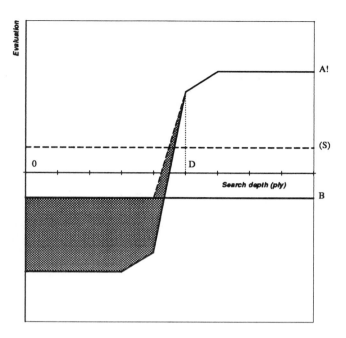

Figure 10.1: Swindle position.

(1)   initial differences with alternatives,
(2)   final differences with alternatives and
(3)   integrated effort until crossing.

Any such measure should incorporate the heuristic that the more alternatives there are with the above characteristics, the larger the "goodness" of the move. It should also include how much better the move is than the alternatives in terms of final values, and possibly how much worse initially (for example, from a 3-ply search), since that determines how likely it is for the move to be pruned by a selective searcher.

We could therefore propose a formula of the following form for the goodness of move m:

$$G(m) = \sum_{j \neq m} \left[f(v_d(m) - v_d(j)) g(v_1(j) - v_1(m)) \sum_{i=1}^{d} (max(v_i(j) - v_i(m), 0) b^i) \right]$$

Here m is the best move after a d-ply search (full search), j any legal move, $v_i(j)$ the value of move j after an i-ply search, b the (effective) branching factor, and f and g two functions to be determined. The factor b^i provides a weighting according to (approximate) search effort required. The formula is a summation over the product of three terms, corresponding to the three parameters mentioned above.

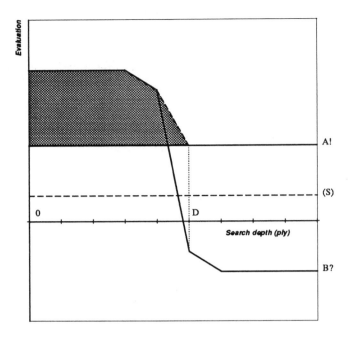

Figure 10.2: Trap position.

One factor of the *difficulty* of the position can then just simply be the goodness of the best available move. However, we may also want to use different functions f and g, and include terms relating to the overall variability of values.

10.3 An Example

To get a feeling for the practical value of the ideas presented in the previous section, the chess machine *ChipTest* was used to gather manually[5] some statistics about the search in a few positions in which the best moves would receive exclamation marks from human annotators. For most of the positions examined, the elements discussed in the previous section show up clearly.

In the following graphs, as well as in the stylized figures of the previous section, the backed-up evaluations for several children nodes of the root position are shown as a function of search depth. The evaluations a standard tournament program (like *ChipTest*) would print out, when searching this position in a game, are indicated by the dashed line (i.e. the maximum value over all legal moves at each depth[6]). The thicker line traces the evolution of the (eventual) best move.

---

[5] By entering all the separate moves to be searched.

[6] Actually, various search extensions complicate this issue in the case of *ChipTest*.

The shaded area is the positive part of the difference between those two curves (indicating how much less than the current favorite the eventual best move is evaluated during the search). Without being in any way numerically accurate, this area gives a good qualitative indication of the proposed measure of problematicity. In general, the larger and more to the right the area, the better the best move.

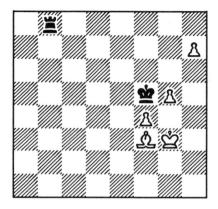

Figure 10.3: Prototypical problematical position.

As an example of a problematic position, consider the position in Figure 10.3. Although white seems to be much better materially speaking, the game could easily become a draw because of black's threat to sacrifice the rook for the white f- and g-pawns, thus obtaining a drawn ending of h-pawn with bishop of the wrong color against king. The best move in the position turns out to be the one that initially looks the worst: 1. Be4+! secures promotion by forcing the black king away from the h-pawn. Figure 10.4 shows that this position has all the required characteristics of a swindle position. Initially the best move has a much worse value than many alternatives, it remains worse for some time, but in the end it is much better.[7] An opponent might easily miss this opportunity.

10.4 Speculative Play

As has been pointed out many times before, making the objectively best move may not give a player the best practical chances in the case where the opponent is fallible: in some situations making a non-optimal move may increase the (practical) chances to obtain a win (or draw).

---

[7] The values for ten of these alternatives are shown in the figure.

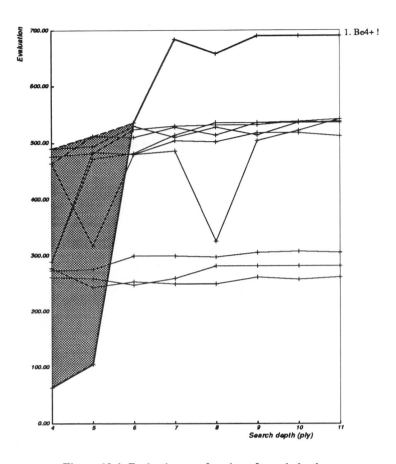

Figure 10.4: Evaluation as a function of search depth.

When one computer program plays another, this kind of *speculative play* is only appropriate when one program is able to look at least 2-ply deeper than its opponent. Indeed, not only does it have to see everything the opponent can see, but it also has to detect major changes in evaluation that happen in the *next* ply of search. Taking into account that, on top of this, extra information has to be gathered, it seems that the right conditions for speculative play are unlikely to occur among computers.

Against human opponents, however, it may be perfectly justifiable to play an inferior move which leads to a problematic position. The following situations (or any combination of them) are candidates for speculative play:

(1) the position is lost anyway,

(2) the opponent is (thought to be) much weaker,

(3) the opponent is in time trouble,

(4) we really need to win this game (for example in the last round of a tournament), or

(5) we have to make a choice between (otherwise) equal looking alternatives.

Since in this last situation it cannot hurt to incorporate some extra information, speculative play may have an absolute value as well. In the case that bonuses are given for problematicity of the opponent's positions at depth 1,[8] one way to incorporate the above elements would be to weigh the bonuses according to some combination of the factors given above. Alternatively two different values can be computed, one of which is the standard minimax value v, and the other the "expected value" v'. Here we could base a decision on the "effective value" $v_e = \xi v' + (1 - \xi)v$ in which ξ is a coefficient which indicates "trappy-ness" and varies between 0 and +1, negatively correlated with the opponent's strength and time and our objective evaluation v of the position, and positively correlated with our ambition/necessity to win.

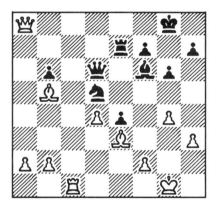

Figure 10.5: *Duchess – Kaissa* (black to play).

The foregoing can be illustrated with Figure 10.5, showing a critical position from a game between the programs *Duchess* and *Kaissa*, Toronto, 1977 (Michie 1986b). In this position *Kaissa* played 1. ... Re8 and lost after another 15 moves or so, sending the desperate *Kaissa* programmers into an all night debugging session. In fact, the move *was* really the best (i.e. prolonged the game the most) in the given circumstances. After the only alternative move 1. ... Kg7, there would have followed mate in five via 2. Qf8+! Kxf8 3. Bh6+ Bg7 (or Kg8) 4. Rc8+ Qd8 5. Rxd8+ Re8 6. Rxe8 mate. That several hundred people, including a former World Champion, missed this mate clearly indicates that this position is problematic and that, against a human opponent, *Kg7 would have been the better move.*

---

[8] By increasing the evaluation of the top-level moves by a value based on the problematicity of each resulting position.

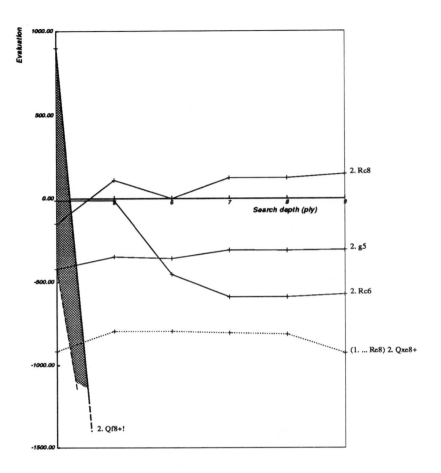

Figure 10.6: Evaluation as a function of search depth.

Figure 10.6 represents the search data from this position graphically in the same style as the previous figures, but with the evaluations from black's point of view. The position after Kg7 is clearly a swindle position: the best move is non-obvious, even though it is really good.[9] Compare Figure 10.6 with Figure 10.1 (taken upside-down as we look from the other player's perspective). Given that the alternative 1. ... Re8 2. Qxe8+ (S) is a clear loss, and 1. ... Kg7 2. g5 (B) is tenable (at least for a while), the decision ought to be clear.

---

[9] This position is even more problematic than would seem from the figure. Since all the moves are checks, *ChipTest* extends to the mate almost instantaneously, making the surprise look more shallow than it would for a human. Also, many programs would not be able to find the mate with the same nominal depth.

10.5 Practical Considerations

There are a number of issues that must be considered if problematic play is to become an integral part of a chess program's search algorithm.

Computing the backed-up evaluation of a large number (or all) of the top-level moves (rather than just a bound for most of them as done by the $\alpha\beta$ algorithm) can be expensive. This need not be a problem when the program is used for annotations, but may considerably slow down a tournament program. Several fast approximations are possible, however. The following is a brief list of possibilities:

(1) If singular extensions (Anantharaman, Campbell and Hsu 1988) are used, a fail-low of the singular favorite indicates a potential swindle *if* the opponent's best move changes. This still requires singularity testing of the top-level move. Also, it is not obvious how to discern traps this way.

(2) Compute exact values for all second-best moves. This has important side benefits (for example for time control algorithms), and the singular extension algorithm almost already does this. Also, this allows a direct approximation of a speculative value.

(3) Approximations for problematicity can also be gathered from a comparison between a (full) shallow search and the regular deep search (for example, search all the children up to 5-ply and compare their ranking with the results of the standard search).

(4) Finally, from simply inspecting the number and depths of fail-highs and fail-lows, useful information may be gathered.

Another issue is the problem of reliably measuring position difficulty. Some measures of position difficulty have been proposed, but all ignore the search history of individual moves. For example, Michie (1986b) argues that the effective branching factor is the main criterion for difficulty. Although this is certainly related to how difficult a player perceives a position to be, it ignores certain important aspects. Indeed, if all moves are essentially equivalent, the position is easy, even when the branching factor is high. Conversely, when only two moves are to be considered, the decision may be difficult and crucial.

The number of singular extensions may be another criterion (also easy to compute if the search does this anyway), but again does not incorporate how obvious the singular moves are. An argument in favor, however, is that when the forced lines to be considered are long, a human player is more likely to make a mistake along the way. This means that there should at least be some correlation with perceived difficulty.

10.6 Future Work

There are several areas where the study of problematic play can make important contributions. The section outlines several promising areas for further work in applying these ideas.

10.6.1 Database Play

For several endgames with up to 6 pieces, the distance to win or mate has been computed and stored for all possible positions (see, for example, Thompson 1986). When a computer program recognizes the board position as one of those positions, it can simply look up the exact value of its successors, and choose the objectively best move.

This works fine when the computer has either the stronger side in a won ending or the weaker side in a drawn position. In the former case, the program will play optimally towards a win, while in the latter (where a win is out of the question anyway), it will avoid decisive mistakes. When the program has a losing position, or the stronger side in a drawn position, however, the fact that the opponent may not be perfect becomes important. If the program could exploit the weaknesses of its opponents in such cases, it could increase its chances for a draw or win respectively.

Levy (1987) proposed to improve a computer's database play by giving bonuses for the number of mistakes the opponent can make in a given position, leading to a preference for moves in which the opponent has a higher likelihood to go wrong. In a similar spirit, we intend to try out a variation of our technique (i.e. using the concept of difficulty based on evolution of the evaluation as a function of search depth) on various endgame databases. Note that in this case efficiency is not an issue, since a game-theoretically optimal decision can be made based on simple table lookup.

10.6.2 Annotating Games

Identifying problematic positions is crucial in automated analysis of chess games as well. In a sense, a computer analysis is a lesson from a computer teacher. For this lesson to be effective it is necessary that the program be aware of the weaknesses of its students.

The advantage here is that the analysis need not be done in real-time and can therefore be much more thorough than what is possible under standard tournament conditions. The program also has the possibility to backtrack when it finds errors in its own analysis.

On the other hand, a teacher has to provide understandable explanations (even of inferior variations), has to be able to judge when and how deep to analyze, needs access to several individual features, and some concept of attack (threat) and defense. In all these cases the program needs to be able to judge the *interestingness* or *importance* of a position under consideration, a criterion which is intimately related to problematicity.

10.6.3 And More ...

Considerable psychology literature is available on how humans play chess. Some of this information could be used to build up a knowledge base about human chess strategies. For example, this knowledge base could contain data about moves likely to be subject to forward pruning by a human (even mate or stalemate can easily be overlooked!), information on what a human is likely to have learned from books, and indications of which positional features a human may attach the most importance to. Finally, there seems to be an interesting application for various machine learning techniques here, related to the identification of opponents (as a group and/or individually), as well as to the game itself.

Acknowledgments. I would like to express my thanks to Murray Campbell, Herb Simon and Jonathan Schaeffer for many stimulating discussions and comments on drafts of this paper, and to the *ChipTest* Team for letting me use their machine for my experiments.

11 Verifying and Codifying Strategies in a Chess Endgame

I.S. Herschberg, H.J. van den Herik and P.N.A. Schoo

11.1 Background

Only a short time ago, the game of chess was a research area in which artificial intelligence (AI) workers without specific chess knowledge could achieve significant results. Notably, AI techniques (representation, search heuristics including their sophisticated refinements, etc.) were tested in endgame domains of three or at most four pieces. Anything beyond this number was practically excluded by the extreme complexity and huge fast-storage requirements. The construction of omniscient databases, as described by van den Herik and Herschberg (1985) and by Thompson (1986), was made possible by the arrival of supercomputers which overcame the previous storage limitations, and which had enough computational power to handle the complexity issue in reasonable time. For a treatment of these issues, see the works of Dekker, van den Herik and Herschberg (1987b), and van den Herik and Dekker (1988).

Although in the construction of small databases for simple endgames complete information can be obtained by an exhaustive enumeration using full-width backward chaining (van den Herik and Herschberg 1985), for larger databases heuristics still seem to have a role. This is especially true in the construction of five- and six-men databases, whenever such an endgame converts to a different one, as Dekker, van den Herik and Herschberg (1987a) and van den Herik, Herschberg and Nakad (1987) report.

Current developments seem to indicate that heuristics, with the uncertainty they are bound to introduce, can be eliminated, at least in some cases. This elimination, automatic in the sense of *programmable,* promotes the domain to which it is applicable from high plausibility to verifiable certainty. The work leading to this reduction of uncertainty for five-men endgames with at most one pawn was done by Stiller (1989). This has recently been generalized by Dekker

This chapter contains minor revisions from one of the same title in the *New Directions in Game-Tree Search Workshop* proceedings, T.A. Marsland (ed.), Edmonton, May 1989, pp. 95-105. It also appeared in the *Journal of the International Computer Chess Association*, vol. 12, no. 3, pp. 144-154, under the title "Verifying and Codifying Strategies in the KNNKP(h) Endgame."

(1989), who allows an arbitrary number of pawns to be included among the *n* pieces, albeit the computer speed limits its applicability to $n \leq 5$ at present writing. Dekker has constructed a generic endgame-database-building program which, in theory, is able to build the 32-piece-endgame database. During construction of a database, his program can be set to consider castling as well as *en passant* capture, though it does not consider the 50-move rule.

To end our digression and to summarize the results of "Complexity Starts at Five" (Dekker, van den Herik and Herschberg 1987b), we recall that the construction of the KNNKP(h) endgame uses a prospective analysis over all subdomains adjacent to the KNNKP(h) domain and reachable by conversion therefrom. These conversions, ten in number, may be grouped into four classes of subdomains: (1) KNNKA, (2) KNKP, (3) KNNK and (4) KNKA, in which A stands for Any of Q, R, B, N. Determining potential final positions is considerably simplified by noting that class 3 and class 4 can be safely excluded. This assertion is proved by classes showing that the set of continuations in class 3, *in so far as it results from KNNKP(h)*, is empty in a certain sense; so is class 4. This assertion is proved by Dekker, van den Herik and Herschberg (1987a) by eight *lemmatics*, where the latter term is defined as involving theorems and proofs of heuristic assumptions. The emptiness of the classes is equivalent to the statement that within the classes excluded, while it is true that white can mate, this side cannot do so without black's departing from optimal counterplay. Since prospective endgame analysis assumes optimal play by both sides, the classes are safely excluded from the analysis. Processing the result of this prospective analysis, the retrospective relations between the KNNKP(h) domain and its adjacent domains are depicted in Figure 11.1. An arrow indicates a possible conversion from KNNKP(h) to the adjacent domain involved in the inverse sense. The result of the backward-chaining enumeration is a database of 57,802,752 positions (i.e., $7 \times 64^2 \times \binom{64}{2}$).

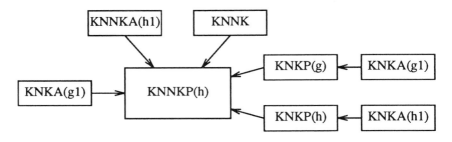

Figure 11.1: Retrospective view of KNNKP(h) and its adjacent domains.

The implementation of the database is a *packed linear one-dimensional array*, say M, in which the index, say j, of each array element is a suitably chosen bi-unique mapping of a board configuration. The contents of M[j] (eight bits) by convention are:

        −1   for an illegitimate position,
        0   for a drawn position and
        n   for a win-in-*n* position, $n \leq 254$.

The 50-move rule draw has been dealt with separately by Dekker, van den Herik and Herschberg (1987a). Once the (~60Mbyte) database has been constructed, it is a trivial matter to determine the (an) optimal move for any position. (There may be several equipollent optimal moves.)

The major issue, though, is to find an acceptable justification for the database-derived move being optimal. In this sense acceptability is defined in terms of Grandmasters' notions; after all, these are the human experts in the domain. To paraphrase, while it is true that *locally* the database explicitly holds perfect information, *globally* speaking it is incapable of formulating a strategy. Yet it is our belief that such a strategy *must* exist, however implicitly.

11.2 Human Expert Analysis

A.A. Troitzky (1866-1942), whose fame rests on the endgame studies he composed, has spent a major part of his life in Russia in the investigation of the intricacies of the KNNKP(h) endgame. We quote two of his principal results as statements A and B below (Troitzky 1934).

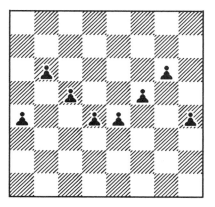

(a) The extreme black pawns' positions.   (b) The Troitzky zone.

Figure 11.2: Properties of the Troitzky endgame study.

11.2.1 Statement A: Safe Blocking of the Pawn on h4

Following Troitzky (1934) we refer to Figure 11.2(a), effectively condensing eight different endgames (or four if symmetry with respect to the mid-board vertical is considered). Troitzky's statement A reads:

The endgame is won for white provided the black pawn is no more forward than the positions indicated for the various pawns in Figure 11.2(a) <u>and</u> the pawn is *safely blocked.*

Again following Troitzky, the notion of being *safely blocked* amounts to two simultaneous conditions:

- that white can protect the blocking knight when the latter is attacked by the black king <u>and</u>
- that neither of the knights can be the victim of a forced capture by black.

11.2.2 Statement B: The Troitzky Zone

By statement A, the position is *always* a win for white provided the pawn is *safely blocked* on h4, h5, h6 or h7. Blocked pawns on h3 and h2 are special cases. Troitzky (1934) has made a profound analysis of positions with the pawn on h3 and concluded that some of these still are won, whereas some others are drawn, but only just! The crucial discriminant is whether the black king can move to the corner square a8 *in time.* Troitzky asserted that there is a contiguous area for the black king to occupy such that black can reach the safe square a8 without problems. This area, dubbed the safety zone by Troitzky, has since become known as the Troitzky zone (see Figure 11.2(b)). Troitzky's second statement B can be paraphrased as:

> Whatever the positions of the mobile knight and the white king, the game is drawn whenever the black king is within the Troitzky zone.

11.3 Computer Verification of Troitzky's Statement A

More than once in the past few years, the chess world has been faced by computer analysis that essentially improved accepted chess theory. The works of Thompson (1986), and van den Herik, Herschberg and Nakad (1987) provide typical data. This circumstance made it plausible that human statements about complex problems would contain some, possibly minor, errors. This circumstance motivated us to investigate to what extent Troitzky's statements would stand against the omniscient database constructed previously. Describing the steps of this investigation below, we have attempted to draw the reader into the spirit of our quest as it developed.

11.3.1 Determining the Winning h-Pawn Ranks

In the chess world, the statement that a certain type of position is "always" won regrettably often means that the position is generally won except for special circumstances. These special circumstances have been found to occur in the precise interpretation of the notion *safely blocked* in statement A. A trivial instance of such a special circumstance forcing a different interpretation of *safely blocked* is hinted at by the position [WK a1, WN h3, WN a8; BK c6, BP h4], in which white is bound to lose his knight. This shifts the problem from the definition of *safely blocked* to the definition of a *forced capture*. This example, trivial to a chess player, arouses the suspicion that more such special circumstances may be found and may be less trivial to the human expert. This gives rise to a subproblem of how to list (exhaustively!) all positions to which the special circumstances apply. Evidently, manual determination of the special circumstances is out of the question and the task before us is constructing a program effectively capable of listing, more generally, all configurations satisfying a given (special) class characteristic. As a tentative definition of these special circumstances, we intuitively singled out four classes of special configurations:

(1) black captures a knight;
(2) black chases away the blocking knight;
(3) enforced repetition of positions;
(4) the immobility of both knights.

Initially, only classes 1 and 2 were identified as classes of special configurations (i.e., classes to which special circumstances would apply), because they most obviously sprang to mind. However, as the investigation progressed, we stumbled on classes 3 and 4, even though these arose in a different context. To us, these findings imply that the possibility of other classes remains. Still, we did not see our way to define them conceptually on the mere existence of the database available to us.

11.3.2 The Tablebase Technique

An exhaustive enumeration of the positions of class 1 may, in principle, be done by any of three techniques.

(a) We singly consider all drawn positions from the database and determine whether an n-ply prospective search involves losing a knight. This technique is profligate of computer time, firstly because we have to search to n-ply with n unknown in advance and possibly large, secondly because perusing the database may well lead to useless repetition of search by reason of identical subtrees having to be searched time and again.

(b) We construct a database in the usual representation, the goal state not being "white mates" but "black captures a white knight." This again requires some 60M bytes of storage. The attendant disadvantage here is that almost all entries will contain a 0 (zero), corresponding to configurations in which no knight can be captured. The reason simply is that there is only a handful of configurations in which a knight *can* be taken.

(c) We build a *tablebase* containing relevant positions only. In this context a *relevant* position is a position in which either one of the knights can be captured or in which the knight is *forced* to take the pawn. (Databases confirm chess theory that the successor game KNNK is then drawn.)

We have opted for the *tablebase* approach. The tablebase is a two-dimensional array, named C for capture information. In the first column of C, the *key field,* we record the configurations' representation, and in the second column of C, the *distance field*, we note the corresponding number of moves to either knight capture or pawn loss. The number of paired entries is not known in advance but is strictly limited to the number of rare configurations where these captures or losses can occur. The number of paired entries is not known in advance but is strictly limited to the number of rare configurations where these captures or losses can occur.

Building the tablebase is closely analogous to building a conventional endgame database. Initialization is by recording all configurations leading to the capture/loss indicated in one move. Subsequently we search for all positions leading to this result in *two* moves. The process extending the number of moves terminates as soon as no new such positions are found for the next tentative value of the distance field.

11.3.3 Combining Tablebases

For the special configurations of class 1, the tablebase *takeknight* was constructed. Similar to the procedure in the database, the convention obtains that in the position stored in the key field, white is to move (WTM). With *takeknight* in hand, it was found expedient to renounce construction of a distinct tablebase for class 2, because it may well happen that black aims a combination of goals. For instance, black may first threaten to enclose a knight in a corner (the class 1 goal) and, if prevented from doing so by white, may still pursue the goal of chasing away the blocking knight. This type of position (goal 1 having been frustrated shifting to goal 2 or conversely) could well fail to be recorded in any tablebase, barring special devices. Schoo (1988) has shown that the problem can be overcome by the construction of a tablebase which allows for such a combination of goals. Accordingly, *badblocked* was built.

11.3.4 Resolving the Tablebase with the Database

By construction, *badblocked* enumerates all *not safely blocked* positions common to classes 1 and 2. It is now a valid research goal to try to find additional drawn positions in which the pawn is *not safely blocked*. For this purpose we inspect all positions in the database in which the knight is blocking the pawn and which have been recorded as drawn. Next, these positions are searched for in *badblocked*. There are now precisely two mutually exclusive possibilities:

(a) if the position in question occurs in *badblocked*, we evidently have a configuration which is drawn by reason of the pawn being *not safely blocked*;

(b) if the position in question fails to occur in *badblocked* we have a drawn configuration, which by our preliminary interpretations of *safely blocked* would be a *safely blocked drawn* position!

Positions coming under (b) intrigued us. Their occurrence might point to:

(i) the incorrectness of the characterizations we chose for *safely blocked*;

blocking WN	black pawn	# of positions
h6	h7	61
h5	h6	9
h4	h5	21
h3	h4	28

Table 11.1: Discrepancies between the database and *badblocked*.

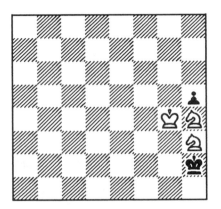

(a) White to move, loses a knight.

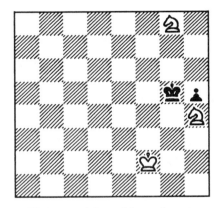

(b) A surprising white stalemate.

Figure 11.3: Two types of drawing situation.

(ii) the existence of concepts other than those so far considered which yet play a decisive role in the outcome;

(iii) the falsity of Troitzky's statement A.

The resolution of the database with *badblocked* resulted in finding 119 positions absent from *badblocked* that the database indicated a draw. Table 11.1 presents them, broken down by the positions of the blocking knight and the pawn.

With only 119 discrepant positions visual inspection was possible. It turned out that both (i) and (ii) were at the root of these discrepancies. When investigated more closely the following was found:

(1) When constructing *badblocked* we had blithely assumed that, provided no unprotected knight is under attack, none of the knights can be captured on the next move. The position of Figure 11.3(a) shows that this assumption was unjustified. (In the diagram the black king does not threaten the knight on h3 by definition, because the latter is protected by the white king. Yet the black king is able to capture the knight on the next move because the white king is in check. After white's move, the knight no longer is protected and may then be captured by the black king.)

(2) The remainder of the positions turn out to be drawn by an amazing stalemate strategy: one of the knights is under attack and white, on trying to preserve this knight, stalemates black. An example is provided in Figure 11.3(b): white may protect the blocking knight by moving Kg3, resulting in black's being stalemated "pat in the middle of the board."

An exhaustive check showed that on this closer analysis, all 119 positions should have been characterized as *not safely blocked*. This is because of the loss of a knight in group (1) and the sacrifice of a knight in group (2), if white is to avoid stalemate.

Moreover, we may infer that there are no positions coming under class 3 of Section 11.3.1 *Determining the Winning h-Pawn Ranks*, which implies repetition of positions. Similarly, the nullity of class 4 is evident, because there are only two mutually exclusive possibilities:

- either one of the mutually protecting knights blocks the pawn, in which case the position is won with the pawn on h4, h5, h6 or h7, or
- neither of the knights (again providing mutual protection) blocks the pawn, in which case the position is irrelevant for the investigation.

11.3.5 Troitzky's Statement A Confirmed

The foregoing has shown that every *drawn* position with a blocked pawn on h4, h5, h6 or h7 always is *not safely blocked*. Rephrasing this, we have found that there are *no* positions which are both drawn **and** *safely blocked*. As a corollary, there is no position disproving Troitzky's statement A. For completeness sake, we still have to prove that draws exist in which the pawn is *safely blocked* on h3. Troitzky's statement B, constructively defining the existence of a safety zone, however, is a strong pointer to the occurrence of draws with a *safely blocked* pawn on h3.

As a result of our research, we are in a position to append a qualification to Troitzky's statement A:

> The maximin[1] of all combinations in which black may capture a knight or may chase away the blocking knight is 4 moves for a blocked pawn on h4 to h7 inclusive (Schoo 1988, p. 21).

11.4 Computer Verification of Troitzky Statement B

11.4.1 The Verification of the Extent of the Troitzky Zone

Verifying or falsifying the correctness of the extent of the Troitzky zone, with a fixed pawn on h3 and therefore a blocking knight on h2, is a simple problem in computer terms. In passing we note that discrepancies as per Table 11.1 do *not* arise with the pawn on h3. For each black king (BK) position we determine the

---

[1] The maximum of the minimums.

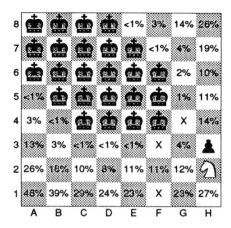

Figure 11.4: Troitzky's zoning laws as confirmed.

number of legitimate won positions with arbitrary but legal placements of the
white king (WK) and the non blocking white knight (WN). When divided by
the total number of legitimate positions involving the BK position under
investigation, we obtain a fraction which may be regarded as the probability of a
win. Converting to percentages and rounding to the nearest integer, the results
are inscribed in Figure 11.4. Where the diagram shows a black king, the
percentage is exactly zero. To rephrase, should the black king (BK) be found on
such a square, the position can *never* be won for white. The crosses (on f1, f3
and g4) indicate the illegitimacy of the BK ever being found there under our
assumption of WTM.

We find that the BKs as shown in Figure 11.4 *exactly* correspond to the
Troitzky zone as given in Figure 11.2(b). This in turn implies the *complete
correctness* of Troitzky's statement B, published as long ago as 1934 and hence
without the benefit of computer assistance. This is an impressive achievement,
the more so because the area outside of the Troitzky zone contains squares
which have less then 1% chance of winning. We can safely infer that Troitzky
must have discovered these rarest of all positions and must have been aware of
how to convert them into a win. Our admiration knows no bounds.

11.4.2 A Basic Strategy for Searching the Troitzky Zone

In Section 11.4.1 *The Verification of the Extent of the Troitzky Zone* we have
effectively proved that with the h3-pawn *blocked* and the BK in the Troitzky
zone, the position is drawn. It follows that positions from which the BK can
reach the safety zone are also drawn. A fascinating investigation now arises:
under what conditions, given a blocked h3-pawn, can a position be characterized
as a draw? To provide a partial answer to the question we stipulate from results
previously obtained in this paper that given a blocked h3-pawn, the following

n	# of positions	n	# of positions
1	39028	7	252
2	25024	8	86
3	12983	9	64
4	4915	10	114
5	1537	11	22
6	387		

Table 11.2: Count of positions and their distance (n) to the Troitzky zone.

classes of positions are *certainly* drawn:
  (a) the BK is within the Troitzky zone, or
  (b) the BK can reach the Troitzky zone, or
  (c) the black pawn (BP) is *not safely blocked.*
It is well worth remarking that if a position comes under none of (a), (b) or (c), it should be regarded as **not** (*yet*) classified and definitely **not** as automatically won. For positions under (a), the inclusion under (a) is immediate: we merely have to read off the position of the BK. Likewise, positions under (c) are available immediately from the tablebase *badblocked* which served us earlier in this investigation (Section 11.3.3 *Combining Tablebases*).

To determine the set of positions coming under (b), a tablebase *runsafety* was built. Without going into details, we must note that the problem signalled in Section 11.3.3 *Combining Tablebases* recurred: some positions threatened to escape classification under (b) because they would, in a good strategy, alternately pursue the goals implied by (b) and (c). In its final version, *runsafety* therefore combined the characteristics of *badblocked,* of the BK being in the Troitzky zone and the h3-pawn being blocked by a WN. Table 11.2 exhibits the results from *runsafety* where *n* is the number of moves needed by black to achieve its goal, assuming mutually optimal play. Consider, though, the validity of the notion of optimal play in these circumstances (Levy 1987). From Table 11.2 it follows that the maximin for reaching the Troitzky zone or chasing away the blocking knight is 11 moves. Figure 11.5 shows one of the 22 maximin instances. An optimal path is 1. Kf3 Kd1 2. Ke3 Kc2 3. Kd4 Kb3 4. Kc5 Ka4 5. Kb6 Kb4 6. Nd6 Kc3 7. Kc5 Kd3 8. Kd5 Ke3 9. Ke5 Kf2 10. Ke4 Kg2 11. Ng4 h2 and white is forced to capture the pawn, whereupon the game is drawn.

It is worth noting that black attempts to reach the Troitzky zone as the first objective. Having been frustrated in this purpose by white's king pursuit, black switches to the subsidiary strategy of chasing away the blocking knight. This example is apt to show why a naive *runsafety* tablebase will not suffice.

Figure 11.5: A maximin example leading to a draw.

11.5 Strategies for Mate-in-n Positions

In Section 11.4.2 *A Basic Strategy for Searching the Troitzky Zone* we have presented a sample result of a strategy for black indicating, be it only by way of example, *how* a drawn position can be handled in such a way that it will result in an actual draw, the latter being defined as a position which is an undoubted draw to all expert observers. A much more interesting problem (and correspondingly more difficult) is to formulate a strategy for white indicating *how* to handle a *won* position (van den Herik and Herschberg 1986). Several approaches for the KNNKP(h) endgame have been proposed (Schoo 1988), but none of them so far has led to explicit rules-to-be-followed. This is not utterly surprising when we remember that the maximin of the won KNNKP(h) endgame is no fewer than 115 moves.

11.5.1 Strategies from Depth Charts?

A depth chart for an n-men endgame is a chess diagram showing $(n-1)$ men in well-defined positions. The notion of *depth chart* was introduced by Roycroft (1986a). The n-th piece is free to be located on any of the unoccupied squares. The number recorded in the square is the distance-to-mate, assuming WTM. The occasional X denotes an illegitimate placement of the missing piece. Such depth charts may serve as heuristics to discover strategies. Examples, again specializing to KNNKP(h), follow.

Figure 11.6(a) is a depth chart with a *safely blocked* h5-pawn, similarly Figure 11.6(b) is for the h4-pawn. Let us consider square a4, just above the BK. The h5-chart yields the value of 10, the h4-chart shows 61. (Depth charts for h6, h7 show 9 and 10, respectively.) Clearly, there is something afoot with the pawn

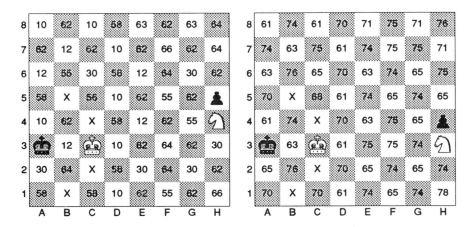

(a) Depth chart for the h5-pawn.   (b) Depth chart for the h4-pawn.

Figure 11.6: WTM mating distances for the other knight places.

position, which we surmise from the dramatic increase in mating distance. To some extent this becomes explicable after placing the missing white knight on a4. The move 1. Na4-b2 keeps the BK confined. This being so, with the *safely blocked* pawn on h5, h6 of h7, the knights will have little trouble in mating the BK. This is no longer true for the *safely blocked* h4-pawn. Clearly, this relates to the number of tempi required to mate without allowing the pawn to promote to a queen. This is confirmed by producing an optimal winning sequence: it transpires that the BK is not mated in the a1-corner, but will have to be chased all over the board until it meets its fate in the h8-corner. We may therefore conclude that the a1-corner is far from ideal for black, given that the pawn is located on h4. This in itself does not constitute a strategy but could be regarded as containing the germ of one.

11.6 Tentative Generalizations

From the blow-by-blow description of our research activity, it is readily deduced how difficult it is to verify extant statements about chess knowledge and to formulate strategies when truth down the last detail is a requirement. Finding new heuristics is even more difficult, and this has not yet been attempted. Rather, we have made a start in developing new techniques for verifying existing heuristics, especially when these have been cast in rule form, which amounts to the construction of *tablebases*. What we *have* achieved is a generalization of *tablebase* construction, which proceeds automatically after two procedures have been suitably initialized:

- the procedure *relevant* indicating the types of positions in question, and
- the procedure *goalwards* specifying the goals black aims to achieve.

11.7 Conclusions

The conclusions listed below are limited in scope, having been derived from an investigation of the KNNKP(h) endgame, in which it has been attempted to formulate rules guided by an omniscient database. The finding of rules is delicate, so the research has been largely confined to testing extant rules. Applying new techniques and greatly improved hardware, the present rules have been checked for their correctness. The techniques employed are generally suitable, in our view, for the purpose of extracting knowledge from endgame databases. The results obtained are summarized in the conclusions hereafter.

(1) Whenever the BP is *safely blocked* on any of h4, h5, h6, h7, the position is won for white (Section 11.3.5 *Troitzky's Statement A Confirmed*).

(2) The maximin to a draw of a *not safely blocked* position is 4 moves (Section 11.3.4 *Resolving the Tablebase with the Database*); this statement applies to blocked pawns on any of h4, h5, h6, h7.

(3) The Troitzky zone as defined by Troitzky (1934) turns out to be unassailably correct (Section 11.4.1 *The Verification of the Extent of the Troitzky Zone*).

(4) The maximin for reaching the Troitzky zone (and thus drawing) is 11 moves (Section 11.4.2 *A Basic Strategy for Searching the Troitzky Zone*).

(5) Depth charts only give limited indications for the strategy to be followed. While they are a potential aid in formulating strategies and classifying positions, exploiting this aid is far from easy for experts and programs alike, chiefly because it is far from clear what characteristics are important enough to be a prime consideration. Here again, the fundamental difference between knowing *that* and knowing *why* is revealed.

Acknowledgments. The construction of a first version of the database has been made possible by the Netherlands Organization for the Advancement of Pure Research (ZWO, now NWO, file number 39 SC 68-129) by their donation of computer time on the SARA (Amsterdam) Cyber 205. Until early 1987 the Delft University of Technology was the home base for the research described. Thereafter, the home base shifted to the Computer Science Department of the University of Limburg. It took only some 52 hours to reconstruct the nearly 60-Mbyte database on an Apollo DN-4000 workstation (autumn 1988), the availability of which is gratefully recognized. So is the contribution of the research in the framework of the ACHILLES project (Automation of CHess Intelligence using Expert Strategies), part of a joint research effort between IBM and the University of Limburg. Finally, we are glad to state our great indebtedness to Mr. Chr. M. Bijl, librarian of the Bibliotheca Van der Linden-

Niemeijeriana in the Royal Dutch Library for making available his bookmanship and familiarity with the intricate endgame domain.

12 Learning in Bebe

T. Scherzer, L. Scherzer and D. Tjaden

12.1 Introduction

Most chess programs are deterministic. They will always play the same move for a given position, and so may experience problems in tournaments when an opponent follows a line of play that produced a loss for the chess program in an earlier round. In 1982 we noticed this phenomenon when *Bebe* lost the same game repeatedly during extended (8 hours) speed chess sessions against humans. *Bebe* has depth controlled access to a transposition table (T-table) (Slate and Atkin 1977), but during a speed game it would only use about 25% of the table, because the depth limit was 5 plies. Thereafter the T-table was left intact between games, hoping to startle opponents when *Bebe* played moves different from the previous game. The psychological effect on the opponent of a computer that appeared to be learning was often devastating enough to give *Bebe* a victory. The effect was short-lived because after 5 games little remained in the T-table from the first game. We did not explore this idea further until 1986, when the danger of losing the same game twice during the 5th World Computer Championship was large enough to warrant action.

We decided to try the idea of saving the board positions that occur during a game in a special section of memory that would be copied to the T-table at the beginning of each search. Effectively this gave *Bebe* deeper look ahead if an opponent tried to repeat a game from a prior round. This scheme is similar to that described by David Slate (1987), and is related to the rote learning introduced by Arthur Samuel (1959,67). We were able to determine from case studies that for specific examples the method would achieve the desired results. The larger question was, if the scheme was implemented for all positions in a game, would there be measurable improvement in *Bebe*'s play against an opponent? The answer to that question is the subject of this paper.

12.2 Terminology

The algorithm presented here was implemented in our chess-playing program. Some of the phenomena observed from our learning algorithm may be peculiar to that program, although it is a typical full-width, iterative-deepening, alpha-beta chess program with a quiescence search. One significant difference is that the positional score value is computed at a fixed nominal depth of search, i.e., ply 5 in a 5-ply search. The quiescence search only adds or subtracts material to the basic positional score determined at the nominal leaf node. This gives *Bebe* a positional horizon effect as well as the usual material horizon effect. Another difference is the inclusion of checking moves in the first few levels of the quiescence search. Also included at all levels of the quiescence search are pawn moves to the 6th and 7th ranks (pawn moves to the 8th rank are considered as captures, and so are automatically included). The quiescence search also requires that getting out of check must be proved, not assumed. Finally, *Bebe* can only search to odd numbered depths. This is partially because the asymmetric scoring functions make it difficult to compute a score at an even ply. As is increasingly popular, the program also retains the T-table between moves during a game.

12.2.1 Short-Term Memory

The algorithm depends on having T-tables that are accessed by the program during searches. The T-table will be called Short Term Memory (STM) in this paper because of the short life expectancy of the entries, at most several minutes. These entries are from internal and leaf nodes in the search. Each entry is 16 bytes, of which 12 bytes are stored, and 4 bytes are used as the memory address. An STM entry consists of:

4 bytes	Hash code used as STM memory address.
4 bytes	Hash code used for match verification.
2 bytes	Search height.
2 bytes	Position score lower limit.
2 bytes	Position score upper limit.
2 bytes	The move.

One STM entry is created for every node reached during a search, and so without special controls the table can easily be flooded. *Search height* holds the height of the subtree on which the score is based. The search height of the leaf node is always 0. The search height of the node just above the leaf node is 1, and so on. *Position score lower limit* and *upper limit* are the lower and upper bounds of the score for the position. Both values are needed for the easiest implementation of the learning algorithm. *The move* is the move that achieved the position score at this node.

12.2.2 Long-Term Memory

The algorithm also requires a special memory for storage of game positions. This is called Long-Term Memory (LTM). The entries in LTM are retained between games and, if a disk drive is available, can theoretically be retained forever. The LTM entries have a 16 byte format similar to the STM entries, but all 16 bytes are stored in a simple linear table. An LTM entry consists of:

4 bytes	Hash code to be used as STM memory address.
4 bytes	Hash code used for match verification.
2 bytes	Depth of search.
2 bytes	Move number.
2 bytes	Position score.
2 bytes	The move.

One LTM entry is created for each root node during a game. *Depth of search* is the search depth that was completed at the root node. Iterative-deepening is used, and only information from the highest completed search is stored in the LTM. *Move number* is the number of the move within the game. *Position score* is the score that the search returned from the root node. *The move* is the move that was actually played at this point in the game.

12.3 The Algorithm

The basic algorithm consists of two processes. One creates LTM entries at the conclusion of searches. The second transforms and copies LTM entries to STM at the start of searches. LTM is never examined by the search process itself.

12.3.1 Creation of LTM Entries

After the search of the position at the current root node, an LTM entry is created to hold the score at the root node, the depth of search and the move played. The score must be adjusted by any "contempt factor" (a measure of the estimated superiority/inferiority of the program over its opponent) that is being used, to bring it to a zero contempt equivalent. This entry is then added to LTM by a linear search. The search checks each entry for a complete hash code match and, if equal, overwrites the older entry. If no matching entry is found, the new entry is added to the end of the list. Storing by move number (lower move numbers have priority) is not a good technique, but we could not devise an algorithm that expressed the concept of 'usefulness.' All game positions are stored. No attempt was made to decide which positions were critical to the game.

This method only uses one LTM entry per position stored. Therefore a 40-move game only requires 40 entries in LTM, regardless of the number of times that game is played. If there is no room in the table, the new entry is allowed to overwrite any entry with an equal or greater move number. Although storage space would seem to be no problem with disk, the load time (Section 12.3.2 *Transformation from LTM to STM*) would quickly become large in relation to the allowable time per move. We also allowed the algorithm to create LTM entries during ponder searches from a predicted opponent move, even when the opponent did not make the predicted move. This requires some extra table space, but speeds up searches during game replays.

12.3.2 Transformation from LTM to STM

The transformation of LTM entries to STM entries is done at the start of each
search. The process is simple because of the similarity of the formats of the two
entries. The hash code is left unchanged. Depth of search in LTM entries is
identical to search height in STM. Position score from LTM must first be
adjusted from its zero contempt equivalent to reflect the current contempt factor.
STM position scores are then calculated by:

Position score lower limit = position score − tolerance, and
Position score upper limit = position score + tolerance.

Tolerance is the amount that the score is "fuzzed out" (Slate 1987). It is used as
an estimate of the error in *Bebe*'s scoring function and allows the algorithm to
'see' through a score in one position to the score in a following position. We
prefer to use the term tolerance for this value because it is the amount that is
added to, and subtracted from the position score to get an upper and lower limit
range. The values of mates and draws are not changed by the tolerance when
transforming from LTM to STM. Draws and stalemates are identified as
positions with a score of zero. Theoretically, other positions could also have a
score of zero, but this happens so infrequently that we just ignored the
possibility. Checkmates are identified by their numerical proximity to the
machine's internal high and low values. For now, the tolerance is preset at the
beginning of a series of games. The tolerance value has many effects on the
searches, and it will be discussed again later in Section 12.5 *The Experiment*.

At this point complications arise. They are caused by time dependent
information in STM. If the current game move number is 20, there are LTM
entries for each move of this game that have been copied to STM, along with
moves and scores. Because these entries are positions that have already
occurred in this game, their scores do not reflect draw by repetition chances. We
therefore require another process after the LTM to STM transformation. It
consists of regenerating all current game positions and putting them in STM
with a draw score. These will then overwrite the transformed LTM entries from
the current game. This is an important step. Without it, the machine could try to
avoid a drop in score by trying to get back to a previous position. These entries
in STM are then referenced by the program's T-table lookup routine during its
normal search. Since they have a search depth from prior games, they give the
program a glimpse of the future.

12.3.3 An Example

Table 12.1 shows some of the effects of the learning algorithm on the play as
black for the first 8 moves of the Queen's Gambit. We played only 8 moves,
quit and then played again. Principal variation moves that were correct in the
sense of actually being played in the game are shown in italic type. Scores in
game 2 that differ from game 1 are in bold.

Game 1			Principal Variation				Score
1.	Pd4	Pd5	Nc3	Pe6	Bf4	Nc6	−0.201
2.	Pc4	Pxc4	*Pe3*	*Pe5*	*Bxc4*	Bb4+	+0.125
3.	Pe3	Pe5	*Bxc4*	Nc6	Nf3	Bb4+	+0.141
4.	Bxc4	Pxd4	Qxd4	Qxd4	Pxd4	Bb4+	+0.267
5.	Pxd4	Nc6	*Nf3*	Be6	Bg5	Bb4+	+0.224
6.	Nf3	Bb4+	*Nc3*	Qe7	Be3	Be6	+0.073
7.	Nc3	Nf6	Pd5	Qe7	Be3	Bxc3+	+0.091
8.	0-0	0-0	Bf4	Bg4	Pa3	Bxf3	+0.160
Game 2			Principal Variation				Score
1.	Pd4	Pd5	Nc3	Pe6	Bf4	Nc6	−0.201
2.	Pc4	Pxc4	*Pe3*	*Pe5*	*Bxc4*	*Pxd4*	**+0.142**
3.	Pe3	Pe5	*Bxc4*	*Pxd4*	Nf3	Pxe3	**+0.142**
4.	Bxc4	Pxd4	*Pxd4*	Nf6	Nf3	Bb4+	**+0.260**
5.	Pxd4	Nc6	*Nf3*	Be6	Bxe6	Pxe6	**+0.198**
6.	Nf3	Bb4+	*Nc3*	*Nf6*	*0-0*	*0-0*	**+0.035**
7.	Nc3	Nf6	Pd5	Qe7	Be3	Bxc3+	+0.091
8.	0-0	0-0	Bf4	Bg4	Pa3	Bxf3	+0.160

Table 12.1: First two plays through a game with learning on, and 0.125 tolerance.

In game 1, *Bebe* has no LTM entries for this opening, and so produces the moves shown. The principal variation lists reasonable moves, except for the 5th ply in moves 2 through 4, as a consequence of giving a bonus to checking moves at the leaf ply. The scores are erratic because of special bonuses and penalties for piece development and center control in the opening. In Table 12.1 the large drop at move 6 is due partially to the loss of the checking move Bb4+ at the leaf node. The increase at move 8 is associated with castling and the asymmetry of *Bebe*'s scoring functions (especially for king safety).

In game 2, the program played the same moves, but many principal variations and scores changed. At move 1, there is no change because none of the positions in the principal variation have an LTM entry. Scores, principal variations and moves selected will not change unless there is at least one LTM entry for a position in the principal variation, and that LTM entry has a score that is different from the search score by the tolerance value. Moves 2 and 3 show the effect of the LTM entry from move 4. In game 1 at move 4, the position was stored in LTM with a score of +0.267. This position is reached in the principal variations of game 2. The STM entry that is found has a score lower limit of 0.267−0.125 = 0.142, and a score upper limit of 0.267+0.125 = 0.392. The lower limit becomes the new score at moves 2 and 3. The score at move 4 drops from 0.267 to 0.260 because ply 2 sees that Pxd4 is better for white than Qxd4.

The score at move 5 drops because of the STM position at move 6 that has a score upper limit of 0.073+0.125 = 0.198. Move 5 also illustrates one form of 'blockage.' The 3-ply score of the sequence Be6, Bxe6, Pxe6 is +0.223, and this is actually the sequence selected by the 3-ply search at move 6. The 5-ply search shows that Be6, Pd5, Bb4+, Nc3, Bxc3+ has a value of −0.002, and therefore Be6 is never played. With no LTM entry with the −0.002 value, the search will continue to over-value move 5. At move 6, *Bebe* entirely rejects the game 1 principal variation in favor of one that matches the actual play in game 1, despite the score being lower than the original principal variation. The score at move 6 is the lower limit from move 8, which is 0.160−0.125 = 0.035. There are no changes for moves 7 and 8 because the scores are within the STM score limits, and there are no LTM entries for moves 9 and 10.

The algorithm also affects search times. In replays, the STM entries with their score bounds will produce faster searches because of the validity of the move in them and the extra cutoffs that their score upper and lower limits cause. Another effect is attributed to better principal variations. In game 1, 4 of the first 6 moves have a principal variation that correctly predicts the opponent's move. In game 2, this has risen to 5 of 6. Here, to keep the example simple, we did not use thinking on the opponent's time. When we enable the option, *Bebe* conducts 4 extra searches in game 1, at moves 1, 4, 7 and 8, while assuming a move that the opponent did not make. These searches also create LTM entries that may affect the searches in game 2. In a third replay (not shown), *Bebe* changed move 5 from Nc6 to Nf6 in an attempt to avoid the score drop at move 6.

12.4 The Theory

The operation of the algorithm will theoretically allow the program to see ahead when it is at or near positions that have occurred in prior games. For example, a 5-ply search at move 20 can see the entry from move 22 in a prior game. If the score from move 22 is substantially lower than the original score from move 20, the program will, hopefully, pick a better move. The program's performance against an opponent should improve with time, because *Bebe* should be able to 'see' farther ahead and change to a better line of play.

12.5 The Experiment

To test the learning algorithm, we decided to play *Bebe* against a commercially available chess computer to see what the long term effects of the learning algorithm would be. We wanted to start with two equal, but different, players because we felt that this would be the toughest test. We wanted *Bebe* and the opponent to be equal because we think that the usefulness of the algorithm may be limited to equally strong players. This is an unproven assumption, but for the purposes of the experiment, equality of opposition seemed like a good place to start. Starting with a score of 5 out of 10 gives an equal range of values to show improving or degrading performance.

To achieve equality, it was necessary to handicap *Bebe* so that it always played black, had no book and used only 5 seconds per move. The opponent always played white, had full use of its book and was given 10 seconds a move. We believe that neither program used a contempt factor. Both units had their thinking on the opponent's time options on, not only because the commercial unit could not turn off that feature, but also to make the test as close to real world play as possible. The T-table was always cleared between games. A series of 40 games was played (without the learning algorithm) to establish that the machines were performing equally well. A drawback to enabling thinking on the opponent's time is that the operators had to play smoothly and consistently to avoid introducing errors in the results associated with the time variability of their responses to the machines.

Games were scored as a loss for *Bebe* when down 5 pawns. Wins were played to checkmate. Draws were by repetition or the 50 move rule, with a single exception, which was adjudicated a draw after 120 moves because it was 23:15 hours on a Friday night and the operators were tired.

Two series of games were played with the learning algorithm on. In both series *Bebe* had 8,000 positions of LTM available. This number appears small, but is large enough to hold about 130 games through move 35. The number of positions required to hold a game cannot be accurately estimated because it depends on how many predicted moves the opponent makes. LTM was cleared at the beginning of each series. The raw data for the two series is available, and in the second series we gathered more information to help support better explanations of the learning.

Figure 12.1 summarizes the results of the first series, which took place in late 1986. Using zero tolerance, 180 games were played and the results plotted for sets of 10 games each. The game zero point, which represents the tested starting value of 5, is included. The line is the linear regression of the data point set. The opponent's programmed opening choices were Pe4, Pd4, Pc4, Nf3 in order of decreasing probability. *Bebe* almost always responded Pe6, except for a few early games where Pe5 was experimented with before changing back to Pe6. The results of the second series are summarized in Figure 12.2. The series took place in 1989, and we used 0.125 as a tolerance. The results are plotted as for series 1. The game zero point was re-tested and the result 5.5 was used. The change in the game zero value is due to other changes in the program since 1986. In an attempt to get clearer results, we restricted the opponent's opening move to Pe4. *Bebe* responded Pe5 for all games in the series. For series 2 we also noted whether black or white changed to a move that lead to a new game, and at which move number the change occurred. The results are summarized in Figure 12.3. The opponent is attributed with a 'change' at move 1 of game one, because that creates the first occurrence of that position from the learning algorithm point of view. Opponent changes at moves 2, 3 and 4 are caused by randomizing its book selection. *Bebe*'s changes occur primarily between moves

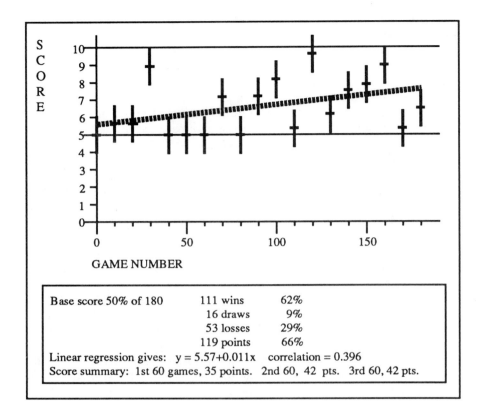

Figure 12.1: Tolerance = 0.0 for series 1 tests.

12 and 30, where it changed 50 times. This is relatively early in comparison to the average game length of 68 moves.

12.6 What Does it All Mean?

We expected smoother results, with a steeper slope. Some scattering of the points in Figure 12.1 is attributed to the opponent's book options. The opponent does not play its opening book variations with equal frequency, and so the algorithm will require differing numbers of replays to learn how to win different openings. If we had taken move lists for the games, we could plot scores versus time for individual openings. In the second series, we tried to minimize this problem by restricting the opponent's first move to Pe4, but only achieved more scatter, as Figure 12.2 shows. The confidence levels for the linear regression were 90% for series 1, and 75% for series 2. The positive slope of the line is encouraging, even though it is only 0.1 for 10 games. We doubt that a simple

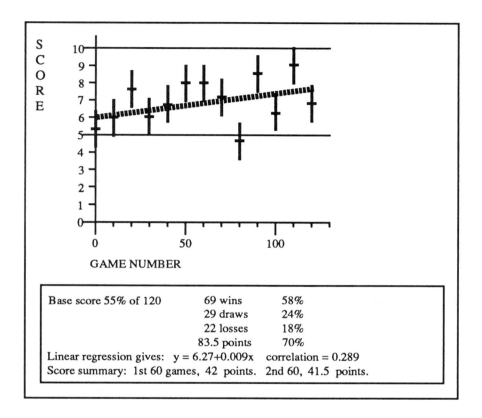

Base score 55% of 120	69 wins	58%
	29 draws	24%
	22 losses	18%
	83.5 points	70%
Linear regression gives: y = 6.27+0.009x	correlation = 0.289	
Score summary: 1st 60 games, 42 points. 2nd 60, 41.5 points.		

Figure 12.2: Tolerance = 0.125 for series 2 tests.

straight line is adequate to explain the results, because the intercepts of both lines are above the base point, and the counts of sets of 60 games makes us think that there may be a limit to the algorithm that is reached at about 70% wins (42/60). 70% wins is about 150 Elo points. Whether there is an upper limit or not, the algorithm seems to be working. The low degree of success that the opponent achieved when it changed its mind suggests that *Bebe* was pressuring it (Section 12.7.6 *Time and Speed*).

Bebe's good degree of success is attributed to changes associated with avoiding bad positions (Section 12.7.8 *Score Flow*). We noticed that the win percentage in the two series was close, 62% to 58%, while the draw and loss percentages were very different. We do not know if the increased number of draws in series 2 was caused by changes in the program, or was associated with the change in the tolerance from series 1 to series 2.

Another question is, how many games were identical? In series 1, there was only 1 game that was repeated (a win for *Bebe*). It was repeated about 8 times in the 180 games, thus overestimating the program's true strength. But in series 2,

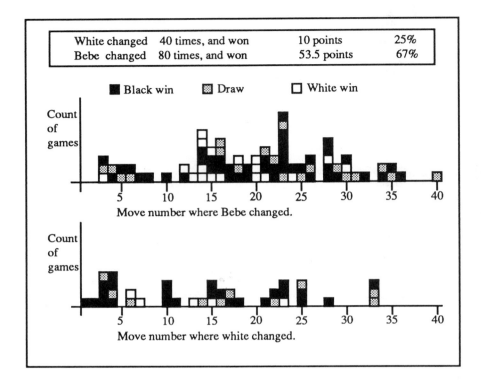

Figure 12.3: Series 2 tests, which side changed.

no game was repeated! Either *Bebe* or the opponent changed at some point. We initially expected to have many repeat games in both series. Now we feel that the algorithm introduces many side effects that add variability to the play of both sides. This variability introduces 'new' games that the algorithm must then learn. The level of opponent variability was particularly high, to the extent that it changed its move at move 14 in game 120, the last of the series.

12.7 Unanticipated Side Effects

After analyzing the data and re-examining the learning algorithm, we have been able to discover many side effects and intrinsic flaws both in the basic chess program, and in the algorithm itself or what it invokes from the search. Some of the issues are so complex that we cannot even come to a general conclusion whether they increase or decrease performance. We can only give a general discussion, and leave questions for further tests.

12.7.1 Tolerance and Culprit Moves

When the presence of LTM entries causes *Bebe* to select an alternate move, the original move made the first time has effectively been assigned *culprit status*. *Bebe* treats the move as if it was the cause or "culprit" of the low scores that followed. This may or may not be a good assumption. If the move is toward the end of a forcing sequence it probably isn't the culprit. It may take several runs through the sequence for a better culprit move to be found. If the falling score is associated with some positional factor, such as developing a knight to the wrong square 15 moves earlier, *Bebe* will probably never back up enough of a low score to assign culprit status to the knight move. The tolerance value is the primary controlling factor for the selection of culprit moves. There are two distinct aspects associated with culprit selection. We call them *game level* and *search level*. Game level refers to how early or late in the game a different move is selected. Search level determines whether an individual search changes the root node move, or a move later in the principal variation.

12.7.2 Game Level Culprit Selection

First an example to illustrate how tolerance affects culprit selection at the game level. In Table 12.2 we list a hypothetical game with scores at each move. The moves themselves are irrelevant, only the score values and tolerance will affect culprit selection. Zero tolerance tends to assign culprit status to any move followed by a position with a lower score. This is a consequence of zero tolerance returning an exact value at ply 3 in the search, leading to termination of the branch and a possible higher value from ply 5 not being examined.

Non-zero tolerance tends not to change a move at the root node unless some position in the search has a score that is more than 1 tolerance lower than the original score at the root node. In a 3-ply search there can only be one such position, in a 5-ply search there can be two, in a 7-ply there can be three and so on. Note that in this example for 5-ply searches, larger tolerances will start to select culprits later and later in the game, until a tolerance of 0.40, which actually selects no culprits and would allow the machine to replay the entire game. Here, the large tolerance would allow the win repeatedly. More typical would be a case where moves 14 through 17 were scored with values from -1.60 through -2.00 and the game would eventually be lost. In this case the large tolerance would allow the loss repeatedly until the score at move 14 changed to a value less than -1.80, which would allow move 12 to have culprit status. We therefore have a problem. In this example, only the large tolerance can see through the low value at move 13 to the high value at move 14 and not assign move 12 culprit status, but this same high tolerance would possibly never select a culprit if the score were to drop consistently by only 1/2 tolerance per move with 5-ply searches. Seven-ply searches would not select culprits if the score dropped by 1/3 tolerance per move, and 3-ply searches would not select culprits if the score dropped by only 1 tolerance per move.

Culprit Status (Yes/No) for 5-ply Searches					
		Tolerance Values			
Move	Score	0.0	.10	.20	.40
1.	+.50	Yes	No	No	No
2.	+.45	Yes	Yes	No	No
3.	+.35	Yes	Yes	No	No
4.	+.30	Yes	Yes	No	No
5.	+.20	Yes	Yes	No	No
6.	+.10	Yes	Yes	Yes	No
7.	+.00	Yes	Yes	Yes	No
8.	−.25	Yes	Yes	Yes	No
9.	−.40	Yes	Yes	Yes	No
10.	−.60	Yes	Yes	Yes	No
11.	−1.00	Yes	Yes	Yes	No
12.	−1.40	Yes	Yes	Yes	No
13.	−1.80	No	No	No	No
14.	+5.00	No	No	No	No
15.	+6.00	No	No	No	No
16.	+10.00	No	No	No	No
17.	+99(mate)	No	No	No	No

Table 12.2: Tolerance effects on culprit status.

Part of the problem here is that the tolerance is a global value. It is probably necessary to have something additional in the algorithm that varies the tolerance of individual LTM entries during the LTM to STM transformation process.

12.7.3 Search Level Culprit Selection

Culprit status for a move in the game does not guarantee that something else will be selected. To choose an alternate, the search must find a move that has a higher value than that returned by the search of the culprit. The culprit move will be played again if all other moves still have lower scores. Forced move sequences have this property. Here, the LTM entry will be updated with the new lower score, which may change the culprit status of earlier moves in the game the next time it is played. If the move is not changed, and only the value in LTM is lowered, new earlier moves in the game will achieve culprit status for the next time the game is played.

How do different tolerance values affect culprit selection in a search for a game move that has culprit status? The answer is more complex than for game level. For zero tolerance, the node at ply 3 gets an exact value, and returns that value. Therefore, the only option available to the search is to change the move

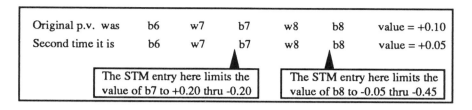

| Original p.v. was | b6 | w7 | b7 | w8 | b8 | value = +0.10 |
| Second time it is | b6 | w7 | b7 | w8 | b8 | value = +0.05 |

The STM entry here limits the value of b7 to +0.20 thru -0.20

The STM entry here limits the value of b8 to -0.05 thru -0.45

Table 12.3: STM entry effects on returned search value.

at the root node. This will occur if the drop in value is sufficient to cause the search to find another 'best' move. For non-zero tolerance, the search (of 5-ply) usually has two option points for a move change. One is at the root node, the other is at ply 3. Ply 5 is not an option point because the move there is still the best move and there are no LTM entries referenced below ply 5 to affect the value at ply 5. Deeper searches would have more option points, but still only at odd numbered plies. The decision is therefore whether to change this game move or wait until the next game move. The decision will depend on the values returned by the search. For example, assume we are replaying the game above, but with 0.20 tolerance, and that the original 5-ply principal variation is represented by the moves b6; w7 b7; w8 b8. At move 6, which is the first move with culprit status, the search would discover entries in STM that force changes on the returned value of the original move, as Table 12.3 shows.

Three possibilities now arise because of the new lower value of this variation:

Case 1:

There is no variation at move 6 with a value larger than -0.05. Move 6 will be played as before, but with the LTM entry value updated to -0.05.

Case 2:

Some other move is found at ply 3 that is not black's original move 7, with a value greater than -0.05 and less than or equal to $+0.10$. The value cannot be larger than $+0.10$ because the search would have found and used that value the first time the game was played. The LTM entry value is updated. Here, although move 6 has culprit status, the search has selected a principal variation that is deferring change to move 7. In forced move sequences this happens frequently.

Case 3:

Some other move is found at the root node that is not black's original move 6, with a value greater than -0.05 and less than or equal to $+0.10$. This time, move 6 is changed, and a 'new' game will be played. Again the LTM value is updated.

In all cases, the exact value updated to LTM will have an effect on the culprit status of moves 4 and 5 for the next time the game is played. Table 12.4 illustrates these possible effects.

New move 6 value		−0.05 to −0.01	+0.00 to +0.09	+0.10
Culprit status of:	Move 4	Yes	Yes	No
	Move 5	Yes	No	No

Table 12.4: Returned search value on culprit status.

Note that some values give move 4 culprit status, but not move 5. The move 4 culprit status can be particularly annoying with an update value of +0.09. This is only a small change to the value of move 6, and *Bebe* may go on to a win. But move 4 still has culprit status and the next time the game is played, *Bebe* may change its choice at move 4, getting into a new game with all the inherent risks.

12.7.4 Learning Delays

One unexpected problem is something we call the *ratchet effect*, which occurs when score drops are caused by small positional factors that have slowly filtered back to some game position. Imagine some position where *Bebe* has two moves available, with scores differing by 0.01. The program may play the game several times before the score of the originally chosen move drops enough for it to pick the second. Then the game can repeat several more times with the second before its value drops enough for *Bebe* to switch back to the first. The process can cycle several times before either a third move is selected, which has a score that does not decline, or the lower scores at the current position filter back enough to cause *Bebe* to change to some earlier move. The process can even continue at the earlier position. Thus the method ratchets the score down in a position at a rate slower than desired.

In the second series of games, *Bebe* reached a position where two different moves had equal scores and were played randomly. One move was played 12 times, winning 8 points (67%), the other was played 10 times, winning 7.5 points (75%). If either had been played exclusively, the positions following from it would have been 'learned' more thoroughly and would probably have produced a higher overall score. In another case, *Bebe* had been playing and winning a certain game. But the score at move 14 was slowly dropping. An alternate was chosen and it was poor, but the eventual loss was far enough away that the learning process needed time to reduce the values of the positions following the new move 14 to the point where the original move could compete. This time, the scores were lowering actively enough that *Bebe* alternated between the two moves for the next ten games and scored only 5 points (50%). In effect, *Bebe* was learning 2 sets of games slowly instead of 1 set quickly.

12.7.5 Another Kind of Horizon Effect

When the machine decides to change a culprit and play a different move, it will often change to a move that would be made later in the game. For example, if black's moves 10, 11 and 12 are b10, b11 and b12, the search recognizes that swapping to b11, b10, b12 is just a transposition, but the sequences b10, b12, b11, or b11, b12, b10 are too deep for a 5-ply search to see as transpositions to the original game. It should be remembered that the machine in some sense 'likes' the original game position and will find ways to approach that position as closely as possible.

That actually happened in several games. In one, *Bebe* changed at move 15 then drifted back into a previous game, then changed again at move 20 to go into a new game. In game 69, *Bebe* changed at move 20, drifted back into a previous game, changed again at move 26, and again drifted back into a previous game, then changed a third time to a new game. This happens because the program's scoring function is effectively saying 'these are good positions,' while the LTM entries are saying 'no they are not.' It is also possible that this type of game level transposition activity is not bad, and that the transposed new game is in some sense 'better' by disallowing some options for the opponent.

12.7.6 Time and Speed

The most dramatic side effect of the algorithm is the speedup of searches through a game that has been played before. This is unexpected because there are usually only 3 to 7 LTM entries that affect the current search. However, these few entries are in the principal variation, which consumes 20% to 40% of the search time. Even with non-zero tolerance, the $\alpha\beta$ window is partially closed, speeding the search. For example, if the node at ply 5 in the search starts with a search window of $(-0.10, +0.20)$ and finds an STM entry with score limits of $(+0.10, +0.30)$, that node will actually search with limits of $(+0.10, +0.20)$. This smaller window will produce more cutoffs, and yield a faster search.

Unfortunately, *Bebe*'s search depths go up by two for each iteration, producing searches only for odd numbered depths. Had an increment of one been used, 6-ply searches would have started by game number 50 in the series. We did not monitor the exact speedup factor, but did note that in games beyond number 50, the program had only consumed 60 seconds for the first 20 moves (3 seconds per move), while during the control series, with learning off, 90 seconds would typically be used for the first 20 moves (4.5 seconds per move).

Faster searches still help because of the unusual nature of *Bebe*'s search policy. With 5 seconds per move time control, the program always starts a 5-ply search (after completing the 3-ply search). The available clock time may allow it to search only 15 of the 30 moves at the root node the first time in a specific position. The next game with that position may allow 25 of the 30 moves to be searched at the root node, and one of the extra 10 may be played. The third time through the position, all 30 moves at the root may be searched because of the number of LTM entries from the prior games. Thus, the speedup alone can be enough to cause *Bebe* to select different moves. If the searches go faster, the opponent has less "ponder time" (time to predict a reply), theoretically reducing slightly the quality of its play. This is the primary source of opponent variability, besides its book options. This conjecture is supported by the fact that the opponent is expected to win 45% of new positions, but only won 25% when it chose moves that lead to new games. This substantial difference is probably caused by poor move selection under time pressure.

12.7.7 Predicted Move Accuracy

If *Bebe* is replaying a game that has ascending scores, almost all of its 'predicted' moves will be wrong, because the search has 'learned' that the moves made previously by the opponent are bad in the sense that they give *Bebe* higher than expected scores. Therefore, in the replay the program will have virtually no ponder time. If the position is complex, *Bebe* may have insufficient time to select the correct move at some point and so lose the game. If this happens, however, a new set of LTM entries is created, and the next time the position is reached, these LTM entries may effect a search speedup enough to allow *Bebe* to re-select the correct move this time.

The opposite is true while replaying a game that has descending scores. The search has learned that the move made previously by the opponent was good, and therefore the prediction will be correct, and *Bebe* gets more ponder time. In effect, the program is rewarded with extra clock time in bad positions, and penalized with less clock time in good positions. We do not have data to decide if this 'predicted move effect' had any significant impact on the results of the experiments.

12.7.8 Score Flow

By letting *Bebe* see a little further, the algorithm generally produces a flow of scores back up the game tree. However, the minimax nature of the search allows low scores to filter up the game tree much easier than high scores. If the game has descending scores the even numbered nodes accept the lower scores, passing them up the search tree toward the root node. This gives the move at the root node a lower score, which is then reflected in the LTM entry for the position. If the game has ascending scores, the even numbered nodes do not accept the higher scores and try to find alternate moves with lower scores. However, whenever the move chosen at ply 2 in the search is not played by the opponent, the value of that position can permanently prevent a higher score from filtering up the game tree.

The best example of high scores not filtering back up the game tree is in mating situations. Assume a position at move 40 from which a 4-move forced mate exists. Assume the mate cannot be seen with a 5-ply search. If *Bebe* makes the correct move anyway, at move 41 it will discover the mate in 3 and the position is cataloged in LTM with a score of +97. If in another game the program reaches the same position at move 40, the node at ply 2 will change to another of the opponent's options and the score at the root node will only show the positional disadvantage the opponent accepts to 'avoid' the mate. It may take a dozen or more passes through the position at move 40 before the mate in 4 is fully recognized and cataloged.

Score flow, like culprit selection, is dependent on the tolerance value. A score for an LTM entry will only be changed if scores of nearby derivative LTM entries are different by more than 1 tolerance. The rule is similar to the rule for culprit selection. Also important is the fact that the tolerance value allows only part of the score change to flow back in the game. If a game consists of a series of slightly decreasing scores, there may be no score flow at all. This further complicates the issue of tolerance selection. Large tolerances allow the program to 'see' through temporary score drops, but produce too little score flow, and possibly no culprit selection. Small tolerances produce more score flow, but too much culprit selection. It is interesting to note that the series 1 experiment with zero tolerance produced somewhat better results than the series 2 experiment with 0.125 tolerance.

12.7.9 Finding Ways to Lose Games Previously Won

Our assumption at the start of the experiment was that moves would only change in lost games. We quickly discovered that the algorithm would also cause *Bebe* to change moves in won games, because of temporary drops in score values. If we list the scores associated with each position in a game, there are usually points where the score drops. If the drop is large compared to the tolerance, then *Bebe* selects different moves, even when the original game was won.

Another way to lose a previously won game is for the program to discover, usually via the ponder of the predicted move, that the opponent has some combination that wins material. Because the results of the ponders also go to LTM, *Bebe* will avoid the position in the future because the opponent has this option. The subtlety here is that it may take 2 to 30 plays through the position to discover this resource of the opponent, selecting a new predicted move each time, until one is found that is good for the opponent. Consequently there can be a string of wins followed by a string of losses while *Bebe* searches for a new way to win. Given that the program is able to do 5-ply ponder searches of the predicted move, the LTM entries that are associated with these searches become the equivalent of 6-ply searches by the opponent. Thus *Bebe* can 'see' some things that a 5-ply searching opponent cannot.

12.7.10 Second Best Moves

Whenever there is going to be a move, the selected move will be 'second best' by *Bebe*'s standards. We have never examined the quality of *Bebe*'s second best move, and in most cases don't know what it would be because the $\alpha\beta$ algorithm does not provide it. For example, in one game *Bebe* played Qd8-e7 which lead quickly to a poor position. When the same game came up again, *Bebe* played Qd8-d7 and then Qd7-e7, using two moves to get to the same place. The poor position previously achieved was now even worse because the opponent had a whole extra move. At first we thought this should not happen because the position was the same, but the extra move forced on the opponent guarantees that all subsequent low score positions will differ by 1 opponent move. Thus, *Bebe* has avoided all the LTM entry positions associated with the original game.

12.8 Other Implementation Issues

There are some other points of significance, which are associated with the specific implementation of the learning algorithm. If any change is made to the program that alters the scoring values, the current set of LTM entries is theoretically invalid. After a program change, positions can be re-scored by re-searching and assigning them new values. Were this process run continuously in a 'background' mode, it would be a form of retrospective analysis.

The LTM entries could also be invalidated by a change in the hash key algorithm. A change, via a new software release to the system random number generator, could invalidate LTM if system random numbers are used to build the hash key table. In general these problems could be solved if the LTM entries are stored with board positions instead of hash keys. The hash key would be regenerated as a part of the LTM to STM conversion process.

12.8.1 Game Level Feedback

Bebe's learning algorithm is a method of feedback applied to the current position by using score values from future positions. This works well for some short-term tactical positions, but not well enough for long-term play when scores get lower before a win. Essentially, the present algorithm has the machine searching for games where the move by move scores are steady, increasing, or only slightly decreasing. Always in doubt is whether such games actually exists?

We feel that the game outcome should affect some of the LTM scores. Too many games were played and then avoided, because of a score drop in one position before the win. Some form of retrospective analysis is needed to smooth these scores out. The serious question is whether this can be done without extensive time consuming searches. Part of the difficulty here is that the program already has all the chess oriented knowledge that is practical for us to do, and the only additional information available with the algorithm is the scores at each move of the game.

12.8.2 A Proposed Giant Back-up Scheme

Bebe stores the current game being played as an initial position and the series of moves that has been played. In an attempt to enhance the performance of the learning algorithm, we wrote a special *unplay* routine that could be called at the end of a game. The routine would start at the last move (that *Bebe* played) of the game. It then re-searched the position to the same depth of search as was recorded in the LTM entry for the position. The re-search would update the LTM entry. Then it unmade 2 plies of the game, and re-searched that position, again updating the LTM entry. This process would be repeated until the beginning of the game was reached. The idea is that score flow is enhanced by playing the game in reverse move number order. When forward playing (the normal mode), a score at move M can only be affected by LTM entries 1 or 2 moves following M.

Unplaying the game updates LTM entries at the higher moves first, then backs up, allowing the updated scores from higher moves to have immediate impact on lower number moves. This is particularly the case for long forcing move sequences. The enhanced score flow should provide quicker learning responses (changed moves) than forward playing. Unplaying a game is one of many possible forms of offline post-mortem or retrospective analysis that is possible. We did not use it in the experiments because of the increased amount of time it would take at the end of each game.

12.8.3 Dead Entries

Another problem that needs to be addressed is the accumulation of LTM entries that will never be used because the machine has 'learned' to avoid those positions. In the experiment we used 8,000 positions of LTM. This was enough to catalog all 120 games through move 37, averaging 67 positions per game. But many of these positions are unreachable because either their scores were low, or because they are derived from positions with low scores. The current algorithm cannot identify useful positions from those that are not. Eventually, the number of dead entries would exceed the number of live, useful entries by many orders of magnitude. We hope to try a new method in the future which can identify the useless positions, and give us options for game level scoring.

12.8.4 Double Probing

Our perception of the technique to address the issue of useless positions is incorporated into a new *double probing* learning method, so called because the search would be modified to probe STM and LTM independently, in that order. The LTM entry format would be changed slightly to allow for additional fields, and would be accessed by a pointer in the STM entry (identified by a negative depth of search). These new fields would allow for changes to the learning algorithm in an attempt to reduce some of its shortcomings.

One field, *hit count*, would provide a measure of the usefulness of the entry. It would be incremented (to some maximum) each time the LTM entry was a match during the search process. New entries would be cataloged with some small value, and would be allowed to overwrite the LTM entry with the lowest hit count. A similar field, *play count*, would record how many times the position occurs at the root node, in other words, how many times the position is actually part of a game. Positions resulting from ponder searches that are never reached would have a play count of zero. The program could ignore these positions if they identify winning moves for the opponent that are never used by any opponent that the machine has played so far.

Another field, *direction*, would be set by an end of game process that would 'unplay' the game, and store a value in the direction field that took into account whether the game was won or lost, and the values of the positions leading up to the end of the game. Direction would be initialized to zero when an LTM entry was created, and would be set non-zero by the end-of-game function. The search could use *direction* by applying asymmetrical tolerance to the score based on the direction value. When the search finds a matching LTM entry, it can then create score limit values based on current depth of search, and the LTM entry fields direction, play count and value.

12.9 Conclusions

We have described a simple technique that allows a tree searching chess program to improve its play against an opponent. The experimental results show that when playing against a single specific opponent, a 150 point improvement in play is possible by playing that opponent 100 to 200 games. Improvements against new opponents would depend on whether those new opponents played games that were similar enough to take advantage of earlier LTM entries. Shorter term results are not clear. A serious problem is the necessity of an algorithm that is better able to help the program identify culprit moves.

One specific advantage to the routine is its usefulness in tournament play. We have used it several times to prevent *Bebe* from duplicating lost games in tournaments. We can now go to tournaments and let *Bebe* play all its matches without making program or book changes between rounds.

13 The Bratko-Kopec Test Revisited

T.A. Marsland

13.1 Introduction

The twenty-four positions of the Bratko-Kopec test (Kopec and Bratko 1982) represent one of several attempts to quantify the playing strength of chess computers and human subjects. Although one may disagree with the choice of test set, question its adequacy and completeness and so on, the fact remains that the designers of computer-chess programs still do not have an acceptable means of estimating the performance of chess programs, without resorting to time-consuming and expensive "matches" against other subjects. Clearly there is considerable scope for improvement, as the success of test sets in related areas like pattern recognition attest.

Here the performance of some contemporary chess programs is compared with earlier results from 1981, to help identify the properties of those cases that computers cannot handle well by search alone and to show the relative progress that has been made. Even though use of standard tests is still not widespread, many chess programming groups built such sets and a few have been circulated. One of the earliest was the NY1924 data set (Marsland and Rushton 1973) of about 800 positions, later used in a minor way to assess the performance of *Tech* (Gillogly 1978), and to develop evaluation function weighting factors (Marsland 1985). At about the same time Ken Thompson was building far larger test suites (Thompson 1979) and more recently Dap Hartmann worked with some 63,000 positions to extract knowledge from Grandmaster games (Hartmann 1987a,b). The Hartmann suite was used to tune the evaluation parameters of such programs as *Phoenix* and *Deep Thought*. When one considers that even 63,000 positions is a minuscule fraction of the estimated 10^{43} unique chess positions, what role can the small set of 24 B-K (Bratko-Kopec) positions play? Aside from being too small, the positions can be criticized because they consider only tactical and pawn lever moves, with many other important ideas and structures not covered. The tactical moves are now thought to be simple for computers, and also much larger test sets exist (Reinfeld 1945). Nevertheless, the true importance of pawn moves for high calibre play is brought out by the B-K positions better than by any other test set.

This chapter is an expanded version of a paper in the *New Directions in Game-Tree Search Workshop* proceedings, T.A. Marsland (ed.), Edmonton, May 1989, pp. 135-139. Later it appeared in the *Journal of the International Computer Chess Association*, vol. 13, no. 1, pp. 15-19.

Recognizing the narrow scope of the B-K suite, Jens Nielsen is developing a more sophisticated test with a greater range of features and is using it to estimate the Elo rating of commercial chess computers. Nielsen's (1989) system has many facets, using not only time taken to help measure a program's merit, but also testing the program's ability to reject moves. His system includes tests of endgame play, positional play, tactics and traps. At present some 145 problems are posed from 80 positions (many positions require the generation of a sequence of moves). Even though the test is time-consuming to apply, more than 40 programs have been tested and their Elo rating estimated with remarkable correlation to other accepted measures (Nielsen 1989). Like the B-K test and others, this system is of considerable benefit in the development of new chess programs, since it probes for the presence of specific knowledge and for the absence of common conceptual errors.

13.2 Previous Results

The original paper by Kopec and Bratko (1982) was also criticized for its unrealistic requirement that the program produce an ordered list of up to three choice moves. Although ordering moves is easy for humans, the pruning algorithm in most chess programs precludes consistent generation of such a list. That objection could have been overcome easily had the experiment been run slightly differently: by providing an ordered list of choice moves and rating performance according to the relative strength of the principal move proposed.

The last and final complaint aimed at prepared test sets is that programs can be tuned to perform well on the suite, perhaps at the expense of their overall playing strength. In principle, this objection is valid and serious, but in practice the pawn lever positions in particular have led to an appreciation of the importance of knowledge assessing critical pawn configurations. Also the harder tactical problems led to the development of selective search extensions (Anantharaman, Campbell and Hsu 1988) to identify and follow forced variations. Further, far more critical to the playing strength of programs than performance on any test suite are other factors, such as good use of time (Hyatt 1984; Anantharaman 1990), and effective use of transposition tables in the endgame (Nelson 1985). Nevertheless, it is clear from the results that the recognized best chess programs exhibit superior performance on the B-K test.

Consider Table 13.1 (Kopec and Bratko 1982), which shows an extract from the original results. Although the weakest programs fared badly when this test set was sprung upon them, some brute-force programs, notably *Belle*, *Duchess* and *BCP* did well even by today's standards. In particular, in 1981 *Belle* achieved a score of 18, which today is only exceeded by a handful of programs. Nevertheless, there can be no doubt that the comparably performing programs of today are stronger than *Belle*'81.

Computer Subjects					
	Program	Rating	Score	T	L
1.	Chess Challenger '10'	Unr	1	1	0
2.	Chess Challenger '7'	Unr	5	2	3
3.	Sensory Chess Challenger	Unr	5	3	2
4.	Sargon 2.5	1720~	5	2	3
5.	AWIT	1400	5	4	1
6.	OSTRICH81	1450~	6	4	2
7.	CHAOS	1820	6	5	1
8.	Chess Champion Mk V (E)	1885~	6.83	5	1.83
9.	Morphy Encore	1800~	9.33	6	3.3
10.	BCP	1685~	13	10	3
11.	DUCHESS	1850	16.50	10.5	6
12.	BELLE	2150	18.25	11	7.25

Key: (E) Experimental version; ~ Rating is an estimate; (Unr) Unrated;
      (T) Tactical score; (L) Score on pawn lever positions.

Note: Programs running off mainframe computers have names entirely in upper case
       letters. Others are stand-alone microcomputer programs.

Table 13.1: An extract from the original (1981) Bratko-Kopec results.

13.3 Interpretation of Current Performance

Turning now to the results of eight years later, Table 13.2 and Table 13.3, present the data supplied by by applicants to the 6th World Computer Chess Championships, plus some 1986 data for *Awit*'83. Of the twelve tactical positions, Table 13.2, about half the programs can solve nearly all (thus equaling the *Belle*'81 score). Further, virtually all the programs can solve far more than half the tactical positions. As these results show, the harder problems are positions 10 and 22, which are presented in Figure 13.1. However, there was no pattern to explain why the eight programs which successfully solved 11 tactical problems could not solve them all, since their failures were uniformly distributed across five different problems (positions 7, 10, 16, 18 and 22). Also, there can be little doubt that these top programs could be "tuned" to solve all twelve B-K tactical problems, but at what cost to their average playing strength? Equally it would seem that problems 1, 12, 14, 15, 16, 19 and 21 are within reach of solution by all contemporary programs, given enough effort. So in some sense those positions are a measure of minimal acceptable strength.

For the lever positions shown in Table 13.3, however, few programs can solve more than half, and only three positions can be solved by almost all the programs. In particular, problems 4, 6 and 8 seem easy enough for those programs that have the right knowledge. Interestingly, 13 of the 22 programs solved all three problems and the others only failed to solve one each! On the other hand, almost no program can solve the three most difficult (namely positions 2, 9 and 23), all of which involve a pawn sacrifice for positional gain, either specifically, or as part of the analysis of the principal variations. Figure 13.2 shows two representative positions. Not only are these problems difficult, but also it is possible that the few programs which were successful in solving them may just have been lucky. Even so, there are possibilities for improvement, since although 15 programs solved neither problem 9 nor 20, *Mephisto* was able to solve both! This suggests that *Mephisto* might contain special pawn knowledge not found in other programs.

13.4 Conclusion

Our data leads to the final questions. Is the B-K test good enough for estimating the performance of chess programs? Clearly not, since the suite is too small and not wide-ranging enough. Despite that shortcoming, are there still things for programmers to learn from the B-K test? Clearly yes, especially for new programs and those programs which are alone in failing a particular problem. Conversely, when several programs solve one problem, some programming error or lack of knowledge is preventing correct solution by the others. Finally, although more and more chess programs are incorporating selective extensions and dynamic width control in the deeper portions of the search, the results show that at least one fully selective search program, *Awit*'83, achieved a respectable score on the test suite even though it was selective at every level in its search, and even though in over-the-board play it had a checkered career. This suggests that in the middlegame one can do quite well with selective search, but in the endgame totally different knowledge, time control and more dynamic search depth limits are required. Lack of these features accounted for *Awit*'s relatively poorer endgame play.

To conclude, the data presented here provides an opportunity to consider whether the calibre of a chess program is measured not so much by how many correct moves it makes in any test suite, but rather by the quality of the moves it proposes as alternatives to the acknowledged best choices. That is, the quality of a chess program is measured not so much by the frequency with which it plays optimal moves, but by the strength of its less than perfect choices.

Position Tactical (T)	1 Qd1	5 Nd5	7 Nf6	10 Ne5	12 Bf5	14 Qd2	15 Qxg7	16 Ne4	18 Nb3	19 Rxe4	21 Nh6	22 Bxe4	Ttl 12
AI Chess	ok	ok	ok	ok	ok	ok	ok	ok	ok	ok	ok	ok	12
Awit'83	ok	ok	Bd6	Qc5	ok	ok	ok	ok	ok	c5	ok	ok	9
Bebe	ok	ok	ok	Rd7	ok	ok	ok	ok	ok	ok	ok	ok	11
BP	ok	ok	Rg3	Qc5	ok	ok	ok	ok	ok	ok	ok	Nh5	9
Centaur	ok	e5	ok	Qc5	ok	ok	ok	ok	ok	ok	ok	e5	9
Cray Blitz	ok	ok	ok	ok	ok	ok	ok	ok	f5	ok	ok	ok	12
Dappet	ok	Bf4	ok	Qc5	ok	ok	ok	ok	ok	ok	ok	e5	8
Deep Thought	ok	ok	Ra2	ok	ok	ok	ok	Qh5	ok	ok	ok	ok	11
Hitech	ok	ok	ok	ok	ok	ok	ok	ok	ok	ok	ok	ok	11
Lachex	ok	ok	ok	ok	ok	ok	ok	ok	f5	ok	ok	ok	11
Mach 4	ok	ok	ok	ok	ok	ok	ok	ok	ok	ok	ok	Ne5	11
Mephisto	ok	ok	Qc1	ok	ok	ok	ok	ok	ok	ok	ok	ok	11
Merlin	ok	ok	ok	Qc5	ok	ok	ok	ok	Be6	ok	ok	ok	10
Modul	ok	ok	ok	ok	ok	ok	ok	ok	ok	ok	ok	ok	12
Much	ok	Bf4	ok	Qc7	ok	ok	ok	ok	Bg4	ok	ok	Rd8	8
Pandix	ok	Rad1	Rg3	Qc5	ok	ok	ok	ok	Qb6	ok	ok	e5	7
Phoenix	ok	ok	ok	ok	ok	ok	ok	ok	Qb6	ok	ok	ok	11
Rebel	ok	ok	ok	ok	ok	ok	ok	ok	ok	ok	ok	Ne5	11
Shess	ok	Rad1	Bb4	Qc5	ok	ok	ok	Be7	Bg4	ok	ok	e5	5
Waycool	ok	ok	Ra2	ok	ok	ok	ok	ok	ok	ok	Qe3	Nh5	10
Y!89	ok	ok	Bb4	ok	ok	ok	ok	ok	Qb6	ok	ok	e5	9
Zarkov	ok	ok	ok	Qc5	ok	ok	ok	ok	f5	ok	ok	Rd8	9

Table 13.2: Results for the B-K tactical positions.

Position / Lever (L)	2 d5	3 f5	4 e6	6 g6	8 f5	9 f5	11 f4	13 b4	17 h5	20 g4	23 f6	24 f4	Ttl 12
AI Chess	e5	ok	ok	ok	ok	Re1	ok	Rac1	h6	Kb1	Bf5	ok	6
Awit'83	Rb1	a5	ok	ok	ok	Re1	ok	ok	e6	Qh5	ok	ok	7
Bebe	Ke3	ok	ok	ok	Nc3	Rc1	ok	ok	ok	Kb1	Bf5	bxc5	6
BP	e5	Qd8	ok	Kg4	ok	Bb5	Rfb1	Rac1	ok	Nb5	Bf5	c5	3
Centaur	e5	Qc7	ok	c4	ok	Re1	Nf5	Rec1	Qc8	Nc5	Bf5	exf5	2
Cray Blitz	g5	ok	ok	ok	ok	Bd3	ok	ok	c6	ok	0-0	ok	8
Dappet	e5	ok	ok	ok	ok	e5	ok	ok	h6	Nb5	Bf5	ok	7
Deep Thought	Kf3	Qd8	ok	ok	ok	Re1	ok	ok	c6	a3	Bf5	ok	6
Hitech	f5	Bd8	ok	ok	ok	Bd3	Nf5	ok	a5	ok	Bf5	exf5	5
Lachex	e3	Rg8	ok	ok	ok	Re1	ok	ok	h6	Qh5	Bf5	ok	6
Mach 4	Kf3	Rd8	ok	Kg4	ok	Re1	Nf5	ok	c6	Kb1	Bf5	exf5	4
Mephisto	Kf3	Bd8	ok	ok	ok	ok	Nf5	ok	c5	ok	Bf5	ok	7
Merlin	Kf3	ok	Nf3	ok	ok	g3	Nf5	ok	ok	Nb5	Bf5	ok	6
Modul	Kf3	Bd8	ok	ok	f6	Bb5	Rb1	ok	c5	ok	Bf5	ok	5
Much	e5	Rd8	ok	ok	ok	g3	Qa2	Rac1	Nb8	Nb5	Bf5	bxc5	2
Pandix	Kf3	Qd8	ok	Kg4	ok	Re1	ok	ok	c6	Qb5	Bf5	ok	6
Phoenix	Kf3	ok	ok	ok	ok	Re1	ok	ok	c6	Qh5	Bf5	ok	6
Rebel	Kf3	Bd8	ok	ok	h4	Re1	ok	ok	h6	ok	Bf5	ok	7
Shess	e5	ok	ok	ok	ok	Re1	ok	ok	b6	Nb5	Be6	bxc5	5
Waycool	f5	ok	ok	ok	ok	ok	Rfb1	Rac1	b6	Qh5	Bf5	f5	5
Y!89	e5	ok	ok	a4	ok	Bb5	Rfb1	Qe2	h6	Nb5	Bf5	exf5	3
Zarkov	e5	ok	ok	ok	ok	ok	ok	b3	h6	h3	Bf5	exf5	6

Table 13.3: Results for the B-K lever positions.

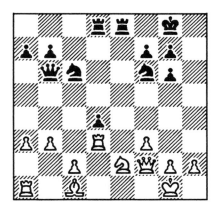
Posn. 10, black plays Ne5.

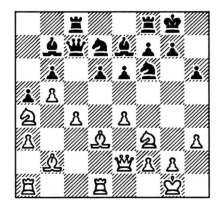
Posn. 22, black plays Bxe4.

Figure 13.1: Two difficult tactical positions.

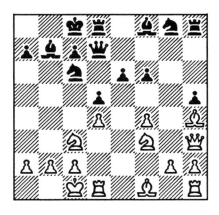
Posn. 9, white plays f5.

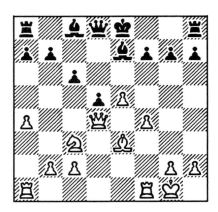
Posn. 23, black plays f6.

Figure 13.2: Two difficult pawn lever positions.

Part IV. Computer Chess and AI

The first two parts of the book covered historical issues, reported on important events and progress in man-machine play, and provided details of three major chess programs. This part has a more philosophical tone with papers by noted authors. John McCarthy opens by considering why chess was regarded as the first *Drosophila* of artificial intelligence (AI), and supports this view with examples drawn from variations of a typical elementary ending. Here humans find the winning strategy by elimination, and yet computer programs experience various degrees of difficulty. Thus chess clearly provides a wealth of fundamental problems for computer and human alike to address. McCarthy goes on to consider some other *Drosophila*, like the Yale Shooting Problem and the use of chess-book knowledge, as sources of material for considering issues like whether some situations are better or worse than others (this remains a fundamental problem for AI). Finally the issue of whether the game of Go poses some different and perhaps computationally harder problems relating to the recognition of groups is raised.

The following, longer, chapter by Donald Michie with the engaging title of *Brute Force in Chess and Science* examines some of the computer successes in playing chess, despite a seemingly minuscule amount of knowledge—and attributes this success to brute-force means. Similarly in the area of endgame databases the computer has successfully overcome complexity barriers that daunt even the best human experts when playing a basic endgame like KQKR, or the difficult KQP(7)KQ ending.[1] Several 5-men endgames have now been exhaustively studied and human analysis, like the Kling-Horwitz work, has been found wanting. Although this has often led to revised human thinking on these topics, greater understanding has been slower to come. The chapter closes by examining how brute-force methods are now being successfully applied in the biological sciences, and concludes that the "intellectual traffic [of ideas] in both directions is bound to increase."

Finally the interesting paper by Mikhail Donskoy and Jonathan Schaeffer considers why computer chess, which once was at the center of artificial intelligence research activity, now seems to have drifted into a side line. Partly the shift is attributed to computational successes, leading people to think that few fundamental problems remain, and partly it is attributed to the rapid expansion of artificial intelligence itself, diminishing much of the early AI work.

---

[1] The notation here is also written KQvKR and is read as king and queen versus king and rook. Also KQP(7)vKQ is king, queen and pawn on the 7th rank against a king and queen.

Also part of the problem has been that it proved too hard to make the conventional knowledge-based approaches to search work as effectively as simpler, more direct methods. The impact on the computer-chess community of this apparent falling by the wayside is thoroughly explored, but always there remains the thought that one day computer chess programs will overcome all human opposition, thus vindicating the dedication of those who have sought the "golden grail" for so long.

14 Chess as the Drosophila of AI

J. McCarthy

14.1 Introduction

The phrase *Chess is the Drosophila of Artificial Intelligence* is not my own invention. To the best of my recollection, I owe it to the late Alexander Kronrod, who may have used it as a defense against physicists when they complained that he used so much of their precious computer time in a *mere* chess match. This was probably in 1966 during the year-long computer chess telegraph match between Stanford University and the Institute of Theoretical and Experimental Physics in Moscow. Let me say that initially my thoughts were not entirely clear when choosing this topic, but now I can expand the subject slightly so as to allow discussion of the *Drosophila* of AI (artificial intelligence) in a more general sense.

One of the pressures I was under came from people in computer science. They sometimes urged me to tackle topics of practical importance and to concentrate on experimental and theoretical work in precisely these applicable areas, as opposed to a backwater such as computer chess. This echoes a remark that might have been made to Thomas Hunt Morgan in 1910: "Elephants are far more useful than fruitflies and who wants better fruitflies? So why don't you do your work in genetics on elephants rather than on fruitflies?" To which Morgan could have countered: "It takes no more than two weeks to breed a generation of fruitflies, you can keep thousands of them in a bottle and they are cheap to feed."

14.2 To Various Audiences

With the choice of *Drosophila* out of the way, I can now address my remarks to several groups. First, consider the *philosophers*, some of whom hold that intelligence is impossible for a machine to achieve. They should consider the gradual and sometimes not so gradual climb in performance of chess machines. The best program has just beaten its first Grandmaster. Who knows, in 1992 the World Champion may be next, as Newborn (1979) predicted.

An earlier version of this chapter, "The Fruitfly on the Fly," appeared in the *Journal of the International Computer Chess Association*, vol. 12, no. 4, pp. 199-206. We thank the editors of the Journal for permission to use their transcription of Professor McCarthy's talk at the Canadian Information Processing Society Conference, Edmonton, 30 May 1989.

My next few remarks concern the computer-chess community. By and large, they come in two flavors: sportsmen and businessmen (makers of commercial chess machines). Neither group is primarily motivated to produce scientific papers explaining how the results were achieved and how others might build upon them for further improvement. Because of these factors, computer chess has not succeeded in its *Drosophila* role and I must entreat the community that computer chess be made more scientific: publication is what we need.

To computer scientists in general I have only one wish to express: let there be more of these *Drosophila*-like experiments; let us create some more specific examples! Finally, I hold that government and industry often take an extremely short-range view towards AI and towards computer science in general. For example, in 1971, the Defense Advanced Research Project Agency (DARPA) cancelled a robotics project they had been sponsoring, because quick results could not be promised. However, DARPA continued sponsoring the same workers in a different field. Eighteen years later, it is clear that this switch of objective was accompanied by a decline in quality. The 1970 and 1971 papers are still being cited in the literature (including the applications literature) as significant advances; not so for their 1973-1975 publications (since 1971, nine two-years periods have passed). I claim that for applications to be developed, basic research is essential and must be supported in whatever form, be it done by companies, government or universities which, after all, specialize in basics.

14.3 The First Drosophila

Switching my focus slightly, let me recall my own paper *Some Expert Systems Need Common Sense*, which gave a fairly detailed critique of the technology of contemporary expert systems (McCarthy 1983). There I addressed the possibility that the MYCIN expert system could be proficient at diagnosing bacterial infections without even knowing what a bacterium, a doctor or a hospital is. In fact, MYCIN did not even consider time-dependent processes (not allowing even the question: the patient yesterday died, what do you recommend for today's patient with the same symptoms?). Despite these crippling limitations, we now possess a useful expert systems technology.

Concentrating on computer chess, I would like to consider the position of Figure 14.1(a) from Hans Berliner's Ph.D. dissertation (Berliner 1974). (For all four diagrams the convention that white moves first applies.) He used it to show the need for a *global strategy*, and argued that a chess program conducting a 5-ply search would play 1. Ke3. He then gave a summary of the findings during the tree search for which I refer to his thesis, and concluded by stating:

> Most of the problems in chess are tactical (immediate) problems and for this reason, the lack of global ideas is frequently obscured in today's [1974] programs.

I think that is still true.

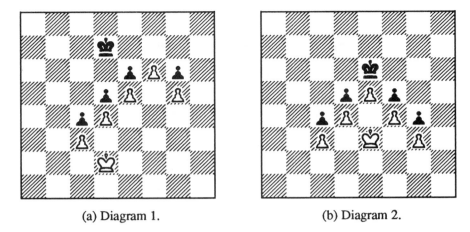

(a) Diagram 1.   (b) Diagram 2.

Figure 14.1: Two variations on a theme.

Returning to 1989, I asked some participants of the 6th World Computer Chess Championship, on the morning before my lecture, to submit this problem to their programs. All found the solution, needing from three to twenty seconds, and all did it by brute force considerably mitigated by transposition tables (Nelson 1985). Transposition tables are particularly effective for this problem because only the kings and the white pawn at f6 have any moves, and therefore only a small set of distinct positions arise in the search process.

Perhaps some people would justify the use of brute force in programs by claiming that: Humans use brute force too, except that they are unaware of the massive parallelism built into their brains. However, it seems to me that humans use a much simpler thought process that does not involve brute force. First, the player forms the goal of going around the pawns to the left and capturing the pawn on e6. He notes that the black king (BK) must stay on squares where it can prevent the white pawn (WP) on f6 from queening and this allows the white king (WK) to reach c5 without interference. Then, unless the BK is on d7, the WK advances to d6, but if the BK is on d7, the WK can advance to d6 in three moves anyway. With the WK on d6, it can capture e6 unless the BK is on f7, but anyway the pawn can be captured in two more moves. Thus white captures the pawn in at most 10 moves. If the WK were initially on h3, capturing the pawn would take 14 moves, but solving the problem would be no more difficult for a human chess player.

The interesting part for me is the 5 (or 9, with WK on h3) move advance to c5. The key is determining that specific BK moves are irrelevant provided that the BK stays within the set of eight squares, $A = \{d7, d8, e8, f7, f8, g8, h7, h8\}$, preventing the WP at f6 from queening. Maybe some parallelism is involved in the human pattern recognition that suggests the goal of going around the pawn formation. It probably is not required, but human chess playing might be the

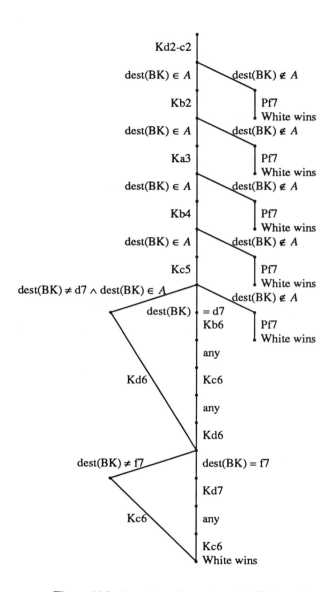

Figure 14.2: A condensed search tree for Diagram 1.

beneficiary of parallel pattern-recognition capabilities evolved in support of
vision. Parallelism certainly is not required to justify the plan.

The "pawn hold king" solution to the problem can be formalized using
condensed move trees. The formalization should make clearer what human
intelligence does and what AI will have to do. Maybe it will also help the
writers of chess programs. We consider two versions. In the first version,

moves are still represented by edges, but a set of moves can correspond to a single edge and a set of positions, equivalent from the point of view of the strategy being evaluated, corresponds to a node. The size of the tree is enormously reduced compared to the actual move trees. In the second version, an edge corresponds to a sequence of moves, but then we have to allow branching from the middle of an edge. So, still greater economy is achieved.

Figure 14.2 shows a move tree as described by the first version. The labels on its edges are propositions about the moves rather than the moves themselves. One should probably also attach propositions about the positions to the nodes. In exchange for a more complex concept, we get an significantly smaller tree.

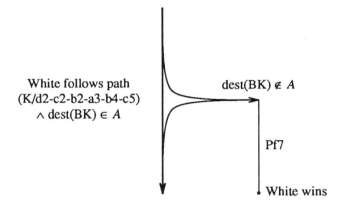

White follows path
(K/d2-c2-b2-a3-b4-c5)
$\land$ dest(BK) $\in$ A

dest(BK) $\notin$ A

Pf7

White wins

Figure 14.3: An edge-branching tree for Diagram 1.

However, we can abstract further as in Figure 14.3. Here the arrow denotes the white king following the path to c5 and the black king staying within the eight squares $A = \{d7, d8, e8, f7, f8, g8, h7, h8\}$. One arrow represents the behavior of both players. Since black can deviate from this behavior, the figure shows a multi-tailed arrow leaving the edge followed by the pawn move Pf7 that refutes it. We do not carry Figure 14.3 beyond getting the WK to c5, because the rest is exactly the same as in Figure 14.2. We call trees such as the one of Figure 14.3 *edge-branching trees*, since edges can have branches as well as nodes. This representation is even more compact and does not even bother to note how many moves there are in the sequence. I think it corresponds more closely to human reasoning.

Vladimir Lifschitz suggested that, instead of an edge-branching tree, we put a node in the middle of the edge from which 'moving the BK out of the set A' branches. This gives a conventional tree at the cost of making the edges before and after the node of indefinite length, since the same node has to represent whatever point black deviates. Figure 14.4 represents Lifschitz's idea. There needs to be a mathematical theory of the correspondence between move trees and these more abstract condensed move trees. Although chess is a game in

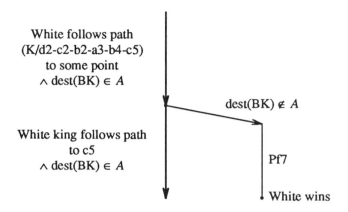

Figure 14.4: A Lifschitz tree for Diagram 1.

which the players move alternately, we see that in this position it is worthwhile to regard them as moving simultaneously. Fortunately for chess players, simultaneous action is the more common in life, and we can adapt our non-chess habits to understand this position. To be able to model consecutive moves as processes involving concurrent actions is a challenging task which may make the programs better.

In the proper sense of using chess as a *Drosophila*, an important requirement is a satisfactory theory of concurrent actions. This is a theory of how to achieve goals with the opponent moving concurrently rather than in alternation with you. Such a theory, as it happens, is relevant to the naval battle-management project; in the world of naval warfare, ships *do* move concurrently. However, this is one more project which DARPA is currently dropping. Very likely in the course of this battle-management project there are some useful scientific results. Maybe these results will be published in an abstract way serving as a foundation for further work. But I am concerned about the more likely outcome that whatever has been done in this area will have been done half-heartedly, or merely done to the extent it is applicable to this specific naval battle-management problem and, even so, abandoned half-way through.

Suppose we wish to investigate the true relation between the position of Figure 14.1(a) and the human strategy given above. Is the strategy valid in analogous positions? Assume we consider the position of Figure 14.1(b), a slightly amended version of Berliner's position. To human beings, the same strategy applies: players form the analogous goal of going around the pawns to the left and capturing the pawn on d5. Meanwhile, noting that the BK must stay on squares of a set $B = \{$b5, b6 b7, b8, c6, c7, c8, d7, d8, e6, e7, e8, f7, f8, g6, g7, g8, h5, h6, h7, h8$\}$. However, the set B (with BK on b5) allows the WK only to reach a3. Hence, there is a two-way split in reasoning as the variation below shows.

Nevertheless, as we will see, the main idea can be maintained 1. Kd2 Kd7 2. Kc2 Kc6 3. Kb2 Kb6 4. Ka3 Kc6 (after Kb5 white wins by 5. e6; for human beings the ideas are similar) 5. Kb4 Kb6 6. Ka4 Kc6 7. Ka5 Kc7 8. Kb5 Kd7 9. Kb6 Ke7 10. Kc7 Ke6 11. Kc6 Ke7 12. Kxd5. In fact, we have to supply a justification for our statement after 4. ... Kb5. Here we suppress a further debate and assume the strategies for the Figure 14.1 Diagrams 1 and 2 to be analogous.

In our search for the true relation between the position of Diagram 1 (or Diagram 2) and the human strategy as given above, we now add two pawns to the position of Diagram 2, a black pawn on a7 and a white pawn on a6, as depicted in Figure 14.5(a), to create another analogy.

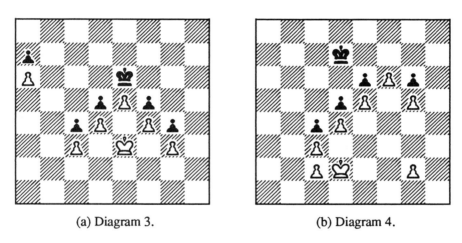

(a) Diagram 3.   (b) Diagram 4.

Figure 14.5: The effect of additional material on the solution.

Following the same strategy as outlined for Figure 14.1(b), the conclusion is that it does not work. In particular, we are unable to play 9. Kb6 in the positions that follow from Diagram 3. However, white can win anyway. So the game-theoretic value is again preserved. Moreover, it is also possible to extend the line of reasoning so that the strategy to follow coincides with the strategies described above. This need not always be the case. Berliner gave in Figure 14.1(a) the addition of two pawns on b4 (white) and b5 (black) as an example, which turned the position into a draw. Another fine experiment in relation to the original strategy in Figure 14.1(a) is the addition of white pawns on c2 or g2 or both (see Diagram 4, Figure 14.5(b)). All I can state is that when adding one white pawn the chess machine *Bebe* found the solution quicker than when adding two white pawns. This ends my discourse on small *Drosophilas*.

14.4 Another Drosophila

The second *Drosophila* worth mentioning is not taken from chess. But again, it is one which roused the impatience of practical-minded people who were saying: "You theoreticians are wasting too much time on this Yale Shooting Problem." I have a different opinion, namely that the Yale Shooting Problem is a kind of key to understanding the practical use of non-monotonic reasoning. It is a problem in *generality*. I would like to have a general database of common-sense knowledge, such as the general fact about getting somewhere is by going, and the general fact that when people die they remain dead. I would like to see that all sorts of trivial facts of that kind would be available to *any* computer program to use in a general form. In monotonic reasoning, deduction follows from premise without the possibility of refutation and, indeed, with absolute necessity. However, monotonicity is not a realistic model of the world. In the well-known problem of the missionaries and cannibals, the problem solver is bound to retract conclusions in the face of certain facts contradicting these all-too-simple assumptions.

In terms of the Yale Shooting Problem (Hanks and McDermott 1987), what does the sequence of loading, waiting and shooting mean? What is added by the common-sense knowledge database? We may state by definition that
- loading loads and
- shooting kills if loaded; but what about waiting?

Moreover, we may define
- one remains alive unless shooting happens and similarly
- a gun remains loaded unless shooting happens.

Hence, during the process of loading, waiting and shooting, the gun came unloaded. However, a gun having run out of ammunition, cannot be assured to stay unloaded. A spent gun will not always remain spent.

Non-monotonicity, as in the above, is typical of human reasoning. It involves the need to modify plans or strategies seen later to embody unwarrantable assumptions. In more formal terms, what we would like to have is a scheme starting from

$A \vdash P$ (i.e., A syntactically necessitates P)

and

$A \subset B$ (A is implied by B)

therefore

$B \vdash P$

with the latter alternatively written as

$[(A \subset B)] \supset [\text{Th}\,(A) \subset \text{Th}\,(B)].$

That is, if A is implied by B this implies that any theorem derived from A is implied by any theorem derived from B. This neat formulation, unfortunately, is not always achievable by either a human or a smart robot.

This is merely one of too many examples, and as a research area in computer reasoning, non-monotonic problems and common-sense knowledge problems have hardly been explored. In my opinion, if a bird can fly the fact need not be mentioned, because that would be part of the common-sense knowledge database. By contrast, if a bird cannot fly, the fact must be mentioned and the fact should take precedence over the database.

14.5 A Third Drosophila

Returning to chess, over the years we have seen that all chess programs rely on evaluation functions. Since Nimzovitch we possess rules intelligible for human beings, and along the lines of which a game will proceed adequately. Hence, next to the rules of adequacy we have the value of a position (or of its successors) produced by the evaluation function. A two-fold problem now arises:
- this value may not correspond to a human's action in such a position, and
- this value may not correspond to what a program must do in such a position.
Chess players always compare related positions, they never evaluate them independently. Chess programs evaluate each position, usually disregarding previous evaluations. Therefore, chess programs, were they able to take a leaf out of the human book, should be much simpler than they are now by relying on prior evaluations of related positions. I think that the models as described by my former student Barbara Jane Huberman (1968), now named Barbara Liskov-Huberman, is close to the model of Capablanca (1935) in his endgame book. Of course, the model has only been proved to be appropriate for the KRK, KBBK and KBNK endgames and, admittedly, the ideas are not applicable for the full game, but perhaps we can gain something out of the comparison of positions with the predicates *better* and *worse*. Figure 14.6 shows an example of a forcing tree (Huberman 1968, p. 5):

> The program has the move in p; it must make a move leading to a position q judged *better* than p for every sequence of moves by the opposition. Each iteration of the program will produce a tree like this; several iterations will be required to reach checkmate.

The difficulty in this procedure comes in deciding what pattern features of the positions are important.

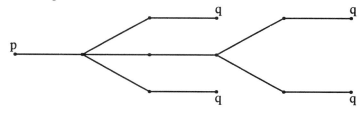

Figure 14.6: Example of a forcing tree.

Huberman's first hypothesis was that the model used in the program is a good representation of the abstract model assumed by chess books. It has resulted in insights about translation from book problem-solving methods into computer program heuristics. The relation between methods and heuristics are embodied in the functions *better* and *worse*.

Huberman's second hypothesis was that the information in the chess books is sufficient for the definitions of *better* and *worse*. Speaking for myself, I consider a combination of the right attributes, the idea of comparing positions instead of evaluating them and the introduction of *better* and *worse* predicates to be yet another true *Drosophila* in computer science research.

14.6 A Fourth Drosophila

As a final *Drosophila*, I would like to mention the research on Computer Go. Let me first state that there is a fundamental difference with chess. Comparing the playing strength of the best Computer-Go program with the playing strength of the Go World Champion, I estimate such a program to be twenty levels behind the Champion, whereas I believe that the best among computer-chess programs is "only" three levels behind Kasparov. The deepest issue about intelligence is its very foundation; it seems to be based on some collection of intellectual mechanisms, however embodied. Of some we know they exist and they are in the collection. From others we do not know they exist, let alone whether they are in the collection or not.

In human chess, a position is considered as a whole; it is not divided into parts (sometimes, an example of a part of the board helps illustrate a concept, but it is not vital). In Go, separation is absolutely vital.[1] Searching all legal moves in a Go game tree must be discarded after a few plies only, because of their many ramifications and the consequences of their combinatorial explosion. Therefore, a Go program ought first to identify small groups of stones and conduct searches and evaluations regarding each of these groups separately. The research of Go programs is still in its infancy, but we shall see that to bring Go programs to a level comparable with current chess programs, investigations of a totally different kind than used in computer chess are needed.

14.7 A Conclusion

A plethora of conclusions can be drawn about the impact of the four *Drosophilas* listed. As research develops, the possible conclusions have a habit of proliferating. I will refrain from anticipating but, speaking personally, expect

---

[1] For man because of limited mental capacities, for machine because of space and time limits (although assists like transposition tables and parallel search techniques may be particularly helpful here). - Editors.

the more fruitful results to emphasize some of the following ideas: "local" estimations on groups (Go), configurations (*better* and *worse*), databases with common-sense knowledge, and distinguishing phases in plans (as in dealing with endgame positions). Some combinations of these, I believe, are a potentially fertile basis for the much-needed global strategies for solving a general problem of any sort.

Acknowledgments. I thank Prof. H.J. van den Herik and Prof. I.S. Herschberg (Editors of the ICCA Journal) for writing up their notes on my talk. The present version contains some ideas, inspired by their feedback, that were not in the oral presentation.

15 Brute Force in Chess and Science

D. Michie

15.1 Introduction

It would be easy to imagine that at this 6th World Computer Chess Championship we shall learn more about how well today's computer programs play chess. What we will actually learn is more restricted, although none-the-less interesting, namely: How well do today's chess programs play against each other? Levy (1986a) has written:

> One of the unique aspects of programming a computer to play chess is the fact that concrete methods exist for calibrating the success or failure of the program.

Perhaps one should say "almost unique," since there are many skilled tasks for which concrete methods do exist, including weather forecasting, economic modeling, or identifying and describing molecular structure in biotechnology. This last field is particularly relevant in being combinatorial and chess-like in its formal properties. However, the calibration task in chess is more difficult than in any of these other problem domains, as I shall explain. Let us return to Levy:

> In chess it is easy to determine whether your program is stronger or weaker than someone else's — you simply play a series of games between the two programs and the program which wins the series can reasonably be assumed to be the stronger.

So far, so good; but stronger at what? At playing other programs, or at playing chess masters? If the latter, then what kind of a chess master? Are we talking about a strong Grandmaster (GM) who has never faced superior brute-force analysis before? Or do we mean a weak International Master (IM) who specializes, as does David Levy, in beating computer-chess programs by encouraging them to beat themselves? Levy's passage continues:

> In the same way it is possible to compare the strength of a chess-playing computer program with that of a human player — the best man (or machine) will be the winner.

This chapter is a revised and updated version of "Brute Force in Chess and Science," Procs. CIPS Conference, Edmonton, May 1989, pp. 82-111. Also, *Journal of the International Computer Chess Association*, vol 12, no. 3, pp. 127-143. It is reproduced here with the permission of the Canadian Information Processing Society and the International Computer Chess Association.

15.2 Computer-Hostile Chess

Suppose that the winner of the series of games postulated by Levy (SW for *series winner*) is similarly tested against some *third party* (TP). Suppose also that we know that TP is regularly defeated by the *series loser* (SL). Can we infer the outcome? Given that:

>TP usually loses to SL
>
>and SL usually loses to SW
>
>can we infer that TP usually loses to SW?

If and only if all three parties are human, or all three are programs, then the answer is: "Yes, it is inferable that the Third Party usually loses to the Series Winner." Otherwise transitivity fails and nothing can be inferred. The outcome then depends on, among other things, whether the humans involved have incorporated in their repertoire certain "computer-hostile" modes of play historically pioneered by David Levy himself.

When pitted against a chess program, Levy adopts a style which he has described as "Do nothing: but do it well." Although not effective against human masters, it scores heavily against computer opponents. By going for blocked positions devoid of tactical mobility, he invites his computer opponent to reveal its threadbare positional sense and lack of long-range strategic ideas. Sooner or later the machine drifts into some position which it is incapable of recognizing as strategically doomed. Before this happens, however, a stronger but less computer-exposed player than Levy may yield to the temptation to try some tactics, and become lost in the calculational complexities. This is what happened at the Software Toolworks Chess Championship held at Long Beach, California, which saw the first-ever defeat of a Grandmaster by a chess program in a full-scale tournament.

15.2.1 Upset at Long Beach

The top section of this Swiss tournament had an entry of about 100 players, 76 of whom were rated over 2300 on the USCF scale and seven were Grandmasters. The two-processor version of *Deep Thought* tied for first place with GM Anthony Miles. *Deep Thought*'s eight games went as set out in Table 15.1 (opponents arranged in decreasing order of USCF rating).

Impressive though this outcome is, we should not necessarily find it surprising. Based on various calculations Newborn's (1979) predictions can be seen in Table 15.2. Moreover, Levy (1986b) tabulated the USCF performance ratings, achieved by the leading chess programs in human tournaments in various years since 1967, and found the best linear fit to be:

$$rating = 49.2 \times (year - 1900) - 1697$$

Using Levy's (1986b) plot of rating data (circles) in Figure 15.1, we find that the 2740 Software Toolworks performance result (the square) contributed by *Deep Thought* fits the line.

Opponent	USCF Rating	Result for *Deep Thought*
GM Walter Browne	2640	Lost
IM Vincent McCambridge	2599	Drawn
GM Bent Larsen	2590	Won
FIDE Master Alex Fishbein	2572	Won
IM Jeremy Silman	2507	Won
FIDE Master Salgado	2388	Won
Mr. Glicksman	2388	Won
Mr. Alexander Lesiege	2334	Won

Table 15.1: *Deep Thought*'s opponents at the 1988 Software Toolworks tournament.

Computer victory over IM	:	1984
Computer victory over GM	:	1988
Computer victory over World Champion	:	1992

Table 15.2: Newborn's 1979 predictions of computer success.

Walter Browne heads the list as the highest-rated player, and was unique in defeating *Deep Thought*. Browne was also the only player out of our eight known to have had previous experience of opposing computer play. In the spring of 1978, he made an exhibition tour in the USA and, before stopping at Twin Cities, Minnesota, had accumulated a record of only two losses and six draws in seventeen exhibitions of simultaneous chess, each involving several dozen games. He had already been US Champion for three consecutive times and at the time had a USCF rating of 2560. Atkin and Slate's *Chess 4.6*, running on a Control Data Cyber 176, was allowed to be one of Browne's 44 opponents. The program defeated him in 63 moves. For the game record, see Michie (1980) with a commentary by D. Kopec. Browne had also on two occasions attempted public demonstrations of winning within the 50-move limit against an exhaustive move-optimal database of the ending KQKR. He failed on his first attempt and succeeded (but only just) on the second.

Such previous experience is highly relevant. If GM Bent Larsen had been briefed beforehand with the elementary do's and don'ts of play against computers, the consensus is that the outcome would have been different. The same comment is no doubt applicable to some of *Deep Thought*'s other opponents.

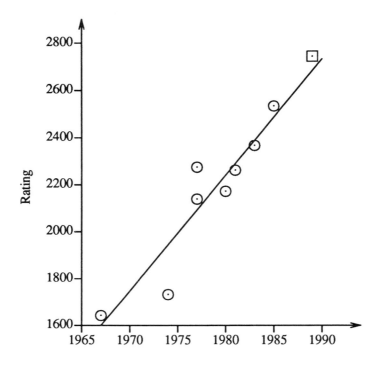

Figure 15.1: Levy's plot of leading chess program ratings (circles) as a function of time.

15.2.2 Deep Thought versus Bent Larsen

The Bent Larsen – *Deep Thought* game is reproduced below from the *Spectator* (17 December 1988) by kind permission, as annotated by GM Raymond Keene, former British Champion.

White: GM Bent Larsen (2590 FIDE) – Black: *Deep Thought* (~2550 USCF)
1988 Software Toolworks Open Championship
1. c4 e5 2. g3 Nf6 3. Bg2 c6 4. Nf3 e4 5. Nd4 d5 6. cxd5 Qxd5 7. Nc2 Qh5 8. h4 Bf5 9. Ne3 Bc5 10. Qb3 b6 11. Qa4 0-0 12. Nc3 b5 13. Qc2 Bxe3 14. dxe3 Re8 15. a4 b4 16. Nb1 Nbd7 17. Nd2 Re6 18. b3 Rd8 19. Bb2 Bg6 20. Nc4 Nd5 21. 0-0-0 N7f6 22. Bh3 Bf5 23. Bxf5 Qxf5 24. f3 h5 25. Bd4 Rd7 26. Kb2 Rc7 *Now Larsen becomes impatient and goes astray. He should quietly consolidate with Ka2 before attacking on the other wing. Instead, he challenges the machine to a battle of calculating wits and is cut to ribbons.* **27. g4 hxg4 28. Rhg1 c5** *White's bishop has no retreat square, since Larsen neglected to create a haven for it on b2. So white is forced into complications.* **29. fxg4 Nxg4 30. Bxg7** *See* Figure 15.2. **Rg6** *It is most impressive that black delays capturing the white bishop until the optimum moment. If instead Kxg7 then 31. Rxd5 Qxd5 32. Rxg4+ with compensation for the lost exchange.* **31. Qd2 Rd7 32. Rxg4 Rxg4**

33. Ne5 Nxe3 34. Qxd7 Nxd1+ 35. Qxd1 Rg3 *Another fine move. Again the machine sidesteps a premature capture, thus depriving white of the counterplay he must have been expecting after Rxg7 36. Qd8+ Kh7 37. Nd7.* **36. Qd6 Kxg7 37. Nd7 Re3 38. Qh2 Kh7 39. Nf8+ Kh8 40. h5 Qd5 41. Ng6+ fxg6 42. hxg6+ Kg7 43. Qh7+ Kf6 0-1.**

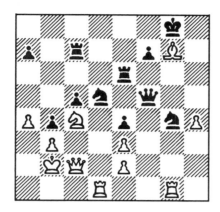

Figure 15.2: Larsen – *Deep Thought*, after 30. Bxg7.

15.2.3 Good in Parts

To appreciate the lack of wisdom of a human deciding to embark on tactical complications as Larsen did, one should recall that *Deep Thought*'s search of over 700,000 nodes of lookahead per second was giving a solid horizon of 10-ply in the opening phase and 9-ply in the middlegame, rising to 10-ply and beyond in the endgame. A *singular extension* (Anantharaman, Campbell and Hsu 1988) feature searches forceful variations out to a depth of 16 to 18 ply, taking the average over the maximum depth of each search. Such an opponent, just as the proverbial curate's egg, might be called "good in parts." What about the other parts?

About a month after the Software Toolworks Open Championship, an informal exploration of *Deep Thought*'s other parts revealed a surprising lack of resource in dealing with a relatively weak player who was, however, trained in the Levy style. Mr. Dominic Lawson is a former British county player who has not played serious chess for some years, informally assessed by GM Raymond Keene as being in the USCF 2200 - 2250 range. He was given an hour or so's "computer-hostile" briefing by Levy, prior to engaging *Deep Thought* in a 30-minute game by transatlantic telephone. The total time on each chess clock was thus set to 30 minutes.

Eventually Lawson got into severe time trouble and resigned, but not before his "do nothing" policy had elicited from *Deep Thought* sufficiently poor positional play to place the program in extreme jeopardy. Admittedly, the time constraint reduced *Deep Thought* to about a fifth of its normal search capability. On the other hand, such speedup of play is usually reckoned to bear more heavily against the human than the machine side.

Subsequent confirmation that study of past machine games can open the door to computer-hostile chess was provided by World Champion Gary Kasparov himself, who trounced *Deep Thought* in a two-game match in October, 1989 (see Chapter 2 *Advances in Man-Machine Play*). Having earlier played through many of *Deep Thought*'s past games, he commented that he could steer his opponent into lines it did not like. Interestingly, by move 25 of game 1 every chess master present could see that *Deep Thought* was already strategically lost, whereas the program's own evaluation was still reporting the position as even.

15.3 Use of Knowledge

The brute-force programs of today, then, are patchworks of tactical strength and strategic weakness. To remedy the weaknesses, through the so-called *knowledge approach,* would seem at this stage to offer better returns on each unit of extra effort than if the same effort were to go to developing more search power.

Deep Thought's introduction of the *singular extension* heuristic (Anantharaman, Campbell and Hsu 1988) illustrates the use of a simple refinement of the program's knowledge (in this case concerning the concept *forcing*) to leverage the limited knowledge content of the existing evaluation function. Singular extension generalizes the standard practice, which is to search beyond the solid lookahead horizon along all forcing lines defined just in terms of captures and checks. The *Deep Thought* heuristic extends this narrow definition of *forcing* to include all cases where a unique opponent's reply is indicated by the pre-eminence of its evaluation score over alternative opponent options.

The core of *Deep Thought*'s stored chess knowledge, tiny by human chess standards, occupies seven tables, as follows:

2 tables	piece placement
1 table	files and blocked pawns
1 table	white pawn structure
1 table	black pawn structure
1 table	white passed pawn
1 table	black passed pawn

Various chess concepts, such as king safety, are encoded by combining different primitive items of information from the tables.

As for anticipated performance gains arising purely from hardware improvements, these can be estimated in a rough fashion from self-play exercises such as Ken Thompson's, in which the calculative resources of the two sides were varied. Levy (1986b) extrapolates from Thompson's measurements to Grandmaster level and estimates gains in the Super-Grandmaster region to taper off at about 10 rating points for each added ply (5- to 6-fold increase in calculation). The advent of machine play of *Hitech* and *Deep Thought* calibre now enables self-play estimation to be extended to the upper range of the scale.

15.4 Grandmaster Backlash

As remarked to me by Jonathan Schaeffer, the immediate next development is likely to be a flurry of interest among IMs and GMs who will be quick to master the essentials of computer-hostile play. We may then pass through a paradoxical period in which programs continue to rise in strength as measured against standardized opposition, while falling in their USCF ratings as calculated from tournament results. Associated with this, in Master Tournaments containing mixed human and computer players one may anticipate partial restoration of the transitivity of the *usually loses to* relation discussed before.

An alternative outcome is that Grandmasters may protest against continued participation of computers in serious tournaments. Shortly after their respective experiences against *Deep Thought*, Mr. Dominic Lawson and GM Bent Larsen compared notes. Larsen remarked that the Software Toolworks Swiss tournament, as is now common practice, had offered an option for those players not wishing to be drawn against computer opponents to give advance written notice to the organizers. Had he been aware of the option, Larsen stated that he would have exercised it. Without attributing points of view to any particular individuals, the following summarizes some objections among master players to computer participation in tournaments.

Objection 1:
Chess is a culture shared among colleagues who form a human community, however adversarial the game may be in itself. After play, opponents commonly analyze the fine points together, and many find in the tournament room the mainstream of their social life. Robot intruders contribute only brute force, not interesting chess ideas. Their admission, it is held, would impoverish the culture.

Objection 2:
For masters, the soul of competitive chess is matching oneself against professional peers, including preparation for encounters by advance study of the opponent's style and foibles. The developers of a computer program can nullify all this by last-minute substitution of one stored opening book for another, alteration of parameters of board evaluation or of play, and the like. Skill and insight in constructing and exploiting models of the opponent is a central part of the craft. To have it thus disabled imposes an unfair handicap, comparable to obliging an opera star to sing an unrehearsed duet on the stage with a voice synthesizer.

Objection 3:
> The intellectual content and significance of the performance of chess masters lies in their mental reduction of vast combinatorial domains to a humanly-structured hierarchy of descriptive concepts, rather as a scientist seeks to reduce the combinatorics of natural phenomena to an orderly and intelligible set of predictive laws. It is intrinsic to chess that theory must also be operationally effective by the test of actual play: "his theory against mine." What if the machine opponent has no theory, or at least nothing recognizable as such to the human chess mind? If machine-generated play is such that it *could* have proceeded from human-type theory, or could be described after the event in terms of such theory, then the human master's power to conceptualize is being fairly tested. But what if the opponent's play is so strange and convoluted that no description is, or ever will be, possible *in terms which could fit into human memory or be interpretable by a human processor*? Rather as a tennis professional facing a robot player able to impart spins which could never come from a human-held racket, Grandmasters will find in such opposition only obscurity. What has this to do with the skill to which they have devoted their life?

Fact-gathering related to such objections would be timely in view of Prof. Lim Kok-Ann's recent interpretation of FIDE rules. He gave a written opinion to the USCF Computer Chess Committee, that "a computer cannot be a player" (Welsh 1988) with the implication of future exclusion from FIDE tournaments.

15.4.1 Obscurity of Machine Strategies

The last of the three objections has the most substance, yet it is not obvious. For human experts the thought of interacting with non-biological, but nevertheless goal-seeking, problem solvers is new. So the unconscious assumption arises that such agents, even though non-human, cannot think up anything which humans could not. Or even if a chess machine *could* think humanly-undiscoverable chess thoughts (principles, rules, strategies etc.), then they would be thoughts which a knowledgeable chess master could at least *digest* and *assimilate*.

The doctrine of necessary assimilability by expert human brains rests on shaky foundations. For some chess maneuvers of machine origin which remain at present mysterious, the reader is referred to the many works of A.J. Roycroft (1986a,b,c,d,88a,88b). To the same point are the comments of van den Herik, Herschberg and Nakad (1987) who compared Grandmaster analysis of the KRP(a2)KbBP(a3) ending with their exhaustively computed database for this endgame. The latter comprises nearly 5 million legal positions of which about four fifths can be won by white, the worst case requiring 54 moves. Among the fundamental questions which arose from the comparison, these authors list:

- "To what extent can optimal play and counterplay, assuming these to be uniquely given by the database, unambiguously be translated into strategic terms? In other words, is there an alternative, for the human player, to rote learning of a huge number of special cases?"

• "Is there a means of compressing the database so as to make it more readily understandable to a human player?"

For simplicity in conveying the main point, I prefer to use the example which historically was the first to attract attention, namely the KQKR endgame. Mention was earlier made of GM Walter Browne's two brushes with Ken Thompson's exhaustively computed database of minimax-optimal moves for the queen against rook endgame. Recently GM Nigel Short (2655 FIDE rating, approximately USCF 2750) attempted, and failed, on five separate occasions to win within the 50-move limit from starting positions set up for him by GM John Nunn (1988). These were selected to be in the range 26 - 29 minimax-optimal moves from the win (defined as safe rook capture or mate). The most adverse starting positions in the space lie at a distance of 31 moves. Note however (and this is crucial) that Short, in common with other Grandmasters, can demonstrate without difficulty the win under such conditions *against any human opponent*. What, then, is the true issue?

15.4.2 Grandmasters Sheltered from Complexity

Nigel Short, like any other GM, has had a sheltered life with respect to opposing play. His exposure has been confined to that small subset of strong play which is driven by simplifying heuristics. These simplifiers are what human masters adopt in order to contain in their minds the *combinatorial explosion* which would otherwise overwhelm them. It is precisely in terms of these same simplifiers that they comprehend the meaning and purpose of the play of a Grandmaster opponent. In other words, human masters have had no past practice against unintelligible computer strategies. A quick example of a simplifier which necessarily characterizes human master play of the queen-against-rook ending, is the assumption that the defending player will never separate his rook and king. To do so precipitates complexities and dangers which it is good human sense to avoid. A machine opponent, not requiring any such heuristic, has only to separate rook and king to confront the attacker with novel and tricky skirmishing on which human playing experience has nothing to say. Examples in this vein could be multiplied.

15.4.3 Machine Strategies Not Necessarily Explainable

With the relatively small queen-versus-rook ending it is not impossible that a human could eventually understand, explain and perhaps even master for his own use the bizarre intricacies of machine play. But only a small step up the ladder of complexity, to queen and pawn (on g7) versus queen, is sufficient to exceed such a possibility. Komissarchik and Futer (1974) built an exhaustive database for this ending. A computed minimax-optimal strategy takes the white king on a labored and mysterious journey, circumnavigating the board more than once, before the preconditions for safe pawn promotion are finally established. Figure 15.3 from Komissarchik and Futer (1974) is here reproduced. Roycroft

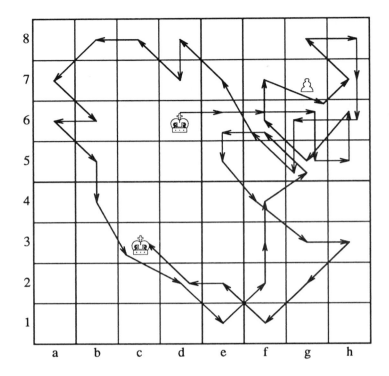

Figure 15.3: A king's labored and mysterious journey.

comments on " ... the white king's contorted peregrinations throughout the
solution's full length". Qualified students of this result believe that human
insight into the detailed rationale is unlikely to be attainable (Roycroft 1986d).

    These ideas can be approached through a memory/calculation trade-off
graph as in Figure 15.4. Two optimal-strategy plots of calculation against
memory are shown. In each case points on the line represent the fastest-running
program which can fit into the given memory allocation (X-axis) given the
calculational resource-bound (Y-axis). Equivalently, the smallest memory
allocation which can support a program to run within the resource-bound shown
on the Y-axis is the number of store-bits read off from the X-axis.[1] For the

---

[1]   Both scales should be thought of as logarithmic, running to more than, say, 10^{25}
bits along the horizontal axis and to more than, say, 10^{25} binary discriminations along the
vertical. A point on a curve means: for the given amount of memory this is the fewest
calculation-bits needed for worst-case evaluation of any position, and conversely for the
given amount of calculation this is the smallest memory needed. The "rectangle of feasibility" enclosed by the dotted lines is determined by the known limits to human memory
storage ($10^{10} - 10^{11}$ bits filled in a lifetime) and to calculation (20 bits/sec).

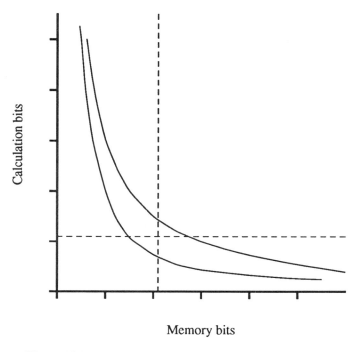

Figure 15.4: Memory-versus-calculation plot for two chess endgames.

"easier" ending (such as queen versus rook) the memory-to-calculation relation has been graphed assuming the possible existence of "human-digestible compromises" between opposite types of indigestible machine solution, that is lookahead-intensive and lookup-intensive. For the more difficult ending (say queen and pawn (g7) against queen), the line joining optimal representations has been drawn to pass clear of the rectangle of human resource, to indicate for this machine-soluble problem a conjecture of human infeasibility. No domain for which such a conjecture is true can ever yield a strategy that is both humanly memorizable and humanly executable.

In summary, the third Grandmaster objection is based on fear that machines could pollute the tournament game with obscure and humanly meaningless styles of play. The possibility cannot be dismissed, and the emergence of the phenomenon should be watched for. However, when asked to say from inspection of game records which player is the chess master and which is the chess machine, experts continue to fail the test. It seems that the feared stylistic pollution is not yet with us.

15.5 Chess and Science

It is a hard but inescapable fact that the neurobiology of the brain imposes limits on human describability of complex phenomena, in applied science as in chess. Television weather forecasters might decide to describe the basis for their predictions in the terms used by the meteorological computer programs from which they came. But if they did, neither viewers nor colleagues would understand them. If, however, they were to take pen and ink and attempt the predictions themselves, complexity condemns them to a choice of evils: either

(1) to attempt the hopeless task of executing the computer models inside their head, or

(2) to attempt the currently hopeless task of constructing simplified yet effective qualitative models which *can* be executed in the head.

Scientists who today undertake the modeling of complex domains usually opt to cut their losses. Intelligibility and mental checkability of models are then sacrificed for machine computability. This forced move towards obscurity has implications for future scientific practice. Careful study of the trade-offs involved is indicated, and computer chess is ideally placed to act as the needed test-bench.

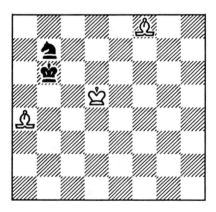

Figure 15.5: The Kling-Horwitz position, either side to move.

15.5.1 Limits to Human Theory-Construction

Consider in this connection the project to analyze the KBBKN (two bishops against knight ending). Nearly 140 years ago, Kling and Horwitz (1851) contributed a celebrated but (as it has turned out) flawed theory, illustrated by the position shown in Figure 15.5. They concluded erroneously that, provided black can set up this pattern, the position is drawn. Later, using the Thompson database, A.J. Roycroft identified Diagrams (a), (b), (c) and (d) of Figure 15.6

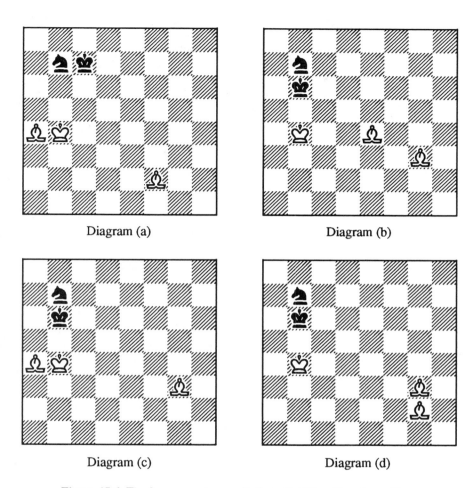

Figure 15.6: The four compulsory exits from the Kling-Horwitz position.

and showed that these critical positions form the *compulsory exits* for black when faced with optimal play. They are believed to comprise an exhaustive set such that when white drives black out from the shelter of the Kling-Horwitz pattern, play must pass through one of the four. Kling and Horwitz had no way of knowing that their attempt at a decisive analysis of the KBBKN domain was fated to fail. The cause of failure is the same as in pre-computational meteorology, namely, that beyond a certain level of complexity, fully effective theories which a human brain can use cannot be found by the unaided brain itself. The computational complexity of a given domain has to be defined relative to some specified system. If that system is a computer, then the limits are set by such parameters as instruction set, clock rate, size and speed of _memory and I/O transfer rates. If the designated system is the brain, then the limits are set by analogous facts of neurobiology.

Such limits, be they computer-bound or facts of biology, have always been there. But in the first flush of the scientific revolution it seemed that the new tools of formal description, calculation and proof would allow the trained mind to solve all questions which can be framed in the language of science. This inspiring, if somewhat megalomaniac, conception was formulated in 1619 by Descartes on the eve of his 23rd birthday, and it was to motivate the whole of his subsequent life and work. Whether, like his successors, he meant to assert total describability of phenomena is unclear. He spoke of "a completely new science which would be capable of solving *in a general manner* all problems which could be proposed in all the quantitative fields ..." The italicized phrase (my italics) carries a connotation of generic as opposed to domain-specific methods. It may also imply an element of allowable approximation. If this is what he meant it is just as well. In his *Discourse on Method* (1637) one of three worked examples chosen to illustrate the new principles was the construction of a scientific explanation of the weather! No such caution inhibited Leibniz in his 1677 preface to *The General Sciences* which set out his proposals for a mechanizable logic to support human thinking:

> For all inquiries which depend on reasoning would be performed by the transposition of characters and by a kind of calculus, which would immediately facilitate the discovery of beautiful results. For we should not have to break our head, as much as is necessary today, and yet we should be sure of accomplishing everything the given facts allow. ... And if someone doubted my results I should say to him: "Let us calculate, Sir," and taking pen and ink we should soon settle the question.

15.5.2 Limits to Graspability of Solutions

Science today has been reluctantly awakened from Leibniz' dream by the computational achievement (as in meteorology) of "brute-force" solutions which can be used to great effect (as also can Ken Thompson's chess databases) but which are not fully graspable by the user. Weather prediction is an example of solutions gained by numerical computation. There remains a feeling that these domains somehow constitute a special case, and that solution obscurity is perhaps something to do with the numerical aspect. The human brain was surely not fashioned for arithmetic, but to hold sway over knowledge and reasoning. Moved by this thought most scientists (after making due exception of the numerical part of their task) still side with Leibniz. Hence one cannot over-stress the importance of the demonstrations now arising from computer chess that, in non-numerical domains too, the discoveries of brute force can break the bounds of human ability to achieve comprehension.

For one more example, let us go back to the ending KRP(a2)KbBP(a3) of van den Herik, Herschberg and Nakad (1987). Having encountered this ending in play against Velimirović (Rio de Janeiro, 1979) GM Timman's subsequent analysis identifies the position of Figure 15.7 as crucial and adds: "White wins the a-pawn in at most 21 moves." The computed database shows this to be attainable in at most 11 moves, and reveals no fewer than 13 errors in the 41-ply main variation of Timman's published analysis. So we are obliged to discard the human analysis. How graspable then is the machine-generated analysis? In this case the question remains open. But as we have seen in the Futer and Komissarchik domain, machine-generated solutions can exist which, for the time being at least, lie totally beyond human grasp.

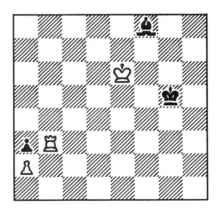

Figure 15.7: Timman conjecture: White almost always passes through this position.

15.5.3 Complexity Impasse

Combinatorial domains of importance in empirical science are today facing something of the same impasse as computer chess. That is to say, solutions to particular instances of a scientific problem (analogous to particular legal positions in a complex domain of chess) can be laboriously obtained, perhaps by prohibitively costly analysis, yet the solutions are opaque. What is required is the extraction from such solved cases of manageable sets of general rules by which solutions to newly encountered instances can expeditiously be obtained, the extraction, preferably on a computer-aided basis, of operational theories.

A successful chess exercise on this theme was recently reported by Muggleton (1988). An inductive-learning methodology was used to generate automatically a playing strategy from example sequences of play. From the extremely complex KBBKN ending mentioned earlier, the starting position shown in Figure 15.8, with white to move, was selected. With the aid of Thompson's exhaustively computed database for this ending (Thompson and Roycroft 1983), the endgame specialist A.J. Roycroft was able to supply an exposition of the initial phase of optimal play for white from which Muggleton could construct sets of positional attributes, actions and example sequences of play. To these an algorithm was applied for inducing regular-language grammars, in combination with an ID3-like decision-tree induction algorithm, resulting in the construction of a finite-state automaton. The latter embodied the machine's discovery of an effective strategy, duly presented to Roycroft for appraisal, which was positive.

Figure 15.8: Initial position for Muggleton's inductive acquisition of a strategy.

Arising from his interactions with the Thompson database and involvement in inductive-learning work of the kind described above, Roycroft has been able to transform the theory of the KBBKN ending from the state of stagnation and error in which it had so long been becalmed, into one of the most deeply researched endings known (Roycroft 1983,86a,b,c,88b). Comparable perhaps is Troitsky's monumental and unparalleled analysis of the KNNKP ending (Troitzky 1934), itself the subject of a striking computer-aided confirmation and extension by Herschberg, van den Herik and Schoo (Chapter 11 *Verifying and Codifying Strategies in a Chess Endgame*).

There is, I feel, an indication in all of this of a future style of work involving three-way co-operation of inductive-learning programs, machine-learning specialists and domain specialists, with a different role for the computer from that which we find computers playing in science today. For a picture of the conventional style, let me quote Michael Gunn (1988) of the UK's Rutherford Appleton Laboratory:

> Theoretical physicists classify the style of their work, loosely, into three categories: formalistic — in which they do accurate calculations with pencil and paper; intuitive — in which they carry out crude calculations, often with rather sophisticated ideas underlying them; and computational — in which they do calculations, frequently of an exploratory nature on problems not amenable to the other two types of thought.

The context makes it clear that Gunn had in mind brute-force varieties of computations, comparable to those performed by Thompson in the initial database construction. Muggleton's use of sequence induction is perhaps more closely related to the style designated by Gunn as intuitive.

It is a common objection to chess as a model of scientific investigation that it forms a fully specified and determinate world. In contrast, the scientist's subject matter is veiled in layers of obscurity introduced by unavailability of relevant measurements, instrument error, environmental perturbations, biological variation and so forth, in a word "noise." This state of affairs is not universal. Some of the most important domains of contemporary molecular biology are fully specified and determinate in the same sense as chess. Yet their logical complexity wraps them in a fog of what appears to the investigator to be random noise, but in reality is not.

I end this review by discussing the prediction of secondary structure in proteins from a knowledge of their primary structure.

15.6 The Protein Prediction Problem

There are some 100,000 different types of protein in the human body, and they are collectively responsible for almost all the vital tasks. The conformation of a protein, its three-dimensional shape, determines its function. For a given physico-chemical environment the conformation is uniquely predictable from the precise sequence of amino-acid building-blocks of which the molecule is composed, that is, from the protein's *primary structure*. It is now possible to create a gene to order, and have this gene supervise the construction of the precise amino-acid sequence which it codes for, in effect writing a "message" using an alphabet of some twenty symbols. But it is not possible to know whether a sequence will constitute a new useful protein, since the rules governing the conversion of the one-dimensional information into three-dimensional information, and the rules relating conformation to function, are not understood. A protein folds up into a macro-sequence of "alpha-helices," "beta-sheets," and "turns." Precisely which of these three structures a given amino-acid in the sequence will find itself belonging to is strictly computable from quantum chemistry, but only in the "in principle" sense that it is strictly computable for any chess position whether it belongs to the category "won" or "drawn" or "lost." The practical problem is the same in either case: how to utilize an existing database of sample cases which have already been assigned to their proper classes so as to construct rules for predicting the class membership of new cases of the same general kind. In chess endings this pre-assignment can be laboriously carried out by exhaustive computation. For selected proteins it can be carried out, also laboriously, by crystallographic analysis.

I mention the protein problem because of Ross King's (1989) recent work carried out in the Turing Institute, which specializes in algorithms for inductively inferring rules from data (King and Sternberg 1990). For protein prediction the number of cases which have been fully solved by crystallographic methods is of the order of 100, mainly to be found in the standard Brookhaven database (King 1989). These comprise altogether some 10,000 positions. A position is a "slot" in the polypeptide sequence which in principle could be occupied by any one of the 20 amino-acids. Each position is allocated in the database to one of the three decision classes, roughly about 25-30% are in alpha-helices, 20% in beta-sheets and 50-55% in turns. For computer-induction purposes this is the totality from which "training sets" have to be drawn. Based on the presence or absence of specified chemical properties (e.g., "carrying an electrical charge") in the individual members of the given subsequence, King's rules map from short local subsequences to decision classes. For example, using the rule:

$$(\text{pos, neg, pos}) \rightarrow A$$
with the pos class = {h, k, r} and the neg class = {d, e}

then the primary sequence (h, d, r) is predicted to have the secondary structure (A, A, A). That is, when the protein folds, h, d and r in this sequence all end up in an alpha-helix.

King's inductively extracted rules compared reasonably well in accuracy of prediction with other state-of-the-art methods of rule-extraction. They scored an additional "plus" on the basis of their comprehensibility to molecular biologists, and indeed they represent theories about the formation of protein secondary structure. As a corrective to optimism, however, "state of the art" in this domain means a mere 60% correct prediction, compared with about 30% for random guessing. We are now considering whether significant further improvement might come from applying some of the latest inductive engines developed in our chess work. Meanwhile automated rule learning is beginning to extend the rule-formulation abilities of protein specialists. The same applies to chess endgame analysis, as indicated in recent studies such as those of Shapiro (1987).

15.7 Endgames of Molecular Science

In chess analysis as in molecular science, I see an era of mutual tuning of two classes of instrument: well-stocked brains and artificial intelligence (AI) software tools. A logical step now would be the identification of combinatorial problem domains in molecular chemistry and genetics as suitable for treatment with the new induction tools. There is opportunity here to press further along the road of AI-assisted discovery opened by Joshua Lederberg and Edward Feigenbaum in the early 1960s with the Dendral project. Whether on balance we speak of gains to the methodology of science from computer chess, or vice versa, is beside the main point. The significant point is that intellectual traffic in both directions is bound to increase, and can bring nothing but good to both communities.

Acknowledgments. Experimental work at the Turing Institute referred to in this paper was made possible by Contract number DAJA45-86-0047 from the US Army Research Institute for the Behavioral and Social Sciences through its European Research Office of the US Army, London, UK. The opinions expressed are those of the author and do not necessarily represent those of the US Army. I am indebted to GM Raymond Keene and to the Deputy Editor of the *Spectator*, Mr. Dominic Lawson, for permission to reproduce Mr. Keene's annotations of the game involving *Deep Thought*, and for helpful facts and discussion. I owe a similar debt for information and comments to IM David Levy, to GM John Nunn and to Mr. John Roycroft — also to Mr. Charles Sweeney of the Turing Institute chess research group who helped me with the graphics and with checking the game records.

16 Perspectives on Falling from Grace

M.V. Donskoy and J. Schaeffer

16.1 Introduction

Research in computer chess has progressed over the past three decades to the point where programs will soon be Grandmaster strength. Superficially this accomplishment seems impressive. However, the building of a chess program that is better than all humans is a scientific pursuit, and it is relevant to ask what the lasting scientific contributions of achieving this result are. Perhaps the ends justify the means, but what are the means by which the computer-chess community strives for this lofty goal? Rather than evaluating the accomplishments of computer-chess research, here we consider the methods by which the results have been obtained.

For the fledgling area of artificial intelligence (AI) chess was viewed as an important test application. Some researchers regarded computer chess as the *Drosophila* of machine intelligence. However, three decades of progress has relegated the problem of building chess programs to only a peripheral relationship with AI. Mainstream artificial intelligence has moved on to other applications, even though the chess problem is still far from being solved. Instead, computer chess seems to have become a separate research area, with only historical ties to AI. To many researchers, it is regarded as mere "game playing." Why has computer chess fallen from grace from the mainstream research community?

These questions cannot be completely addressed here; there are many points of view and different sides to be argued. This chapter examines computer chess from the research perspective, attempting to understand it better as a science. A retrospective look at what has been accomplished is presented with a view to examining where the field is today and where it is headed tomorrow. Whereas the past has often been clouded by engineering passing as science, misspent effort for short-term gains, and research results with little applicability to other domains, there is evidence that computer chess is emerging from the shadow of its past and may be recapturing some lost stature in the research world.

This chapter contains minor revisions from one of the same title in the *New Directions in Game-Tree Search Workshop* proceedings, T.A. Marsland (ed.), Edmonton, May 1989, pp. 84-93. It also appeared in the *Journal of the International Computer Chess Association*, vol. 12, no. 3, pp. 155-163.

16.2 Historical Trends

The development of computer-chess programs can be divided into three distinct eras. The first, or *pioneering* era, spanned the 1950s to the mid 1970s. It was characterized by the extensive use of chess knowledge to both guide the search and assess chess positions. By today's standards, many of these programs used *ad hoc* techniques.

The second phase, or *technology* era, began in the mid 1970s and was marked by the exploitation of brute-force alpha-beta ($\alpha\beta$) search. The observation that there was a strong correlation between machine speed and program performance meant that one had only to use faster computers to improve performance. The advent of fast sequential processors, followed by special-purpose machines and parallel systems, resulted in a dependence on advancing technology to solve the chess problem. To some extent, this era is not yet over but it is clear that with massively parallel VLSI chess programs (for example, *Hitech* (Ebeling 1986) and *Deep Thought* (Hsu 1987)) there is not much further one can go in this area, although there are still interesting problems to be solved (such as how to use parallel processors effectively).

Recently, a new era of computer-chess work has been begun. With current technology being pushed to its limits, it was time to go back and re-discover the ideas and motivations of the pioneering era. This *algorithm* era is resulting in a variety of innovative ways of searching (for example, Beal 1989; McAllester 1988; Rivest 1988; Anantharaman, Campbell and Hsu 1988; Schrüfer 1988) and uses of knowledge (see, for example, Chapter 6 *Hitech*).

One way of distinguishing between the eras is by the search methods that dominated each one. Most programs of the pioneering era used selective search methods. Their search algorithms were unstable, required extensive application-dependent knowledge, were difficult to debug, and it was hard to predict their performance. The technology era preferred the simplicity of brute-force $\alpha\beta$, which was easy to implement, reliable and had predictable performance. The new era is still dominated by $\alpha\beta$, but the ideas of *selective deepening* have complicated the search procedure (for example, Anantharaman, Campbell and Hsu 1988). This era represents a compromise in search strategy over the extreme positions of its predecessors.

Perhaps the preceding discussion best illustrates why computer chess fell from grace. With brute-force $\alpha\beta$ searching, chess became an uninteresting problem to AI. The solution to improve performance was to just build faster machines. However, some of the fundamental problems of playing good chess (such as those outlined by Berliner (1973)) are beyond the reach of hardware technology alone. After a decade of chasing the faster machine mirage, it now appears necessary to return to the basics, finding better search algorithms and better ways of using chess knowledge to solve the problem. In some sense, research in computer chess has come full circle.

16.3 Scientific Credibility

Here we outline some of the obstacles to computer chess achieving credibility in the scientific community. The topics mentioned do not exhaust the points for discussion, but illustrate some of the major obstacles.

16.3.1 Beyond Alpha-Beta

In the technology era, work on finding new search algorithms almost ceased. The emphasis was placed on finding ways of improving $\alpha\beta$ search. Then several researchers discovered that chess programs were building trees which were within a factor of two of the minimal tree (Schaeffer 1986; Campbell and Marsland 1983). Where was there to go, if perfect search efficiency was only a factor of two away?

Happily, the past few years have seen a resurgence of interesting new approaches to game-tree search. Null moves, actually an old idea (Adelson-Velsky, Arlazarov and Donskoy 1988) but with new applications (Beal 1989; Chapter 9 *Experiments with the Null-Move Heuristic*), and singular extensions (Anantharaman, Campbell and Hsu 1988) have enhanced the productivity of $\alpha\beta$ search by concentrating effort where it is most likely to succeed. Entirely new approaches to minimax search include conspiracy numbers (McAllester 1988; Schaeffer 1989a), min/max approximation (Rivest 1988) and Solution Tree and Costs Search (Schrüfer 1988). Perhaps it is also time to revive some of the (relatively) older search ideas such as B* (Berliner 1979b; Palay 1982), the method of analogies and the notion of influence (Adelson-Velsky, Arlazarov and Donskoy 1975,88). All these ideas merit serious reconsideration.

For many years, the strength of the $\alpha\beta$ cutoff caused the computer-chess community to ignore alternate search algorithms. The idea is simple and yields an exponential savings in tree size. It is unfortunate that computer chess was given such a powerful idea so early in its formative stages. Conspiracy numbers has provided the insight that there is important information to be gained at nodes where one would normally cut off. The singular extensions algorithm is the first algorithm that uses this information to find its way into practice.

To the average researcher in AI, yet another way to search minimax trees is of little interest. It is an algorithmic problem, not an AI problem. Until we develop algorithms where the search is guided by knowledge, this area will be of little interest outside the small community of computer-chess aficionados.

16.3.2 A Little Knowledge Can Go a Long Way

It is amazing how far computer-chess programs have progressed using minimal chess knowledge. In fact, it is not uncommon to observe *better* performance in a program with *less* knowledge.[1] Unfortunately, this apparent paradox is often

---

[1] For example, deeper searches compensating for less detailed knowledge (see Chapter 6 *Hitech*).

used as a rationalization for avoiding the issues of knowledge representation and usage in chess programs.

Computer chess programs have been stymied by the *knowledge acquisition* bottleneck. Chess Grandmasters have a large store of knowledge at their disposal. It is difficult to extract that knowledge in machine usable terms. Humans often describe chess positions in abstract terms that are hard to quantify. Further, the influence of intangibles on a Grandmaster's play, such as intuition, are not to be under-estimated. These problems are not dissimilar from those encountered by an expert system designer, this being a fundamental problem of AI.

There are at least three major problems here. First, there is the quantity of knowledge required. Simon and Gilmartin (1973) have estimated that chess Grandmasters have as many as 100,000 patterns or *chunks* of knowledge at their disposal. Second, there is the quality of the knowledge. Some pieces of knowledge are adequate for improving the play of non-masters, but as the strength of the opponents increase, the quality and complexity of the knowledge required increases. The third problem is the way the knowledge is represented. Many common chess notions are easily understood by humans but are hard to capture in machine usable form (e.g. initiative). Often one resorts to approximations that capture some of the effect without understanding the implications of the loss of accuracy.

Perhaps the difficulty in using chess knowledge is best summed up as follows. Canadian Grandmaster Kevin Spraggett stated that he spent the first half of his career learning the basic principles of chess, and the second half trying to unlearn them! The problem encountered when using chess knowledge (or any non-factual knowledge for that matter) is that for every heuristic, there is an exception. For some heuristics, the exceptions are so infrequent that most chess programs ignore them. Yet, it is precisely under these conditions that human players excel. In this area, so closely akin to other problems in AI, computer-chess researchers have made little progress. It is probably fair to say that most ignore the problem.

Given the enormity of the task of acquiring, representing, and using knowledge, why haven't more computer-chess researchers tackled the problem? Some recent attempts are basically simplistic and somewhat naive while avoiding the real (harder) problems (Hartmann 1987a,b; Schaeffer and Marsland 1985; Marsland 1985). Some progress has been made recently in this area (see Chapter 6 *Hitech*), but this can only be viewed as a constructive start.

One can view AI as having to tackle three main problems: representing knowledge, searching for solutions, and the interactions between search and knowledge. For effective search, some knowledge must be applied. On the other hand, to use applicable knowledge in large problem domains one needs good search methods. The two are not separable. The majority of computer-chess research is on search algorithms, with the issues of knowledge and the search-knowledge interaction largely neglected.

Will brute-force search be enough to achieve World Championship level play? If so, then such a program would tell us little that could be of use in the wider field of AI. If not, then perhaps chess programmers should be addressing the fundamental problems of acquiring and using knowledge now!

16.3.3 A Conflict of Interest?

Unlike most other fields of computer science (and indeed, unlike most other sciences), computer chess publicly exhibits its progress. Since 1970, there have been annual tournaments that measure the rate of program improvement.[2] The consequences are both good and bad.

The desire to have one's chess program perform as well as possible in the public spotlight is strong motivation for many to work ardently on their programs. The potential returns for success in these tournaments is large, whether the benefits are monetary, publicity, or prestige. There is no doubt that these tournaments have been a tremendous boost to computer chess.

However, there is a serious disadvantage to this continuous public attention. As a scientist, one searches for the solution to difficult problems, even if success may take many years. How does one resolve this with annual spectacles where one has an obligation to have an improved program each year? This encourages small, short-term projects whose results will have a direct bearing on program performance. Long-term research projects, the difficult problems that remain to be solved, get neglected as being long shots that are unlikely to help program performance. It really is a matter of perceived return for time invested. Many chess programmers choose short-term gains at the expense of long-term success. Perhaps the best computer-chess researchers are the ones with no interest in writing their own competitive programs.

Since the benefits of winning are high, there is little incentive for quickly disseminating new research results. Many chess programmers hold back on new ideas to ensure that their programs maintain a competitive edge. Consequently, each team of chess programmers may have to discover ideas that are well known to other teams. This can only slow down progress in computer chess.

16.3.4 Experimental Computer Science

One notable aspect of computer-chess work, not typical of most research in computer science, is the large experimental component. For example, demonstrating the effectiveness of a new search idea may require the searching of hundreds or thousands of trees to acquire enough data to be able to pass judgment on the idea. The probabilistic nature of search trees means that experimentation will always be a large part of the study of search algorithms.

---

[2] Monty Newborn asserts that this is the longest ongoing scientific experiment in Computer Science.

Although the importance of experimentation in developing chess programs is not to be under-estimated, some programmers rely too heavily on the experimental results without necessarily understanding the underlying theory. One has only to look at an experimental domain such as physics to realize that experiments are usually only conducted for testing the strength of a theory. In computer chess, it is often the other way around; one does experiments and only then tries to understand what is happening.

A major problem is the lack of a theory of computer chess. There is lots of theory on search algorithms ($\alpha\beta$ in particular), although only a small portion is relevant for a practitioner. However, there is no theory of chess knowledge and its interactions with the search. Chess programmers alter their program and have no means for understanding what the potential consequences of the change are. They then usually conduct experiments to see if the change is beneficial. Without fully understanding the subtleties of the problem we are trying to solve, it is no wonder that much work is wasted on blind experimentation.

16.3.5 Coping with Error

Chess programs must cope with at least three types of error. First, there is error in leaf node evaluations, implying incorrect or inadequate chess knowledge. Minimax search has the insidious property of hiding such errors. Second, there are errors in decisions as to where to search in the tree. Fixed depth $\alpha\beta$ (with static search extensions) does not have this type of problem (which is one of the reasons why it is so popular), but selective search does. Third, there are search efficiency errors (such as move ordering) that affect the rate of search, but usually not its outcome.

Of the three types of search errors, the first two are the most serious since they can influence the quality of the move chosen by the program. Do we have any measures of how serious these problems are? It has been said that chess programs are the world's most sophisticated random number generators. How can we argue with that statement when we have no idea what the significance of the results produced are? A numerical analyst could not judge the quality of a numerical computation without knowing some bound on the error. Why should chess programs be exempt? How often have chess programs made the right move (our sole measure of "correctness") for the wrong reason? How often has a chess program correctly solve a problem, only to have a bug fix result in the program now giving an incorrect solution?

Work in error analysis has been sadly lacking. Error estimates for chess programs are based solely on empirical observations. There are no techniques for measuring or compensating for errors. Many numerical analysts make their livelihood from precise mathematical analysis of error properties. The result is faster, more stable numerical algorithms. Is the same close analysis not possible for computer chess?

How much error are we willing to live with in a chess program? One cannot answer that question without knowing how much error we are currently dealing with. Human chess players live with error; the less error, the better the player. Even the human World Champion is not immune from trivial mistakes. Error is not to be feared; only to be kept under control. Chess programs should not necessarily be striving for perfection.

16.3.6 But Is it Useful?

Is computer chess, as currently practiced, artificial intelligence? Maybe. It really depends on your definition of AI; there are some people who think that what most AI researchers do is not AI (Parnas 1988). Many of these researchers may be guilty of the same errors as computer-chess people are: building large systems that are capable of performing well on one problem but whose generality is questionable. Unfortunately, most people working in computer chess have done a poor job of selling their ideas to any community other than their own. There are more important research problems in the world than making computers play chess. Chess researchers cannot live in an ivory tower and solve a problem without concern over the generality of the ideas. A lot of good work has been done in computer chess and may have applicability in other areas. Regrettably, most of this work remains hidden from view and not generalized.

Theorem proving is a problem that has much in common with computer chess. Both can build large trees to solve problems, but theorem proving is without as powerful a tool as $\alpha\beta$ cutoffs. Monty Newborn has successfully applied his experience with searching chess trees to theorem proving (Newborn 1988b). Many of the algorithmic ideas first developed in computer chess are relevant to other tree search based problems, and it is surprising that they are not used more extensively. Why is theorem proving an acceptable research problem and computer chess not? One reason is that people can see where to use theorem provers, whereas they can only see computer chess as game playing. Theorem provers are used as tools to solve what are perceived as more important problems.

The stigma of mere "game playing" must be overcome. Part of the problem lies with the commercial side of computer chess; some equate research in computer chess with sales of chess machines. Computer chess remains a restricted domain ideal for artificial intelligence research. However, the emphasis on performance, best epitomized by the annual tournaments and the competition for commercial sales, has clouded the view of many.

16.4 Engineering Credibility

There is no doubt that chess programs can be large, complex programs. Most chess programmers are proud of their accomplishment and the programming skills that made it possible. Many outside (and some inside!) the computer-chess community will argue that building a chess program is more an engineering feat than one of scientific interest. So how does the work on computer chess measure up to engineering standards?

16.4.1 Building Without Tools

David Slate and Larry Atkin, writing on the difficulties of developing their chess program, state that:

> Our problem is that the programming tools we are presently using are not adequate to the task. ... This lack of programming tools has plagued the whole field of computer chess. With the proper tool one might accomplish in a day a job that had been put off for years. Although serious efforts are underway to overcome this deficiency, the number of people working on this is surprisingly small, and their research is still in its infancy. (Slate and Atkin 1977, pp. 116).

In the intervening 14 years since that was written, little, if anything, has been done to improve the number and quality of tools used to build, debug and test chess programs.

Why is there so much effort spent on building chess programs and not much on tools to build chess programs? One answer, again, is the performance demands. Programmers are always striving for immediate gains, lacking long-term insight. Another, more subtle, performance aspect is what the tools produce. A tool that allows one to succinctly describe chess knowledge may be capable of expressing all sorts of wonderful things in a human readable form. Unfortunately, these tools will produce code that is not going to be as fast as hand-written code. The poorer the code, the slower the program runs, and (painfully) the worse the program performance. Can one afford the performance cost? The dilemma is akin to that encountered by ardent assembler programmers who argued that compilers would never succeed since the quality of code produced by them was inefficient. History has proven them wrong. With the increasing speed of today's processors, the "overhead" of using tools is small compared to the cost of programmer time.

It is a shame better tools are not available. As a result, a lot of talented people spend a great deal of time wrestling with basic chess program problems that might be more easily solved with the right tool.

16.4.2 If it Works Once, it Works

One of the most serious problems faced by chess programmers is testing. Since there are roughly 10^{43} chess positions, it is not possible to do exhaustive testing. Given that adequately testing a chess program is a difficult task, many chess programmers take the easy way out and disregard the problem. Too many programs are developed by testing things once, or perhaps (extravagantly) a few times, and concluding that it works. Alternatively, there is the so-called "tournament experience;" the more games the program plays, the better the programmer feels about his program. This does not engender a high degree of confidence!

The writers of production quality compilers are faced with a similar problem but, in their case, the number of possible test programs is not finite. The compiler writing industry has solved this problem by establishing large collections of test programs for each language. Although such a test suite can never certify that the compiler is bug free, a program that successfully handles the test suite must be reasonably reliable.

There are few test suites available for chess programs and there are only two in common use. The 300 positions from Reinfeld's (1945) *Win At Chess* book are exclusively tactical problems while the Bratko-Kopec set consists of 24 positions that test a program's ability at tactics and at finding pawn levers (Kopec and Bratko 1982). A test suite of only 324 positions is inadequate to properly cover a problem space of 10^{43} positions. Moreover, both problem sets have serious deficiencies. The *Win At Chess* set is such that most programs easily solve more than 80% of the problems. Of what significance is a program that solves 86% instead of 84% of the problems? At least the Bratko-Kopec set is valuable because of the 12 positional problems. However, since this is an oft-used benchmark, many programs have been tuned to perform well on this set, perhaps to the extent of degrading their overall performance.

Why has the computer-chess community not started an effort at assimilating test data used by individual programmers and constructing a useful test suite? Perhaps 10,000 problems? Maybe that is too small. Without such a test suite or better software testing methods, many chess programmers' time is needlessly wasted.

16.4.3 Where Should One Place One's Efforts?

The discovery of a correlation between speed and performance may have set computer-chess research back a decade. The metrics of computer speed and nodes per second have been regularly used as an approximate measure of the strength of a program. As a result, programmers often devote enormous amounts of time and resources towards optimizing their programs: finding tricks to make routines run slightly faster, or hand optimizing assembler code. The net gains, usually only a small percentage speedup, cannot have a significant impact on the program's chess ability.

This effort is largely wasted. Not only is there a high likelihood of introducing a bug (and consequently wasting additional effort trying to find it), but it is not clear that the effort is well spent. If an equivalent amount of effort were spent on finding better search algorithms or better ways to use knowledge, the potential gains would be significant. For example, better search algorithms offer a chess program orders of magnitude more in gains than trivial optimizations. After all, if computer chess is a research project then time is best spent on research, not hacking.

16.5 Conclusions

It is perhaps unfortunate that αβ came along so early in computer-chess history. It has a lot of nice properties that would make it an ideal search algorithm for computer chess, but for the exponential growth in the search tree. Much effort has been concentrated on this algorithm, as though it were the chess programmer's panacea. Now, more so than ever before, computer chess must break out of the fixed-depth, αβ search frame of mind and consider alternatives. Brute-force αβ may have done as much damage to the progress and credibility of computer-chess research as it has given chess programs high ratings.

Should an artificial intelligence system solve a problem using methods similar to the human approach (the cognitive view) or should it just solve the problem using any approach (the engineering view) (Parnas 1988)? The prevailing attitude is that it is not AI unless the former approach is used. Computer chess is an important problem worth solving, regardless of the methods used. Making computers play chess is both engineering and science, and one should draw on all resources for solving the problem. Perhaps this is the path that AI will eventually also have to follow.

In retrospect, it is not surprising that computer chess has fallen from grace. Since the research has strayed from the main stream and has neglected many of the mandatory scientific aspects, it is only natural that computer chess should be shunned by our AI colleagues. Of course, there is still time to make amends!

Acknowledgments. We greatly appreciated the constructive criticism from Greg Rawlins, Randy Goebel and Murray Campbell. This work was supported in part by the Canadian Natural Sciences and Engineering Research Council and the University of Alberta's Central Research Fund.

Part V. A New Drosophila for AI?

The preceding chapters have reviewed three decades of work on computer chess. Success in that area has been attributed to several factors including its interest as a fundamental problem in artificial intelligence, the development of better searching techniques and memory functions, considerable public testing under competitive conditions, major improvements in hardware speed and memory capacity of computers and an active public interest in electronic products— making extensive commercial investment in better programs economic.

Many of these advances have been beneficial to the study of computer Go too, but in the past that problem has not attracted as much interest either from university research groups or from commercial vendors. All this may now be changing. Although only a few people have equally strong interest in chess and Go, with the growing economic strength of the Pacific Rim countries, one can expect the oriental game of Go to attract more resources and attention. This is especially true since many people think that the brute-force methods, so successful in chess, will not work for Go. Of course similar claims were made for chess more than a decade ago, only for those pundits to be quickly proved wrong.

Thus these two chapters are especially timely. The first one by Chen, Kierulf, Müller and Nievergelt reviews the state of Go by considering the development of their programs. They show how search and knowledge can work together. The following chapter by Shirayanagi presents a proposal for a new generation of Go-playing programs. He uses a tutorial-based solution to the knowledge problem. It is built around the use of priority trees as the basic data structure for ordering plans and strategies, ensuring their application in a systematic way.

In time we will see if Go succeeds in becoming the new *Drosophila* of artificial intelligence, as many expect, but certainly the challenge is there. Since Go can be considered as several mini-games in play concurrently, perhaps this is also a problem that is well-suited to a parallel programming approach.

17 The Design and Evolution of Go Explorer

K. Chen, A. Kierulf, M. Müller and J. Nievergelt

17.1 Introduction

The Smart Game Board, a software workbench dedicated to the development of game-playing programs, has been used to implement half a dozen programs that play different games. We describe its use in the development of three Go-playing programs: *Explorer* and its two offspring, *Go Intellect* and *Swiss Explorer*. It took four years to build and refine the Smart Game Board; this powerful programming environment now makes it possible to implement in less than a year a Go program that is strong by current standards. In the Fall of 1988, in its first test against other programs, *Explorer* tied for 2nd among 16 programs that competed in the 4th Computer Go World Championship in Taiwan. *Explorer* proved to be a fierce if somewhat unsteady fighter. The programming and development team split soon thereafter, each group trying out its own cure to avoid *Explorer*'s predictable lapses. Both successors run on the Smart Game Board and improved on their parent's record in their very first encounter. In the summer of 1989, *Go Intellect* won the North American Computer Go Championship, and *Swiss Explorer* won the Go Tournament at the first Computer Olympiad in London (Kierulf and Nievergelt 1989). We attribute these results to a mixture of good luck and a solid dose of sound software engineering practice.

The three parts of this paper have the following goals. In Section 17.2 *Smart Game Board* we describe enough of the Smart Game Board to document the decisive importance of a powerful development environment. A large investment of effort in building the best software engineering environment we were able to devise, out of components that are well understood, made it feasible to experiment extensively in the poorly understood realm of knowledge engineering. In Section 17.3 *Go and Computers* we summarize the most important characteristics of Go and survey the history of computer Go. This should enable readers who do not play this game to appreciate some of the

We are grateful to the ACM for permission to extract parts of the paper by Kierulf, Chen and Nievergelt (1990), published in Communications of the ACM, vol. 33, no. 2, pp. 152-166. Copyright Feb. 1990, Association for Computing Machinery, Inc.

problems Go programmers face. In Section 17.4 *Explorer and its Evolution* we present the forces and ideas that have shaped our three Go programs. The software engineering and knowledge engineering lessons learned from this project have been presented by Kierulf, Chen and Nievergelt (1990).

17.2 Smart Game Board

The Smart Game Board package supports two kinds of experiments with game-playing programs. First, as a hypertext medium, its *user interface* is designed to help serious players study the game in ways that are impossible without a computer. Second, as a workbench for programming games, its structure encourages experimentation with different search algorithms and strategies. Neither of these functions is bound to any one game; originally designed for Go, the Smart Game Board now includes Othello, Nine Men's Morris, and chess.

17.2.1 A Tool for Players of Various Games of Strategy

The Smart Game Board is a tool to assist game players in the many activities they now perform on a wooden board and paper: playing, teaching, discussing, analyzing, studying, recording and organizing game collections and printing. Several software packages offer such features for chess or Go separately, but we are not aware of any other program that attempts to support a broad range of games. A snapshot in Figure 17.1 shows that the user can open windows dedicated to any of the games supported by the Smart Game Board. This generality comes from exploiting common features of two-player board games. Functionally, it is an editor and database system specialized for game trees. A game is a tree-structured document that can be opened, viewed, modified and saved. The tree may degenerate into a sequence of nodes, but the generality of a tree is needed to let the user experiment with different move sequences while keeping the original game intact. Each node represents a position and its attributes, such as the move that leads to this position, comments and markings of the board, or the time left at this point in the game.

A game is replayed by traversing the tree. Advancing by one node executes the move stored at that node. General tree editing commands allow one to copy properties, nodes and entire subtrees from one game to another. More powerful operations on game trees include backing up values in min-max fashion, or sorting the branches according to the number of leaf nodes in each subtree. The Smart Game Board also provides data management functions such as ordering games by opening or by player. It has been used, for example, to organize 1300 Othello games and therefrom create a library of standard Othello openings.

A control panel common to all games (a window at the top left of the screen in Figure 17.1) embodies most of the user interface. Game-independent operations are defined as motions on a game tree. Game-specific operations (e.g., setting up positions in chess, entering marks for annotating Go games) and

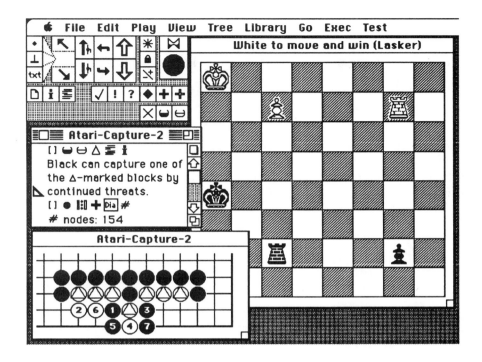

Figure 17.1: Example display.

status information (e.g., number of captives in Go) are provided in a game-specific menu.

17.2.2 Structure of the System

Figure 17.2 shows the structure of the Smart Game Board. It is designed to separate game-specific from game-independent aspects, and provides slots where each game can plug in its specific routines for the rules (legal move recognition and execution), the user interface (board display, move input, menu functions) and an optional playing algorithm. A search engine provides depth-first search and iterative-deepening based on game-specific routines for move generation, position evaluation and time control.

The program is written in SemperSoft™ Modula-2 under MPW (Macintosh Programmer's Workshop) and runs on the Apple® Macintosh.™ So far, Go, Othello, Nine Men's Morris (Mühle, programmed by Ralph Gasser) and chess have been implemented. Go and Othello programs that run on the Smart Game Board have competed successfully in several tournaments. The chess module is not intended to play, only to manage game collections.

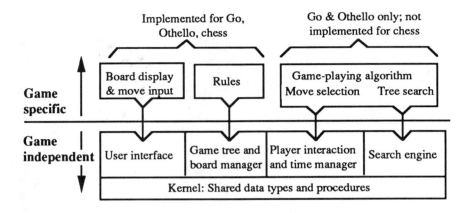

Figure 17.2: Smart Game Board.

17.2.3 Testing and Monitoring Game Algorithms

Game programmers require many of the same features as do expert players. A user interface that lets one replay and annotate games also serves for setting up positions and record the results of the program's performance in those positions. A collection of games serves as a source of problem positions, or as raw material for a statistical analysis on which to base program strategy.

Game programmers also have special requirements. They need instruments to measure what is going on inside the program: for example, windows showing current goals, estimated scores or the state of the search. The Smart Game Board provides general tools for that purpose, and some assistance for game-specific test functions, including a log file to store results and statistics for later study and operations for playing and replaying a set of games. The format of the log file (lines with items separated by tabs) is easily read by spreadsheets and statistical analysis programs.

The command 'Analyze Game' compares moves actually played with moves the computer would play. It goes through all positions that satisfy certain selection criteria, and calls a game-specific routine at each position. This is useful in several phases of program development:

- to test program performance on problem collections,
- to identify those moves the program doesn't find in a collection of expert games, either caused by bugs, wrong parameters, or lack of some specific knowledge, and
- to examine a collection of earlier blunders to make sure the bugs that caused them have been permanently removed.

The command 'Tourney' plays a round-robin tournament between different programs. We often pit slightly different versions of the same program against each other to study the effect of a single modification. The user can choose the number of rounds, the time limit and the program versions to play against each other. Tourney and Analyze can be used together to detect good moves.

17.3 Go and Computers

Assuming the reader knows little or nothing about Go, we attempt to provide some intuition for this game's domain of knowledge, in part by comparing Go to chess. Several excellent introductory books are available from Ishi Press International. Go is a two-person game of perfect information in the sense of game theory; at all times, both players know the entire state of the game. The players alternate placing a black and a white stone on some empty intersection of a 19 by 19 grid. Once played, a stone never moves, but it may disappear from the board when captured. A player's objective is to secure more territory than his opponent, counted in terms of grid points. In the process of surrounding territory by laying down a border of stones that must be 'alive,' fights erupt that typically lead to some stones being captured ('killed'). Much of the difficulty of Go comes from the fact that during most of the game, few stones are definitively alive or dead. Stones are more or less vital or moribund, and their status can change repeatedly during the course of a game, as long as the surrounding scene changes. Only when the game has ended can all stones be classified definitively as alive or dead. Thus 'life or death,' the key concept of Go, exhibits a split personality. As an operational concept during the game, it is the most important factor in estimating potential territory and for assessing the chances of battle, but is rather fuzzy. It becomes more and more precise as the game progresses, and is a well-defined concept used for counting territory when the game has ended. The game ends when neither player can find a profitable move and all points are classified as one of black, white, or no-man's-land. This situation typically arises after about 200 to 300 moves have been played, with anywhere between 60% and 90% of the 361 grid points occupied. Whereas in chess we count a move (by a white piece) and counter-move (black piece) as a single move, in Go we count the placement of each single stone as a move. Even keeping in mind that a Go move corresponds to half a chess move (a 'ply'), it is evident that a Go game can take a long time.

If chess is a model of a single battle (as fought thousands of years ago), Go is a model of war. Typically, several loosely interacting campaigns and battles for space proceed concurrently. Go is a great game of synchronization: stronger players are better able to coordinate campaigns and disrupt the coordination among enemy forces. Multipurpose moves are the most effective, such as a 'splitting attack' that wedges in between two enemy groups, or a move that threatens to kill an enemy group and extends one's own territory at the same time. Typically one player has the initiative, called 'sente,' which enables him to play strong threats that leave the opponent little choice but to respond locally. Thus players with sente can choose the field of action to suit their goals, whereas the opponent, said to be in 'gote,' "follows the play around the board." The

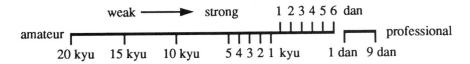

Figure 17.3: Rating levels of Go players.

sente/gote relationship alternates between the players, but among opponents of different skill, the stronger player will manage to keep sente most of the time.

The interaction of loosely related campaigns and the consequent importance of timing makes Go a superb practical example for the theory of sums of games (Milnor 1953; Hanner 1959; Conway 1976). During the endgame, independent regions on the Go board contribute component games, and the full-board game is the sum of these games. At each turn, a player selects one component game in which to play a move and passes in all others.

Intuition and experience let players estimate the numerical value of each move considered. In the opening, a typical move is worth 10 to 20 points of territory. Move values may be highest in the middlegame, but then they decrease steadily towards the endgame, where fights erupt over a single point, or even 'half a point.' This phenomenon of decreasing value of a typical move as the game progresses causes timing to be of the utmost importance. If a move is estimated to be worth x points in a local context, it must be played at just the right moment, when the value of other moves is also about x. If played too early, the opponent may ignore this move and reply with a bigger one elsewhere, perhaps gaining sente. If played too late, when the value of other available moves has diminished, the opponent may prevent it, even at the cost of ending in gote. Players analyzing a game are always debating which move, among several good ones, is 'the largest.'

A handicap system makes it possible to balance players of different skill without changing the nature of the game much. The weaker player starts by placing anywhere from 2 to perhaps 13 stones on the board. In Japanese Go, these stones are placed in a fixed pattern on 'handicap points.' In Chinese Go, the weaker player places them anywhere, starting with x free moves, providing an advantage estimated at 10 points per move. Player A is x stones better than B if the chances become equal when B receives x handicap stones. Thus the handicap system defines a fairly accurate rating scale, as Figure 17.3 illustrates. Playing strength of amateurs is measured on a scale where one unit corresponds to a handicap stone. A weak player may be 20 kyu, implying receipt of 10 handicap stones from a 10 kyu, who in turn receives 9 handicap stones from a first kyu. A first kyu 'takes black,' i.e. plays first, against a first dan, who receives 5 stones from a 6 dan. That's about as high as the amateur scale goes. Above that, there is a separate scale for professionals. A strong amateur might earn professional 1-dan status after several years of intensive study. The professional scale has a finer grading: its 9 skill levels are compressed into a difference of about two handicap stones.

Because computer Go is in its infancy, one would like to build on the mature experience gained from other games, but such experience does not transfer readily. At chess, for example, computers owe their spectacular prowess more to the computer's speed at searching than to its knowledge of chess lore. Experience with the computer-chess approach of full-board search does not apply directly to Go, for two reasons:

Branching factor.

Because Go is played on a 19 by 19 board, the number of legal moves decreases from 361 at the start to several dozen at the end, creating a tree with an average branching factor of about 200, as compared to a branching factor of about 40 legal moves from a typical chess position. This larger fan-out may be compensated partly by the fact that transpositions (different move sequences leading to the same position) are more frequent in Go than in chess. (This phenomenon arises because almost all Go moves onto an empty grid point are legal, thus they can be played at any time, whereas many chess moves cease to be legal after some other pieces have moved.) Thus transposition tables that detect positions analyzed earlier promise to be relatively more effective in Go than in chess. Still, we must assume that the vastly larger search space of Go greatly reduces the depth of feasible search.

Position evaluation.

Material and mobility, the dominant factors in chess evaluation functions, are easily computed. In Go, possession of territory is the closest equivalent to material possession in chess, but its evaluation is much more subtle, and except at the very end of the game, a player's claim to territory can always be challenged. Go has no clear analog to chess mobility; perhaps 'shape' comes closest, but good and bad shape are hard to measure.

Success in computer chess was achieved mostly by using fast search to compensate for meager chess knowledge, thereby sidestepping the issue of knowledge engineering. The analogous recipe is unlikely to lead to comparable success in Go. The insight that both *domain-specific knowledge* and *search* are of critical importance makes Go a more diverse and balanced test-bed for artificial intelligence research than chess. Computer Go may well become the new *Drosophila* of artificial intelligence.

Despite the large branching factor of Go, strong players routinely look 10 to 20 moves ahead when a fight demands it, an activity called 'reading.' This perplexing term suggests that a player, at that moment, is not free to let his imagination roam, but simply has to discover what is given—whether a plausible, perhaps forced, sequence of moves works or doesn't. Go does know the concept of *narrow and deep search,* as does chess, but with a difference. 'Reading' is limited to a local scene, say a 5 by 7 corner, and never extends to the full board. Even if reading guarantees a win in a local battle, that does not necessarily mean much; the enemy might ignore this battle and get compensation elsewhere. A separate, more intuitive mental act is required to assess the relevance of such a local search to the overall situation.

17.3.1 The Development of Computer Go

A brief survey of the history and current state of computer Go serves to place our project in perspective. Compared to other games of strategy, in particular checkers and chess, computer Go started late and, until recently, progressed slowly. The future may tell whether this is because of a late start or because of the inherent difficulty of Go.

Work in computer Go started in the early sixties (Remus 1962) and intensified with the Ph.D. dissertations of Zobrist (1970b) and Ryder (1971). Zobrist relied on pattern recognition, Ryder on tree search. Both of these approaches had already been explored in chess, where the latter, in particular, has proven its value beyond doubt. Although these approaches capture part of what Go is about, neither program played as well as a beginner plays after just a few games. Humans use pattern recognition to a large extent, but their patterns are more complex and abstract than those used by Zobrist. Also, pure tree search runs into the hurdle that the branching factor of Go is significantly larger than that of other games on which this approach has been tried. Selective search is more important for Go than it is for chess, and setting goals to focus the search calls for insight into the position.

Reitman and Wilcox (1979) made a step forward with a program based on a representation that reflects the way good players perceive the board. They concentrated on strategy, adding some tactical analysis late in the project. Their program only reached the level of a novice player. Bruce Wilcox (1985) analyzed the strong and weak points of that first program, then rewrote it. Later he gave insights to that work with his history of computer Go (Wilcox 1988).

Since 1985 activity in computer Go has mushroomed. A strong Go-playing program was a goal of the Japanese "Fifth Generation" project, but was dropped (too hard?). Several dozen small teams are now involved in programming Go, and these efforts are beginning to bear fruit. The annual International Computer Go Congress, organized by the Ing Foundation of Taiwan, has provided an arena for competition and a yardstick for assessing progress. We are aware of 6 computer Go tournaments held around the world during 1989. Each of the top Go programs participated in at least two of these, so it is possible to compare their prowess with some confidence. The top half dozen Go programs are of comparable strength. They play at the level of 12 to 15 kyu, distinctly better than human beginners. In any one tournament, chance, including the 'bug-of-the-day' phenomenon, decides the winner (Kierulf and Nievergelt 1989).

17.4 Explorer and its Evolution

Explorer is designed for rapid experimentation in the realm of Go knowledge engineering. We wish to observe how the formalization and capture of different Go concepts affects the style and strength of the program. Thanks to its modular structure, *Explorer* was able to go through dozens of versions and two major redesigns in less than a year.

17.4.1 Go Concepts and Position Analysis

Among the Go concepts designed into *Explorer*, *influence* is the most basic. Any stone radiates influence across the board; its influence peaks at the location of the stone, and decays exponentially with distance. The super-position of the influence of all the stones on the board creates a field of force, a terrain that determines the structure of the board at this moment.

Another basic concept of Go is that of a *block:* A set B of stones of the same color such that any two stones in B are connected by a sequence of stones in B, with any consecutive pair horizontally or vertically adjacent. A block is 'strongly connected,' and its stones die and are removed in unison when they lose their last 'liberty,' i.e. when there is no free point adjacent to any stone in the block. Blocks, more than single stones, are the basic building blocks in Go.

A *block* is a rigorously defined concept essential for checking the legality of moves, but a block is too small a unit when discussing the quality of moves. For this we use two higher concepts, 'chain' and 'group,' that turn out to have fuzzy definitions, although the intent of these concepts is clear.

A *chain* is a set of blocks that, normally, can be connected into a single block at will, even against (most) measures taken by the opponent. A chain is a 'potential block,' and for purposes of planning can be treated as such. Many chains will turn into blocks as the game progresses, but there are exceptions. Higher level planning may decide that the connectivity of a particular chain is not worth preserving, because there are other more valuable moves.

A *group* is a set of chains that typically fight together; an attack on any chain in a group is an attack on all of them. Like an army that can operate and survive independently, it has a claim to territory, and many groups will turn into the boundary of a single territory as the game progresses. But there are many exceptions, since groups split and merge routinely, perhaps according to the players' plans, often dictated by the unpredictable whim of the fortunes of war.

Influence and chains serve to identify groups. *Explorer* defines a group as a set of chains of the same color connected by points with friendly influence above a certain threshold (Chen 1989). The influence measure was tuned to produce a reasonable result for groups in some standard configurations. Unlike a collection of explicit rules or patterns that can never capture all situations, influence applies to all configurations, and gives reasonable results for most. Figure 17.4 shows an example with the groups labeled by safety ranges from 0 (hopeless) to 64 (totally safe). The two black chains labeled 64 in the lower left are joined into a single group, a fighting unit. So are the two white stones labeled 47 along the lower edge. The territorial claim for each group is shaded.

This analysis of the board is updated after each move. Figure 17.5 shows the effect of two additional moves. A black invasion (left) lowers the safety of white's 2-stone group from 47 to 13, and enhances the safety of black's group to the right from 47 to 49. A white 'peep' (right) breaks a black chain and drastically reduces the safety of its parts from 46 to 28 and 4.

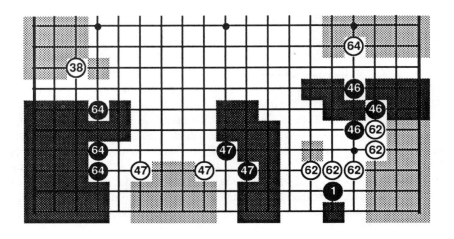

Figure 17.4: Groups, their safety and their claim to territory.

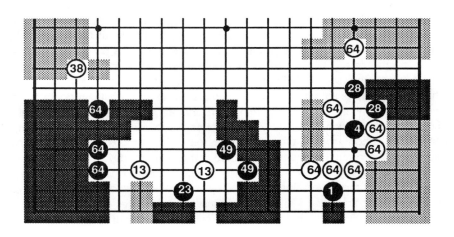

Figure 17.5: Effect of a black invasion and a white peep on group safety.

17.4.2 Move Generation, Evaluation and Selection

The move-decision process starts with the position analysis described above which identifies static relationships among stones: blocks, chains, groups and important properties of these objects (e.g., liberties and importance of blocks, relative number of liberties and potential cutting points of chains, and safety and value of groups). The move generators and evaluators use this information as Figure 17.6 shows.

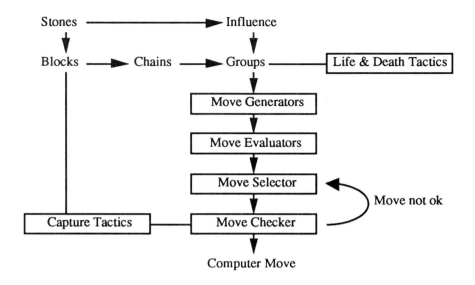

Figure 17.6: Move generation and selection process.

Some move generators are based on properties of blocks, chains and groups recognized by position analysis, e.g. 'attack weak group.' Others recognize local patterns of stones, such as connections, shapes and standard endgame sequences near the edge. There are also generators specialized for specific stages of the game such as the opening or a *ko* fight. Each move generator suggests a set of moves, with a specific value for each proposed move. All values are added together and the move with the highest total value is picked, after passing a check to avoid the worst blunders.

Note that the move selection process is based on a static analysis of the current position; lookahead is only used for special tactical situations, and even there its scope is limited by lack of time. Without full-board lookahead, some decisions must remain guesswork. For example, how important it is to cut depends on the strength of the two resulting groups *after* the cut, and from which side to play a threat can only be decided by taking the opponent's response into account. Even ignoring the lack of lookahead, this move selection process is unsatisfactory. Although it handles double-purpose moves well (they get the sum of two values), in most positions it is practically impossible to balance the weights given to different moves and different motives. The main problems are value inflation, overlap between move generators and that the position analysis is simply too rough to determine reliable move values.

17.4.3 Evolution of Explorer

When the design team split in Spring 1989, *Explorer* served as a starting point for two programs that evolved in different directions. Ken Chen redesigned the position analyzer and produced *Go Intellect*, a program with a much improved understanding of Go. Anders Kierulf and Martin Müller produced *Swiss Explorer*, a relatively solid player that improved on the components *Explorer* already had. In August 1989, *Go Intellect* won the North American computer Go championship at Rutgers 4 to 0, and a week later in London *Swiss Explorer* won the Computer Olympiad in a 10-player round-robin tournament 8 to 1.

Go Intellect uses strategic lookahead to avoid some of the difficulties mentioned above. A highly selective lookahead routine is the main move decision-maker, with search depth and width dynamically determined. Ken Chen also re-engineered the Go knowledge and redesigned the move generators with emphasis on both territory and safety, instead of predominantly around safety as in *Explorer*. For the next version of *Go Intellect*, he plans to concentrate on developing knowledge-guided tactics routines and improving the efficiency and accuracy of the global strategic lookahead routine.

The structure of *Swiss Explorer* is closer to that of the old *Explorer*, but it has been refined in several ways:

- The instrumentation of the Smart Game Board was used to find out where the good and the bad moves really come from—that is, which routines contribute most to playing strength and to bugs. For this purpose, move generators were split into smaller units with a single motive or purpose. Statistical analysis of many games caused us to concentrate work on a few move generators and to throw away several others.
- New move generators were added for the opening phase of the game: extensions along the edge and toward the center, faster developing moves instead of simple block extensions. Other generators were improved, e.g. attacking and protecting weak groups.
- The combination of move values was generalized. In some cases of known overlap between move generators, only part of the value was added. This also eliminated problems with move generators that suggested the same move twice, leading to doubled values.

Explorer could still be improved significantly along these lines, maintaining the current structure, but that leads to a dead end. Experience with brute-force chess programs and Go programs using lookahead (*Goliath* and *Go Intellect*) has shown that lookahead can significantly improve weak evaluation functions. Thus we are currently working on a new control structure that facilitates the interplay of lookahead with knowledge-based move generators. The new elements in the next generation of *Explorer* include:

- Local search to generate tactically sound moves and global lookahead to combine the results from different local areas.
- Partition of the board into meaningful components such as territory, moyo (potential territory) and boundary. This helps generate moves to enclose territory and to capture invading stones.

17.4.4 Knowledge Selection and Use: Conflicts and Gaps

It is interesting to reflect on the fact that most progress in computer chess was made by amateurs of medium playing strength—strong chess players were evidently not essential to the development of champion chess machines. This shows that computers can play amazingly powerful chess without much explicit chess knowledge. We expect that explicit representation of game-specific knowledge will be more important for Go than for chess. We estimate that *Explorer* contains significantly more game-specific knowledge than today's chess programs, but of course it is only a tiny fraction of standard Go lore. We have more than the necessary Go knowledge at hand in the form of project members who are both strong amateur players and experienced computer scientists, but we face the difficult problem of selecting a small subset of Go knowledge that is *consistent and self-contained*. Emphasizing fundamentals, we try to make *Explorer* understand concepts such as: what stones are dead and should be given up, what groups are unsafe and should be protected or attacked, what blocks are important and deserve high priority. These concepts compete for resources, since one move cannot satisfy all goals. For example, the goal of maximizing territory is in conflict with a dozen other goals, such as influence, safety, making good shape, attacking or restraining opponent forces.

Some knowledge may be of little value to a machine. For example, human players memorize standard corner opening sequences, called joseki, because they are safe and save much thought. *Explorer* has a large joseki library, but we don't use it at tournaments because the program lacks strategic understanding to extend sophisticated opening sequences.

The Olympiad version of *Swiss Explorer* had a small repertoire of moves and a stable, balanced set of knowledge:
- Although it had no concept of territory, it built some just by placing stones (pattern-generated moves) on the third line during the opening.
- It liked to extend blocks, a slow way of playing that creates solid connections; thus it did not need to know much about jumps and weak connections. *Explorer* generated reasonable moves in the type of positions it frequently got into, but might blunder disastrously in situations far off its preferred domain.

When trying to expand *Explorer*'s domain of reasonable behavior by adding more knowledge, we observed that even a consistent set of knowledge creates problems if it contains gaps. Seemingly safe knowledge extensions did not necessarily lead to better play. After adding new move generators and improving others, we found that the program often got itself into situations it didn't know how to handle. The knowledge was out of balance:
- Loose moves in the opening and in attempts to protect weak groups lead to errors in group recognition and in connectivity not observed earlier.
- Opening moves, oriented towards potential territory instead of plodding along on the third line, gave *Explorer* territory that was nearly, but not completely, safe. But *Explorer* lacked any idea of how to fight or limit an invasion of its potential territory.

Most of these problems were corrected by plugging the gaps with new knowledge. Now the program's knowledge is once again reasonably balanced, with a much broader repertoire of moves than at the Olympiad. Full-board lookahead in future versions of *Explorer* will also help in bridging gaps and reconciling knowledge conflicts.

17.5 Conclusion and Outlook

Reviewing the games of *Explorer* and its descendants, we observe that our knowledge-based approach to computer Go is feasible for developing a low-rated amateur. *Explorer* is now a non-voting member of the American Go Association rated 15 kyu based on its performance in two human tournaments.

Almost all Go knowledge is heuristic, and thus imprecise. We continually attempt to refine our programs' knowledge in order to reduce conflicts and improve performance, and investigate additional Go concepts that can profitably be captured and used. As computer chess has proven repeatedly, game playing is an experimental subject where predictions are difficult.

Tactics is the one aspect of game playing amenable to exact calculation. *Explorer*'s computing power is woefully inadequate for solving the tactical problems it recognizes. Improving tactical prowess is an open-ended route to a stronger Go program—no inherent limitation can be seen as yet. Strong chess machines use special-purpose hardware to generate and evaluate 100 to 1,000 times more positions per second than a conventional microprocessor could. We are not aware of any work on Go hardware, but that's an obvious approach to investigate.

What motivates researchers to pursue this never-ending race for stronger computer players? Computer game playing is one of the few cases in the fuzzy area of knowledge engineering where performance and progress can be measured with remarkable accuracy, and the causes that affect performance can be identified. Computer chess, for example, has shown that you don't need to understand much about chess at all in order to play at the level of an international master; all you have to do is look at 1 million positions per second. This insight may not generalize beyond chess, but it is an impressive statement about the power of computation.

In conclusion, computer Go stands today where computer chess was 20 years ago. Among dozens of programs, each one seems to follow its own approach, and the most visible characteristics they share are a low amateur level of play, and a lot of hope. It was impossible, two decades ago, to predict with any degree of assurance how far and how fast computer chess would progress, and it is impossible today to predict how successful computer Go will be, and what it takes to get there. The only road to insight and progress is hard, trial-and-error experimentation. The various versions of *Explorer* are data points along this road.

Acknowledgments. Thanks to Monty Newborn, Jim Stein and Ken Thompson for helpful comments. This work was supported in part by NSF under grant DCR-8518796.

Appendix: Fragment from an Explorer Game

White: Bob Felice, 12 kyu   Handicap: 3 stones
Black: *Go Explorer*, 15 kyu   Black wins by 4 points

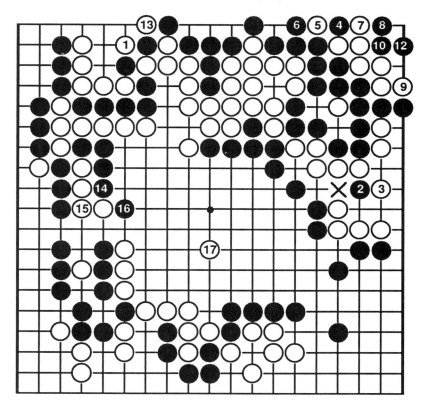

Figure 17.7: Tulsa Midwestern Go Tournament, February 25/26, 1989.

This is one of *Explorer*'s better performances. White may not realize that his group in the upper right corner needs an additional move to live. It is surrounded by a big one-eyed black group, which white proceeds to attack with 1. *Explorer* realizes that it can only live by capturing some enemy stones and ignores the atari. Black's move 2 threatens '×' and the entire white group along the right edge. White defends well at 3. With 4 and several skillful follow-up moves black kills the white corner (11 is played at 5). *Explorer* correctly ignores white 13 to capture some important stones.

18 Knowledge Representation and its Refinement in Go Programs

K. Shirayanagi

18.1 Introduction

It is often said that, unlike chess, an exhaustive search of the game tree for deciding the next move for Go is impossible, because of the huge search space. Therefore, in Go search is limited to local fields only. For more global decisions, various strategic human knowledge should be applied. Almost all Go playing programs (for example, Zobrist 1970b; Ryder 1971; Sanechika *et al.* 1981) settle on an evaluation function to represent this knowledge. These programs decide on the next move by selecting candidates with maximum evaluation function values. However, Go programmers often judge that the program's maximum-value moves are bad or unsuitable for a situation (a board state, or placement of stones on the board), so that the only way to get the proper result is to refine the evaluation function. But a temporary refinement for one situation may cause a contradiction for another.

Evaluation functions are often linear combinations among various strategic factors, in other words, an *ad hoc* arithmetic expression. They do not explicitly represent human knowledge, thus making it difficult to decide which factors of the function to refine or how to refine them. This is one reason why Go programs have not yet properly exceeded the 15 kyu level of Reitman and Wilcox's program (Reitman and Wilcox 1979). Consequently, this *arithmetic* approach cannot improve the strength of Go programs further.

Our new approach to programming Go is to represent knowledge explicitly without evaluation values of moves as necessary. As the representation primitives, we use only specialized terms, notions, or pattern knowledge in Go. In other words, we represent knowledge not *arithmetically* but *symbolically* so that the representation is easy to refine. We illustrate these ideas in a program called *YUGO* (*Y*ou can *U*pdate the *GO* program).

Section 18.2 *Tree Representation and Refinement* describes how to represent knowledge symbolically, in a tree expression, and how to refine the tree representation. In programming Go, programmers should use this method to represent and refine knowledge which is not known precisely in advance.

This chapter is a revised version of "A New Approach to Programming Go—Knowledge Representation and its Refinement," in *New Directions in Game-Tree Search Workshop* proceedings, T.A. Marsland (ed.), Edmonton, May 1989, pp. 53-65.

Section 18.3 *Go Programming* describes how the tree expression actually represents three kinds of knowledge: global decision algorithms, common-sense knowledge about names and about local meanings of moves. They are stored in the Go playing program, *YUGO*.

Section 18.4 *Fundamental Tools* presents two basic tools of Go programming: naming and meaning understanding. They are necessary for local responses to name and meaning of the opponent's most recent move. Regarding knowledge about them, we can almost precisely represent it in advance. The two ideas are also implemented as a part of *YUGO*.

Section 18.5 *Evaluation of YUGO* discusses how to improve the program. Moreover, the usefulness of our representation and refinement methods are shown.

Finally, Section 18.6 *Conclusion* summarizes our new approach to programming Go.

18.2 Tree Representation and Refinement

Numerical values for weighting or evaluating candidate moves do not imply any information about the Go programmer's thought process. Human players often decide the best move by combining knowledge such as "in this situation, this move has priority over that move." Therefore it is natural to represent our knowledge as a set of moves having priority. Symbolic (combinatorial) relations, not numerical values of moves, are necessary because we often need to refine the representation of knowledge.

We propose a representation method using a tree called a *priority tree* [1] as a graphical expression. This method is suitable for refinement in programming Go, as we will explain in Section 18.2.2 *Tree Refinement*.

First, nodes of this tree denote one of three procedures: DO, JUDGE, or SELECT:[2]

• DO procedure: Executes the procedure named by the node. That is, it plays a move on the Go board according to the procedure.
• JUDGE procedure: Evaluates various local or global situations according to the predicate named by the node.
• SELECT procedure: Selects the most suitable procedure from all the candidates which are put on nodes just below @, where @ is called the *antenna* and always put on this node.

Here the antenna @ receives a message of plans from a planning module (if it exists) of a Go program. The default of @ is empty.

Next, the order of this tree specifies the priority among the procedures, where "node A has priority over node B" means that "node A should be considered or executed sooner than node B." A top priority node is put on the

---

[1] Note that a priority tree is different from a game tree.
[2] The other possibility is another priority tree as a subtree.

root of the tree. Additionally, a JUDGE node is a fork which splits into two branches and a SELECT node is also a fork which can continue with two or more branches.

18.2.1 Tree Execution

A Go program has to include a module which executes a tree representation. The method of executing a priority tree is defined as follows:

ONE-WAY:

> Assume that A is just above B in priority. If the results of executing A are not empty and there exist moves in them which are suitable for a current plan or are obviously not bad, then return the moves, otherwise execute B next.

FORK:

- Predicate: If the judgment of the predicate named by the fork is YES, then proceed to the left node immediately below. Otherwise, proceed to the right node immediately below.
- Antenna (@): Assume that $A_1, A_2, \cdots, A_n$ are immediately below @. If @ receives a current plan P, select the most suitable A_i for P. If @ does not receive any message (@ is empty), select A_i at random or by comparing the situations resulting from executing different A_i.

18.2.2 Tree Refinement

In Go, knowledge representation depends on the surrounding situations (placements of stones). Therefore, we cannot say that a priority tree is a complete representation, because often the tree execution result is a bad move. Even so, the following tree refinement models the process of a Go beginner becoming more skillful by taking a teacher's advice. Using P_Ω to denote a feature of a situation Ω, as explained by the programmer, and $*P_\Omega$ to denote a predicate indicating whether a situation has P_Ω or not, then in a situation Ω:

- tree creation: When a program has no suitable priority tree, the programmer creates a new priority tree: (δ) or $(*P_\Omega(\delta)$ (something)). If there are two or more good DO procedures, $\delta_1, \cdots, \delta_k$, then the tree is written (@ $(\delta_1), \cdots, (\delta_k)$) using the antenna @.
- tree refinement: When δ is better than δ', the programmer replaces the δ' node of an existing priority tree by $(\delta\ (\delta'))$ or $(*P_\Omega\ (\delta)\ (\delta'))$ to create a new tree (Figure 18.1).

The contradiction that any refinement often produces a bad move is common to an evaluation function and a priority tree. But while refining an evaluation function may cause more contradictions, tree refinement causes fewer.

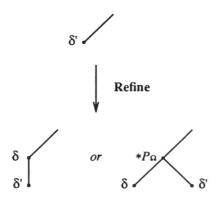

Figure 18.1: Priority tree refinement.

18.3 Go Programming

We have been constructing a Go playing program by representing some knowledge in a priority tree and by repeating the tree refinement. Currently in *YUGO*, the following three forms of knowledge are represented by priority trees and is refined as necessary.

- Core Algorithm: Global decision algorithm for playing Go.
- Name Knowledge: Knowledge about quick response to name by name.
- Meaning Knowledge: Knowledge about quick response to meaning by meaning.

The first is global and the latter two are local. A Go program has to represent at least these three by means of priority trees.

18.3.1 Core Algorithm

Human Go players first look at the opponent's most recent move and unconsciously name it and understand its local meaning. Next they consider whether a quick response to the name or meaning is suitable for a current placement of stones. However, after that, a thought process for deciding the next move may vary according to a player's ability or taste. We call the decision process the core algorithm. Go programmers cannot completely represent the core algorithm the first time, so a priority tree representation is used.

Figure 18.2 shows three priority trees representing core algorithms of the current version of *YUGO*. A favored algorithm can be selected and executed in Lisp using the simple command

$$YUGO \; "algorithm\_name".$$

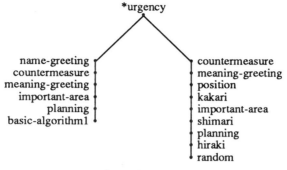

Core Algorithm 1

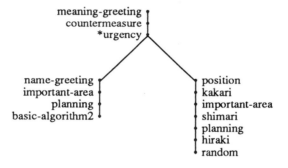

Core Algorithm 2

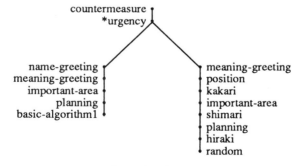

Core Algorithm 3

Figure 18.2: Priority tree examples of core algorithm.

Here we briefly explain each procedure at nodes of these tree examples.

*urgency:[3]

> Judges whether an opponent's move is urgent or not, that is, should the move be directly responded to or not. Currently, YUGO judges the urgency simply and locally from the move name.

name-greeting:[4]

> Quick response to name by name (e.g., doing *hane* to *tsuke*) as detailed in Section 18.3.2 *Name Knowledge*.

meaning-greeting:

> Quick responses to meaning by meaning (e.g., *escaping* to *being blockaded*), see Section 18.3.3 *Meaning Knowledge*.

position:

> Putting a stone on a corner of the board, mainly in opening game (e.g., *hoshi, komoku*).

important area:

> Extraction of strategically important areas or points. YUGO's method has been detailed by Shirayanagi (1986).

countermeasure:

> Looking ahead (reading moves) to create moves defending a friendly basis[5] against an opponent's attack.

planning:

> Construction of plans of offense, defense, *moyo*-destruction, *moyo*-construction and *yose* (territory reduction and extension). YUGO's idea is to extract weak and important bases which blockade and/or are blockaded.

kakari, shimari and hiraki:

> These are procedures for doing several kinds of *kakari, shimari* and *hiraki* respectively.

random:

> Random selection out of the remaining (and appropriate) moves.

basic-algorithm1 and basic-algorithm2:

> These have priority trees
>
>   (position (kakari (shimari (hiraki (random))))) and
>   (position (kakari (shimari (important-area (hiraki (random))))))
>
> in the list expression, respectively.

It is interesting that we cannot tell which of these algorithms in Figure 18.2 plays Go better. The choice is a matter of taste. However, of course, there seems to be an even better algorithm, and we may construct it by the scheme in Section 18.2.2 *Tree Refinement*.

---

[3] This is a JUDGE procedure. In this way, YUGO always puts '*' at the head of the predicate name.

[4] From now on, all procedures belong to DO.

[5] Basis is a unit of the same color stones not cut by enemies.

18.3.2 Name Knowledge

Human Go players often consider a quick response (greeting) to a move name. The name greeting is fundamental in Go, although humans abandon the greeting move if it is bad or unsuitable for a situation. We call the knowledge about the name greeting *name knowledge*. Almost all name knowledge is based on the well-known knowledge about the name called Go proverbs or Go maxims such as "Do *hane* to *tsuke*." However, this knowledge is considered incomplete for all situations. So we should represent it by priority trees. Here move names are put on DO nodes and a DO procedure creates one or more such moves.

Figure 18.3 shows an example of a priority tree representing name knowledge to an opponent's *ate*[6] where *shicho* is a capturing method and **shicho* denotes a binary predicate indicating whether or not the enemy's stones can be captured by *shicho*. Both *ate* and *nige* are move names and *tenuki* means to make no direct response to an opponent's move.

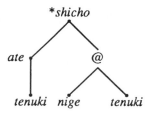

Figure 18.3: A priority tree of name knowledge.

When *YUGO* names a white move *ate*, the tree tells how to respond to the move. Namely, the execution of the tree is equivalent to the following algorithm, assuming that @ is empty.
(1) "Does the *shicho* work?" If the answer is YES, go to (2), otherwise go to (4).
(2) If there exists a move named *ate* in the surrounding area, then play it (that is, do *ate*), otherwise go to (3).
(3) Do *tenuki*.
(4) Select at random one procedure from "Do *nige*" and "Do *tenuki*."
See Shirayanagi (1988) for implementation details, and the paper by Kierulf, Chen and Nievergelt (1990) for a good introduction to computer-Go terminology.

Table 18.1 shows a part of initial and current priority trees of the knowledge in *YUGO*.[7] The initial trees were given by the programmer in advance. The current trees have been refined based on ten games I played with *YUGO*. Some of the refinement results did not change, but they may change after more games.

---

[6] See Section 18.4.1 *Naming a Move* for how to name a move.
[7] We do not detail the contents of Table 18.1.

YUGO currently has 23 elements of name knowledge and is implemented in TAO Lisp (Takeuchi, Okuno and Ohsato 1986). The frame system KRINE (Ogawa *et al.* 1984) manages the knowledge base of *YUGO*.

Name Knowledge	Initial Tree	Current Tree
To *tsuke*	(@ (*hane*) (*nobi*))	(@ (*hane*) (*nobi*))
To *ate*	(*nige*)	(**shicho* (*ate* (*tenuki*)) (@ (*nige*) (*tenuki*)))
To *oshi*	(*nobi*)	(**2moku* (*hane*) (*nobi*))
To *nozoki*	(*tsugi*)	(@ (*tsugi*) (*oshi*))
To *boshi*	(@ (*keima*) (*tenuki*))	(@ (*keima*) (*tenuki*))
To *katatsuki*	(*oshi*)	(*oshi*)
To *hane*	(*hane* (*kiri*))	(*osae* (*nobi* (*hane* (*kiri*))))
To *kirichigai*	(**kirichigai* (*nobi*) (*tenuki*))	(**kirichigai* (*nobi*) (**ate* (*ate*-tree)(*tenuki*)))

Table 18.1: Initial and current priority trees of name knowledge in *YUGO*.

18.3.3 Meaning Knowledge

A meaning greeting is also fundamental. This responds directly to an opponent's move according to the simple knowledge about its local meaning called *meaning knowledge.* Unlike move names, local meanings have few Go proverbs. So, meaning knowledge is based on a common-sense knowledge such as "Do *escape* when *blockaded.*" As with the name knowledge, it is natural to use a priority tree to represent the meaning knowledge. Here a DO procedure creates moves having the meaning.

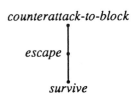

Figure 18.4: A priority tree of meaning knowledge.

Figure 18.4 shows an example of a priority tree representing meaning knowledge to an opponent's *blockade,* where *counterattack-to-block, escape* and *survive* are DO procedures. At present, Yugo has four pieces of meaning knowledge. When *YUGO* recognizes that a white move means *blockade,* and understands that a black basis B is blockaded by white bases $W1, \cdots, Wn$,[8] the tree execution implies the following algorithm:

(1) If there exist moves counterattacking at least one of $W1, \cdots, Wn$, then return the moves as candidates of the next move. Otherwise, go to (2).

(2) If there exists moves that let B escape from the block net $W1, \cdots, Wn$, then return them. Otherwise, go to (3).

(3) If there exists moves giving B a *living* style, then return them. Otherwise, return empty.

Like a core algorithm representation, it may be a matter of taste to determine a procedure priority.

18.4 Fundamental Tools

Let us give two fundamental capabilities for Go programming: naming and meaning understanding. They are necessary for name greeting and meaning greeting respectively. Regarding knowledge about them, we can almost precisely represent it in advance since it does not depend on a global situation. These two capabilities are implemented as a part of *YUGO*.

18.4.1 Naming a Move

Almost all move names are uniquely determined by their visual pattern. We can classify move names into three groups: *relationship, style* and *position*. The relationship group shows the relationship to the nearest enemy stone and the style group shows the relationship to the nearest friendly stone. The position group describes a position on the board.

A strong human player can correctly name almost every move. We represent this knowledge using the following ideas: 1) finely classifying move names into types, members of which are move names with close meanings in Go, and 2) giving a weight of naming to these types. Table 18.2 shows the types, and their weights and members. The smaller the number, the larger the weight. Note that some of the move names are not included in Table 18.2.

YUGO stores standard patterns of the move names in Table 18.2 in the form of two-dimensional coordinates and logical formulae showing the surrounding conditions. It also recognizes each move name in Table 18.2, including symmetrical and rotated positions. By matching against standard patterns, *YUGO* can name about 50 moves almost as well as strong human players.

In general, the weight relation among the three groups of move names is "relationship" > "style" > "position" except for (11) the guzumi type, as seen in Table 18.2. When a move belongs to two or three groups, we select the most appropriate name according to the weight. Let's look at some simple examples:

---

[8] See Section 18.4.2 *Meaning Understanding* for how to understand local meanings of a move.

Group	Type	Move Name
Relationship	(1) nuki	*nuki*
	(2) kiri	*kiri*
	(3) ate	*ate, ryo-atari*
	(4) tsugi	*tsugi, katatsugi, kaketsugi*
	(5) osae-to-de	*osae*
	(6) fukurami	*fukurami*
	(7) magari	*magari*
	(8) hane	*hane, atekomi, warikomi, horikomi, osae*
	(9) oshi	*oshi, osae, hai*
	(10) tsuke	*tsuke, kosumitsuke, hasamitsuke, tsukiatari*
	(12) nobi	*nobi, hiki, sagari*
	(13) nozoki	*nozoki*
	(14) kakari	*kakari, keimagakari, ikkengakari,* *ogeimagakari, nikengakari*
	(15) keshi	*katatsuki, kake, boshi*
	(16) sansan-iri	*sansan-iri*
	(17) uchikomi	*uchikomi*
	(18) hasami	*hasami,* n*ken-basami* $(1 \leq n \leq 3)$
	(19) tsume	*tsume*
Style	(11) guzumi	*guzumi*
	(20) shimari	*keimajimari, ikkenjimari, ogeimajimari,* *nikenjimari*
	(21) hiraki	*hiraki,* n*ken-biraki* $(1 \leq n \leq 3)$
	(22) **basic**	*narabi, kosumi, ikkentobi, keima,* *hazamatobi, nikentobi, ogeima*
Position	(23) **basic**	*hoshi, komoku, sansan, mokuhazushi,* *takamoku, tengen*

Table 18.2: A classification of move names with weights.

Figure 18.5 shows that a stone Ⓐ at the exactly same position is given different names, depending on the weights.

Figure 18.6 gives a trickier example. The white Ⓐ was played after the black ■. What is the name of the white Ⓐ move? This pattern has aspects of magari, hane, nozoki and osae-to-de in the relationship group. Osae-to-de means *osae* with respect to the move ■ called *de*. According to the weights of types in Table 18.2, we have (5) osae-to-de > (7) magari > (8) hane > (13) nozoki. Thus, the correct name of the white Ⓐ move is *osae*.

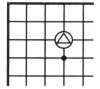 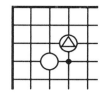

(a) *Komoku* in the position group.   (b) *Kosumi* in the style group.

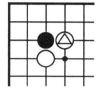

(c) *Hane* in the relationship group.

Figure 18.5: Changing relationships with stone placement.

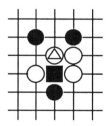

Figure 18.6: What is the name of the marked white move?

18.4.2 Meaning Understanding

Local meanings of a move are understood by the influence of the move on a placement of stones in the surrounding area. A key idea is to look at a change of the situation caused by the move. We define a situation by a set of lists arranging bases, their completeness as territories or territory sizes, and their *eye-richness* for black and white. For example, one situation might be:

{(B1 (incomp 0)) (B2 (incomp 0)) (B3 (12 0)) (B4 (4 0))
(B5 (incomp 0)) (B6 (4 0))
(W1 (15 0)) (W2 (incomp 0)) (W3 (invaded 0))
(W4 (invaded 0)) (W5 (5 2))}

where Bi's and Wj's are basis names, "incomp" means an incomplete territory and "invaded" is a territory invaded by an enemy. *Eye-richness* is represented by the number of "V-shape" triples of points.

Local meanings of all moves except *blockade* are understood by looking at the difference between a situation before the move and after the move in the following manner, assuming the move M is white.

Local meanings of M to white:
- *connect* ⟺ the number of white bases decreases,
- *consolidate* ⟺ some Wj changes from "incomp" into a number in territory completeness,
- *expand* ⟺ some Wj increases in territory size,
- *prevent* ⟺ some Wj changes from "invaded" into a number or "incomp" in territory completeness, and
- *eye-make* ⟺ some Wj increases in *eye-richness*.

Local meanings of M to black:
- *cut* ⟺ the number of black bases increases,
- *invade* ⟺ some Bi changes from a number or "incomp" into "invaded,"
- *eye-break* ⟺ some Bi decreases in *eye-richness*.

When no changes are seen, no local meanings are understood. For *blockade* the meaning is understood by recognizing whether a basis lies inside a convex hull of three or more enemy bases.

A Go program should update a situation whenever an opponent's move is made and should remember the most recent situation. The more precisely the program computes territory completeness or size and *eye-richness,* the better it understands a local meaning. *YUGO* now understands the meaning well enough to play Go from opening to middlegame.

18.5 Evaluation of YUGO

YUGO rapidly surpassed the beginner's level and currently plays Go as well as about a 15 kyu human player. We cannot say that this level is much better than the existing Go programs (such as, Zobrist 1970b; Ryder 1971; Reitman and Wilcox 1979; Sanechika *et al.* 1981,88). But most of them are not expected to become much stronger, since human knowledge is reduced to something static, like evaluation functions or values. On the contrary, *YUGO* represents human knowledge explicitly in a symbolic expression so that the representation is precisely refinable. Consequently, despite a little difficulty in implementation, *YUGO* can be updated according to a Go programmer's taste or teaching, and we expect further improvements to occur as we continue with our refinements.

The priority tree used in *YUGO* is one of the most useful symbolic expressions for Go programming.

(1) The tree is easy to write and read, and can also be written as a list. Additionally, if we represent, for example, the tree

$$(*shicho\ (ate\ (tenuki))\ (nuki\ (nige)))$$

by if-then rules in Lisp, we have

(if *shicho*-p

    (if *ate*-p *ate*-moves *tenuki*-moves)

    (if *nuki*-p *nuki*-moves *nige*-moves))

which becomes more complicated. Here, *N*-moves is a Lisp function for playing the move named *N*.

(2) The tree is suitable for refinement, and it is easy for a programmer to determine which parts of trees to refine. New nodes can be added and relationships changed at leisure. Conversely, the refinement is difficult when using another tool, such as the if-then rules in Lisp.

18.5.1 For Further Improvement

We have shown a new direction for programming Go. However, there are many challenging problems for further improvement of a Go program:

Perception

    We claimed that arithmetic evaluation functions should not be used for weighting a move, more generally, for representing the knowledge required for thinking strategies. But, regarding a perception for territory size, basis strength, thickness (*atsumi*) and so on, we believe that we have to represent them by numeric values. The perception is also necessary for thinking strategies in Go, and thus we must propose a good method for representing it (see also the works of Zobrist (1970b) and Ryder (1971)).

Situation Evaluation

    Evaluating a board state is also required for local game-tree search with a given tactical goal. We should also settle on a good static evaluation function for situations in a minimax search under alpha-beta pruning (for such a function see the work of Sanechika *et al.* (1981,88)).

Predicate

    Predicates in a priority tree should be precisely represented. For example, **urgency* of an algorithm tree currently in *YUGO* is only superficially recognized by a move name. It should often be more deeply or globally recognized. Also, to refine a priority tree, the programmer must first extract a feature of the situation and precisely represent it.

Antenna

    In a sense, enriching antennas is one of the most important ideas for improving the performance of a Go program. This is because the antenna accepts a program's global or local plan to determine which of the candidate moves are suitable for the plan or are consistent with common senses about good moves. Currently, *YUGO* makes it empty and thus only selects one of the candidates at random, or sometimes receives and accomplishes plans resulting from the planning procedure explained in Section 18.3 *Go Programming*.

Joseki and Move Sequence

    YUGO has several Josekis, which are common good move sequences, in the knowledge base. However, it now uses none of them during play because it is difficult to decide when they should be used. We expect some improvement, as we can put many Josekis, or other good move sequences, below a predicate or an antenna in a priority tree.

Multiple Intention

All the priority trees used in the global decision algorithm in *YUGO* are too simple to represent a program's multiple intention of strategy. For example, a defensive move sometimes has the next or future aim of attacking an enemy basis. To play such a move, more procedures must be added to the tree, changing the order.

Parallel Processing

It sometimes takes a long time (about three minutes) to execute a priority tree. Because the tree of the core algorithm is more complex, we may introduce parallel processing to get better response.

Go Programmer

We assume that a Go programmer has knowledge of Go to some extent. The stronger the player, the better the priority tree will be refined. Indeed, like human beginners, a Go program needs refinement not only by the programmer but also by other human teachers.

18.6 Conclusion

We have represented the important knowledge required for playing Go by means of a priority tree. Nodes of the tree are procedures for deciding the next move and an order is the priority for executing these procedures. We can easily and precisely refine the representation by adding new nodes and changing the order between nodes. Additionally, as fundamental tools of Go programming, we presented a method for naming a move and understanding moves in a local context.

We have been constructing a Go program by refining trees of the global decision algorithm and common-sense knowledge about a quick response to an opponent's move. The program has not yet exceeded 15 kyu level, but we expect our direction of Go programming will enable significant progress.

Acknowledgments. I am grateful to Shigeki Goto and Kime H. Smith for their valuable comments and advice, and also appreciated helpful discussions with group members in the NTT Software Laboratories.

Bibliography

Ackley, D.H. and H.J. Berliner (1983), "The QBKG System: Knowledge Representation for Producing and Explaining Judgments," technical report CMU-CS-83-116, Department of Computer Science, Carnegie Mellon University.

Adelson-Velsky, G.M., V.L. Arlazarov, A.R. Bitman, A.A. Zhivotovskii and A.V. Uskov (1970), "Programming a Computer to Play Chess," *Russian Mathematics Surveys,* no. 25, pp. 221-262, Cleaver-Hume Press, London. (Translation of Proceedings 1st Summer School Mathematics Program, vol. 2, pp. 216-252, 1969).

Adelson-Velsky, G.M., V.L. Arlazarov and M.V. Donskoy (1975), "Some Methods of Controlling the Tree Search in Chess Programs," *Artificial Intelligence,* vol. 6, no. 4, pp. 361-371.

Adelson-Velsky, G.M., V.L. Arlazarov and M.V. Donskoy (1988), *Algorithms for Games,* Springer-Verlag, New York.

Akl, S.G., D.T. Barnard and R.J. Doran (1982), "Design, Analysis and Implementation of a Parallel Tree Search Algorithm," *IEEE Transactions on Pattern Analysis and Machine Intelligence,* vol. 4, no. 2, pp. 192-203.

Anantharaman, T.S., M.S. Campbell and F-h. Hsu (1988), "Singular Extensions: Adding Selectivity to Brute-Force Searching," AAAI Spring Symposium Proceedings, pp. 8-13. Also published in the *Journal of the International Computer Chess Association,* vol. 11 (1988), no. 4, pp. 135-143 and in *Artificial Intelligence,* vol. 43 (1990), no. 1, pp. 99-110.

Anantharaman, T.S. (1990), "A Statistical Study of Selective Min-Max Search," Ph.D. thesis, Department of Computer Science, Carnegie Mellon University.

Babaoglu, O. (1977), "A Hardware Move Generator for Chess," technical report, University of California, Berkeley.

Barth, T. (1988), "Neue Varianten von Suchverfahren und Stellungsbewertungen im Computerschach," Doctoral dissertation, Institut für Praktische Informatik, Technical University of Vienna (in German).

Baudet, G.M. (1978a), "The Design and Analysis of Algorithms for Asynchronous Multiprocessors," Ph.D. thesis, Department of Computer Science, Carnegie Mellon University.

Baudet, G.M. (1978b), "On the Branching Factor of the Alpha-Beta Pruning Algorithm," *Artificial Intelligence,* vol. 10 , no. 2, pp. 173-199.

Beal, D.F. (1980), "An Analysis of Minimax," in *Advances in Computer Chess 2,* M.R.B. Clarke (ed.), Edinburgh University Press, pp. 103-109.

Beal, D.F. (1982), "Benefits of Minimax Search," in *Advances in Computer Chess 3*, M.R.B. Clarke (ed.), Pergamon, Oxford, pp. 17-24.

Beal, D.F. (1989), "Experiments with the Null Move," in *Advances in Computer Chess 5*, D.F. Beal (ed.), Elsevier Science Publishers, Amsterdam, pp. 65-79. A revised version is published under the title "A Generalized Quiescence Search Algorithm" in *Artificial Intelligence*, vol. 43 (1990), no. 1, pp. 85-98.

Bell, A.G. (1978), *The Machine Plays Chess?*, Pergamon, Oxford.

Berliner, H.J. (1973), "Some Necessary Conditions for a Master Chess Program," 3rd International Joint Conference on Artificial Intelligence, pp. 77-85.

Berliner, H.J. (1974), "Chess as Problem Solving: The Development of a Tactics Analyzer," Ph.D. thesis, Department of Computer Science, Carnegie Mellon University.

Berliner, H.J. (1979a), "On the Construction of Evaluation Functions for Large Domains," 6th International Joint Conference on Artificial Intelligence, pp. 53-55.

Berliner, H.J. (1979b), "The B* Tree Search Algorithm: A Best First Proof Procedure," *Artificial Intelligence*, vol. 12, no. 1, pp. 23-40.

Berliner, H.J. (1979c), "Backgammon Computer Program Beats World Champion," *Artificial Intelligence*, vol. 14, no. 2, pp. 205-220.

Berliner, H.J. (1981), "An Examination of Brute Force Intelligence," 7th International Joint Conference on Artificial Intelligence, pp. 581-587.

Berliner, H.J. (1986), "Computer Chess at Carnegie Mellon University," in *Advances in Computer Chess 4*, D.F. Beal (ed.), Pergamon Press, Oxford, pp. 166-180.

Berliner, H.J. (1989), "Some Innovations Introduced by of Hitech," in *Advances in Computer Chess 5*, D.F. Beal (ed.), Elsevier Science Publishers, Amsterdam, pp. 283-294.

Berliner, H.J. and C. Ebeling (1989), "Pattern Knowledge and Search: The SUPREM Architecture," *Artificial Intelligence*, vol. 38, no. 2, pp. 161-198. An updated, abbreviated version appears in this book.

Bernstein, A., M. deV. Roberts, T. Arbuckle and M.A. Belsky (1958), "A Chess Playing Program for the IBM 704," Proceedings Western Joint Computer Conference, Los Angeles, pp. 157-159.

Bratko, I. and M. Gams (1982), "Error Analysis of the Minimax Principle," in *Advances in Computer Chess 3*, M.R.B. Clarke (ed.), Pergamon, Oxford, pp. 1-16.

Brudno, A.L. (1963), "Bounds and Valuations for Abridging the Search of Estimates," in *Problems of Cybernetics*, vol. 10, pp. 225-241. Originally appeared in *Problemy Kibernetiki*, vol. 10, pp. 141-150 (in Russian).

Byrne, R. (1989), New York Times chess column, Tuesday, 26 September.

Campbell, M.S. (1981), "Algorithms for the Parallel Search of Game Trees," M.Sc. thesis, Department of Computing Science, University of Alberta. Also available as technical report TR 81-9.

Campbell, M.S. and T.A. Marsland (1983), "A Comparison of Minimax Tree Search Algorithms," *Artificial Intelligence,* vol. 20, no. 4, pp. 347-367.

Capablanca, J.R. (1935), *A Primer on Chess,* Harcourt & Brace, New York.

Chen, K.H. (1989), "Group Identification in Computer Go," in *Heuristic Programming in Artificial Intelligence: The First Computer Olympiad,* D.N.L. Levy and D.F. Beal, (eds.), Ellis Horwood, Chichester, pp. 195-210.

Condon, J.H. and K. Thompson (1982), "Belle Chess Hardware," in *Advances in Computer Chess 3,* M.R.B. Clarke (ed.), Pergamon, Oxford, pp. 45-54.

Conway, J.H. (1976), *On Numbers and Games,* Academic Press.

Darwish, N.M. (1983), "A Quantitative Analysis of the Alpha-Beta Pruning Algorithm," *Artificial Intelligence,* vol. 21, no. 4, pp. 405-433.

Dekker, S.T., H.J. van den Herik and I.S. Herschberg (1987a), "Perfect Knowledge and Beyond," report 87-37, Delft University of Technology, Delft. See also (1989), *Advances in Computer Chess 5* D.F. Beal (ed.), Elsevier Science Publishers, Amsterdam, pp. 295-312. Also published in *Artificial Intelligence,* vol. 43 (1990), no. 1, pp. 111-123.

Dekker, S.T., H.J. van den Herik and I.S. Herschberg (1987b), "Complexity Starts at Five," *Journal of the International Computer Chess Association,* vol. 10, no. 3, pp. 125-138.

Dekker, S.T. (1989), personal communication.

Dreyfus, H.L. and S.E. Dreyfus (1986), *Mind Over Machine,* MacMillan, New York.

Ebeling, C. (1986), "All the Right Moves: A VLSI Architecture for Chess," Ph.D. thesis, Department of Computer Science, Carnegie Mellon University. See also (1987), book with same title, MIT Press.

Elo, A.E. (1978), *The Rating of Chessplayers, Past and Present,* Arco Publishing, New York.

Euclid (1895), *Analysis of the Chess Ending King and Queen Against King and Rook,* E. Freeborough (ed.), Kegan Paul, Trench, Trubner & Co.

Feldmann, R., B. Monien, P. Mysliwietz and O. Vornberger (1989), "Distributed Game-Tree Search," *Journal of the International Computer Chess Association,* vol. 11, no. 1, pp. 65-73.

Fine, R. (1941), *Basic Chess Endings,* David McKay Company, New York.

Fishburn, J.P. and R.A. Finkel (1980), "Parallel Alpha-Beta Search on Arachne," technical report 394, Computer Sciences Department, University of Wisconsin, Madison.

Fishburn, J.P. (1981), *Analysis of Speedup in Distributed Algorithms,* Ph.D. thesis, Computer Sciences Department University of Wisconsin, Madison. See also (1984), book with same title, UMI Research Press.

Frey, P.W. (ed.) (1977), *Chess Skill in Man and Machine,* Springer-Verlag, New York. See also 2nd edition (1983) with two extra chapters.

Fuller, S.H., J.G. Gaschnig and J.J. Gillogly (1973), "Analysis of the Alpha-Beta Pruning Algorithm," technical report, Department of Computer Science, Carnegie Mellon University.

Gillogly, J.J. (1978), "Performance Analysis of the Technology Chess Program," Ph.D. thesis, Department of Computer Science, Carnegie Mellon University.

Goetsch, G. and M.S. Campbell (1988), "Experiments with the Null Move Heuristic in Chess," AAAI Spring Symposium Proceedings, pp. 14-18. A revised version of this paper appears in this book.

Good, I.J. (1968), "A Five-Year Plan for Automatic Chess," in *Machine Intelligence 2*, E. Dale and D. Michie (eds.), Elsevier Science Publishers, New York, pp. 89-118.

Greenblatt, R.D., D.E. Eastlake and S.D. Crocker (1967), "The Greenblatt Chess Program," Proceedings of the Fall Joint Computer Conference, pp. 801-810.

Groot, A.D. de (1965), *Thought and Choice in Chess*, Mouton, The Hague.

Gunn, M. (1988), "The Challenge of the New Materials," *New Scientist*, no. 1646, Jan. 7.

Hanks, S. and D. McDermott (1987), "Nonmonotonic Logic and Temporal Projection," *Artificial Intelligence*, vol. 33, no. 3, pp. 379-412.

Hanner, O. (1959), "Mean Play of Sums of Positional Games," *Pacific Journal of Mathematics*, vol. 9, no. 1, pp. 81-99.

Hartmann, D. (1987a), "How to Extract Relevant Knowledge from Grandmaster Games, Part 1," *Journal of the International Computer Chess Association*, vol. 10, no. 1, pp. 14-36.

Hartmann, D. (1987b), "How to Extract Relevant Knowledge from Grandmaster Games, Part 2," *Journal of the International Computer Chess Association*, vol. 10, no. 2, pp. 78-90.

Hayes, J.E. and D.N.L. Levy (1976), *The World Computer Chess Championship*, Edinburgh University Press, Edinburgh.

Hearst, E. (1983), "Man and Machine: Chess Achievements and Chess Thinking," in *Chess Skill in Man and Machine*, P. Frey (ed.), Springer-Verlag, pp. 167-198.

Herik, H.J. van den and I.S. Herschberg (1985), "The Construction of an Omniscient Endgame Data Base," *Journal of the International Computer Chess Association*, vol. 8, no. 2, pp. 66-87.

Herik, H.J. van den and I.S. Herschberg (1986), "Omniscience, the Rulegiver?," Proceedings of L'Intelligenza Artificiale Ed Il Gioco Degli Scacchi, III° Convegno Internazionale, B. Pernici and M. Somalvico (eds.), pp. 1-17.

Herik, H.J. van den, I.S. Herschberg and N. Nakad (1987), "A Six-Men-Endgame Database: KRP(a2)KbBP(a3)," *Journal of the International Computer Chess Association*, vol. 10, no. 4, pp. 163-180.

Herik, H.J. van den and S.T. Dekker (1988), "Uitputtende Enumeratie Schaakeindspel," in *Het Gebruik van Supercomputers in Nederland*, J. Hollenberg (ed.), SARA, Amsterdam, pp. 127-132 (in Dutch).

Horacek, H. (1984), "Some Conceptual Defects of Evaluation Functions," Proceedings ECAI, Elsevier Science Publishers, Amsterdam, pp. 269-272.

Horacek, H., H. Kaindl and M. Wagner (1986), "Decision Making in Unclear Situations," Proceedings 2nd Austrian Meetings on Artificial Intelligence, Springer-Verlag, Informatik-Fachbericht 124, pp. 17-27.

Horacek, H., H. Kaindl and M. Wagner (1987), "Probabilities in Game-Playing: Possible Meanings and Applications," Proceedings 3rd Austrian Meetings on Artificial Intelligence, Springer-Verlag, Informatik-Fachbericht 151, pp. 12-23.

Horacek, H. (1989), "Reasoning with Uncertainty in Computer Chess," in *Advances in Computer Chess 5,* D.F. Beal (ed.), Elsevier Science Publishers, Amsterdam, pp. 43-63. Also published in *Artificial Intelligence,* vol. 43 (1990), no. 1, pp. 37-56.

Hsu, F-h. (1987), "A Two-Million Moves/s CMOS Single-Chip Chess Move Generator," *IEEE Journal of Solid-State Circuits,* vol. 22, no.5, pp. 841-846. Portions of this paper can be found in Chapter 5 *Deep Thought.*

Hsu, F-h. (1990), "Large Scale Parallelization of Alpha-Beta Search: An Algorithmic and Architectural Study with Computer Chess," Ph.D. thesis, Department of Computer Science, Carnegie Mellon University.

Huberman, B.J. (1968), "A Program to Play Chess End Games," technical report no. CS 106, Ph.D. thesis, Computer Science Department, Stanford University.

Hyatt, R.M. (1984), "Using Time Wisely," *Journal of the International Computer Chess Association,* vol. 7, no. 1, pp. 4-9.

Hyatt, R.M., A.E. Gower and H.L. Nelson (1985), "Cray Blitz," in *Advances in Computer Chess 4,* D. Beal (ed.), Pergamon Press, Oxford, pp. 8-18.

Hyatt, R.M. (1988), "A High-Performance Parallel Algorithm to Search Depth-first Game Trees," Ph.D. thesis, Department of Computer Science, University of Alabama, Birmingham.

Hyatt, R.M., B.W. Suter and H.L. Nelson (1989), "A Parallel Alpha/Beta Tree Searching Algorithm," *Parallel Computing,* vol. 10, no. 3, pp. 299-308.

Ibaraki, T. (1986), "Generalization of Alpha-Beta and SSS* Search Procedures," *Artificial Intelligence,* vol. 29. no. 1, pp. 73-117.

Jansen, P. and J. Schaeffer (1990), "Seconding a Grandmaster," *Journal of the International Computer Chess Association,* vol. 13, no. 1, pp. 29-33.

Kaindl, H. (1982a), "Quiescence Search in Computer Chess," SIGART Newsletter, no. 80, pp. 124-131. Reprinted in *Computer Game-Playing: Theory and Practice,* M.A. Bramer (ed.), 1983, Ellis Horwood, Chichester, pp. 39-52.

Kaindl, H. (1982b), "Dynamic Control of the Quiescence Search in Computer Chess," Proceedings EMCSR-82, North-Holland, 973-978.

Kaindl, H. (1983), "Searching to Variable Depth in Computer Chess," 8th International Joint Conference on Artificial Intelligence, pp. 760-762.

Kaindl, H. (1988a), "Useful Statistics from Tournament Programs," *Journal of the International Computer Chess Association,* vol. 11, no. 4, pp. 156-159.

Kaindl, H. (1988b), "Minimaxing: Theory and Practice," *AI Magazine,* vol. 9, no. 3, pp. 69-76.

Kaindl, H. (1989), *Problemlösen durch Heuristische Suche in der Artificial Intelligence,* Springer-Verlag, Vienna.

Kaindl, H., M. Wagner and H. Horacek (1989), "Comparing Various Pruning Algorithms on Very Strongly Ordered Game Trees," New Directions in Game-Tree Search Workshop, T.A. Marsland (ed.), Edmonton, pp. 111-120. A more comprehensive version is available as technical report 50, Institut für Statistik und Informatik, University of Vienna, 1988.

Kierulf, A. and J. Nievergelt (1989), "Swiss Explorer Blunders its Way into Winning the First Computer Go Olympiad," in *Heuristic Programming in Artificial Intelligence: The First Computer Olympiad,* D.N.L. Levy and D.F. Beal, (eds.), Ellis Horwood, Chichester, pp. 51-55.

Kierulf, A., K.H. Chen and J. Nievergelt (1990), "Smart Game Board and Go Explorer: A Case Study in Software and Knowledge Engineering," *Communications of the ACM,* vol. 33, no. 2, pp. 152-166.

King, R.D. (1989), "PROMIS: Experiments in Machine Learning and Protein Folding," in *Machine Intelligence 12,* J.E. Hayes, D. Michie and E. Tyugu (eds.), Oxford University Press, Oxford.

King, R.D. and M.J.E. Sternberg (1990), "A Machine Learning Approach for the Prediction of Protein Secondary Structure," to appear *Journal of Molecular Biology.*

Kister, J., P. Stein, S. Ulam, W. Walden and M. Wells, (1957), "Experiments in Chess," *Journal of the ACM,* no. 4, pp. 174-177.

Kling, J. and B. Horwitz (1851), *Chess Studies, or Endings of Games, Containing Upwards of Two Hundred Scientific Examples of Chess Strategy,* Skeet, London.

Knuth, D.E. and R.W. Moore (1975), "An Analysis of Alpha-Beta Pruning," *Artificial Intelligence,* vol. 6, no. 4, pp. 293-326.

Komissarchik, E.A. and A.L. Futer (1974), "Ob Analize Ferzevogo Endshpilya pri Pomoshchi EVM," *Problemy Kybernetiki,* no. 29, pp. 211-220 (in Russian); translated as: "Computer Analysis of a Queen Endgame," *Journal of the International Computer Chess Association,* vol. 9 (1986), no. 4, pp. 189-198.

Kopec, D. and T. Niblett (1980), "How Hard is the Play of the King-Rook-King-Knight Ending?" in *Advances in Computer Chess 2,* M.R.B. Clarke (ed.), Edinburgh University Press, Edinburgh, pp. 57-80.

Kopec, D. and I. Bratko (1982), "The Bratko-Kopec Experiment: A Comparison of Human and Computer Performance in Chess," in *Advances in Computer Chess 3,* M.R.B. Clarke (ed.), Pergamon, Oxford, pp. 57-72.

Kopec, D., B. Libby and C. Cook (1988), "The Endgame King, Rook and Bishop vs. King and Rook (KRBKR)," AAAI Spring Symposium Proceedings, pp. 60-61.

Kopec, D. (1989), "Deep Thought Outsearches Foes, Wins World Computer Championship," *Chess Life,* pp. 17-24.

Korf, R.E. (1990), "Real-Time Heuristic Search," *Artificial Intelligence,* vol. 42, no. 2-3, pp.189-212.

Kumar, V. and L. Kanal (1984), "Parallel Branch-and-Bound Formulations for AND/OR Tree Search," *IEEE Transactions on Pattern Analysis and Machine Intelligence,* vol. 6, no. 6, pp. 768-778.

Lehnert, W. (1988), "Natural Language Understanding," in *Exploring Artificial Intelligence,* H. Shrobe (ed.), Morgan Kaufman Publishers, Los Altos, pp. 85-86.

Leithauser, B. (1987), "The Space of One Breadth," *New Yorker Magazine,* March 9, pp. 43-72.

Levy, D.N.L. and M.M. Newborn (1982), *All About Chess and Computers,* Computer Science Press, Rockville, MD. This book is a combined reprint of *Chess and Computers* (Levy 1976), and *More Chess and Computers* (Levy and Newborn 1981).

Levy, D.N.L. (1986a), "Chess Master Versus Computer," in *Advances in Computer Chess 4,* D.F. Beal (ed.), Pergamon, Oxford, pp. 181-194.

Levy, D.N.L. (1986b), "When Will Brute-Force Programs Beat Kasparov?," *Journal of the International Computer Chess Association,* vol. 9, no. 2, pp. 81-86.

Levy, D.N.L. (1987), "Improving the Performance of Endgame Databases," *Journal of the International Computer Chess Association,* vol. 10, no. 4, pp. 191-192.

Levy, D.N.L. (ed.) (1988), *Computer Chess Compendium,* Springer Verlag, New York.

Marsland, T.A. and P. Rushton (1973), "Mechanisms for Comparing Chess Programs," Proceedings ACM National Conference, Oct., pp. 202-205.

Marsland, T.A. and M.S. Campbell (1982), "Parallel Search of Strongly Ordered Game Trees," *Computing Surveys,* vol. 14, no. 4, pp. 533-551.

Marsland, T.A. (1983), "Relative Efficiency of Alpha-Beta Implementations," 8th International Joint Conference on Artificial Intelligence, pp. 763-766.

Marsland, T.A. (1985), "Evaluation-Function Factors," *Journal of the International Computer Chess Association,* vol. 8, no. 2, pp. 47-57.

Marsland, T.A. and F. Popowich (1985), "Parallel Game-Tree Search," *IEEE Transactions on Pattern Analysis and Machine Intelligence,* vol. 7, no. 4, pp. 442-452.

Marsland, T.A. and N. Srimani (1986), "Phased State Space Search," Proceedings of the Fall Joint Computer Conference, IEEE Computer Society Press, pp. 514-518.

Marsland, T.A. (1987), "Computer Chess Methods," in *Encyclopedia of Artificial Intelligence,* vol. 1, S.C. Shapiro (ed.), Wiley & Sons, pp. 159-171.

Marsland, T.A., A. Reinefeld and J. Schaeffer (1987), "Low Overhead Alternatives to SSS*," *Artificial Intelligence,* vol. 31, no. 2, pp. 185-199.

Matanović, A. (editor in chief) (1989), *Chess Informant* series and *Encyclopaedia of Chess Openings, Encyclopaedia of Chess Middlegames,* and *Encyclopaedia of Chess Endgames* volumes, Chess Informant, Belgrade, Yugoslavia.

McAllester, D.A. (1988), "Conspiracy Numbers for Min-Max Search," *Artificial Intelligence,* vol. 35, no. 3, pp. 287-310. See also (1985), "A New Procedure for Growing Mini-Max Trees," AI Laboratory Report, Massachusetts Institute of Technology.

McCarthy, J. (1983), "Some Expert Systems Need Common Sense," internal report, Stanford University.

Meulen, M. van der (1989), "Weight Assessment in Evaluation Functions" in *Advances in Computer Chess 5,* D.F. Beal (ed.), Elsevier Science Publishers, Amsterdam, pp. 81-89.

Michie, D. (1980), "Chess with Computers," *Interdisciplinary Science Reviews,* vol. 5, no. 3, pp. 215-227. Reprinted in Michie, D. (1982), *Machine Intelligence and Related Topics,* Gordon and Breach Science Publishers.

Michie, D. (1983), "Game-Playing Programs and the Conceptual Interface," in *Computer Game Playing,* M. Bramer (ed.), Ellis Horwood, Chichester, pp. 11-25.

Michie, D. (1986a), "Evaluative Comments in Chess," in *On Machine Intelligence,* Ellis Horwood, Chichester, pp. 44-60.

Michie, D. (1986b), "Computer Chess and the Humanization of Technology," in *On Machine Intelligence,* Ellis Horwood, Chichester, pp. 77-86.

Michie, D. and I. Bratko (1987), "Ideas on Knowledge Synthesis Stemming from the KBBKN Endgame," *Journal of the International Computer Chess Association,* vol. 10, no. 1, pp. 3-13.

Milnor, J. (1953), "Sums of Positional Games," in *Contributions to the Theory of Games II,* M. Dresher, A.W. Tucker, P. Wolfe, (eds.), pp. 291-301, Princeton University Press.

Mittman, B. (1977), "A Brief History of Computer Chess Tournaments: 1970-1975," in *Chess Skill in Man and Machine,* P. Frey (ed.), Springer-Verlag, pp. 1-33.

Moussouris, J., J. Holloway and R. Greenblatt (1979), "CHEOPS: A Chess-Oriented Processing System," in *Machine Intelligence 9,* J.E. Hayes, D. Michie and L. Mikulich (eds.), Ellis Horwood, Chichester, pp. 351-360.

Muggleton, S.H. (1988), "Inductive Acquisition of Chess Strategies," in *Machine Intelligence 11,* J.E. Hayes, D. Michie and J. Richards (eds.), Oxford University Press, Oxford, pp. 375-389.

Nau, D.S. (1980), "Pathology in Game Trees: A Summary of Results," AAAI Conference Proceedings, pp. 102-104.

Nau, D.S. (1983a), "Pathology on Game Trees Revisited and an Alternative to Minimaxing," *Artificial Intelligence,* vol. 21, no. 1-2, pp. 221-244.

Nau, D.S. (1983b), "On Game Graph Structure and its Influence on Pathology," *International Journal of Computer and Information Sciences,* vol. 12, no. 6, pp. 367-383.

Nau, D.S., P. Purdom and C. Tzeng (1986), "Experiments on Alternatives to Minimax," *International Journal of Parallel Programming,* vol. 15, no. 2, pp. 163-183.

Nelson, H.L. (1985), "Hash Tables in Cray Blitz," *Journal of the International Computer Chess Association,* vol. 8, no. 1, pp. 3-13.

Nelson, H.L. and R.M. Hyatt (1988), "The Draw Heuristic in Cray-Blitz," *Journal of the International Computer Chess Association,* vol. 11, no. 1, pp. 3-9.

Nemes, R. (1951), "The Chess-Playing Machine," *Acta Technica,* Hungarian Academy of Sciences, Budapest, pp. 215-239.

Newborn, M.M. (1975), *Computer Chess,* Academic Press, New York.

Newborn, M.M. (1977), "The Efficiency of the Alpha-Beta Search on Trees with Branch-Dependent Terminal Node Scores," *Artificial Intelligence,* vol. 8, no. 2, pp. 137-153.

Newborn, M.M. (1979), "Recent Progress in Computer Chess," in *Advances in Computers 18,* M. Yovits, (ed.), Academic Press, pp. 59-117.

Newborn, M.M. (1985), "A Parallel Search Chess Program," ACM Annual Conference Proceedings, Denver, pp. 272-277.

Newborn, M.M. (1988a), "Unsynchronized Iteratively Deepening Parallel Alpha-Beta Search," *IEEE Transactions on Pattern Analysis and Machine Intelligence,* vol. 10, no. 5, pp. 687-694.

Newborn, M.M. (1988b), personal communication, Moscow.

Newborn, M.M. (1989), "Computer Chess: Ten Years of Significant Progress," in *Advances in Computers 29,* M. Yovits (ed.), Academic Press, pp. 197-250.

Newell, A., J.C. Shaw and H.A. Simon (1958), "Chess Playing Programs and the Problem of Complexity," *IBM Journal of Research and Development,* vol. 4, no. 2, pp. 320-335. Also in *Computers and Thought,* Feigenbaum and Feldman (eds.), pp. 39-70, 1963.

Nielsen, J.B. (1989), personal communication, August.

Nilsson, N. (1980), *Principles of Artificial Intelligence,* Tioga Press.

Nitsche, T. (1982), "A Learning Chess Program," in *Advances in Computer Chess 3,* M.R.B. Clarke (ed.), Pergamon, Oxford, pp. 113-120.

Nunn, J. (1988), personal communication.

Ogawa, Y., K. Shima, T. Sugawara and S. Takagi (1984), "Knowledge Representation and Inference Environment: KRINE, An Approach to Integration of Frame, Prolog and Graphics," International Conference on Fifth Generation Computer Systems, pp. 643-651.

Palay, A.J. (1982), "The B* Tree Search Algorithm - New Results," *Artificial Intelligence,* vol. 19, no. 2, pp. 145-163.

Palay, A.J. (1983), "Searching with Probabilities," Ph.D. thesis, Department of Computer Science, Carnegie Mellon University. See also (1985), book same title, Pitman.

Parnas, D. (1988), "Why Engineers Should Not Use Artificial Intelligence," *IN-FOR Special Issue on Intelligence Integration*, vol. 26, no. 4, pp. 234-246.

Pearl, J. (1980), "Asymptotic Properties of Minimax Trees and Game-Searching Procedures," *Artificial Intelligence*, vol. 14, no. 2, pp. 113-38.

Pearl, J. (1982), "The Solution for the Branching Factor of the Alpha-Beta Pruning Algorithm and its Optimality," *Communications of the ACM*, vol. 25, no. 8, 559-564.

Pearl, J. (1984), *Heuristics: Intelligent Search Strategies for Computer Problem Solving*, Addison-Wesley.

Reinefeld, A. (1983), "An Improvement of the Scout Tree Search Algorithm," *Journal of the International Computer Chess Association*, vol. 6, no. 4, pp. 4-14.

Reinefeld, A. and T.A. Marsland (1987), "A Quantitative Analysis of Minimal Window Search," 10th International Joint Conference on Artificial Intelligence, pp. 951-954.

Reinfeld, F. (1945), *Win At Chess*, McKay, New York. Also (1958), Dover, New York.

Reitman, W. and B. Wilcox (1979), "The Structure and Performance of the IN-TERIM.2 Go Program," 6th International Joint Conference on Artificial Intelligence, pp. 711-719.

Remus, H. (1962), "Simulation of a Learning Machine for Playing Go," Proceedings IFIP Congress, North Holland, 1962. See also Levy, D.N.L (ed.) (1988), *Computer Games II*, Springer Verlag, New York, pp. 136-142.

Rich, E. (1983), *Artificial Intelligence*, McGraw Hill, New York.

Rivest, R.L. (1988), "Game Tree Searching by Min/Max Approximation," *Artificial Intelligence*, vol. 34, no. 1, pp. 77-96.

Rosenberg, R.S. and J. Kestner (1972), "Look-Ahead and One-Person Games," *Journal of Cybernetics*, vol. 2, no. 4, pp. 27-42.

Roycroft, A.J. (1983,86a,b,c,88a), "*C* GBR Class 0023," *Endgame*, vol. 5, no. 74, pp. 218-219; vol. 6, no. 83, pp. 12-15; vol. 6, no. 83, pp. 24-25; vol. 6, no. 84, pp. 65-68; vol. 6, no. 93, pp. 418-428.

Roycroft, A.J. (1986d), "Queen and Pawn on b7 against Queen," in booklet no. 7 of *Roycroft's 5-Man Chess Endgame Series*, Chess Endgame Consultants and Publishers, London, England.

Roycroft, A.J. (1988b), "Expert Against Oracle," in *Machine Intelligence 11*, J.E. Hayes, D. Michie and J. Richards (eds.), Oxford University Press, Oxford, pp. 347-373.

Russell, S. and E. Wefald (1988), "Decision-Theoretic Control of Reasoning: General Theory and an Application to Game Playing," technical report UCB/CSD 88/435, University of California/Berkeley.

Ryder, J.L. (1971), "Heuristic Analysis of Large Trees as Generated in the Game of Go," Ph.D. thesis, Stanford University (Microfilm 72-11, 654).

Samuel, A.L. (1959), "Some Studies in Machine Learning Using the Game of Checkers," *IBM Journal of Research and Development,* vol. 3, no. 3, pp. 210-229. See also (1963), *Computers and Thought,* E.A. Feigenbaum and J. Feldman (eds.), McGraw-Hill, pp. 71-105.

Samuel, A.L. (1967), "Some Studies in Machine Learning Using the Game of Checkers II - Recent Progress," *IBM Journal of Research and Development,* vol. 11, no. 6, pp. 601-617.

Sanechika, N., H. Ohigashi, Y. Mano, Y. Sugawara and K. Torii (1981), "Notes on Modeling and Implementation of the Human Player's Decision Processes in the Game of Go," Bulletin of the Electrotechnology Laboratory, vol. 45, pp. 1-11.

Sanechika, N., H. Oki, S. Yoshikawa, T. Yoshioka and S. Uchida (1988), "A Method of the Go System 'GOSEDAI'," ICOT technical memorandum: TM-0618, pp. 1-28 (in Japanese).

Schaeffer, J. (1983a), "The History Heuristic," *Journal of the International Computer Chess Association,* vol. 6, no. 3, pp. 16-19.

Schaeffer, J. (1983b), "Long-range Planning in Computer Chess," ACM Annual Conference, pp. 170-179.

Schaeffer, J., P.A.D. Powell and J. Jonkman (1983), "A VLSI Chess Legal Move Generator," Third Caltech Conference on Very Large Scale Integration, R.E. Bryant (ed.), Computer Science Press, pp. 331-349.

Schaeffer, J. and T.A. Marsland (1985), "The Utility of Expert Knowledge," 9th International Joint Conference on Artificial Intelligence, pp. 585-587.

Schaeffer, J. (1986), "Experiments in Search and Knowledge," Ph.D. thesis, Department of Computer Science, University of Waterloo.

Schaeffer, J. (1987), "Speculative Computing," *Journal of the International Computer Chess Association,* vol. 10, no. 3, pp. 118-124.

Schaeffer, J. (1988), private communication.

Schaeffer, J. (1989a), "The History Heuristic and Alpha-Beta Search Enhancements in Practice," *IEEE Transactions on Pattern Analysis and Machine Intelligence,* vol. 11, no. 11, pp. 1203-1212.

Schaeffer, J. (1989b), "Distributed Game-Tree Search," *Journal of Parallel and Distributed Computing,* vol. 6 no. 2 pp. 90-114.

Schaeffer, J. (1989c), "Conspiracy Numbers," in *Advances in Computer Chess 5,* D.F. Beal (ed.), Elsevier Science Publishers, Amsterdam, pp. 199-218. Also published in *Artificial Intelligence,* vol. 43 (1990), no. 1, pp. 67-84.

Scheucher, A. and H. Kaindl (1989), "The Reason for the Benefits of Minimax Search," 11th International Joint Conference on Artificial Intelligence, pp. 322-327.

Schoo, P.N.A. (1988), "Analyse van een Schaakeindspel-Database," Project thesis, Haagse Hogeschool, Sector Techniek, Studierichting Hogere Informatica (in Dutch).

Schrüfer, G. (1988), "Minimax-Suchen: Kosten, Qualität und Algorithmen," Ph.D. thesis, Technical University Braunschweig, Germany (in German).

Scott, J.J. (1969), "A Chess-Playing Program," in *Machine Intelligence 4,* B. Meltzer and D. Michie (eds.), Edinburgh University Press, pp. 255-265.

Shannon, C.E. (1950), "Programming a Computer for Playing Chess," *Philosophical Magazine,* vol. 41, no. 7, pp. 256-275. See also Levy, D.N.L (ed.) (1988), *Computer Games I,* Springer Verlag, New York, pp. 81-88.

Shapiro, A.D. (1987), *Structured Induction in Expert Systems,* Turing Institute Press in association with Addison-Wesley Publishing Company.

Shirayanagi, K. (1986), "On a Problem Solving Model in the Game of Go," technical report IPS Japan (86-AI-48), vol. 86, no. 58, pp. 81-88 (in Japanese).

Shirayanagi, K. (1988), "Frame Representation and Learning of Proverbs in Go," 36th Annual Convention IPS Japan, pp. 1603-1604 (in Japanese).

Simon, H.A. and K. Gilmartin (1973), "A Simulation of Memory for Chess Positions," *Cognitive Psychology,* vol. 5, no. 1, pp. 29-46.

Simon, H.A. (1974), "The Psychological Concept of ''Losing Move'' in a Game of Perfect Information," Proceedings of the National Academy of Sciences of the USA, vol. 71, no. 6, pp. 2276-2279.

Slagle, J.R. and P. Bursky (1968), "Experiments with a Multipurpose Theorem-Proving Heuristic Program," *Journal of the ACM,* vol. 15, no. 1, pp. 85-99.

Slagle, J.R. and J.K. Dixon (1969), "Experiments with Some Programs that Search Game Trees," *Journal of the ACM,* vol. 16, no. 2, pp. 189-207.

Slate, D.J. and L.R. Atkin (1977), "Chess 4.5—The Northwestern University Chess Program," in *Chess Skill in Man and Machine,* P. Frey (ed.), Springer-Verlag, pp. 82-118.

Slate, D.J. (1987), "A Chess Program that Uses its Transposition Table to Learn from Experience," *Journal of the International Computer Chess Association,* vol. 10, no. 2, pp. 59-71.

Sternberg, W., E. Conway and J. Larkins (1979), "Queen vs Rook," *Chess Voice,* April/May, pp. 8-11.

Stiller, L. (1989), "Parallel Analyses of Certain Endgames," *Journal of the International Computer Chess Association,* vol. 12, no. 2, pp. 55-64. See also (1988), "Massively Parallel Retrograde Endgame Analyses," Computer Science technical report no. 88-014, Boston University.

Stockman, G.C. (1979), "A Minimax Algorithm Better than Alpha-Beta?," *Artificial Intelligence,* vol. 12, no. 2, pp. 179-196.

Ströhlein, T. (1970), "Untersuchungen über kombinatorische Spiele," Doctoral dissertation, Faculty of General Science, Technical University of Munich (in German).

Takeuchi, I., H. Okuno and N. Ohsato (1986), "A List Processing Language TAO with Multiple Programming Paradigms," New Generation Computing, vol. 4, no. 4, pp. 401-444.

Tarsi, M. (1983), "Optimal Search on Some Game Trees," *Journal of the ACM,* vol. 30, no. 3, pp. 389-396.

Teague, A.H. (1988), "Backup Rules for Game Tree Searching: A Comparative Study," AAAI Spring Symposium Proceedings, pp. 23-25.

Thompson, K. (1979), personal communication, Bell Laboratories, N.J.

Thompson, K. (1982), "Computer Chess Strength," in *Advances in Computer Chess 3*, M.R.B. Clarke (ed.), Pergamon, Oxford, pp. 55-56.

Thompson, K. and A.J. Roycroft (1983), "A Prophesy Fulfilled," *EndGame*, vol. 5, no. 74, pp. 217-220.

Thompson, K. (1986), "Retrograde Analysis of Certain Endgames," *Journal of the International Computer Chess Association*, vol. 9, no. 3, pp. 131-139.

Troitzky, A.A. (1934), "Sbornik šakhmatnykh étyudov. S priloženiem kratkoy teorii éndšpilya 'Dva Konya protiv pešek'," Leningrad (in Russian). Partly re-published (1937) as *Collection of Chess Studies, With a Supplement on the Theory of the End-Game of Two Knights Against Pawns*, translated by A.D. Pritzson, David McKay Company, the latter again re-published (1985) by Olms, Zürich.

Turing, A.M., C. Strachey, M.A. Bates and B.V. Bowden (1953), "Digital Computers Applied to Games," in *Faster Than Thought*, B. V. Bowden (ed.), Pitman, pp. 286-310.

Warnock, T. and B. Wendroff (1988), "Search Tables in Computer Chess," *Journal of the International Computer Chess Association*, vol. 11, no. 1, pp. 10-13.

Welsh, D.E. and B. Baczynskyj (1985), *Computer Chess II*, W.C. Brown Co., Dubuque, Iowa.

Welsh, D. (1988), "Bona Fide?" *Journal of the International Computer Chess Association*, vol. 11, no. 2/3, pp. 126-127.

Wilcox, B. (1985), "Reflections on Building Two Go Programs," SIGART News 94, pp. 29-43.

Wilcox, B. (1988), "Computer Go," in *Computer Games II*, D.N.L. Levy (ed.), Springer-Verlag, New York, pp. 94-135.

Wilkins, D.E. (1982), "Using Knowledge to Control Tree Searching," *Artificial Intelligence*, vol. 18, no. 1, pp. 1-51.

Winston, P.H. (1977), *Artificial Intelligence*, Addison-Wesley.

Zobrist, A.L. (1970a), "A Hashing Method with Applications for Game Playing," technical report 88, Computer Science Department, University of Wisconsin.

Zobrist, A.L. (1970b), "Feature Extraction and Representation for Pattern Recognition and the Game of Go," Ph.D. thesis, University of Wisconsin (Microfilm 71-03, 162).

Zobrist, A.L. and F.R. Carlsson (1973), "An Advice-Taking Chess Computer," *Scientific American*, vol. 228, no. 6, pp. 92-105.

Zuse, K. (1945), "Chess Programs," *Der Plankalkül*. Later translated and published as report no. 106, (1976), Gesellschaft für Mathematik und Datenverarbeitung, Bonn, pp. 201-244.

Index

Boldface indicates first-order entries.